Critical Histories of Accounting

Routledge New Works in Accounting History

EDITED BY GARRY CARNEGIE (*Melbourne University Private, Australia*),
JOHN RICHARD EDWARDS (*Cardiff University, UK*),
SALVADOR CARMONA (*Instituto de Empresa, Spain*) and
DICK FLEISCHMAN (*John Carroll University, USA*)

Critical Histories of Accounting

Sinister Inscriptions in the Modern Era

Edited by Richard K. Fleischman, Warwick Funnell and Stephen P. Walker

Routledge
Taylor & Francis Group
NEW YORK   LONDON

First published 2013
by Routledge
711 Third Avenue, New York, NY 10017

Simultaneously published in the UK
by Routledge
2 Park Square, Milton Park, Abingdon, Oxon OX14 4RN

*Routledge is an imprint of the Taylor & Francis Group,
an informa business*

Library of Congress Cataloging-in-Publication Data

Critical histories of accounting : sinister inscriptions in the modern era /
edited by Richard K. Fleischman, Warwick Funnell, and Stephen P.
Walker.
p. cm. — (Routledge new works in accounting history ; 11)
Includes bibliographical references and index.
1. Accounting—History. I. Fleischman, Richard K. II. Funnell,
Warwick. III. Walker, Stephen P.
HF5605.C75 2012
657.09—dc23
2012003567

ISBN13: 978-0-415-88670-3 (hbk)
ISBN13: 978-0-203-10274-9 (ebk)

Typeset in Sabon
by IBT Global.

Contents

Figures

Tables

Introduction

Warwick Funnell and Stephen P. Walker

The critical tradition has come to occupy a prominent place in accounting historiography. Critical accounting scholars have confronted the responsibility of accounting and accountants in precipitating crises in the past and the present. They have revealed how the seemingly innocuous practice of accounting has featured in key episodes of the modern era such as acts of genocide, the operation of slavery, the treatment of indigenous peoples and the exploitation of labour under capitalism. Scholars have also shown that the organizations which represent accounting practitioners and the places in which accountants pursue their craft are locations for the practice of social exclusion on the basis of gender, class, race and ethnicity.

This book presents a collection of eleven previously published, significant articles, authored by prominent critical accounting historians, in the hope of interesting a new generation to consider the intellectual possibilities and rewards of doing research in the area. These chapters are prefaced by an overarching and thematic review, which charts the expansion of critical accounting history research and suggests some future directions. The titles of the four parts of this book—annihilation, subjugation, exploitation and exclusion—recognize that an impressive, expanding body of historical research has shown accounting to be far more than a prosaic, neutral technical practice. Instead, accounting inscriptions can have a pronounced and powerful moral dimension as a sinister political tool used to promote the interests, ideologies and plans of individuals or groups, irrespective of any catastrophic impacts on others. There have been many recurring episodes in the past, observes Fleischman (2004, 12), where "accounting or accounting practitioners stand accused of participation in repressive regimes or dishonest actions".

ANNIHILATION

The chapters in the first part of the book recount some particularly extreme historical episodes when accounting was one means used by governments to implement policies of annihilation. Attempts at annihilation and subjection are actions of states which target particular groups of individuals who have a common characteristic, most especially religious beliefs, race or ethnicity, which allows them to be distinguished from others. Annihilation, extermination or genocide are attempts by a government or a group which possess the power, belief and ability to obliterate another group of individuals and, if possible, to expunge any trace of them. Ethnic cleansing of the modern era differs from genocide in that rather than being a purposeful policy to obliterate individuals sharing a particular characteristic wherever they are to be found, those responsible seek to do so within a particular area, possibly even just a city (Cooper and Catchpowle 2009, 717).

An attempt to annihilate is a political practice most often masquerading as a moral imperative which requires the elimination of a social collective who serve a useful ideological purpose by being vilified as an enemy or, in the case of Germany's Jews, a threat to the purity or future of the Aryan race. This recognizes that an attempt to annihilate a group of individuals will arise from a complex set of most often irrational motives, certainly not for economic and political purposes alone or even primarily. An attempt at annihilation denies the fundamental requirement of all civilized societies: respect for and recognition of the sanctity of human life. Thus, *annihilation* is a term denoting behaviour of the most extreme and obscene form. Most people would find it difficult to associate such iniquitous behaviour with the seemingly non-threatening calculative practices of accounting. Yet, accounting historians have established the tragic, indeed possibly the essential, contributions of accounting to governments and individuals who are determined to carry out policies of annihilation, most notoriously in the implementation of the Nazi's 'final solution' during World War II. In each country that Germany invaded a priority was the obliteration of all Jews. This was to be the Third Reich's divine mission. Unlike other instances of genocide, the Holocaust was the first time when the power of the technology of the modern world had been turned on a group of people, connected only through a religious heritage, to systematically and methodically to murder them to the last person (Bauer 1989, 83–84).

Chapter 2 by Funnell highlights the moral nature of accounting in the practices used by German government departments during the Holocaust to expedite the transportation and processing of Jews and their property, at the same time effectively making them invisible as individuals by supplanting their identities with numbers in accounting reports. Accounting numbers as an instrument of the German civil bureaucracy provided new quantitative visibilities at "centres of calculation" (Miller 1990, 318) which enabled the German civil bureaucracy, military organizations and their masters to control from a distance (Humphrey and Scapens 1996, 89; Fleischman 2004, 19) and capture key dimensions of the extermination process without being in constant attendance. Accounting provided the means by which the individuality and humanity of Jews was supplanted and disguised by a new numerical identity which made them invisible to Germans not directly involved in the attempted annihilation of Jews.

In Chapter 3 Lippman and Wilson also show how accounting was used to deny Jews their humanity and individuality when those imprisoned in concentration camps were employed as slave labour for the benefit of large German firms which included Krupp and Volkswagen. Sophisticated accounting practices valued Jews solely as productive inputs which were used to ensure the greatest financial advantage to these firms and to be dispensed with when they were no longer capable of being productive. Lippman and Wilson conclude that there was never any recognition of the human cost associated with the debilitating conditions under which the Jews worked or the savage manner in which they were finally killed. In the chapters on the Holocaust the moral culpability of accountants as individuals and accounting as a profession is established both for their direct involvement in the attempted annihilation of the Jews and their enthusiastic contributions to early Nazi programmes which were designed to exclude Jews from all aspects of German life. Thus, Lippman and Wilson show how the non-Jewish members of the pre-eminent German professional accounting organization, the Institut der Wirtschaftsprüfer (IdW), introduced policies which progressively excluded Jews from membership and sought to disqualify them from performing any professional accounting work (Markus 1997; Walker 2000). While accounting and accountants did not provide the motivations or even the justifications for attempts to annihilate the Jews, nor did accountants necessarily take part in the process directly, they did provide a means to allow the process once started to be carried out more effectively and efficiently and for its true intent to be hidden.

SUBJUGATION

Part II of the book, which deals with subjugation, or subjection, examines the manner in which accounting was used by a dominant political authority in a variety of circumstances to consolidate and extend its power. In the case of the British government's reaction to the Irish Famine in the 1840s and its administration of poor relief in the early nineteenth century, accounting provided a means to create a maligned identity for some and shape social beliefs advantageous to the imperial power. While the implementation of policies of subjugation by an imperial power may result in many deaths, whether it be purely a consequence of giving primacy to the interests of favoured individuals and corporations from the imperial power or the result of a particular prejudiced, demeaning view of the subjugated, this is not the principal aim of the policy but rather what might be regarded as an unavoidable consequence of the moral duty of the defiler. The imperial power seeks to exercise power to subdue, not to annihilate. Whereas imperialism refers to the exercise of power over another state, most effectively by economic agreements, when this develops to where the external power seeks to use its position to dominate and subjugate by governing and establishing structures of economic, political and social control which favour the invader, including the seizing of property, a colony is established. In a growing body of literature by accounting historians, accounting in numerous historical and geographical contexts has been shown to provide the means to identify and value that which is to be seized by the imperial power and to expedite the process (Cooper and Catchpowle 2009, 718; Annisette 2000; Gibson 2000; Neu 2000b; Said 1993).

The chapters addressing subjugation demonstrate how accounting information was used both to define issues and problems related to the imperial enterprise and also to create political and social discourses or sets of meanings which would then inform and legitimize political debate and strategies essential to the preferred imperial political goals and beliefs. Fleischman (2004, 18) has warned that "accounting is much more constructive than reflective of social values, more active than passive in social ordering". Accounting reports provided those in authority with justifications for their policies, for legitimizing their actions, however catastrophic this may have been for the subjugated, and for implementing their policies (Funnell 2001). They also provided the means by which those who exercised imperial power at the heart of the empire were able to monitor and control the implementation of imperial policies. Accounting "made visible distant locales, thereby, allowing local knowledge to be mobilized by imperial powers" (Neu 2000b, 170).

Whereas annihilation is pre-eminently racial and ideological in motivation, most often, as shown in this volume, subjection has been overwhelmingly motivated by attempts to gain access to the property and territory of another for the benefit of the imperial power. Imperialist powers, such as Britain and more lately the U.S. (Cooper and Catchpowle 2009; Chomsky 1999a, 1999b, 2004), have been especially adept at disguising these motives by providing reasons which are said to constitute legitimate grounds, including those defined in moral terms, which allow their intrusion in the affairs of another. In the late twentieth century, although America has proclaimed a responsibility and obligation to promote democratic values as the reasons for the wars in which it has engaged, most notoriously in Iraq, many critics such as Chomsky (1999a, 1999b, 2004, 2006), Chwastiak (2001, 2006) and Cooper and Catchpowle (2009) have instead accused the Americans of economic imperialism. America's wars were fought to protect and advance the economic interests of American companies and to provide greater opportunities for them, with the control over oil the most obvious reason.

In the case of both imperialism and colonialism, as Neu and Graham demonstrate in Chapter 4, the operative aim is unlikely to be annihilation of all the people conquered, for to do so may defeat the very purpose of the interventions, to gain access to markets or resources. To decimate a land and to destroy all who may have lived and worked there would provide little benefit to a conqueror who seeks more than control over resources, apart from removing a potential competitor and enemy which ultimately the conqueror could enrol as a partner or co-conspirator. Thus, whereas a determination to annihilate another group arises from deeply seated animosities and prejudices which cannot be justified on any 'rational' economic or political grounds, most imperialists would seek to establish a symbiotic relationship with the vanquished to gain the greatest advantage from the conquered lands. This has been the outstanding feature of imperialism from Roman times and most especially the British in the nineteenth century.

Neu and Graham show how Canadian federal legislation which sought to transform the First Nations people into atomized individuals, whose identity as members of a tribe would be destroyed and their existence and well-being determined by market forces, was dependent on coincident accounting practices for its efficacy. Accounting provided the means to give visibility to the alleged failings of the conquered and, therefore, a means to justify subsequent action as redemptive. Accounting was used, in effect, as an imperial practice to translate the legislative intentions of the Canadian government into the day-to-day, or micro, practices necessary for implementation of policies in the field. In Chapter 5 Walker similarly establishes the way in which accounting information was essential to the implementation of British poor laws in the early nineteenth century by providing the means to monitor the poor and manage the provision of poor relief, thereby contributing to efforts to reduce expenditure on poor relief. Accounting practices helped to achieve these aims by providing a means to construct moral identities for the poor to enable and justify their surveillance, control and, where possible, denial of relief. As the population began to increase greatly in the nineteenth century, the propertied classes sought measures to alleviate heightened financial demands of the system of poor relief. The moral dimension of accounting practices, thus, was again in evidence by its use as a form of social control in a society dominated by hierarchical determinations by providing the means to distinguish and differentiate the poor. The poor had to be 'rendered governable' by making them 'visible' as a moral entity.

O'Regan (chapter 6) also demonstrates how implementation of responses to the Irish Famine in the mid-1840s by the British government, which ruled Ireland as a colony, was heavily reliant upon a "vast architecture of accounting". Accounting provided the means by which policies of the government in London could be implemented by the Treasury at a distance in Ireland. Through its accounting reports the Treasury was able to govern through their centres of calculation located at Commissariat depots, principal amongst which were those at Cork and Limerick. Treasury regulations, accounting reports and minutes provided a constant and ever-present means of disciplining behaviour of those entrusted with delivering relief to those who were identified as entitled to help. More importantly, accounting provided the means by which the "oppressor seeks to incorporate the native into its moral universe, a universe alien to the native mind" (O'Regan 2010, 417). Accounting, as Walker also establishes in the context of the administration of the English poor laws, was essential to the development of a discourse of the 'Other', a means by which the Irish could be conceived in terms which distinguished them from the British and which provided the justification for the form of intervention in the crisis favoured by the colonizer. In the case of the Irish Famine, the British government used economic criteria for assistance to the starving Irish to both justify the manner in which they responded to the crisis and to confirm the racial stereotype of the Irish as slothful and indolent and, therefore, the undeserving poor (Fielden 1968; Harris 2004; Harrison 1957; Himmelfarb 1984; Spencer 1851).

The British government's responses to the Irish Famine and the relief of the poor illustrate that the moral agency of accounting is determined and legitimated by prevailing economic and political structures and not by any internal logic or calculus. Abject need, which, in the absence of financial means, could not be translated into an economically enforceable entitlement, had no relevance to the most efficient disposition of food supplies, as opposed to distribution based upon humane considerations. The strict rendition of the principles of nineteenth-century political economy, which both the governments of Peel and Russell insisted on moralistically applying at the time of the Irish Famine, meant that the only entitlements which were morally and economically defensible were those exercised in and derived from market exchanges (see Sen 1981, 161, 162). Ultimately, accounting numbers were a means of providing financial criteria for deciding on assistance to those who suffered, over one million of whom died either directly or indirectly from the British policy of providing assistance only to those who deserved it, that is, those who could work for money. Those who could meet the qualifications of entitlement by having sufficient money to buy food would be fed while others would starve. Accounting provided the technologies to enforce the exclusion of those who were condemned as undeserving of assistance. Entitlements justified on economic grounds were the natural domain of accounting calibrations. Uncalculating compassion had no place in Treasury policies and practices, which were the administrative manifestation of the prevailing, intolerant attitude towards the poor and the righteous appreciation of the virtues of property ownership.

EXPLOITATION

The third part of the book explores the interfaces between accounting and exploitation. As a moral concept *exploitation* is understood as "taking unfair advantage" (Sample 2003, 7) as in, for instance, paying an abnormally low price for a good or service (Wertheimer 1996, x). According to Sample (2003, 88), exploitation takes place "when a person interacts with another for the sake of taking . . . advantage in a way that degrades the other person in virtue of her vulnerability". The exploiter may be motivated by the prospect of deriving (undeserved) benefits or gains from a transaction or relationship with the exploitee. Theorists of the subject probe the distinctions between harmful and mutually advantageous exploitation, consensual and non-consensual exploitation, and between impersonal and interpersonal exploitation (Wertheimer 1996, 14–24; Sample 2003, 9). For Marxists, exploitation is rooted in the economic rather than the moral and comprises the extraction of surplus product by the owners of the means of production. The attention of Marxist scholars focuses in particular on the surplus value appropriated by the owners of capital from the labour expended by the proletariat. Workers are deemed to be exploited "if they work longer hours than the number of labor hours employed in the goods they consume" (Elster 1986, 121).

Researchers have identified various connections between exploitation and accounting. For example, they have observed the exploitation of women in the performance of the accounting function (Cooper and Taylor 2000; Walker 2003b) and used accounting representations to chart shifts in the manner in which that exploitation has responded to various crises of capitalism (Tinker and Neimark 1987). As revealed in part II of this book, studies have identified the role of accounting in the exploitation of indigenous peoples. Researchers have also shown how accounting can be employed to facilitate imperial projects in ways that exploit the human and other resources of the colonial periphery (Davie 2000, 2005a; Hooper and Pratt 1995; Kalpagam 2000). In recent times the impositions of international accounting standards have been described as "vehicles of colonial exploitation" (Aras and Crowther 2008). In contexts such as Maoist China, Western accounting concepts have been deemed instruments of capitalist exploitation (Ezzamel, Xiao and Pan 2007). In the field of collective bargaining, studies have suggested that negotiations between management and unions may be conditioned by workers' perception that accounts are devices used "to dominate and exploit employees" (Gotlob and Dilts 1996).

Indeed, wage labour is conditioned by the relations of capitalism and the capitalist system is founded on exploitation. Writing from a labour process perspective (which, as will be shown in Chapter 1, does not find universal favour among historians of accounting), the chapter by Hopper identifies four epochs of capitalism which form the shifting structural arenas in which the conditions were created for the emergence of new forms of management accounting and control in the U.S. Hopper argues that during industrialization the subordination of labour to capitalist modes of production and the extraction of surplus demanded the compilation of internal accounting records by the new factory owners. The quest for profit maximization encouraged the introduction of increasingly sophisticated accounting systems to minimize labour costs and improve worker productivity. During the epoch of mature industrialization mounting competition encouraged further assaults on labour via the techniques of scientific management and standard costing. A growing army of managers and the practitioners of the new profession of cost accounting applied these innovations.

Hopper contends that during the subsequent Fordist epoch increasing industrial concentration, economic depression and labour resistance formed the backdrop to further innovations in accounting and managerial control. Among the new techniques of this epoch were transfer pricing, return on investment measures and delegated budgets. He shows that in more recent times the crisis of Fordism and the emergence of global capitalism have encouraged the deployment of other techniques 'apposite to the epoch' such as strategic management accounting, target costing and the balanced scorecard.

While the capitalist exploits the proletarian by accumulating the surplus value of her/his labour, the worker does at least remain in a position to sell that labour for a wage. In chattel slavery, where people become the property of others and are bought and sold as commodities, there is no such right to compensation. Slavery invariably comprises a harmful, forced and non-consensual form of exploitation. As will be revealed in Chapter 1 of this volume, and as Chapter 8 by Oldroyd, Fleischman and Tyson attests, historians have shown that on plantations in the U.S. accounting "was instrumental in commodifying, objectifying and dehumanizing an entire class of people" through its processes of valuation, classification, performance measurement and disciplining. Equally as disturbing was the manner in which the routinized processes of accounting inscription constructed the exploitation of slaves as a normalized business practice.

But the chapter by Oldroyd, Fleischman and Tyson also illustrates another dimension of accounting—its potential to moderate and even challenge exploitation. The need for agents and officials to account for the human assets under their charge encouraged efforts to preserve the health of slaves and served to curb the extent of their ill treatment. Accounting was also mobilized in the discourse of abolition and could feature constructively in the transition from slavery to waged labour. The chapter serves as a reminder that accounting can be deployed as a basis for emancipatory interventions. For example, disclosures in modern-day corporate annual reports may reveal the stark contrasts in the remuneration of company directors compared with employees. Such accounting data can be used as the foundation of demands to address inequality (Sikka, Wearing and Nayak 1999). Conversely, inadequate accounting has been implicated in the persistent exploitation of child labour (Mukhopadhyay 2002).

In more historical contexts Gallhofer and Haslam (2003, 30–65) have shown how the philosopher and social reformer Jeremy Bentham envisaged that comprehensive accounting publicity in democratic society would offer a protective mechanism for the disadvantaged by rendering the actions of the powerful visible and thus challengeable. Socialist agitators of the late nineteenth century recognized the potency of accounting disclosures for revealing injustices and the exploitation of labour (ibid.,

66–99). Evidently, what histories of accounting reveal is that while its technologies may be deployed in campaigns to arrest exploitation, liberate the oppressed or to legitimate demands for progressive reform, when it is captured by the powerful accounting may be mobilized in ways which are antithetical to such aims.

If we comprehend exploitation as the injustice associated with taking unfair advantage of those who are vulnerable, or the exploited as the party disadvantaged in a transaction generating asymmetrical benefits, then Chapter 9 by Hooper and Kearins offers a potent illustration of the role of accounting and accountants in such arrangements. The authors show how accounting expertise was captured by the dominant interest in colonial New Zealand and utilized to appropriate land assets from the Maori population and transfer them to European settlers. The case reveals the operation of exploitation in the context of liberalism, where economic rationalities prevailed over the interests of 'the Natives'. Hooper and Kearins confirm what we have seen in other arenas, that accounting technologies rendered acts of exploitation less overt by facilitating action at a distance, generating an aura of neutral objectivity and enabling detachment between accountants and the human objects of their calculative manipulations and interventions. The extent to which the Maori were subject to an unfair bargain becomes apparent when Hooper and Kearins relate how Maori assets were deliberately undervalued and extortionate transaction costs were levied, culminating in a dramatic decline in Maori landownership during three decades of Liberal government.

EXCLUSION

Exclusion is the theme of the final part of the book. In its broadest sense social exclusion refers to the manner in which individuals, groups or communities are denied participation in, or access to, relations, networks, institutions, rights, resources, opportunities and services. The processes of social exclusion are multidimensional. They operate in diverse arenas and both reflect and reinforce the unequal distribution of power. The denial of participation may result in social differentiation, blocked mobility and the alienation, marginalization or disenfranchisement of the excluded (Popay, Escorel and Hernandez 2008; Taket et al. 2009).

It is important to make the rather obvious point that exclusion is dependent on human agency—it "is something that is done by some people to other people" (Byrne 2005, 2). Blocked or restricted access may be founded on the possession of characteristics identified as undesirable by those who control organizations. The processes which operationalize exclusion and the bases on which it is predicated can be single or multiple. Among such criteria are race, ethnicity, caste, gender, sexual orientation, social origin, age, ability, physical appearance, language, religion and geographical location.

These bases of exclusion may be activated intentionally and formally—through, for example, codification in organizational rules and policies—or unintentionally and informally in more subtle ways rooted in institutional practices values and beliefs.

In the context of this book exclusion does not relate to sinister dimensions of accounting inscription. Rather it concerns those who practice the craft, in particular, professional accountants. The emphasis here is on the operation of exclusion by the institutions which dominate the profession, its qualifying associations and recruiting firms in particular.

Silver (1994, 532) identifies three paradigms within which social exclusion is "embedded". These are solidarity, specialization and monopoly. It is the last of these that resonates most strongly with the experience of the accountancy profession. Accounting historians have frequently deployed the Weberian concept of social closure in this connection. Here a status group with a distinctive identity (such as an occupation) seeks to maximize rewards by restricting access to valued resources (such as the provision of services) to a limited number of eligibles. The pursuit of this monopolistic project depends on an occupational group defining its boundaries and identifying attributes which secure inclusion. This process results inevitably in the creation of excluded 'outs' and the perpetuation of occupational inequality. Professions are effectively 'gated communities' which seek to restrict access to those who satisfy formal or informal conditions of entry (Burchardt, Le Grand and Piachaud 2002; Berlant 1975; Collins 1990; Larson 1977; Murphy 1988; Macdonald 1995). Maintaining the economic and social advancement of those who pass through the gate is dependent on keeping it closed to numerous others.

Hence, for professions the "essence of closure is the definition of membership at a particular point in time, and the setting of criteria for deciding who may subsequently join" (Macdonald 1995, 541). Determining the criteria for inclusion and exclusion and drawing occupational boundaries are not always straightforward exercises for professions (Chua and Poullaos 1998; Walker and Shackleton 1998). In the context of a qualifying association it might be expected that such criteria would focus entirely on merit and the possession of the requisite knowledge and skills necessary to practice the vocation. However, when ascription is deployed exclusionary practices appear more sinister.

Critical histories of the accounting profession suggest that exclusionary processes in the pursuit of closure not only impact on the lives of those included and excluded from the vocation. They have also been a major factor in shaping the organizational configuration of the profession and the creation of intra-occupation hierarchies and differentiated markets for accounting labour. They have conditioned relations between organizations within the profession and interactions with the agencies external to it, particularly the state. A focus on exclusion also offers historical insights to the various ideologies and cultures which have permeated the institutions of the accountancy profession in different jurisdictional contexts. Such insights can result in a serious questioning of the supposed altruistic intent of accounting professionals and the organizations which represent and employ them.

It can be seen, therefore, that exclusion is fundamental to understanding professionalization projects in accounting. As Khalifa and Kirkham (2009, 445) state, "Professional exclusionary and marginalising practices, which adversely affected women, some men . . . and minority groups, were essential to the definition of expert knowledge in accounting and the development of professional legitimacy". With this in mind, what bases of exclusion have been explored in historical studies of the accounting profession? Most attention has focused on gender, race and class.

Historical studies of accounting and gender suggest that in patriarchal society women have often been deemed suitable to perform accounting in a number of times and places. These include feminized arenas such as households and philanthropic organizations; serving as a useful adjunct to the male owner of a family business; operating as a reserve army of accounting labour in periods of national emergency; or providing a source of cheap labour in routinized, menial work settings (Black 2006; Cooper and Taylor 2000; Kirkham and Loft 2001; Walker 1998, 2003b, 2003c, 2006; Walker and Carnegie 2007; Wootton and Kemmerer 1996, 2000; Wootton and Spruill 1994). In contrast, women were long excluded from the upper reaches of the masculinized occupational hierarchy in the accounting profession. The exclusion of women from the profession and the discriminatory practices they encountered in attempting to access it and progress within it have been an enduring focus of historical analysis (Lehman 1992; Thane 1992; Shackleton 1999; Walker 2011). While the numbers of women who crack the 'glass ceiling' and occupy the highest positions in the accounting firms remain so stubbornly low, interest in the antecedents of gender and blocked mobility is likely to continue.

The mechanisms of exclusion on the basis of gender have often become visible through biographical studies of pioneer women who overcame barriers to entry (Spruill and Wootton 1995, 1996; Slocum and Vangermeersch 1996). Collective biographies which deploy oral history, such as that by McKeen and Richardson (1998) for Canada, also provide compelling insights to the manner in which the foundations of gender-based closure in professional organizations could shift from the formal-legalistic to the socio-cultural. Oral testimony from New Zealand gathered by Emery, Hooks and Stewart (2002) also point to the absence of formal barriers to the recruitment and career progression of women but the existence of masculine values in firms which work to effectively exclude them from positions of leadership and access to organizational knowledge and networks. Interviews with pioneering women accountants in Australia similarly illuminate the mechanics and experiences of exclusion and the operation of gender discrimination (Linn 1996). Most studies on gender and exclusion have concerned Anglo-American sites. Exceptions, such as the investigation by Carrera, Gutiérrez and Carmona (2001) into women's access to the audit profession during the Franco dictatorship in Spain, also find that exclusionary practices reflected gender discrimination in wider society, particularly as cultivated by powerful institutions such as the Catholic Church.

The work included in this book that illustrates the dynamic processes of gender-based exclusion is Kirkham and Loft's (1993b) highly influential study on "Gender and the Construction of the Professional Accountant". In the years previous to its publication papers had appeared on the gendered division of accounting labour in industrial society and the discriminatory practices which restricted the access of women to the accountancy profession in the U.S. and UK (Lehman 1992; Thane 1992). These contributions were attended by calls for a broadening of the research agenda beyond a narrow focus on the profession (Loft 1992) and approaches which placed gender at the centre of analyses of the professionalization of accounting (Kirkham 1992). These calls were answered by Kirkham and Loft (1993b). Chapter 10 by Kirkham and Loft deploys concepts of gender to explore the discourses used to legitimate the exclusion of women from the accountancy profession in England and Wales. By focusing on a sixty-year period commencing with the formation of qualifying associations, the authors show how the exclusion of women was a central element of the male professionalization project itself. Kirkham and Loft illustrate that women were excluded from the profession by virtue of their sex. While their contribution to the war effort in 1914–1918 culminated in women winning the right to vote and in the statutory removal of their formal exclusion from the memberships of professional organizations, very few women subsequently built careers in public accountancy. Informal obstacles to the recruitment and progression of women ensured that by 1931 the accounting profession continued to be gendered masculine. In contrast, the more routinized and menial forms of accounting work performed by book-keepers and clerks were becoming increasingly gendered feminine.

Compelling studies of the operation of exclusion on the basis of race and ethnicity have been authored by Hammond (1997a, 2002) and Hammond and Streeter (1994). The last of these, focusing on the American pre–civil rights era, features in Chapter 11. Hammond and Streeter's (1994) study commenced with the startling revelation that in 1965 only one hundred of the one hundred thousand certified public accountants in the U.S. were African Americans, and their number has never exceeded 1 per cent of the professional population. By deploying the oral testimony of the few who overcame the formidable obstacles to their recruitment, the authors reveal the overt and subtle forms of racism that blocked the entry of most African Americans to certified public accountancy. Further, as was the case with early generations of women who managed to enter the profession, once admission had been secured, those from minority groups encountered occupational institutions and ideologies that served to frustrate career advancement in the professional mainstream. Like Hammond, other studies have focused on the exclusion of a particular group from the profession in multiracial societies. For example, Kim (2004a) identified the role of cultural difference in the exclusion of Chinese from accountancy in New Zealand.

A notable feature of a number of studies of exclusion on the basis of race and ethnicity is the impact of socio-political change, particularly in the form of transformations from colonial to post-colonial states. The formative contribution here is Annisette's (2003) investigation of the accountancy profession in Trinidad and Tobago. This features in the book as Chapter 12. Annisette shows that under colonial rule accountancy was associated with 'Britishness' and 'whiteness', to the exclusion of the majority population of African and East Indian decent. Following independence from Britain attempts to encourage inclusion by indigenizing professional institutions and educational processes opened the profession to a limited degree, but also served to construct new, racially defined credentials and work practices, as well as the emergence of more subtle forms of racial exclusion. Similarly, Sian (2007) has shown that before independence the British-dominated accountancy profession in Kenya was closed to indigenous Africans and immigrant Asians. Here, too, attempts to reverse exclusion post-independence through affirmative action could be frustrated by the persistence of informal means of racial exclusion. Poullaos (2009) contributes here by investigating attitudes to race in the imperial centre rather than in the colonial periphery. He concludes that in the 1920s the admission of non-British males of 'race or colour' was perceived as inconsistent with the preservation of professional status. This encouraged the maintenance of barriers *de jure* to prevent the entry of "the racialised, subordinated Other" from the vocation.

According to Larson (1977, 66), the exclusion of low-status groups in the social hierarchy contributes towards a profession's effort to achieve "respectability and social standing". Newly formed professional organizations, anxious to establish their status in the professional firmament, often emphasized socio-cultural attributes as a condition of membership. Such attributes, which might include trust, respectability and character, were often assumed to be found among the middle and upper classes, especially those networked with established professional elites (O'Regan 2008; Ramirez 2001; Chua and Poullaos 1998; Richardson 1989). Although their formation offered opportunities for upward social mobility, the earliest professional organizations in Britain often recruited heavily from the middle classes (Anderson and Walker 2009; Kedslie 1990b; Lee 2000, 2010; Walker 1988). Recruitment processes encouraged the admission of those with requisite financial, social and cultural capital. Apprenticeship and membership fees, the emphasis on the display of gentlemanly attributes, the operation of nepotism and the need to develop client networks all tended to encourage recruitment from the middle classes. In the UK the need to 'open' the vocation and establish a more meritocratic basis of recruitment encouraged the proliferation of accountancy bodies.

Increasingly, authors recognize the operation of multiple, as opposed to single, bases of exclusion to the profession. For example, oral histories of African-American CPAs in the U.S. (Hammond 2002; Hammond and Streeter 1994) and of Maori (McNicholas, Humphrey and Gallhofer 2004) and Chinese women (Kim 2004b) in the New Zealand profession illustrate that female experiences are not only conditioned by gender, but also by race, ethnicity and class. In the highly racialized society of South Africa, Hammond, Clayton and Arnold (2009, 705) recently concluded that "processes of professional closure and credentialing excluded the majority population from the ranks of the profession on basis of race and class throughout the period 1976–2000".

Having compared the demographic profile of accountants in late nineteenth-century Canada with that of the population as a whole, Edwards and Walker (2008) concluded that the dominance of those with origins in the British Isles and affiliation with the Anglican and Presbyterian Churches implied the operation of exclusion on the basis of ethnicity and religion. Likewise, Richardson (1989, 15) concluded that "accountancy in its formative years in Canada does not appear to have been open to all members of society, factors such as gender . . . religion and ethnicity affected the ability to enter the professional associations, gain an accounting education and achieve success (elite status) in the profession". On religion specifically, Annisette and O'Regan showed that the characteristics of the founders of the Institute of Chartered Accountants in Ireland rendered their organization "a Protestant Unionist body" (2007, 13–15).

As the foregoing suggests, there is much that remains to be investigated in relation to histories of exclusion in accountancy on the basis of the 'trinity' of gender, race and class. Not only has the operation of these been investigated in limited temporal and spatial dimensions, but the significance of other potential foundations of closure referred to at the beginning of this section have barely been touched upon by critical historians of accounting.

1 A Review of Critical Histories of Accounting

Richard K. Fleischman

INTRODUCTION

This review aspires to chart the meteoric rise of critical scholarship broadly and offer a synthesis of the research findings of critical accounting historians and those critical accounting scholars who have investigated contemporary issues with recourse to history.

The last three decades have featured an exponential growth in the volume of what has come to be called most frequently "critical accounting research," although other names may be applied to constituent segments of the greater whole (e.g., "alternative research," "paradigmatic theorizing," "enabling accounting research," "interventionist accounting," "new accounting history," etc.). The range of research topics and methodologies has proved remarkably broad. One only has to reference the number of new journals that have come into existence devoted almost entirely to critical research (*Accounting Forum, Accounting and the Public Interest, International Journal of Critical Accounting, Social and Environmental Accounting Journal*), as well as many other journals in which critical accounting research is published with varying degrees of regularity (*Abacus, Accounting and Business Research, British Accounting Review, Business History, European Accounting Review*). However, for the purposes of this review, the contents of six journals that have emphasized history over the two decades from 1990 to 2010 supplied the majority of the critical literature discussed. These journals were the flagship critical research publication *Critical Perspectives on Accounting* (CPA); two highly regarded, eclectic, international journals, *Accounting, Auditing & Accountability Journal* (AAAJ) and *Accounting, Organizations and Society* (AOS); and the three accounting history specialist journals in the English language—*Accounting, Business & Financial History* (ABFH) (now *Accounting History Review*), the *Accounting Historians Journal* (AHJ), and *Accounting History* (AH).[1]

This review is organized as follows. The next section provides a broad definition of the major principles of critical accounting scholarship. Attention will then turn to critical accounting historiography specifically with subsections on available resources for doing accounting history and the various paradigms that collectively form the theoretical basis for much of critical accounting history research. Under the heading of the "Suppressed

Voices", major subject areas of critical accounting history will then be discussed in detail—the Holocaust, slavery, the victims of imperialism and issues of race and gender. This is followed by a lengthy section on the "profession under siege" in which various constituent groups of accountancy are critiqued (public accountancy, management accounting, standard-setters, government accountants and accounting academics). We will consider, in the last major section, ways forward for critical accounting historians with subsections on social/environmental (green) accounting and interventionist strategies.

CRITICAL ACCOUNTING: GENERAL PRINCIPLES

Let us begin by having several prominent critical scholars provide an overview of the parameters and goals of their research. Laughlin (1999, 73) encouraged engagement with the accounting profession in this definition of critical accounting:

> A critical understanding of the role of the accounting processes and practices and the accounting profession in the functioning of society and organizations with an intention to use that understanding to engage (where appropriate) in changing those processes, practices and the profession.

Sikka and Willmott (1997, 158) went further and urged confrontation with the profession and its leadership:

> The accountancy profession has surrounded itself with narratives of even- handed public behaviour, professional ethics and discipline through which it rehearses and sustains the dominant fable of 'progress' embedded in accounting history . . . heroic professional bodies and their leaders battle against the odds and, amidst this chaos, introduce and protect the public from diverse troubles and dangers. Such myths can be questioned by involving alternative sources, exhuming buried documents, reviving forgotten and abandoned histories (Said, 1944) to question whether the profession is all that it claims to be.

Broadbent (2002, 436) has cautioned that "critical accounting should . . . argue for the provision of information sets that resist the *status quo*." Of great value is work that "has demonstrated resistance to the patriarchal and gendered values that lie behind accounting's taken-for-granted construction."

Baker and Bettner (1997, 305) have likewise supported the concept that accounting is not the value-free, neutral portrait of reality that many would have us believe: "Critical researchers have convincingly and repeatedly argued that accounting does not produce an objective representation of economic 'reality,' but rather pursues a highly contested and partisan representation of the economic and social world."

The editors of the then newly founded *CPA* editorialized in the maiden issue: "Most of all, we reject methodological secularism and academic obscurantism, and support new forms of dialogue and tolerance that encourage catholic, eclectic and interdisciplinary approaches. The only methodological endorsement we will make is that 'anything and everything' should be open for 'Critique'" (Cooper and Tinker 1990). Accordingly, Moore (1991, 770) defined critical accounting as "a set of discursive practices . . . embodying a radical epistemology (or political) state which questions objectivity in the first place, finds 'accurate representation' an impossible goal, and seeks alternative descriptions for what accountants do and the role accounting plays" (quoted in Roslender and Dillard 2003, 339). Gallhofer and Haslam (1997a, 82) wrote of the important characteristic of accounting's enabling "ability to act as a force for radical emancipatory social change through making things visible and comprehensible and helping engender dialogue and action towards emancipatory change" (quoted in Roslender and Dillard 2003, 341).

CRITICAL ACCOUNTING HISTORY

In the past two decades, the study of accounting has have been immeasurably enriched with the flowering of critical accounting history. At this early juncture, it is appropriate to distinguish critical accounting history from an older historical traditionalism that has a venerable past and present. Many accounting historians provide a valuable service by reporting the events of accountancy's past without necessarily linking their findings to contemporary issues or engaging in paradigmatic discourse. Those who label these efforts as 'antiquarian' demonstrate a perception of accounting history which is both limited and limiting in its understanding of the subject and fails to appreciate the importance of history in our comprehension of the present. Critical accounting historians, by contrast, have different agendas. Some bridge the gap between past and present by using history to expose historical injustices that have continued unabated into the present. Others have exposed episodes totally contained in the past which nevertheless expose enduring values and practices that demonstrate accountants acting unethically or immorally. Finally, other critical accounting historians study the past in order to advance the explanatory power of philosophical paradigms to which they subscribe. This book and this chapter will examine the contributions of critical accounting historians of all these varieties.

Historical Resources

For novitiates to researching and the writing of history, whether critical or traditional, there exists a wealth of resources available—collections of articles, "how-to" manuals, bibliographies and even an encyclopaedia of accounting history (Chatfield and Vangermeersch 2006). The largest compendia of accounting history articles are edited by Edwards (2000) and Fleischman (2006). Each contains a selection gleaned from historians of all persuasions—"new" and "old"; positivist and normative; traditionalist, modernist and postmodernist scholars—all influenced by a variety of paradigms or none at all.

In recent years, a number of handbooks on accounting history have appeared with chapters written by leading scholars in the field (Funnell and Williams 2005; Chapman, Hopwood and Shields 2006; Hopper, Northcott and Scapens 2007; Edwards and Walker 2009). Methodological studies include Previts, Parker and Coffman (1990a, 1990b); Carnegie and Napier (1996); and Fleischman, Mills and Tyson (1996). Bibliographic assistance is available from Parker (1988), Fleischman and Radcliffe (2005) and Napier (2006). If one has neither the time nor the inclination to consult this rather prodigious amount of material, a single scholarly work, Mattessich's 2008 opus, *Two Hundred Years of Accounting Research*, is recommended.

Paradigmatic Debate

Much of the critical accounting history of the last three decades under review involved scholarship informed by a pronounced theoretical grounding. Frequently, paradigmatic discourse was so passionate that Hoskin (1994) colourfully called it "academic antler clashing." The ensuing debates were at times antagonistic, but collectively they led to a greater understanding of the events of accounting's history.

Positivist Accounting Research (PAR) became the mainstream theoretical approach, at least in the US, during the 1980s. The emphasis was to identify the natural laws of accounting, a paradigm articulated for the sciences by Kuhn. In America, it resulted in academic closure as teaching positions at prestigious universities were denied to those who did not conform to PAR standards and publication denied in the elite journals. The most prominent voices of positivism were members of the "Rochester School" (Watts and Zimmerman 1978, 1979, 1986).

More importantly, critical scholarship, otherwise known as normative or interpretive, arose in opposition, and a decade later, in an historical context, the "new" accounting history was christened. A classic critique of PAR (Tinker, Merino and Neimark 1982) asserted that positivist and empirical theories had normative origins and were thus value-laden. Hopper, Storey and Willmott (1987) identified the shortcomings of traditional mainstream history, particularly its failure to contextualize accounting, and contended that interpretive perspectives would be superior.

Mouck's (1989, 1992) two articles make the points that PAR merely parrots the rhetoric of science and that accounting historians should shed all guilt for being normative and controversial. Reiter (1998), in a strong indictment, says that PAR has produced no strong empirical results or positive applications for financial reporting. As that failure has not apparently posed a problem for the mainstream, it has become dysfunctional. Neu and Simmons (1996) challenge the hegemony of PAR in explaining managerial behaviour and thus a need to broaden social relations perspectives. Hooks

(1992b) demonstrates the inadequacy of empirical analysis alone to explain the "expectations gap." Whitley (1988) critiques Watts and Zimmerman for creating doubts as to PAR's epistemological and practical values. In similar vein, Kaplan and McEnroe (1991) point out a decade after the heyday of positivism that the Rochester School was moving in more normative directions in its analysis of agency theory. However, agency theory fails to predict accounting regulatory developments. Shapiro (1998) argues that only a normative model provides criteria for evaluating arguments, such as the rationalization of the standard-setting process.

Notwithstanding these critiques, PAR had its supporters in the critical press—most especially for accounting scholars in *AOS* and *CPA*. McKernan (2007) challenged Shapiro's support of a normative model by asking whether desirable objective (positivist) or politically distorted (normative) accounts were preferable. Ahrens (2008) claimed that interpretive research increasingly required objectivist findings. Finally, Mattessich (1995) demonstrated the way to a synthesis of the two theoretical approaches to the recounting of accounting's past and present.

The 1980s and 1990s were exciting decades as accounting scholars increasingly supported their research findings with reference to paradigms drawn from other disciplines (e.g., philosophy, sociology, economics, etc.). However, despite Walker's (2008c) perception that paradigmatic debates have waned as the century turned in favour of new directions he identified, commitments do remain strong. This section will not attempt to recount the foundation concepts of the "isms," but will focus on discourses between adherents of rival paradigms. For an overview of the major paradigms that have informed critical accounting scholarship, see Lodh and Gaffikin (1997).

The three most prominent paradigms in accounting history are economic rationalism (Neoclassicism), Marxism/labour process and Foucauldianism. The origins of these three, chronologically approximately a century apart, date from Adam Smith (1776), Karl Marx (1867) and Michel Foucault (1980a, 1979), respectively. Each has prominent academics who have bridged the transition to accounting history: Chandler (1977), Williamson (1985) and Johnson and Kaplan (1987) for economic rationalism; Tinker (1985, 1988, 1991), Bryer (2000a, 2000b) and Hopper and Armstrong (1991; see also Chapter 7, this volume) for Marxism; and Hopwood (1987; Burchell, Clubb, Hopwood, Hughes and Nahapet 1985), Hoskin and Macve (1986, 1988) and Miller and O'Leary (1987) for Foucauldianism.

Lest other paradigms go unrecognized, the following is a listing of theories developed by thinkers from other disciplines whom accounting scholars have referenced as pertinent to their studies. These are offered as references for students who wish to see how established scholars deployed these paradigms. By far the most influential is Habermas, who inspired all the following and many others not mentioned: Arrington (1997); Arrington and Puxty (1991); Broadbent and Laughlin (1997); Broadbent, Gallop and Laughlin (2010); Lehman (2006); Lodh and Gaffikin (1997); and Power and Laughlin (1996). Other influential paradigms include:

Scholar	Theory	Article(s)
Baudrillard	Postmodernism	Mattessich (2003), Macintosh (2009)
Derrida	Deconstruction	Arrington and Francis (1989)
DiMaggio/Powell	Institutional sociology	Carmona, Ezzamel and Gutiérrez (1998), Sargiacomo (2008)
Gadamer	Hermeneutics	Francis (1994)
Giddens	Hegemony theory	Macintosh and Scapens (1990)
Gramsci	Structuration	Spence (2009)
Kuhn	Science paradigm shifts	Cushing (1984), Mouck (1993)
Latour	Actor-network theory	Robson (1992)
Lyotard	Postmodernism	Martin (1998)
Weber	Socio-political economics	Colignon and Covaleski (1991)

One of the great strengths of *CPA* over the years has been its dedication to special issues for debate among critical scholars. One of these, volume 5, issue 1, featured discourse among representatives of two of the most prominent historical paradigms. After Neimark (1990) had lamented the challenge to Marxist orthodoxy by Foucauldianism, the new "king," Grey (1994), in the special issue's first article, responded and defended Foucault's work. Armstrong (1994), in a carefully reasoned critique from a Marxist perspective, conceded that the current generation of Foucauldian scholars had improved the paradigm's theory. Hoskin (1994), in another response to Neimark, argued that Foucault's work was far from being idealistic, neo-conservative and anti-rational as charged, and had the potential to be a new and significant approach to understanding ourselves and the world. Neimark (1994) concluded the issue by critically examining the Foucauldian understanding of Marx, the Marxist tradition and even Foucault himself. An article in which Marxist class-based theoretical research is promoted was authored by Cooper (1997) in which she observes that postmodernist paradigms such as Foucauldianism do not give voice to the working classes. A paper in *CPA* (volume 10, issue 5) soon followed this where Bryer (1999) launched a Marxist claim that the FASB's conceptual framework was based on the marginalist conception of economic value, which was subjective and vague, whereas had Marxist theory been deployed, it would have been more scientific. There then followed five critiques of Bryer's offering, authored by Macve, Robson, Samuelson, Tinker and Whittington, with a Bryer rejoinder. Macve (1999) points out that a critical Marxist review should focus more on the subsumption of labour in the production process rather than the profit realized from sales. Tinker (1999) protests Bryer's invoking of Marx in a narrow context here rather than the diverse range of more compelling problems that exist under capitalism. An accusation that Marx has been misunderstood, launched by both Bryer and his critics, causes the discourse to remain inconclusive.

An interesting and extended Neoclassical–Foucauldian historical debate spanned the decade of the 1990s. Hoskin and Macve (1988) provoked a vigorous debate when they identified the Springfield Armory, a government munitions instillation in the early nineteenth century, as the genesis of modern managerialism within a Foucauldian context. They attributed the establishment of a disciplinary (piece-rate) regime that rendered labour calculable and observable to the arrival of West Point graduates, who brought with them values and practices which had been inculcated in them by the examination system at the military academy. An economic rationalist rejoinder came from Tyson (1990, 1993) and from Edwards, Boyns and Anderson (1995) and Boyns and Edwards (1996). Tyson's response, based on his examination of the same archival evidence as Hoskin and Macve, was that the events at Springfield were explained by business complexities, economic pressures and social forces unrelated to the West Point connections. Taking a wider perspective, Boyns and Edwards argue that managerialism developed in a variety of places and times related to differing social, economic and cultural influences.

In the later 1990s, Hoskin and Macve (1996) and Tyson (1998a, 1998b) had a similar debate involving the early New England textile industry. In 2000, Hoskin and Macve published a lengthy statement of the Foucauldian perspective on the origins of managerialism to which Tyson (2000) and Boyns and Edwards (2000) provided brief responses.

During the 1980s, Johnson and Kaplan (e.g., 1987) launched a crusade in which American managerial accounting was blamed for the country's loss of world economic hegemony. In response, Ezzamel, Hoskin and Macve (1990) and Hopper and Armstrong (1991) appeared. In the first instance, these two seminal works were critiques of *Relevance Lost* from the Foucauldian and Marxist perspectives, respectively. But as befits seminal works, these articles are much more than book reviews, and, with Johnson and Kaplan's book, they represent the most compelling discourse involving all three of the most familiar paradigms in critical accounting historiography.

There has been a modest amount of debate about transaction cost theory, one of the cornerstones of economic rationalism as voiced by Williamson (1985). Neimark and Tinker (1986) contained a dialectical critique of transaction cost. Covaleski, Dirsmith and Samuel (2003) attempted to extend its value to the management control literature, and Spraakman and Davidson (1998) employed transaction cost to rationalize the management accounting practices of the Hudson's Bay Company.

Marxist critical scholars are very prolific, as Bryer and Tinker have been for decades and Toms is currently, although he prefers to be identified as a Marxian. One of Marxism's great strengths is its adaptability to changing economic and social environments through history. Thus it is that the current labour-process parameter of Marxism illustrates its revisionist potential. Braverman's (1974) book, detailing the process through which labour was "deskilled" in the US, has given rise to a rich interdisciplinary literature that features sociologists, psychologists and economists, as well as accounting scholars of all paradigmatic persuasions. A small sample of works dealing with the labour process as it evolved from Marx's alienation to various manifestations of shop-floor consent include Bryer (2006); Burawoy (1979, 1985); Cooper and Taylor (2000); Ezzamel, Willmott and Worthington (2004, 2008); Knights and Collinson (1987); Knights and Willmott (1986); Levant and Nikitin (2009); and Walker and Mitchell (1998). A related emphasis for debate has been the labour theory of value, originally articulated by classical economists (e.g., Adam Smith) but more integral to Marxist theory. Representative works are Bryer (1994, 2006), Toms (2006, 2010a, 2010b) and Bowman and Toms (2010).

Several important critical papers that do not fit conveniently into the preceding discussion, four each from the two leading critical paradigms—Marxism/labour process and Foucauldianism—are offered here. Armstrong (1991) critiqued agency theory, a favourite economic rationalist control mechanism, claiming that a more radical theorization was necessary. Cooper (1997) argued that Marxism gives voice to working-class people, which postmodernism is unable to do. Sikka (2008) contended in similar vein that mandatory disclosures were needed if there was to be any hope of ending corporate inequities (wage and gender discrimination). Typical of the differing interpretations of Marxism, Toms (2010a, 2010b) questioned Bryer's view of the "capitalist mentality" and the calculation of profit.

Three important Foucauldian studies—Loft (1986); Burchell, Gordon and Miller (1991); and Stewart (1992)—were pivotal in applying Foucault's philosophical, sociological and economic theories to the accounting discipline even although Foucault himself never made that extension. Walsh and Stewart (1993) made this connection explicit in their study of Owen's model factory community during the British Industrial Revolution. More recent commentators, such as Carter, McKinlay and Rawlinson (2002) and McKinlay (2006), continue to reveal the potential for applying Foucault to histories of accounting and management.

As the paradigmatic debates intensified, an article (Miller, Hopper and Laughlin 1991) appeared that introduced the phrase "new accounting history" into the popular parlance. The credo of the "new" history appeared very welcoming and conciliatory, supporting a "proliferation" of methodologies, "a heterogeneous range of issues and theoretical approaches" and a greater interdisciplinarity. These tenets seemly invited "old" accounting historians to engage with their critical colleagues, but other points raised dispelled that notion. Accounting historians were urged to abandon commitments they might have to perceived traditional ideas, such as the progressive march of history, the existence of facts in history, traditionalists' confidence in their own objectivity and the primacy and neutrality of primary sources. The gulf between the "old" and "new" accounting history was widened further when Miller and Napier (1993) roundly condemned traditional historians for using history only as a vehicle to search for the origins of contemporary practices. In this context, the past had meaning only as it impacted the present. On a more positive note, the article demonstrated genealogy, a new methodological approach particularly favoured by Foucauldians that focused more on the outcomes of the past than the origins of the present. Again the reaction was negative in some quarters. Tyson (1995, 30) wrote: "Studies which contend that accounting was a social or political construct as an economic response to competitive business practices are untenable and misleading." Fleischman and Tyson (1997), citing historians and philosophers, argued that referencing the present in analysing the past brings the reader more into the picture. Moreover, it is contended that historians are unable to disassociate themselves from present-day biases. They also wondered if this was the same Napier who in a 1989 article had seemingly dichotomized the historical process into the "discovery" and "contextualizing" phases so that traditional historians could contribute meaningfully by unearthing the grist for the critical paradigmatic mills.

In a *CPA* special issue, Keenan (1998) defended traditional history and attempted to dismiss two issues raised by advocates of the genealogical approach; namely, the supposition that past innovations represent linear progress to the present (the Whig theory of history), and that historical knowledge is important only as it informs the present. Bryer (1998) writes approvingly of Miller and Napier's attack on traditional methodology because economic rationalism, unlike Foucauldianism and Marxism, had not been rigorously tested as a paradigm. Napier (1998) also responds to Keenan in the special issue.

In the same venue, there are three other articles that were not part of the exchange between Keenan and his critics. All three addressed the interface between the traditional mainstream and the "new" critical accounting history. Merino (1998) wrote that the new history should be celebrated for bringing diversity and "making the familiar strange." She urged tolerance and willingness to listen. Chua (1998) makes the interesting point that since history is allegory, differences between old and new are irreconcilable so that overly zealous and evangelical stances should be avoided and interpretive differences celebrated. Gaffikin (1998) argued that the new historical discourses are not only desirable but also essential for the survival of the (sub)discipline. Arnold and McCartney (2003) subsequently observed that the gulf between "old" and "new" is a false dichotomy occasioned by the newness of accounting history as a discipline.

In confronting contrast to calls for tolerance, Sy and Tinker (2005), with arresting frankness, accuse mainstream historians of carrying a "defunct methodological shield," parading evidence without providing its validity or relevance and deploying "antiquarian archivalism." Tyson and Oldroyd (2007), in a more temperate refutation, demonstrate with evidence from the three specialist accounting history journals, 2001–2005, that all of Sy and Tinker's charges were untrue with the exception of traditional accounting history's Eurocentrism.

Conciliation

The paradigmatic confrontations of the past two decades have also prompted numerous scholars to call for mutual respect for rival paradigms. Fleischman, Kalbers and Parker (1996) urged joint visitation to archives in hopes that resulting synergies would enrich the findings. Davila and Oyon (2008) accuse critical researchers of seeking to benefit their own particular research school and urge cross-paradigm collaboration for the advancement of knowledge. Such calls for interactions have resulted in only a few studies (Fleischman, Hoskin and Macve 1995; Fleischman and Macve 2002). Likewise, Parker (2008a) advocates theoretical and methodological pluralism in seeking the new and the risky. Funnell (1996, 1998b), at a practical level, pointed out the similarities between old and new accounting historians. Both use the same basic methodology (narrative or counternarrative), and since all are ultimately seeking truth, different approaches should be tolerated. Laughlin (1995) makes the point that no one perspective can provide a complete picture of accounting reality since choices have to be made along three continuums—theory, methodology and change.

Other researchers have attempted to integrate the possible contributions of multiple paradigms into the explanation of a single issue or event. For example, Fleischman (2000) tried to demonstrate how Taylorism embodied aspects of economic rationalism, Foucauldianism and Marxism; Rodrigues and Craig (2007) theorized international accounting harmonization using Hegelian dialectics, isomorphism and Foucauldian philosophy. Bricker and Brown (1997) and Bricker and Chandar (2003) suggested how empirics and interpretive research could be combined to produce a richer accounting history.

The words might differ but the calls for conciliation are frequently heard. "Tolerance" was the word of choice for Clarke, Craig and Amernic (1999); Clegg (2006); Merino and Mayper (1993); and Oldroyd (1999). "Diversity" was selected by Merino and Mayper (1993), Chua (1998) and Dillard (2008). Gomes (2008) opted for "acceptance" and "conciliatory." Carmona, Ezzamel and Gutiérrez (2004, 25) are accorded a final positive word: "We argue that although traditional accounting history and new accounting history approaches exhibit fundamental differences, both contribute significantly to the field, and indeed to the sharpening of each other's research agenda." Notwithstanding, Walker (2008c) countered that conciliation is not necessarily a good thing given the important role controversy plays in historical debate.

SUPPRESSED VOICES

Critical accounting historians are most anxious to give voice to suppressed groups who are so powerless that their needs are not conceivably addressed in historical accounting records. Here we will examine the plights of the victims of the Holocaust, the oppressed under slavery regimes, the indigenous populations toiling under an imperialist yoke and those who have and continue to suffer racial and gender discrimination.

The Holocaust

There exists a relatively small but extraordinarily powerful critical literature on Holocaust accounting. Funnell's (1998a; see also Chapter 2, this volume) article on German accountants' service to the Third Reich chronicles how they used accounting numbers to deny the humanity of Jewish prisoners and to "render the 'final solution' invisible and efficient. The accounting numbers were also used to 'purify' the actions and motives of those who sought the annihilation of European Jews." Walker's (2000) exposé of the activities of the British delegation to the Fifth International Congress of Accountants held in Berlin in 1938 was an example of 'appeasement' in miniature. These representatives succumbed to Nazi propaganda, condoned the activities of the Fascist state, and fraternized with future war criminals. Lippman and Wilson (2007; Chapter 3, this volume) told of the heart-rending calculations made by German accountants for corporations that established factories within the concentration camps. These included the daily cost of food and medical attention provided, the life expectancy of the slave labour and the use of cheaper gas that saved a pittance but lengthened the suffering of the exterminated. Lippman (2009) also authored a case study for classroom use based on Holocaust data in which discussion was encouraged on the responsibility of accountants for the information they report. A large team of investigators (Booth, Clark, Delahaye, Procter and Rawlinson 2007) wrote about the repercussions when it was revealed in 1998 that Bertlesmann, a large German publishing company, had published anti-Semitic literature during the Nazi regime. The reputation of the firm as being socially responsible was badly jarred. Cinquini (2007), writing about the same era, related how accounting educators in Italy cooperated with the Fascist regime to teach students how to adhere to the methods of the new "corporative" economy.

Slavery

Economic historians have critically dissected every aspect of slavery for well over a century, whereas the subject is relatively new for critical accounting historians. Virtually all the work that has been done with an eye to plantation accounting has focused on the American South and the British

Caribbean. The earliest accounting scholarship, which was not particularly critical in tone, featured articles by Flesher and Flesher (1981), Razek (1985) and Heier (1988) on US plantation accounting and Cowton and O'Shaughnessy (1991) on absentee ownership in the British West Indies. Barney and Flesher's (1994) article on the Locust Grove Plantation did point out the way owners dehumanized their labour force by seeing slaves as mere instruments of capitalist wealth enhancement. A greater moral outrage at the evils of slavery was evident in a series of articles by Fleischman, Oldroyd and Tyson (Fleischman 2004; Fleischman and Tyson 2004; Fleischman, Oldroyd and Tyson 2004; Tyson, Fleischman and Oldroyd 2004; Tyson, Oldroyd and Fleischman 2005; Oldroyd, Fleischman and Tyson 2008; see also Chapter 8, this volume). Moral questions considered in this literature relate to whether those performing accounting functions should be held to a higher standard of justice for sustaining slave regimes which, although not abhorrent to many at the time, may be construed as a form of genocide since demographic evidence has shown conclusively that the life expectancy of slaves was considerably shortened by its rigorous oppression.

A number of other papers in recent years have contributed to the critical literature on slavery. Vollmers (2003) studied slavery in an urban, industrial setting; Hollister and Schultz (2010) contrasted slavery in rural New York State with the more infamous "peculiar institution" of the South; and Stewart (2010) investigated slavery on Carolina rice plantations, the most physically taxing of all American slave venues, and found that African slaves contributed vitally to the cultivation there. McWatters (2008) used archival evidence to demonstrate the profitability of the slave trade, while McWatters and Lemarchand (2009) related how standardized methods utilized in slave-trade accounting contributed to the rise of capitalism. Donoso-Anes (2002) examined how the accounts of the South Sea Company in the early eighteenth century resolved conflicts between it and Spain over their agreement to regulate the slave trade (asiento).

Imperialism: ANZ's Indigenous Peoples

There has been a healthy critical literature emanating from the Antipodes with respect to the difficulties encountered by the Australian Aborigines and the Maoris of New Zealand, historically and in the contemporary world. The historical issue was the manner in which the indigenous populations were dispossessed of their land. In Australia where land is more plentiful, the issue was not as severe as in New Zealand. Gibson (2000) wrote of how accounting was used as a tool to dispossess Aboriginal landholders. In the New Zealand case, the triumvirate of Hooper, Kearins and Pratt (Hooper and Kearins 2004, 2008; see Chapter 9, this volume; Hooper and Pratt 1995, 2003) revealed various techniques the government used to achieve dispossession (e.g., forced sale, a wealth tax, courts that would accept only documentary rather than oral evidence).

In the contemporary world, the major issues in Australia were discrimination against ethnic minorities as reflected in two regards—(a) the entrance and advancement of ethnic minorities in a variety of accounting-related occupations, especially Aborigines and Chinese (James and Otsuka 2009; Kim 2004a, 2004b), and (b) the culture clash between European and Aboriginal ways of thinking as expressed by Greer and her co-authors (Greer 2009; Chew and Greer 1997; Greer and Patel 2000). Meanwhile, the critical agenda in New Zealand similarly recognized the cultural dichotomy between colonizers and Maoris as it impacted race relations, but here the focus was more specifically on the accounting profession and its clients (Gallhofer, Haslam, Kim and Mariu 1999; McNicholas, Humphrey and Gallhofer 2004). A different critical approach is reflected in Gallhofer, Gibson, Haslam, McNicholas and Takiari (2000), where it is suggested that rather than use accounting to suppress indigenous cultures, perhaps valuable insights can be derived from them.

Imperialism: Canada's First Nations

In a powerful series of articles, Dean Neu and his collaborators (Neu 1999, 2000a, 2000b; Neu and Graham 2006; see Chapter 4, this volume; Neu and Therrien 2003) chronicle the despicable process by which the Canadian government fashioned its indigenous people (First Nations) into "governable" populations. The methodologies employed included (in chronological order) conquest; annihilation; containment; and, finally, assimilation.

Other Imperialism Studies

There has been a considerable volume of critical work on imperialism in Africa ("the scramble for Africa"). Hoogvelt and Tinker (1977, 1978) studied the Sierra Leone Development Company as a case study of imperialism and the role of colonial and post-colonial states under imperialism. Maltby and Tsamenyi (2010) disclosed how English gold-mining companies used accounting to defend their labour policies versus trade union resistance in the former Gold Coast in the first half of the twentieth century. Elad (1998) looked at colonial West Africa to determine whether accounting and taxation of colonists rendered them more subjective and less likely to resist. It did not. Rahaman (2010) reviewed critical research in Africa and suggested additional areas for study.

Most studies of imperialism relate to the post-colonial epoch as nations around the globe continue to suffer imperialism directly or its legacy. Studies of professionalization in such contexts have often proved illuminating. Annisette (1999, 2000, 2003; see Chapter 12, this volume), researching the professionalization movement in Trinidad and Tobago, revealed racial discrimination against blacks (who constituted 80 per cent of the population) and how the entrenched organizations of the colonial power (Britain) dominated the accounting profession. Bakre (2005, 2006) told a similar story for Jamaica where, following independence, the Chartered Accountants of Jamaica was founded but floundered because of internal and external interference from the British accounting profession. Sian (2006a, 2006b, 2007) traced the closure of the profession to the indigenous population as Kenya moved from a British colony to an independent nation. The government eventually revised its policy of exclusion but not its acceptance of segregation.

Davie (2000, 2005a) found an even more diabolical situation in Fiji, where British imperialists colluded with native chieftains to suppress and exploit the vast majority of Fijians. Davie (2005b) and Nandam and Alam (2005) wrote on how the colonial regime in Fiji used accounting to perpetuate racism and exclusion. Dyball, Chua and Poullaos (2006) and Dyball, Poullaos and Chua (2007) asserted that the US delayed the coming of independence to the Philippines on the questionable pretensethat the Filipino accounting profession was unable to manage the country's economic affairs without American supervision.

Three other works of importance need be mentioned to bring this section to a close. Although not an historian, Said's (1944) classic *Culture and Imperialism* is invariably mentioned by critical scholars working in the area of imperialism. Hammond (2003b), whose work spans race and gender, calls for a greater attention to the political motivations behind the marginalization of groups under imperialism. Cooper and Catchpowle (2009) say something that needs be said in today's world—the expending of millions of dollars of Iraq's oil revenues without proper controls, intended to establish US hegemony, is unquestionably "imperialism in action."

Racism: Apartheid in South Africa

Imperialism in Africa, in contrast to the Americas, featured a small, ethnic minority, backed by distant military powers, dominating the majority, indigenous population. Here, the theme that appeared in the critical accounting literature was the South African environment where the white ruling regime had institutionalized Apartheid (not unlike segregation in the US but lacking a white majority). It is for these reasons that South African Apartheid is included in a racist subsection although its origins were clearly imperialistic. Hammond was once again in the vanguard of scholars who studied South Africa in the aftermath of Apartheid. Arnold and Hammond (1994) researched the US congressional debates on investment divestiture and the articulation of the Sullivan Principles, concluding that accounting had both potential and limitations to serve the interests of subordinated groups. Hammond, Arnold and Clayton (2007) and Hammond, Clayton and Arnold (2009), using oral history, found that racism endured even after Apartheid, and that blacks were effectively closed out of the accounting profession. Cooper and Catchpowle (2009) explained the role of accounting in the post-Apartheid privatization programme, but qualified its economic benefits because the democratic transition was threatened.

Racism: America's Ethnic Minorities

The US has much to answer for in its treatment of minority populations. Theresa Hammond has dedicated much of her career to exposing the injustices faced by African Americans attempting to enter the accounting profession (Hammond 1997a, 2002; Hammond and Streeter 1994; see Chapter 11, this volume). Others have contributed as well to this crusade. Viator (2001) studied African-American employees in public accounting and found they were less likely to obtain informal mentoring, particularly as related to protection, resistance and social support. Furthermore, they indicated a stronger intention to leave public accounting. Glover, Mynatt and Schroeder (2000) surveyed African Americans on the job and found their perception to be that their firms were less than totally committed to diversity and that a glass ceiling handicapped their opportunities for advancement.

Scholarship on the subject of Indian affairs in the US is centred at the University of New Mexico. Two articles (Preston and Oakes 2001; Preston 2006) deal with the governmentally mandated reduction of Navajo herds, which proved an economic and social disaster for the tribe. Oakes and Young (2010) dealt with legislation of 1887 intended to fragment the tribal structure by establishing private ownership of land. This action was followed by a century of fraud, mismanagement and accounting failure. A conclusion reached was that accounting fails to restore justice when the parties to a dispute are so unequal in terms of power. Holmes, Welch and Knudson (2005) researched the Coahuiltecan Indian tribes who lived in the area now Texas, then part of New Spain. The exploitation and subjugation of them led to the disappearance of their culture and absorption into Spanish society.

There is a smattering of scholarship dealing with other American ethnic minorities. An article by Blanco and de la Rosa (2008) portrays the underrepresentation of Hispanics in business schools, providing explanations for the shortfall and remedies for its correction. Fleischman and Tyson (2000) write of the interface between accounting and racism that so negatively impacted the lives of Asiatic indentured labourers brought in to work the Hawaiian sugar plantations (cf. Burrows 2002). Finally, Fleischman and Tyson (2006), expecting accountants to be implicated in the heinous episode of the forced relocation of Japanese American citizens during World War II, found that they were actually the most helpful of any administrators to the "evacuees."

Gender: Historical Studies

A number of powerful historical exposés of the genderization of the accounting profession appeared in the early 1990s. Loft (1992) and Kirkham and

Loft (1993a), writing about a time when the US accountancy profession was in its infancy, related the story how only men could become "accountants" while women could aspire to nothing more prestigious that "book-keeper" or "clerk." Kirkham and Loft (1993b; see Chapter 10, this volume), in a subsequent article, studied the feminization of accounting in England and Wales during the period 1870–1930 and found that the degrading of "clerk" to women's work was accompanied by the elevation of "accountant" to a masculine domain. Walker (2003b) found a similar sexual stereotyping and exploitation of women in the UK, where they could aspire occupationally to "book-keeper" but not to "accountant." Shackleton (1999) had a similar tale to tell of gender segregation among the early Scottish professional societies occasioned by masculine fears of female competition in the workplace. Cooper (2010) accounted for the forty-year process of exclusion of women from professional organizations in the UK and Australia arising out of the very same fear. Hammond (2003b), in an article on discrimination based on both race and gender, was of the opinion that the exclusionary plight of Spanish and Maori women was essentially politically motivated. For those more quantitatively oriented, Wootton and Kemmerer (2000) presented empirical data tracking the changing genderization in the US accounting workforce, 1930–1990.

Lehman (1992) chronicled how male accountants constructed an environment in which women had to struggle culturally, educationally, economically and politically. Given this early discrimination, Kirkham (1992) urged critical scholars to re-examine the historical influence and power of the profession and its knowledge base with reference to gender. Hooks (1992a) proposed a research agenda to rationalize the andocentric culture of public accounting, its patriarchal nature, its cultural expectations and the dynamics of praxis in accounting. Gallhofer (1998) accused mainstream feminist research of failing to question the racial and gendered biases of western ethnocentrism and to develop a critique of patriarchal arrangements.

Literature can also illuminate accountancy's past. Rutterford and Maltby (2006) used Trollope's novels to demonstrate how women in earlier times were able to control their own property without the aid of men, providing evidence of a business acumen easily transferred to accounting. Czarniawska (2008) utilized the novels of Douglas Adams to show how perceptions of accounting and gender went through many changes in central Europe between the late eighteenth century and today's global economy.

Nichols, Robinson, Reithal and Franklin(1997) conducted a survey of how professional accountants would respond to actual court cases involving sexual harassment. The findings suggested that male CPAs were less apt to find men guilty compared to females and that females were more likely to prefer in-house investigation than males when episodes arose. Hammond (1997b) and Kirkham (1997) critiqued the project and found the methodology and the theoretical framework wanting.

Komori (2007, 2008) has done considerable work studying the relationship between Japanese women and accounting. Her earlier article examined the beneficial effect of women doing private accounting in the home, paralleling the work of Walker and Llewellyn (2000). The later article dealt with the public sphere where women had made few inroads entering the profession although progress had occurred in the managerial accounting field. Hammond and Preston (1992) have also studied power differentials and exclusion based on class, race and gender in Japan as suggested by the work of Kondo.

This subsection concludes with the mention of two articles that provide food for thought. Dwyer and Roberts (2004a) blame the economic imperialism of the giant international accounting firms for spreading globally the genderization policies prevalent in the US Finally, Fearfull and Kamenou (2007) ask and attempt to answer the poignant question of why ethnic minority women continue to struggle for corporate acceptance and progression after three decades of legislation outlawing discrimination.

Gender: Is a Woman's Place in the Home?

Stephen Walker (1998, 2003c, 2008a; Walker and Llewellyn 2000; Walker and Carnegie 2007) has undertaken a major research project on how household accounting prescriptions confirmed the operation of patriarchy. In Walker and Llewellyn (2000), the distinctions between private life (home) and the public realm (accounting work generally) are discussed and how gendered spheres of influence are created thereby. While the focus has been on Victorian England, Walker and Carnegie (2007) extended the study to Australia and the "budgetary earmarking and control of the extravagant woman." Walker (2008a) also offered a research agenda to further historical gender studies. Topical subjects include the oppression and subordination of women, the dichotomy between their private and public lives, the construction of identities and the restoration of women to the pages of history.

Closely related is the issue of motherhood. Haynes (2008) and Lightbody (2009) discuss how motherhood and career are intertwined, using oral history as a data source. Dambrin and Lambert (2008) objectively point out that motherhood is an economic cost to accounting firms and forces women to seek different career "trajectories." Consequently, the entry-level issues for women of decades past have mitigated somewhat, but the shortfall of female senior managers and partners remains chronic. Windsor and Auyeung (2006) speak to the difficulties faced by minority women with dependent children, some of which might be resolved if flexible hours and other such programmes were to be made public knowledge. Kornberger, Carter and Ross-Smith (2010) had an opposite opinion of flexitime, feeling that demands for it have increased the gender problem.

Gender: The Glass Ceiling

A popular focus of critical scholars researching gender-related issues is the invisible obstacle of the glass ceiling, a roadblock placed in the paths of women (and minorities) that forestalls their elevation in accounting firms and universities to positions commensurate with their abilities. Two papers related to the academic glass ceiling are those of Walker (2008a), who points out the relative lack of female professors and activists, and Emery, Hooks and Stewart (2002) in which the shortfall of high-ranking, female accounting professors in New Zealand is identified. Ciancanelli, Gallhofer, Humphrey and Kirkham (1990) undertook a quantitative analysis of female access to hierarchal positions within UK accounting firms and found insufficient numbers. French and Meredith (1994) optimistically concluded that women were being promoted but only in terms of the percentage entering the profession at the point of recruitment.

Parker (2008a) suggests that a possible way forward for mitigating this problem is to research the importance of women to the profession by virtue of the differing perceptions they bring to bear that are both important and distinct from their male counterparts. Hull and Umansky (1997) critiqued the sex-role stereotyping that justifies in men's minds the right to deny women access to positions of leadership. Several scholars have discussed the differences between the sexes that would make women particularly valuable assets to accounting firms. Haynes (2008) had a similar idea, arguing that it was time to get off the gender issue in favour of feminization, the value of what women accountants could contribute. Dillard and Reynolds (2008) articulate the possibilities of integrating the feminine-intuitive and masculine-rational processes for making business decisions. Hooks and Cheramy (1994) revealed some of the facts and myths about women in the profession. The most significant findings revealed in their surveys were that 89 per cent of female professionals returned to work after having a child and that the same percentages of men and women were promoted to partner if they achieved the rank of senior manager. Since entry-level equity has been achieved, the problem was retention at lower levels. Hammond and Oakes (1992) did not buy into the proposition that the feminine perspective, viewpoint, intuitive talent, etc., could really be defined since these attributes vary so greatly among women.

ACCOUNTANCY UNDER SIEGE

Critical accounting researchers have scrutinized all constituencies that comprise accounting, both historically and currently. This section will review the literature critiquing the performance of public accounting practitioners, standard-setters, management accountants, public-sector accountants and academicians. This section is organized as follows. First, the occupational groups will be considered individually, followed by three areas where the indictment is sufficiently broad that all constituencies stand accused: the subordination of the public interest, the lack of accountability and the deployment of rhetoric to delude those users who depend on accounting information.

Public Accounting Practice

In the past decade, a focal point of public, if not critical, attention has been the major audit failures, which appear to be more numerous than ever before. These frauds have been so extensively covered that there is no need for a full recounting here. Two early scandals predated the articulation of modern audit standards. Hooper, Pratt and Kearins (1993) relate how creative accounting practices and questionable audit decisions led to business failures in colonial New Zealand. An American fraud that immediately predated the more famous McKesson & Robbins scandal led to audit reform with the establishment of the first standard-setting body in the US (Heier and Leach-López 2010). The wave of savings and loan failures of the early 1990s in the US was explained by Margavio (1993) as resulting from inconsistent regulation that ran contrary to GAAP. Merino and Kenny (1994) argued that auditors of savings and loans failed to transcend weak rules and assess the economic substance of transactions. Notwithstanding past history, the profession has yet to respond to the urging of Cullinan and Sutton (2002) that the toughening of fraud detection and the elimination of the current laxness are necessary because these failures are clearly not in the public interest.

Critical researchers have identified some of the problems with financial reporting and auditing that have led to fraudulent outcomes. A striking indictment was forthcoming from Mitchell, Sikka and Willmott (1998), who accused accountants of creating complex transactions that concealed illegal activities, including money laundering, despite the obligation to report detected fraud. Walker (1996) demonstrated the potential positive or negative impact of disreputable accounting practitioners depending on how the profession dealt with their malfeasances. Fogarty, Helan and Knutson (1991) provided evidence that auditors sometimes failed to inform investors when the financial statements of clients could not be relied upon. Neu (1991) claims that the general public has no choice but to put its faith in auditors even though they are more likely to breach the public's trust rather than that of the client when conflicts occur. Mills and Bettner (1992) argue that the "ritualistic nature" of the audit process and standards are used to mask conflict, maintain social order and legitimate the profession's actions.

The title of Powers' (1997) book, *The Audit Society: Rituals of Verification*, serves as an excellent introduction to the issue of the profession's ongoing struggle to attain legitimacy. Power (2003) discusses four themes of the audit process and formal structure that potentially enhance the public's perception of the profession's legitimacy. Richardson (1987a) authored a general article on accounting as a legitimating institution—existing perceptions of it, its sociological roots and future research directions. Young (1997), in "defining auditors' responsibilities," documents the efforts of the profession to dominate its own rules definition and, thus, its legitimacy.

In an interesting paper, Preston, Cooper, Scarborough and Chilton (1995) compare the significant differences between the US professional codes of ethics in 1917 and 1988 and attribute these to the need to redefine legitimacy to a materially different society.

A number of scholars have focused on problems that make it difficult for auditors to legitimize their function. Martens and McEnroe (1992) charge that auditors neglect "substance" in order to avoid litigation exposure and warn that if this trend continues, legitimacy will erode to nothing. Pasewark, Shockley and Wilkerson (1995) present empirical evidence that in-charge auditors lose objectivity when confronted by powerful client employees. Guénin-Paracini and Gendron (2010) point out that legitimacy is hard to preserve when auditors become the scapegoats for frauds (e.g., Arthur Andersen). However, the continued functioning of capital markets and the preservation of economic order depend on such myths. A related story, detailed in Okike (2004), relates how the Nigerian audit profession responded to the post-Enron challenge to its legitimacy. A case study of an Australasian sugar refinery at the turn of the twentieth century demonstrated how accounting was used to legitimate the exploitation of the work force and a generous return to stockholders (Hooks and Stewart 2007).

The objectivity that positivists claim for their scientific and empirical methodology is shared by the accounting profession as it represents itself as the paragon of objectivity. Lehman and Tinker (1987) stated that accounting practices are more productively regarded as ideological weapons for parties participating in conflicts over the distribution of social wealth. Tinker (1991), building upon a message of *Paper Prophets*, rejected the notion that theories are dispassionate reflections of reality but rather should be viewed as grounded in social conflict. Solomons (1991), having cited *Paper Profits* as an example of the evils of radical accounting analysis, opined that the task of accountants is to achieve representational faithfulness, the absence of which endangers the profession. Tinker (1991) responded that partisanship is inevitable in accounting and that our actions are determined by heightened social contradictions.

Perhaps the harshest broadside against accountancy's legitimizing effort came from Mitchell and Sikka (1993), who accused practice of assuming a godlike aura of impartiality and integrity when it was truly collusive and undemocratic. This article also condemned the profession for its conservatism and dedication to the status quo, a point raised in many attack-mode articles (e.g., Malsch and Gendron 2009). Dwyer and Roberts (2004a) studied campaign contributions of the US accounting profession and found a preference to support conservative agendas with relatively little going to civil rights, labour, liberal and women's groups.

Carnegie and Napier (2010), in a recent article, observed the negative stereotyping accountancy has suffered post-Enron. Here we will review what critical researchers have written over the years about practitioners' ethics that would lead to the conclusion that Enron alone could never have produced this disaster. Preston et al. (1995), it will be recalled, explained the revision of the US profession's code of ethics as an effort to preserve legitimacy, not the most noble of purposes. Chwastiak and Young (2003) accused accountants of maintaining silences about injustices in annual reports to make maximizing profit the only measure of success. Velayutham (2003), looking at Australian and New Zealand codes, saw a shift away from a moral public accountability to a "true and fair" position suggestive of compliance with accounting standards. Reiter (1997) argues that accounting ethics are misguided, that the prevailing "ethic of right," geared toward independence, should be scrapped in favour of an "ethic of care," oriented toward social justice. Ponemon (1990) surveyed professionals individually and found that managers and partners reflected less ethical reasoning ability than staff members.

The "expectations gap" has been a chronic problem for the accountancy profession. Young (1997) wrote that the profession has failed to close the gap, especially as it relates to fraud. This failure would be particularly frustrating since Byington and Sutton (1991) think that the US profession's response to crises in 1938, 1971, 1978 and 1985 was designed *only* to close the expectations gap. Humphrey, Mozier and Turley (1992) explored the gap in the UK and the profession's reaction to it—defensive to educate the public and constructive to change audit activities to meet public concerns. Olson and Wootton (1991) argued that the semantics of audit reports are the primary reason why the expectations gap has remained widely open.

While there has been some progress with the profession's hiring of women and persons of colour, there are other groups who have not captured the attention of accounting firms. Jacobs (2003) noted that firms discriminate in the hiring process against people from lower-class origins. Duff and Ferguson (2007) studied the hiring practices of Big Four firms in the UK and found that they were behind in hiring people with disabilities. Fearfull, Carter, Sy and Tinker (2008) decried the situation of accounting clerical workers and others of low status who were rendered invisible in the scheme of things. Cooper and Taylor (2000) also pointed out how non-qualified, clerical employees of accounting firms are basically "deskilled" (Braverman's term) and are virtually ignored in the literature.

Additional complaints have been launched questioning other sacred cows of public accountancy. Kluger and Shields (1991) relate how firms seek to change auditors in hopes of hiding unfavourable disclosures, what has come to be called "opinion shopping." Hendrickson (1998) chronicled US events post-1933 and found self-regulation to be a failure, especially with respect to independence issues. Green (1999) tells how the auditing profession has lobbied hard for changes that would reduce audit risk without addressing the issue of why audits fail.

A prominent theme in accounting history is the attempt of professional societies to close membership on the basis of race, gender and/or social class. The accounting organizations in the UK have been particularly virulent, primarily as a consequence of closure, but perhaps also because of the large number of professional organizations there and/or the extent of the empire. We have already seen closure on the basis of colour in Kenya, the British Caribbean (Jamaica and Trinidad and Tobago), Australia, New Zealand and South Africa. Mother country interference with newly founded societies was evident in Australia (Chua and Poullaos 2008; Poullaos 2009), Canada (Edwards and Walker 2008) and India (Verma and Gray 2006).

Earlier, the founding Scottish societies closed membership to those who aspired to share in monopolistic profits (Kedslie 1990a, 1990b; Walker 1991; Lee 2010). Walker and Shackleton (1998) exposed the phenomenon in the whole of Great Britain. Walker studied the genesis of professional organizations in Scotland (1995) and local societies in major English cities (2004b). The motivation in the latter case was closure and market protection from interlopers, while in Scotland it was an organizational response to powerful London merchants. Other closure episodes around the globe were reported by Ramirez (2001) in France, Baskerville (2006) in New Zealand, O'Regan (2008) in Ireland and Zelinschi (2009) in Romania. Of course, the heinous racial and gender barriers in the US have been studied in detail.

Standard-Setters

The standard-setting process, especially in a profession-regulating environment as is the case with FASB, is particularly difficult. Every close decision generates a cohort of unhappy people. Some scholars have described this treacherous footing in general terms. Committe (1990) questions whether the delegation of power from Congress to the SEC to FASB is even constitutional. Zeff (1999) makes a telling point with regard to FASB's conceptual framework that within a decade of its promulgation, there were no longer any members who had participated in its passage. Hence, the conceptual framework was seriously weakened from that perspective. 'Weakness" is a prevalent theme in many critiques of standard-setting. Samuelson (1999), in a response to Bryer's Marxist critique of the conceptual framework, observed that FASB was not politically strong enough to do anything other than what is "subjective and vague." Jupe (2000) described the weakness of the UK's Accounting Standards Board, which relies on voluntary compliance and is responsive to the rhetoric of key allies to maintain its tenuous existence. Jeppesen (2010) commented that Danish audit standards are soft to avoid resistance. Camfferman and Zeff (2009) reported that the Dutch profession tried to scuttle the UEC for fear that general European standards would be less rigorous than its own.

Tim Fogarty (1994, 1998; Fogarty, Ketz and Hussein 1992; Fogarty, Hussein and Ketz 1994) has written extensively on US standard-setting topics as diverse as due process, political aspects, research challenges and changing FASB's operating basis from structural-functionalism to conflict theory. Some outstanding "gadflies" have taken on the regulatory hierarchy. Briloff (1993a) accuses the SEC of failing to mete out punishment evenhandedly and FASB of issuing rules rather than standards. He presents evidence from decades of malfeasance. Sikka, Willmott and Lowe (1989, 1991) charged that UK professional bodies fail to be accountable either to their membership or to the general public with respect to audit guidelines. Chandler (1991) replied that it is not clear what constitutes the public interest, and that Sikka, Willmott and Lowe had presented an unbalanced view of standard-setting due process. The team responded that the rebuttal had failed to discuss the political aspects of accounting regulation.

Papers have been written that focus on key buzzwords that standard-setters need to re-address. Puxty and Laughlin (1983) have written about "decision usefulness"; Zeff (1998) about "independence" and how to shore up compliance; Masocha and Weetman (2007) on how rhetoric was used to obscure standard-setters' change of opinion about a "going concern audit" standard; and Young and Mouck (1996) recommending recourse to history to gain "objectivity" in the standard-setting process.

This section concludes with mention of a variety of papers critical of the standard-setting process. Hines (1989a, 1991) claims that conceptual frameworks are designed specifically to protect the profession's legitimacy and the status quo. Young and Williams (2010) provide examples of value judgments made by FASB that raise ethical questions of the standard-setting process. Two papers are critical of decisions that FASB has made in framing standards. Basu and Waymire (2010) claim that FASB was influenced by Sprague to shift focus to a balance-sheet approach when an income-statement orientation would better serve the higher purpose of providing information about exchange possibilities. In similar vein, Williams (2003) contends that regulations permit users to evaluate future *benefits* at the expense of information on current means to measure future *risks*. Finally, De Lange and Howieson (2006) forecast that the FASB/IASB convergence effort will fail because history shows that the US will either dominate the proceedings or, if unable to get its way, will take its football and go home.

Management Accountants

Internal corporate accountants have not suffered as much critical opprobrium as external practitioners because it is not always clear how to separate their responsibility from that of the auditors who allow malfeasance to pass and the greed of the corporations for which they work. A review of different paradigmatic alternatives for management accounting research is provided by Baxter and Chua (2003). Luft and Shields (2003) undertook a mapping study illustrating the connects and disconnects evinced in 275 articles on management accounting in six journals. Tinker and Neimark (1988) compared conservative (transaction cost) historiography with critical (conflict theory) using General Motors's accounting records as data. Tinker, Neimark and Lehman (1991) also found "middle road" theorizing of corporate reporting (relativism, quietism, pluralism) untenable since the middle ground shifts over time because of social struggle and conflicts. Chua (1988) observed two decades ago that the heavy borrowing of management accounting research from interpretive sociology had hampered its own theoretical development. Humphrey and Scapens (1996) urged the need for case-based researchers to become more directly involved in theories of the organizational and social functioning of accounting. However, Young and Preston (1996) warned of the possible dangers of pursuing theoretical eclecticism. C. Lehman (2006) avers that conventional accounting rhetoric suggests that the bottom line reflects transactions, performance and stewardship. But this view obscures certain "deleterious" social relationships that produce these results (e.g., the use of immigrant labour).

Management accounting literature is based on Neoclassical economics, say Neimark and Tinker (1986). Our understanding of control systems would be heightened if inter-organizational and social conflict were incorporated as the primary theory and the social origins and consequences of corporate control systems recognized. Macintosh (1995) examined profit manipulation by managers of large mega-national firms and self-beneficial choice of accounting methods that inflated profits. The ethics of profit control were questioned. In a subsequent article, Macintosh, Sherer and Riccaboni (2009) undertook a case study of GE's takeover of Nuovo Pighone, where "generic" management and control systems were instituted to elevate profits reported to capital markets. A greater accountability than economic efficiency and profits was called for. Munro (1995) exposed a large and successful British corporation that had no accounting controls but was "managed by ambiguity" wherein the higher echelons of management knew nothing of what was happening at lower levels. Oakes, Covaleski and Dirsmith (1999) did an historical study of how management rhetoric was used as a mechanism to weaken the union movement and make workers more governable. Armstrong (2005) did an interesting study of the greater prominence of accountants in corporate hierarchies than other professionals, which he attributed to their creative strategies for controlling labour.

Public-Sector Accounting

Warwick Funnell's (1990, 1994, 1997, 2004, 2006) work on public-sector auditing has spanned nearly two decades. The 1990 and 2006 articles chronicled how poor accounting and control were responsible for Britain's hapless showing in the Crimean and Boer Wars respectively. The 2006 article also involved the military in that War Office spending needed to be curbed necessitating that audit standards be articulated and accountability established for that purpose. Radcliffe (2008) also critiqued governmental auditors for maintaining secrets, not observing that which is unpalatable.

Chwastiak (2008) accused US governmental auditors in terms of human and social costs in order to rationalize war.

A substantial public-sector issue in which governmental accountants were involved, especially in the UK, was the nationalization of industries or other enterprises formerly under private control. The *cause célèbre* was the nationalization of the British coal industry and the accompanying pit closures that left critical scholars as "brassed off" as the colliery bands depicted in the movie of the same name. Berry, Capps, Cooper, Ferguson, Hopper and Low (1985) conducted an analysis of the management control system instituted by the National Coal Board (NCB). Most of the same author team participated in Hopper, Cooper, Lowe, Capps and Mouritsen (1986), published as a chapter in Knights and Willmott (1986), dealing with NCB control and worker resistance thereto. Cooper and Hopper (1988) edited a collection of essays dealing with the colliery closures. When privatization replaces nationalization, things can go seriously wrong with that scenario as well. Arnold and Copper (1999) relate the story of the Medway Ports, where the privatization was engineered by Price Waterhouse and cost half the employees their jobs. Also, the redundant workers were forced to sell their shares to the new owners for a ridiculously low value determined by KPMG Peat Marwick. Jupe and Compton (2006) and Jupe (2009) observed that Blair's promised regulation when the national rail system was returned to private ownership proved to be no more than a smoke-screen to mask a wealth transfer from tax payers to capitalists. This failure highlighted a fundamentally flawed concept of fragmenting and privatizing a loss-making industry in the interests of British capitalism.

A fertile subject for critical review of public-sector institutions has been medical care and hospitals. This is especially true for the UK, where the National Health Service (NHS) has been functioning since the 1950s. Issues raised in the literature include budgeting (Preston, Cooper and Combs 1992); financial and administrative change (Broadbent, Laughlin and Read 1991); local and centralized aspects of the NHS (Robson 2007); distributive conflicts as a basis for funding rather than efficiency (Froud, Haslam, Johal, Shaoul and Williams 1998); and patient rights and accountability (Hill, Fraser and Cotton 2001). Holden, Funnell and Oldroyd (2009) related a heart-warming story of the Newcastle Infirmary in Victorian times. In an age when poverty was looked upon as a sin, accounting was used to convince wealthy contributors that paupers should be treated despite such compassion being a violation of hospital rules.

A smaller number of studies have appeared about US health care—hospital costs (Preston 1992; Chua and Preston 1994); Medicare (Preston, Chua and Neu 1997); and the use of financial controls in different varieties of US hospitals (Rayburn and Rayburn 1991). Given the current turmoil in the US involving Medicare fraud and the prospect of privatization of Medicare, more critical work is to be expected.

Academicians

This subsection deals with two of the major components of an accounting professor's job description—teaching and research. The teaching category features the dual reality of how accounting education is failing the practice community, particularly with respect to ethics training, and how the profession conversely fails academe by insisting that the entry-level product be more technically than liberally educated. In this regard, both fail the public interest. On the research side of the ledger, critical researchers have identified a host of barriers that must be overcome—university restrictions on research, access to flagship journals controlled by the academic mainstream and restrictions imposed by governmental funding agencies and professional organizations.

One of the most renowned critiques of accounting education, at least in the US, is Albrecht and Sack (2000) in which three major points were voiced: (a) courses are too often taught as a series of technical rules; (b) courses are geared toward passing a professional exam and, hence, the *right* answer is stressed; and (c) students are not exposed to a broad business education or real-world examples. This latter point echoed the work of Koeppen (1990), who urged that the concentration should be on issues rather than rote learning. In similar vein, Boyce (2004) observed that accounting education is constrained by misconceived disciplinary boundaries focused on the techniques and skills of professional practice.

The most oft-heard complaint of what accounting education lacks is developing the ethics of future professionals. At a general level, Low, Davey and Hooper (2008) opine that the recent spate of scandals have convinced students that ethics are important, just not necessarily for them. Boyce (2008) believes that ethics education should be taken to a global dimension since most crises occur internationally. An early paper on ethics, Puxty, Sikka and Willmott (1994), spoke to the need to "reform the circle" consisting of education, ethics and accountancy. Other critical scholars suggest more specific ways to improve ethics education. Young and Annisette (2009) recommend using literature to teach ethics, emphasizing Dewey pragmatism. Reiter (1996) avers that ethics education fails to explore societal and institutional causes and solutions. She urges the need for an expanded view of ethics, which she called "ethics of care." Saravanamuthu (2004) claims that the profession seeks to "commodify" accounting education to produce "compliant, hegemonic technocrats." Accordingly, education should strive rather to teach ethical accountability.

Other related suggestions were forthcoming from Lee, Clarke and Dean (2008), who advised that auditors be schooled in the art of assurance risk, a talent that could be materially aided by recourse to history, and Shapiro (2009), who thinks that business education should encourage students to think reflectively, ethically and spiritually about themselves, others and the profession. Humphrey, Lewis and Owen (1996), as do many others, share the opinion that accounting education must include social and environmental accounting. Unfortunately, they urged this expansion of the curriculum a decade and a half ago and precious little advance is in evidence, particularly in green accounting. Tinker and Koutsoumandi (1997) argue that the technical education accounting students receive leaves them ill-prepared for the complexities of the job market, and what is needed is a greater appreciation for the historical and sociological background of the profession. Gray and Collison (2002) argue that what accounting students need is "transcendent" education, one that teaches them to serve the public interest. Only then will education be conveyed rather than training.

As suggested in the introduction to this section, there are many impediments to critical academic research, most of them situated in the US The most frequently heard complaints were directed towards the restrictiveness of mainstream American journals (Baker and Bettner 1997). The *Accounting Review* (*TAR*) has come under particular scrutiny. At one time, at least through the mid-1980s, the journal was eclectic in its range of published articles. It has since become so narrow in focus that all the articles that appear therein reflect a methodological sameness—highly empirical, positivistic and scientific in orientation (Williams and Rodgers 1995). Rodgers and Williams (1996) further claim that *TAR*'s universal use of scientific texts drawn from financial economics restricts rather than enlarges accounting's intellectual potential. Williams, Jenkins and Ingraham (2006) have actually accused the gatekeeper elite of killing behavioural research by denying its access to top-rated journals. Heck and Jensen (2007), in an analysis of articles published in *TAR* over its history to 2005, concluded that its current publishing pattern of mathematical analysis and empirical research ("accountics") is done at the expense of articles that would benefit the practice community and research on more interesting topics. Objectivity mandates that a contrary opinion of *TAR* was voiced in Fleming, Graci and Thompson (2000), who wrote how the journal's embrace of quantitative/empirical research brought methods from other disciplines to bear on accounting. Also, Parker, Guthrie and Gray (1998), gatekeepers themselves, have tried to provide advice as to how editors and boards might be approached by surveying UK and Australian professors and department heads as to what constitutes quality research. A different protest against the gatekeepers of accounting knowledge was voiced by Carmona and Zan (2002), Carmona (2004) and Zan (2004). With English as the *lingua franca* of accounting publication, the work of scholars whose first language is not English has not received the exposure it deserves—a loss to all of us. Walker (2005) wrote of the parochialism of accounting history, both in terms of its lack of an interdisciplinary focus and its failure to incorporate non-Anglo scholars or scholarship into its body of knowledge.

The charges of elitism in the American academic community extend beyond the "gatekeepers" of the most prestigious journals. Lee (1995b, 1997; Lee and Williams 1999) has written extensively about how the

American Accounting Association (AAA) is the organization through which the faculties of elite universities (Williams and Rodgers put the number at fifteen) have "colonized" accounting knowledge in the US One needs only look at the composition of the AAA's executive committee and the editorial boards of its journals to understand how the American academic community is "policed."[2]

Professional bodies in Britain and Ireland have also had to endure critical comment regarding their commitment to their constituencies and to the public interest. Willmott, Puxty and Cooper (1993) wrote of the dilemma faced by the leadership of the ICAEW in this regard, and Lee (1995a) felt accountants did protect the public interest but in a self-interested way. Noguchi and Edwards (2008) showed compelling evidence that the ICAEW leadership was detached from its constituency. O'Dwyer and Channing (2008) exposed the Irish professional accounting body's handling complaints in a self-serving manner.

A number of American education-related initiatives have failed in the estimation of critical scholars. Fogarty, Radcliffe and Campbell (2006) wrote of the demise of the AICPA's vision project when professional bodies tried to expand the domain of practice beyond the expertise of accountants and then distanced themselves from the project. Davis and Sherman (1996) chronicled failed activities of the Accounting Education Change Committee, which was captured by the firms that funded it. Accreditation has come under a more global scrutiny. In a critique of the American Association of Collegiate Schools of Business (AACSB), Fogarty (1997) claimed that its accreditation dictates for institutional research, curriculum revision and continuing professional education have distracted academics from the theories and social awareness that characterize postmodernism. Dillard (2002) likewise sees AACSB accreditation as the way in which universities have thwarted the efforts of academics to carry out their social responsibilities. Australian universities stand accused of placing restrictions on accounting research funding by favouring the sciences over the humanities (Neumann and Guthrie 2002). James (2008) employed a Marxist alienation perspective to protest how universities there pressure young academics to finish their dissertations when they would be better served in pursuits more related to teaching and research.

Morgan and Willmott (1993) speak of the need for research findings to be communicated beyond the academic community, and Inanga and Schneider (2005) discuss how accounting research has failed to improve practice. Moore (1991) argues that critical accounting must go beyond theorizing, to take a "political stance in targeting practice and institutions rather than an intellectual approach." Llewellyn (1996) also urges academics to cease theorizing in favour of engaging practice through active intervention. Puxty, Sikka and Willmott (1994) and Sikka, Willmott and Puxty (1995), cognizant of the constraints placed on academics by universities, implore them to break the chains and participate actively in public policy debates. Finally, the Enron/Andersen debacle has received considerable attention from critical scholars. Williams (2004a, 2004b) advances some interesting ideas in the aftermath of the fiasco. He acknowledges that academe must share in the responsibility since the "monolithic paradigm" of positivist economic science was allowed to deprive researchers of the opportunity for ethical discourses which might have conveyed proper behavioural judgments to the practice community. He goes on to say that the academic community should disassociate itself intellectually from practice.

THE PUBLIC INTEREST

A delicate balance exists between accountants/auditors as the guardians of the public interest and their own self-interest. The protection of the public interest is ultimately the major concern of critical scholars. Francis (1990) keynotes this subsection by claiming that accountants have the capacity to be virtuous but fail to appreciate how their failure to act virtuously can adversely impact the lived experiences of others. All too often, they allow external awards to dominate internal awards. Miller (1999) took a hard line by taking the audit profession to task for failing to live up to the service tradition demanded by society. Threats originate from a variety of antagonists—the state, standard-setters, accounting professional bodies, accounting firms and capitalists. By way of introduction, five articles will be mentioned in the chronological order of their appearance, which called for more critical work in this area and provided suggestions for the way forward. Lapsley (1988) pointed out that critical attention had been so focused on financial accounting and accountability that the financial affairs of public institutions had been neglected. Miller (1990) opined that there were many potential congruencies between the roles of accounting and the objectives of the state and that these relationships needed to be researched. Broadbent and Guthrie (1992) called for more evaluative work in the public sector and the opportunity to make international comparisons. McSweeney and Duncan (1998) closely examined the UK's Financial Management Initiative, a seminal public administration policy change, and found numerous published explanations of it. Thus, opportunities for research are available even for topics and events already studied. Finally and most recently, Dellaportas and Davenport (2008) sought to define the "public interest" and for the profession to provide the meanings and how to apply them in practice.

Another subject of vital interest to the public is the relationship between the state and the accounting profession. Sikka and Willmott (1995) reported an "incestuous" association when the UK government appointed accountants as investigators for the Department of Trade and Industry based on the perception that their independence and objective construction of corporate affairs were sufficient credentials. Roslender and Stevenson (2009) recounted how the British Accounting for People Initiative of 2003, designed to force firms to disclose more information about their human capital, was emasculated by the influence of the powerful accounting profession. Cooper, Puxty, Robson and Willmott (1996) told the story of how the implementation of the European Union's Eighth Directive in 1984 failed in Britain because the government cowered before the powerful image of the auditing profession. The directive attempted to establish rules for the education and certification of auditors.

A different power relationship existed in the US as exemplified by Morrison's (2004) report of the "lynching" of Arthur Andersen. The accusations levelled against the government's rush to injustice included misleading testimony, inappropriate leaks, witness threatening, and failure to review Arthur Andersen's audit work papers. Baker and Hayes (2004) spoke to Enron's use of GAAP's legal form to conceal the economic substance underlying transactions.

Two of the editors of this volume have authored articles highlighting episodes when governmental officials charged with the administration of relief were malfeasant in their duties. Walker (2004a, 2008b; see Chapter 5, this volume) related how the Poor Law Guardians stigmatized and degraded the recipients of Britain's relief system in the nineteenth century. Funnell (2001) reported how representatives of the British Treasury during the Irish Potato Famine cared little about relieving the suffering. O'Regan (2010; see Chapter 6, this volume) exposed how the imperial government took advantage of the Irish crisis to establish a vast accounting apparatus intended to "civilize" the native Gaelic population and recalcitrant Anglo-Irish landlords. Walker (2003a) exposed the complicity of Edinburgh accountants as the trustees of insolvent estates to evict the crofters from the land, causing much suffering (the Highland Clearances).

One might expect that the critical party line would be the greed and rapaciousness of corporations and the complicity of their in-house accountants greasing the wheels as the corporate juggernauts rolled toward profit maximization. Yet, the literature has been more restrained. Killian (2010) related the story of Shell Oil in Ireland, which deployed the language of accounting to unite self-interested supporters to exploit natural resources and marginalize the protests of those opposed. Hooks and Moon (1993) examined the US management discussion and analysis standards and found that they furthered corporate self-interest and that pressure on the standard-setters had rendered them weak. Boyce (2000) related how the banking and insurance industries segmented customers into groups based on their perceived contributions to shareholder wealth while marginalizing the poor and disadvantaged. Shapiro (2002) proposed that auditor reports should include verification of legally binding and ongoing health-plan funding to protect labour from corporate cutbacks and defaults. Cooper and Sherer (1984) claimed that corporate reports emphasized private interests (stockholders) and suggested an alternative function for accounting—to understand the economic, social and political contexts of business entities. Damning with faint praise, Lambert and Spooner (2005) reported the results of a field study concluding that French firms manipulated profits, not for opportunistic reasons as suggested by PAR, but rather to broaden legitimacy and/or to adopt what they claimed to be ethical behaviour. In an interesting historical vignette, Carmona and Gutiérrez (2005) related how the Spanish state outsourced cigarette making to poor nuns. However, it was not an act of compassion but rather an effort to diffuse gender conflict at the factory.

ACCOUNTABILITY

Accountability is, or at least should be, a concern for components associated with accountancy's world. We have seen already how the profession is held to a high standard by critical scholars. We will see in this section that the public interest mandates that government be accountable to the public by virtue of its regulatory function. Corporations and their managerial accountants are likewise accountable to stockholders and the public. Accounting educators have an obligation to their students to prepare them for professional careers, a significant part of which is to understand and practice accountability.

Accountability in History

Starting at the dawn of recorded history, Carmona and Ezzamel (2007) studied accounting and accountability in the Mesopotamian and Egyptian civilizations and identified three levels at which accountability operated—individual/state, state/individual and individual/individual. Critical historians Godfrey and Hooper (1996) analysed the famous Domesday Book of William the Conqueror and its introduction of accountability, decision-making and control elements into English feudalism. Quattrone (2004) chronicled the development of accounting practices and accountability within the Jesuit order, reflecting a compromise among theoretical, political, institutional and social factors. Oldroyd (1998) told the story of a Tudor merchant who was able to maintain control and accountability of his merchants at a distance via postal communication. O'Regan (2003) wrote of how the Irish Whig Party established critical accountability and financial control that changed the dynamics of the constitutional relation between Ireland and England. Funnell (2008) reports how the fiscal exigencies of the American Revolution allowed the British Parliament to increase its independence from the Crown. During the long war against France that spanned the turn of the nineteenth century, the British Parliament took control of the secret service from the monarchy in order to increase its accountability (Funnell 2010). Jones (2008) claimed the modern-day need for greater individual accountability in Britain was very reminiscent of medieval thinking. Finally, Oakes and Young (2008) studied the famous American charity Hull House and the efforts taken to establish accountability with its contributors by adding narrative explanations of significant transactions in their reports.

Governmental Accountability

A special issue of *AAAJ* (volume 6, issue 3), dealing with UK governmental accountability, affords some valuable insights into this topic. Humphrey, Miller and Scapens (1993) provide an overview of the neoliberal, public-sector reforms of the Thatcher years that collectively improved accountability. Mayston (1993) considered the possible justifications for these changes, including the emulation of the private sector as a model of accountability and efficiency. Gray and Jenkins (1993) elaborated a model of accountability as the relationship among principal, steward and the codes on which stewardship is based. Ezzamel and Willmott (1993) were less impressed with the process, claiming that only more democratic forms of governance could reform the public sector.

Two other articles, one specific and one general, conclude this subsection. Andrew (2007) wrote on how the coming of privatized prisons to Australia brought new questions of accountability, new performance measures, contract compliance and monitoring. Lehman (2010) examined critical liberal and postmodern perspectives of accountability and how accounting information can democratize the public sphere.

Corporate Accountability

Corporations are frequently the targets of critical scholarship when they fail to act in an acceptable fashion. Cousins and Sikka (1993) insist that to achieve greater accountability, corporations should be required to publish additional information to achieve visibility on social objectives. This position is reinforced in Sikka (2008), where corporate accountability is linked with a reduction in workers' income inequities. Roberts (2009) thinks this same accountability will be achieved if the divide between ethical and strategic concerns could be reconciled. Brennan and Solomon (2008), in an introduction to another *AAAJ* special issue on corporate governance and accountability, call for broader approaches to these issues, ones that transcend the traditional and primarily quantitative nature of prior research. Specifically, they call for broader theoretical perspectives, methodological approaches and accountability mechanisms.

However, the literature is not very optimistic that corporate accountability is within the realm of possibility. Unerman and Bennett (2004) believe that the internet affords the opportunity for corporations to communicate with stakeholders and thereby enhance accountability, but they caution that the modern technology could also be used to increase corporate hegemony. Cooper and Owen (2007) studied the relationship between social/environmental disclosures and accountability and found that neither voluntary nor mandated ones precipitated stakeholder action, hence not contributing to accountability. Mouck (1994) addressed the lack of a theoretical perspective of corporate accountability that is neither extremely right wing nor anti-liberal. Articles by Messner (2009) and Roberts (2009) conveyed a similar message that there are limits to corporate transparency so that the level of accountability demanded by society cannot be met, if for no other reason, the nature of accounting itself.

RHETORIC

Creative corporate managers and accountants have attempted on occasion to disguise less than good news through the use of deceptive language, rhetoric and metaphor. It is left to critical scholars to unmask this deception. Joel Amernic and Russell Craig are the exposers *par excellence*. Large companies that have had their disclosures analysed with respect to their hidden meanings include Massey-Ferguson (Amernic 1992), Disney (Amernic and Craig 2000a), IBM (Amernic and Craig 2000b) and giants of the aluminium industry (Amernic and Craig 2001). Craig and Amernic (2004) disclosed rhetoric in Enron's 2000 letter to stockholders and Andersen's CEO's 2001 testimony before Congress. On a more general level, Amernic (1996, 1998) spoke to the obligation of accounting educators to make students aware of rhetoric and metaphor in accounting reports and on the internet. In a 2009 article, Amernic and Craig pulled no punches in declaring the use of metaphor to be "insidious, distortive, and confounding," especially in light of the profession's commitment to "representational faithfulness."

The literature on the ways rhetoric has been used historically is very diverse. Maltby (2005) observed how rhetoric was used by corporations to avoid social reporting in the days before it was required. Oakes, Covaleski and Dirsmith (1999) told the story of how management rhetoric in the early twentieth century rendered unionized labour sufficiently governable to accept accounting-based incentive plans. Merino and Mayper (2001) explore how the Securities Acts of the 1930s were written rhetorically to restore public confidence. Walters and Young (2008) show how FASB saved face using rhetoric as it moved from the exposure draft to the final standard on stock-option accounting.

In the more modern world of accounting, rhetoric is omnipresent. Fogarty (1996) shows how the disparity between what is promised and what is delivered in the US peer review process is bridged by "imagery." Hamilton and Ó hÓgartaigh (2009) spoke of "auditor rhetoric" reinforcing the status quo, hierarchy and inequity. When activity-based costing was introduced to the UK police services, rhetoric was deployed to shift public opinion from "concern for crime to cost" (Collier 2006). Davison (2008) highlighted the increased volume of rhetoric that characterized the dot.com era. Two tales of rhetoric in the public sector have emanated from Australia. Christensen (2004) reports how universities manage by rhetoric and ambiguity in response to significant change, and Potter (1999) illustrates how Australian governments use greater efficiency and accountability rhetoric to justify public-sector reforms. Finally, Berland and Chiapello (2009) explain how rhetoric is used to control the capitalist budgeting process as solutions to accounting and economic problems.

CONCLUSION: WAYS FORWARD

This chapter has sought to recognize the significance and variety of the contributions of accounting historians but also the influence of this work. This section seeks to turn our gaze to the future with a survey of two areas of critical accounting in which history-oriented scholars have been involved to a very limited degree but which might prove fruitful. The first of these is social and environmental reporting (SER), a fully developed area of critical research that has borne limited success until now. The second is interventionism, a greater activism that would force scholars to set foot out of their ivory towers in an attempt to influence change. In each case, there are opportunities for critical accounting historians to be involved. The final section identifies some ideas of the way forward suggested in the literature.

Social and Environmental Reporting (SER)

Two topics that tend to be linked in the critical literature are SER. However, concrete results in terms of changes accomplished are widely divergent. Corporate social reporting has improved in recent years, in part due to the reforms critical scholars have championed. However, environmental reporting has hardly kept pace, which must be frustrating to those who have expended great efforts in the hope of helping to save the planet. Reasons for the slow progress are readily understandable—the expense of voluntary action, the weakness of governmentally mandated compliance in most parts of the world and the lack of expertise within the accounting profession for related consulting and auditing services.

Scholarship in environmentalism and sustainability has been pioneered by three academic/activists—Jan Bebbington, Rob Gray and David Owen—who have worked individually, together and with multiple co-authors. Gray (1992), early in the crusade, reflected the author's confidence that improved SER would enhance accounting's potential to increase corporate accountability and transparency. Bebbington (1997) also saw the enabling potential of social and environmental accounting, but warned that engaging with the practice community was a prerequisite for forward progress. Bebbington and Gray (2001) reported on a fascinating project undertaken with a New Zealand land research firm in which as much sustainability as possible in a non-sustained world was attempted. The outcome was a failure primarily because of cost, but insights were identified to provide hope for success in the future. They also joined forces with Owen (Owen, Gray and Bebbington 1997; Bebbington, Gray and Owen 1999) in a project to identify the pitfalls that slowed environmental accounting (EA) progress—lack of empiricism, theoretical unawareness, irrelevance to practice and miscommunication between academics. Gray, Walters, Bebbington and Thompson (1995) set out models of praxis extended to the environmental agenda, but optimism was tempered by fears that the proponents of environmentalism had been too "benign" to date. In the same year, Gray, Kouhy and Lavers (1995a, 1995b) did the movement a substantial service by publishing a two-part research project in which a database of UK social and environmental reports and a discussion of the major theoretical preoccupations and tensions on the subject were articulated. Larrinaga-Gonzales and Bebbington (2001) published a case study of the implementation of an EA system. Finally, Bebbington, Larrinaga and Moneva (2008) explored the interface between social reporting and reputation risk management, while Gray (2010) wrote an update on sustainability, its pitfalls and unrealistic claims. Owen (2008) summarized the accomplishments of the movement up to that time and suggested ways forward.

Environmental Accounting Education

Critical scholars have despaired of inspiring the accounting professional community to embrace environmental reporting and auditing. However, there is a ray of hope if the educational process might bestow upon entry-level professionals an appreciation for environmental issues. Most of the literature that is critical of accounting education's almost total neglect of EA in the accounting curriculum comes from UK researchers. Perhaps this is explained by the fact that EA has at least gained a modest foothold in UK universities but hardly at all in the US

Notwithstanding, EA classes are under-subscribed in the UK both in terms of student numbers and professors willing to teach such a course. Bebbington and Thomson (2001) have studied issues of faculty and student reluctance to staff EA courses. Gray and Collison (2002) found that students who opt to take elective EA courses perceive that critical thinking differentiates such courses from those that are more technical in nature, while Collison, Gray, Owen, Sinclair and Stephenson (2000) discovered in surveys that student interest was peaked by the ethical issues involved. Perhaps the hesitancy of British professors to teach these courses lies in the perception of what an EA course requires in terms of pedagogy. Mathews (2001) writes that such courses must involve "deeper learning" than technical offerings based on accounting standards. Thomson and Bebbington (2004, 2005) observed that professors in EA classes must scrap the illusion that they are the fonts of all knowledge in favour of a "dialogic" technique that makes EA courses "transformative" experiences. For those students whose institutions do not provide an exposure to EA issues, Fleischman and Schuele (2006) have prepared a "primer" on environmentalism that may be used as collateral reading in principles and intermediate accounting courses.

Greater Environmental Activism

As we have seen, despite the research efforts of critical scholars, environmentalism has failed to launch in practice. Many have argued for a greater activism and intervention. Tinker, Neimark and Lehman (1991) urged radicalism in social reporting because middle-of-the-road activism does not work when the middle ground changes. Gallhofer and Haslam (1997b) argue for an interventionist approach lest the status quo will not change otherwise. Kaplan and Norton (1996), in the third iteration of their "balanced scorecard" image, have now incorporated environmentalism as a fundamental focus of the well-managed firm. Burritt and Schaltegger (2010), drawing inspiration from this work, maintain that management needs to be engaged to establish a "balanced scorecard" approach to sustainability. Likewise, Ball (2007) seeks to harness all internal allies in firms and keep them engaged lest they be captured by the opponents of further environmental disclosure. Spence, Husillos and Correa-Ruiz (2010) and Cooper, Taylor, Smith and Catchpool (2005) have focused on the political parameters of SER and urge the need to go beyond mere accountability or at least to harness the support of action groups such as trade unions. Finally, Lehman (1995) encourages accountancy to move beyond environmental reporting to sustainability by theorizing that accountability is only achieved with this greener alternative.

Different Shades of Green

Like the old Irish folk-song, environmentalism comes in different shades of green (Gray 1993; Mathews 1995). Milne (1996) identifies various points of environmental commitment and activism running the gamut from "exploitationism" to "extentionist preservation." Elkington, in his 1998 book *Cannibals with Forks*, coined the phrase "triple bottom line" (economic prosperity, environmental quality and social justice), which became a rallying point for activists (Gray and Milne 2004). Many of the environmental researchers cited in this paragraph have moved beyond simple environmental reporting into a call for sustainability, the darkest green on the spectrum.

Other Social and Environmental Reporting (SER) Topics

Because SER is a relatively new arrival and because there are relatively few standards articulated to guide how it should be reported and how assurance will be rendered, critical researchers have found a plethora of inter-related topics to analyse.

One of the most troublesome issues is whether or not the expertise exists within the accounting profession since assurance on environmental/sustainability reporting mandates knowledge of applied science. Those with the requisite scientific knowledge are rarely also imbued with familiarity of auditing processes (Power 1991, 1997b). Birkin (2000) thinks that the application of traditional audit tools to environmental reporting marginalizes these disclosures, a condition that will only worsen if and when assurance will be required for sustainability disclosures. Darnall, Seol and Sarkis (2009) demonstrate significant variations in the quality of environmental audits associated with stakeholder influence. Neu, Warsame and Podwell (1998) wonder if environmental reporting highlights positive environmental actions while obfuscating negative ones, or both. Wallage (2000) worries that assurance without standards risks the loss of independence.

Critical scholars have observed the frequency with which SER attempts to establish the legitimacy of the firm (Deegan 2002; Mobus 2005; Cho and Patten 2007). The verdict of some is that legitimacy is belied when the reporting is more rhetoric than substance (Laine 2009; Milne, Tregidga and Walton 2009). Aerts and Cormier (2009) found that legitimacy is not enhanced by environmental disclosure in annual reports, but it is in press releases on the subject. Cho, Phillips, Hageman and Patten (2009) have examined environmental disclosures on corporate websites and concluded that the richness of the site engenders trust in the *intention* of the firm but not necessarily *belief* in the information communicated. Deegan and Rankin (1996) looked into the environmental reporting of firms that had been prosecuted successfully by the Australian Environmental Protection Authority.

Critical researchers have been engaged in seeking relationships between environmental reporting and other aspects of the firm's performance (e.g., economic performance, environmental performance, firm size, industry). Burnett and Hansen (2008) found that proactive environment management lowers environmental costs and that lower polluting plants are more efficient than higher. Hackston and Milne (1996) determined that firm size and industry are significantly associated with social/environmental disclosure. Meanwhile, profitability is not. Companies listed on stock exchanges disclose in greater volume. Orij (2010) discovered a significant relationship between SER and stockholder orientation of specific national cultures. Patten (2002) reviewed previous literature that showed no correlation between environmental performance and environmental disclosure, but here there was a negative relationship in terms of toxic releases. Clarkson, Li, Richardson and Vasvari (2008) found a positive correlation between economic performance and voluntary disclosure contrary to findings in previous studies. Freedman and Jaggi (1988) discovered that large firms with poor economic performance provide full pollution information while there was no correlation with smaller firms. Also, large firms in the oil industry did better than those in the steel, chemicals and paper industries.

In the absence of standards, it is difficult for users to know just what a social/environmental report was communicating. Lewis and Unerman (1999) say that there is both good and bad in corporate social reports but that which is good varies according to national culture and time period. Buhr and Freedman (2001) point out that countries as seemingly similar as the US and Canada have materially different environmental disclosures, mandatory and voluntary, reflective of cultural differences (US more litigious; Canada more collectivistic). Adams (2004) identifies a "reporting-performance portrayal gap" in SER that could perhaps be bridged with adherence to the guidelines of the Global Reporting Initiative and/or AccountAbility. Edgley, Jones and Solomon (2010) relate how SER assurance can vary as a function of stakeholder inclusivity (where reporting was not captured by management).

There is much more deserving of critical scholarship in the SER area than space permits mention here. A likely venue to visit for a greater listing is Mathews (1997), whose "celebration?" of SER's silver jubilee includes a twenty-five-page bibliography of scholarship in the field. Also, Owen (2008) has updated Mathews with a twenty-year account of SER appearing in *AAAJ*, the clear pathfinder in the area. Finally, Epstein's (1996) book has a wealth of material on how corporate environmental performance should be measured.

INTERVENTIONISM: THE GREAT GADFLIES

On each side of the Atlantic, there are two prominent academics who have struck fear into the hearts of accounting practitioners; standard-setters; politicians; and, yes, other academics. In the US, these gadflies are Abraham Briloff and Tony Tinker, while in the UK, the burrs under blankets are Prem Sikka and Hugh Willmott. Briloff was accorded the honour of the lead article in the inaugural issue of *CPA* in which he launched a wide-ranging polemic against the thin accountability of FASB, the accounting academic sector, the accounting establishment and the accounting profession. The titles of some of his works show the nature and importance of his contributions: *The Truth about Corporate Accounting* (1981), "Accountancy and Society: A Covenant Desecrated" (1990), "Unaccountable Accounting Revisited" (19993b) and "Garbage In/Garbage Out: A Critique of Fraudulent Financial Reporting 1987–1997" (2001). Sikka (2001) extended Briloff's "Garbage In/Garbage Out" article to the UK by showing how the government there has been captured by the audit firms to shield themselves from regulatory action arising out of audit failures and defective financial statements. If one wants more of the Brilovian critique, one needs only go to *Barron's Magazine*.

References to the work of Tony Tinker, Briloff's colleague, appeared with great frequency in these pages. He, of course, was a founding editor of *CPA* and has now moved on to a new journal, *International Journal of Critical Accounting*. A few of his publications reflect interaction with other "great gadflies." In an article entitled "It May Well Be that Briloff Is the Nearest US Equivalent to Sikka" (Carter and Tinker 2005), he compared the research approaches of Briloff, Sikka and Willmott. He then wrote an article in which he advanced his theory that the critical research project needed scholars to read the classical texts (Tinker 2005). Sikka and Willmott (2005) responded that, on the contrary, the way forward was active intervention. Another vignette illustrates the extent of Tinker's willingness to critique the discipline to which he has devoted his energy. In 1985, his landmark book *Paper Prophets: A Social Critique of Accounting* appeared, and a decade later, in "*Paper Prophets*: An Autocritique," he forthrightly critiqued himself (Tinker 2001).

Sikka and Willmott are an authorship team that has been preaching intervention for decades. Sikka today circulates a global internet newsletter in which he informs critical scholars of what is transpiring in the UK and elsewhere that requires critical research and action. At this point, only one of their many joint articles (Sikka and Willmott 1997) will be mentioned. This piece reflected on their joint work to date, particularly that in partnership with Tony Puxty. The article urged others to engage the UK accounting establishment as they have done. Sikka (2008) has accused accounting firms of colluding with corporations in antisocial practices primarily designed to increase profits.

Interventionist Literature

As one might expect given the slowness of progress in environmental and sustainability reporting, critical scholars in this field particularly urge greater activism and intervention. Rather than revisit references provided in an earlier section, only a few new ones will be offered here. Adams and Larrinaga-González (2007) point out the necessity to engage directly with organizations to influence increased sustainability activity as has occurred with management accounting. Bebbington, Brown, Frame and Thomson (2007) likewise argue that direct engagements by critical theorists would be more likely to contribute to change. Neu, Cooper and Everett (2001) encourage critical accountants to integrate theoretical and praxis components of accounting scholarship through intervention in the public sphere. They ponder the questions of how to bring their expertise to bear on an intervention and how intellectuals are to judge the effectiveness/success of their efforts. Chua and Degeling (1993) reported on an accounting-based intervention into a prospective payment system in the US health-care industry. Cooper (2002), in an article on critical accounting in Scotland, revealed that academics there had not progressed beyond theory into an active engagement with the outside world. However, Scapens (2008) cautions that researchers who seek to intervene in practice must combine theoretical knowledge with the craft knowledge of practitioners.

Accounting History: A Way Forward

Despite the many published historical resources mentioned in the preceding, accounting history is still a young discipline in need of recognition and accreditation, particularly in the US. Richardson (2008) has suggested some ideas for developing and legitimating accounting history as an academic discipline. One is to make its body of knowledge controversial and relevant to education. Another is to institutionalize accounting history (e.g., academic associations, conferences and journals). Parker (1997) calls for researchers of contemporary issues to be made aware of the additive value of historical backgrounds to their areas of study. Also, traditional historians need to see the importance of critical research as a vehicle for the resurgence of the discipline. Cooper and Robson (2006) argue that much work has already been done in standard-setting and regulation so that it might be fruitful for scholars to shift gears and study the internal workings of accounting firms since there is ultimately where standardization and regulation actually occur. It might serve the additional benefit of rendering academic research more relevant to practice.

The pros and cons of oral history methodology have been widely considered in Collins and Bloom (1991), Tyson (1995), Hammond and Sikka (1996), Hammond (2003a), Kim (2008) and Haynes (2010). There is certainly much more that can be done in this area.

There is a vast quantity of critical work to be done in accounting history. Numerous untouched archival repositories are accessible for research and almost daily more are coming onto the internet as funding becomes available for digitization and online catalogues. The publication outlets are plentiful and hungry for quality work. There are also opportunities for critically minded accounting historians to investigate the historical background of topical issues that heretofore have only occupied scholars motivated to research contemporary practices. Your coeditors strongly encourage you to consider critical accounting history as a significant component of your research portfolios.

NOTES

1. It is precisely the wide range of subjects, participants and outlets that makes this review non-inclusive. Consequently, apologies are offered to those whose contributions have been understated or omitted entirely. It is also the case that the gist of most articles is derived from abstracts alone and, hence, interpretive errors and inaccurate emphases are unavoidable.
2. In this author's opinion, the AAA has become significantly more democratic in recent years (e.g., opening its national conventions to accounting history papers although *TAR* remains exclusionary).

Part I
Annihilation

2 Accounting for the Holocaust

Warwick Funnell

INTRODUCTION

The Holocaust, which has been referred to as a "gigantic, murderous operation" (Muller-Hill 1994, 68), involved the systematic annihilation of six million Jews (Eisner 1983, 155; Wellers 1978, 139–43). It is recognized as one of the most momentous events in the twentieth century, if not in recorded history (Dawidowicz 1975, xi; Hilberg 1980; Katz 1989, 354). After the Holocaust there would never be the same level of innocence and faith in the inherent goodness of humankind or previous understandings of the way in which social institutions worked (Hilberg 1980, 102; Eisner 1983, 149; Rosenberg 1983, 8, 9, 14; Wiesel 1988, 11; Browning 1988, 173). Unlike other instances of genocide in history, the Holocaust was the first time when the power of the technology of the modern world had been turned on a group of people, connected only through a religious heritage, to attempt to murder them to the last person, more than ten million (Bauer 1989, 83–84; Talmon 1989, book 1, 185).

The enduring metaphor for the Holocaust is of the operation of an efficient machine with the sole objective of processing millions of people as quickly, costlessly and effectively as possible to produce corpses. The killing of a very large number of people in a relatively short space of time was nothing more than "an efficiency problem of the greatest dimensions . . . With an unfailing sense of direction . . . the German bureaucracy found the shortest road to the final goal" (Hilberg 1985, 9; 1980, 101). The Holocaust would not have been possible, argue Hilberg (1985), Goldhagen (1996) and Browning (1980, 183), without the enthusiastic cooperation of the German civil bureaucracy. Destruction of human life on the scale of the Holocaust "is not the work of a few mad minds. It cannot be accomplished

This chapter is based on the paper "Accounting in the Service of the Holocaust", which originally appeared in *Critical Perspectives on Accounting* 9, no. 4 (1998): 435–64. The author would like to thank the publisher, Elsevier, for permission to use this material.

by any handful of men. It is far too complex in its organizational build-up and far too pervasive in its administrative implementation to dispense with specialized bureaucrats in every segment of society" (Hilberg 1980, 99; also 1972, 3; Dawidowicz 1975, xv). Accounting numbers enabled the civil bureaucracy and their masters to control from a distance and to capture key dimensions of the extermination process without being in constant attendance (Humphrey and Scapens 1996, 89; Miller 1990, 318). In terms of Francis's (1990, 7) description of accounting, as with all sectors and resources within a ruthless totalitarian state, accounting in Nazi Germany was a political practice which was not value free. Rather:

> The rationality of accounting—what we account for, how we account, to whom we account, about whom we account, when we account, and so on—are value choices made with respect to relations between members of the *polis*. (Francis 1990, 7)

The purpose of this chapter is to examine the role of accounting as a component of bureaucratic practices used in the perpetration of the Jewish Holocaust and the implementation of the 'Final Solution' by the National Socialist German Workers Party (NSDAP), or Nazis, in Germany between 1938 and 1945 and, thereby, to highlight accounting as a practice with a clear moral dimension. If accounting is a moral practice, then those who use it are moral agents. Accounting's aura of neutrality and objectivity (Francis 1990; Miller and O'Leary 1993, 190, 192) has been the means to discount the subjective as something necessarily inferior to the products of the rational logic of accounting. It has also been a convenient means of isolating accounting from ethical questioning and consideration of accounting's ethical dimensions and moral consequences (Pois 1989, 1937). Consideration of the plight of the silenced and excluded Jews in Germany between 1933 and 1945 will highlight the ethical and qualitative dimensions of accounting by visiting the tragic consequences when the latter are excluded from consideration. A conspicuous feature of accounting information which makes it so attractive is its ability to create new realities and visibilities (Miller 1990, 316–17). In the service of the state, Miller (1990, 317) notes how "technologies of government materialize and visualize processes and activities to be regulated".

Accounting in the service of the German bureaucracy was not only a means of expediting the annihilation of the Jews, but was also one of the means by which people who had no direct involvement in the murder of millions of Jews were able to divorce themselves from the objectives and consequences of their work. The aggregation, reductionism and anonymity of accounting numbers allowed the forced movement of millions of people great distances from their homes to be drained of any considerations which would imply that the numbers and costings on the pieces of paper which were passed from one bureaucrat to the next related to prescient human beings. Accounting as an instrument of the German civil bureau-cracy provided at "centres of calculation" new quantitative visibilities (Miller 1990, 318) which were able to supplant the qualitative dimensions of the Jews as individuals by commodifying and dehumanizing them, and, thereby, for all intents, making them invisible as people (see Marx 1944, in MacIntosh 1994, 41). When it came time to dispose of the property taken from the Jews, the Nazis attempted to purify their actions and to sanctify their motives by insisting that before any of the property could be available for use by the state it had to pass through rigorous accounting procedures. In the process, the accounts were used as the symbolic means of spiritual cleansing for those at the killing centres and directly engaged in the annihilation of the Jews.

ACCOUNTING FOR THE INVISIBLE

The Holocaust involved the extension of functional reasoning from the factory, where it assists management in the transformation of inputs into desired outputs, to the processing of human beings and their property (see Rubinoff in Rosenberg 1983, 13). More particularly, according to Rosen-berg (1983, 14), it resulted in the "corruption of rationality into ideological forms of functional reasoning". At the heart of functional reason is the use of technologies of calculation, most importantly accounting. In the service of the Holocaust they were used to:

> Reduce human beings to quantified objects, thus eliminating their troublesome qualities of humaneness . . . Functional reason must treat people as objects, as things, as mere numbers that can be easily manip-ulated and casually disposed of . . . It allows individuals to manipulate fellow human beings as things until they were done away with when no longer perceived as useful or needed. (Rosenberg 1983, 12)

Accounting provides a partial rendition of reality whereby "visibili-ties created by accounting become reality and, thereby, those issues that have been stripped away in order to create the metaphor become invis-ible" (Broadbent 1995, 71). To be invisible is to risk becoming valueless. Unfortunately for those adversely affected by the bifurcation of reality by accounting into that which is visible and that which is invisible, by defi-nition that which is not captured by accounting must be without value. Broadbent and Laughlin (1994) have noted that the consequence of cre-ating particular visibilities is that some things are allowed to be seen as tangible and therefore to exist. As a result "they can more easily be decou-pled from the social milieu in which they are embedded and discussion of these issues in the 'public' sphere is enabled" (Broadbent and Laughlin 1994, 7). The conversion of Jews to a one-dimensional metric, an integer as a component of tabulations which could be arithmetically manipulated, stripped the identity and all other qualities from the Jews and gave their tormentors the anonymity for the subjects of their work, which enabled them to avoid divulging the human correspondence of their accounts. The Jews were recognized no longer as social beings, and, thereby, in the absence of this measure they became invisible and ceased to exist. They could then be discussed in the public domain through their surrogates found in the calculations in accounting reports. Unlike other social participants, they no longer had a life history, the potential to make worthwhile contributions, responsibilities as family members or the capacity to love and have feelings. Debased numbers are not able to experience emotions, nor do they have a past. Numbers are contrived for a purpose and then cease to have the same importance beyond that purpose.

In the records of the German civil bureaucracy, accounting as a technology of management is clearly implicated in all stages of the destruction of European Jews. From the creation of lists of victims used to plan railway rolling stock needs and the timetabling of transports to the disposal of Jewish property left outside the gas chambers or near the shooting pits, accounting can be seen to have fulfilled an essential part at each step. Thus, those who diligently used accounting precisely to track and account for over six million people cannot escape their share of responsibility for the success of their undertaking. Fleming (1985, 46) notes that the "planned killing" of the Holocaust "required a procedure thought out with absolute precision down to the smallest detail".

THE WILL OF THE STATE AND THE MAIN PHASES OF THE HOLOCAUST

Exclusion of the Jews in Germany 1933–39

In Eastern Europe throughout the nineteenth century Jews had been the subjects of numerous pogroms, especially in Russia. Unlike the policies of the Nazis, pogroms were limited, although still often deadly, harassments of the Jews. They were not attempts to eliminate Jews or to force them to flee to other countries. Instead, they were responses by governments to the periodic venting of local hostilities towards a vulnerable minority which had become a convenient scapegoat for economic and political problems. The Holocaust was something very different. From within the Warsaw Ghetto in 1940, and shortly before his death, Chaim Kaplan described German Jewish policies as a:

> Gigantic catastrophe, which . . . has no parallel even in the darkest periods of Jewish history. Firstly—the depth of the hatred. This is not hatred whose source is simply in a party platform, invented for political

purposes. It is a hatred of emotion, whose source is some psychopathic disease, in its outward manifestation it appears as physiological hatred, which sees the object of its hatred as tainted in body, as lepers who have no place in society. (Arad, Gutman and Margarliot 1981, 201)

The Nazis had prepared their policy of exclusion towards the German Jews well before Hitler was appointed Chancellor on 30 January 1933. In the presence of the enfeebled president, Field Marshall von Hindenburg, the passage through the Reichstag of the *Enabling Act* on 23 March 1933 gave Hitler almost dictatorial powers which, when combined with the declaration of a state of emergency soon after being elected, enabled Hitler to harass, kill and imprison his political opposition and to mute any criticism. Much of the Nazi vitriol was directed at the Jews who, on the basis of Nazi racial theories, were progressively driven out of public service occupations, the universities and the professions (the Law for the Restoration of the Professional Civil Service and Law Regarding Admission to the Bar, 7 April 1933). In 1935 under the Nuremberg Laws, Jews were stripped of their German citizenship and deprived of all citizenship rights and benefits (see an example in Arad, Gutman and Margarliot 1981, 99–200; Bullock 1973, 339). Once Jews ceased to exist as legal entities who possessed rights at law and no longer enjoyed the benevolence of the state they became easy targets for more extreme forms of Nazi attacks. After 1937 Jews were forbidden to attend most public places, including schools, libraries and swimming pools, and to use some forms of public transport. By the outbreak of World War II a comprehensive system of segregation or apartheid had been forced upon all German Jews.

Not content with excluding Jews from public life, the Nazis passed laws which excluded Jews from operating many types of businesses and gave the government the authority to force the sacrificial sale of existing businesses (for an example, see "Regulation for the Elimination of the Jews from the Economic Life of Germany, November 12, 1938", in Arad, Gutman and Margarliot 1981, 115–16). At the same time that the level of economic persecution increased, the various military arms of the Nazis became more brazen in their attacks on Jews and Jewish property. This culminated on the night of 10 November 1938, *Kristallnacht* or the Night of Broken Glass, with the widespread destruction of Jewish synagogues and property. The opportunity was also taken to round up members of the Jewish community who had displeased the Nazis (Klarsfeld 1978, 29). This persecution was not limited to the Jews. Jehovah's Witnesses, homosexuals, gypsies and most other minority religious groups suffered similar privations to those of the Jews.

The Final Descent 1939–45

With the declaration of war against Poland on 1 September 1939 the fate was sealed of nearly two out of every three Jews in Europe. Between the outbreak of hostilities and the end of the war two phases can be identified in the German treatment of the Jews. From 1939 to the beginning of 1942 the laws already in place were enforced with ever-increasing fervour and ruthlessness. From October 1939 the Nazis commenced the transportation of all Jews under their control to the east, principally to Poland. An order from the Reich Security Main Office (RSHA) was issued on 23 October 1941 which forbade any emigration of Jews (in Arad, Gutman and Margarliot 1981, 153–54). From early 1942 the full effects of a policy of annihilation began to be felt. Goebbels, in his diary on 27 March 1942, makes very clear the intentions of the Nazis towards the Jews, at the same time describing the treatment of the Jews during this period of the Holocaust as:

> Pretty barbaric . . . and not to be described here more definitely. Not much will remain of the Jews . . . No other government and no other regime would have the strength for such a global solution of this question. Here too the Fuhrer is the undismayed champion of a radical solution necessitated by conditions and therefore inexorable. Fortunately a whole series of possibilities presents itself to us in wartime that would be denied us in peacetime. (Goebbels 1942, 147–48)

Initially the killings were accomplished by mass shootings. However, it was soon found that a more effective method of destroying a large number of Jews was the use of gas in a similar manner to the way in which it had been used extensively prior to the war to kill, it is estimated, over seventy-five thousand Germans who suffered from incurable diseases, were mentally retarded or were persistent sexual offenders (Hilberg 1985, 872). The first stage in the gassing of the European Jews was carried out by Einsatzgruppen using mobile vans modified for the purpose of using carbon monoxide from the exhaust (Fleming 1985, 63). Most notably, these Einsatzgruppen, who were not under the control of the local army commanders, were given free rein in the early part of the campaign against Russia to carry out their work (Browning 1985; "Special Duties for the SS in Operation Barbarossa, March 13, 1941", in Arad, Gutman and Margarliot 1981, 375). Mobile vans were later superseded by the establishment of the six main death camps in Poland, many of which used the cyanide-based chemical Zyclon B. It was in one of these killing centres that most Jews were to die.

Extermination Accounting

From the time that the Jews were mustered for deportation in Germany and in the countries that were now occupied they ceased to exist as individuals and instead took on the sole identity of a numbered Jew. The creation of lists of deportees was the final stage in a process which had grown from the Nuremberg Laws in 1935 to make the Jews non-existent. They were not recognized as anything other than an input, of varying degrees of value, in a conversion process. As a member of a class of objects they were denoted as a number; a number which formed the basis of a system whereby the Germans could account for the progress of their policy of extermination. Thus, in reports to Hitler and Himmler, for example, the emphasis is on reporting the *number* of people who had been killed and the number yet to be killed. As an example, in a report prepared by the head of the Statistics Department in Himmler's office in March 1943 detailed figures are given of the number of "moves" from the Sudetenland, Austria and other areas under German control. It concludes euphemistically that total "evacuations" for Special Treatment were 1,786,356 (see "SS Statistics of the Final Solution", in Arad, Gutman and Margarliot 1981, 333–34).

The process of accounting for individual Jews was made possible by the detailed lists of Jews living in most areas which had been kept or created for the Germans by Jewish community organizations. Well before preparations for the Final Solution were put into place the Germans knew the extent of their task. They knew that there were 2,284,000 Jews in Poland; 2,994,684 in the Ukraine; and 742,800 in Hungary. With their lists of Jews all that remained was for the Germans to count the number killed and to deduct this from the number available to be killed. Wellers (1978, 139) calls this "macabre accounting". The lists of Jews were often so accurate that with the assistance of Jewish community leaders the Germans knew precisely how many people lived in each house. If they did not collect the correct number of people from each house then Jewish community representatives would be arrested to make up the numbers. Thus, far from being innocuous, documents which specified numbers of Jews to be collected were effectively death warrants in the form of charge-discharge accounting. Jewish leaders would be charged with the number on requisition documents and would be held personally liable until the charge was discharged with a corresponding number of people transported.

Believing that the owners would never return, civilian government employees immediately confiscated and meticulously accounted for all property left by the Jews, including "personal property, apartments, community assets . . . All these odds and ends . . . were now dropped into the laps of the Finance Ministry's experts" (Hilberg 1985, 471). The process, which was systematic, well organized and extremely thorough, was greatly enhanced by the existence of detailed lists of property and wealth which had been required by the Decree Regarding the Reporting of Jewish Property (26 April 1938). The key provisions of this decree stated that:

s.1(1) Every Jew . . . must report and assess his entire domestic and foreign property as of the effective date of this decree, in accordance with the regulations that follow. . . .

s.3(1) Each item of property is to be assessed, in reporting, at its common value on the effective date of this decree . . .

s.4(1) . . . the property must be tentatively reported with an estimated value by June 30, 1938.

All property disclosed was liable to be used in the interests of the state (Decree Regarding the Reporting of Jewish Property, s.7) according to the wishes of the Reich Minister of the Interior, Herman Goering. In cases where property was not disclosed according to the decree, the owner risked imprisonment for a period of up to ten years and immediate confiscation of all property, including that previously disclosed (Decree Regarding the Reporting of Jewish Property, s.8). Conforming to the decree was in essence an accounting exercise whereby each Jew had to draw up a one-sided balance sheet containing nothing but assets. In order to produce the list the decree made it clear that only values which could be substantiated were to be placed on the property. For Jews with extensive fixed property holdings this would have entailed the assistance of professionals with accounting skills, both to arrive at valuations and to create the reports in conformity with the legislation. Accounting, therefore, was involved in the spread of state surveillance, both of domestic and foreign affairs, and in the identification of resources in the possession of condemned Jews which could be made available to the state.

After the passage of the Eleventh Ordinance of Reich Citizenship Law in November 1941, the property of any Jew who left Germany was immediately lost to the state. Prior to this, confiscation of property could only occur after the courts pronounced, in each case, the Jew to be an enemy of the state (Hilberg 1985, 471). With the prospect of inevitable seizure of their homes and other properties, many Jews were induced to sell these in an attempt to gain at least something. At the forefront of this process "accountants and bookkeepers . . . could busy themselves with contracts that were products of pressure put on Jewish owners to sell their property" (Hilberg 1993, 65).

Crucial to the success of Nazi extermination policies was the ability to gain access to railway rolling stock to transport the Jews and to schedule these transports. Once a train had been allocated it was up to the bureaucrats on the railways and the Gestapo to ensure that each train was fully utilized and that the time for each shipment was rigorously met (Hilberg 1985, 455–65; Hilberg 1989). Prior to the trains being made available it was the responsibility of the Traffic Division of the *Reichsbahn* and its accountants to set the rates to charge for the transports. The Gestapo, who was primarily responsible for providing the cargo for the death camp trains, was charged the third-class *one-way* fare of 4 pfenning per track kilometre for each adult carried. A fare of 2 pfenning was charged for children under ten, while children under four travelled free. A discount of half the normal third-class fare was offered for groups of four hundred or more.

Sometimes transportation bills would be sent to the Gestapo through the official Nazi travel agency, the *Mittelewopaische Reiseburo*. As the scale of the deportations grew, however, the Gestapo found it more difficult to meet the costs of transportation out of their budget. To deal with this problem a charge was levied on the Jewish community for each person deported (Hilberg 1985, 467–68). They in turn charged the deportees 25 per cent of their liquid assets. Thus, in effect the Jews were paying for their own death. This money was to be deposited into a special SS account called Account W at the Reichsbank. At the conclusion of each transport a detailed account was required of movements into and out of Account W associated with the transport ("Instruction of Reich Association of the Jews in Germany to Jewish Community Associations, December 3, 1941", in Hilberg 1972, 115–16). Accounting was the essential ingredient which allowed this sequestration of Jewish property by the Nazis to be comprehensive and exhaustive. In a state where terror was an institutionalized practice of the government, where infractions of onerous laws directed against the Jews were met with severe retribution, accounting provided another weapon of threat and intimidation to police decrees such as the Decree Regarding the Reporting of Jewish Property. Without the complicity of accountants, the laws and decrees which firstly catalogued Jewish property and then denied Jews their rights to the property which had been identified would have been far less effective if not unenforceable (see Miller's comments on the relationship between political programmes and "technologies of government", 1990, 318). It was also accounting which provided the linkages and transitions which cohered the different phases of annihilation without the need to divulge to those responsible at each stage the specifics of previous stages.

In occupied countries the Germans paid for the use of the state railway infrastructure. If there were insufficient funds in accounts which contained proceeds from the sale of confiscated Jewish property a charge might be made on the Reich Finance Ministry. Correspondence between the Ministry of Transport and the High Command of the Army in March 1944, which referred to difficulties being experienced by the Greek state Railways in being paid 1,938,488 Reichmark for shipments of Jews to Auschwitz, provides details of payment arrangements and, possibly more importantly, gives a good idea of the businesslike approach of those responsible for the transports. The Ministry of Transport officer writing the request for payment, presumably well after those who had been transported had been killed soon after arriving at Auschwitz, concludes by asking that:

> This matter be cleared up with the Reichsfuhrer-SS and Chief of the German Police/Command Security Police and possibly the Reich Economy Minister and that care be taken to assure transmittal of the transport costs to the Directorate of the Greek State Railways. Kindly inform me about the progress of negotiations. (Hilberg 1972, 164–65)

Directing the logistics of transportation for the extermination camps, including the work of the RSHA, was Eichmann's office, which euphemistically referred to the trains as Sonderzuge or "special passenger trains" (Hilberg 1985, 410–15). Eichmann confirmed that organizing the transports and ensuring that they were all paid for was an extremely complicated process which became increasingly more difficult towards the end of the war. Consequently, the cooperation of a number of German agencies was required for "no matter how large a German force was present, they couldn't just round up people, put them in freight cars, and ship them out. . . . We had to requisition the trains . . . and contract Administration and Supply headquarters" (Eichmann, in Von Lang 1983, 99).

Upon arrival at the extermination camps, the inmates came under the control of the SS Economic Administration Main Office under Obergruppenfuhrer Oswalf Pohl. In Auschwitz, inmates who were allowed to live long enough to work in the camp were given numbers which were tattooed onto their forearms. Subsequently internees were called *figuren* or simply numbers ("Evidence Given at the Nuremberg Trials", in Arad, Gutman and Margarliot 1981, 358–60), with the numbers recorded in a *Totenbuch* or 'death book'. Other dimensions of their being as individuals were thereby displaced by their number for "once they had been tattooed, the only thing that was important about them was their number. Whatever productive work that was to be had from them was as if from a machine" (Gilbert 1986, 824).

Sanctification through Accounting

As part of the efforts to delude the Jews as to their ultimate fate prior to deportations, everyone was permitted to take a small amount of money and some clothing. After each batch of killings the belongings which remained outside the gas chambers were carefully sorted, including gold extracted from teeth, and sent back to Germany. Great care was taken to obsessively account for each item. Hilberg (1985, 473) notes how everything was collected, "to the last hairpin". Himmler insisted that there be "painstaking exactness" in all dealings with Jewish property, warning that "we cannot be accurate enough" (quoted in Hilberg 1985, 951). As an example, in a secret report in June 1943 from the commander of the SS in Galicia, a detailed inventory is provided of all property confiscated from Jews, including:

25.580kg	copper coins
97.190kg	gold coins
20.952kg	wedding rings
11.730kg	gold teeth
343.1kg	cigarette cases
6.166kg	pocket watches, various
3.425kg	pocket watches, silver
7.495kg	fountain pens and propelling pencils

("Final Report by Katzman, Commander of the SS in Galicia", in
    Arad, Gutman and Margarliot 1981, 335–41)

Himmler's demand for meticulous accounting was mainly to ensure that all possible proceeds found their way into the accounts of the SS. All cash seized both before and after death was deposited in accounts at the Reichsbank along with the safe keeping of a vast amount of precious metals and jewellery (Dawidowicz 1975, 147). Himmler was also concerned that in the absence of clear accountability the way would be open for theft, which would be detrimental to the spiritual well-being of his troops (Hilberg 1985, 951). By enforcing stringent standards of accountability at the centres of execution Himmler believed that "in carrying out this most difficult of tasks . . . we have suffered no harm to our inner being, our soul, our character" ("Speech by Himmler to SS Officers, October 4, 1943", in Arad, Gutman and Margarliot 1981, 345). Indicating the seriousness with which meticulous accounting was regarded, Himmler threatened that:

> Anyone who takes so much as a single Mark, of this money is a dead man. . . . There will be no mercy. We had the moral right, we had the duty towards our people, to destroy this people that wanted to destroy us. But we do not have the right to enrich ourselves by so much as a fur, as a watch, by one Mark or a cigarette or anything else. ("Speech by Himmler to SS Officers, October 4, 1943", in Arad, Gutman and Margarliot 1981, 345)

The Nazis endeavoured to transform accounting into the means by which they could be purged of impure motives and avoid being contaminated by a 'difficult' task which the Jews had 'forced' upon them. Himmler's insistence on punctilious accounting for property seized in the concentration camps and killing centres was the use of accounting for the purpose of *sanctification*. The stolen wealth of the Jews had to pass through the accounts of the SS to transform its corrupt nature, which threatened the purity of those with whom it came in contact, into something which was wholesome and which could be a consecrated servant of the state. The seizure of Jewish property could be blessed by rigorous accounting to demonstrate that the acts which produced the property were motivated not by the material results or selfish greed but by the need to purify the German race. For members of the SS and others, to benefit materially in an indiscriminate, avaricious manner allegedly similar to those who had previously owned the property, and probably obtained it by methods injurious to the German people, would be to become one of the fallen Jewish race and to put into question the right of the Nazis to conduct the crusade against the Jews. Thus, in addition to ensuring that the state benefitted from property seizures, accounting offered the means of redemption, a clear conscience and the protection of the inner self.

CONCLUSION

Accounting is used by interest groups to achieve very particular purposes. The use of accounting cannot be neutral or disinterested if it is to fulfil its mission. It is a dynamic practice with often far-reaching effects, affecting not only the operations of organizations which use accounting, but also the individuals upon whom are visited the results of decisions made using accounting information. Until critical accounting research drew attention to the existence of the multiple roles which accounting plays (Covaleski and Dirsmith 1995, 148; Richardson 1987a) it was unusual to connect social consequences with accounting information. Accountants were cast in the role of insignificant players who were to do the bidding of those who used the results of the accountant's work (Yamey, in Hines 1989b, 58). The link was rarely made between broader social consequences and the role of accounting as a constituent element in engendering existing social and political arrangements.

Accounting research over the past two decades has progressively exposed these perceptions of accounting as inadequate and favourable to the status quo. Hopper and Powell and Humphrey and Scapens (1996) are amongst those who have urged that accounting can only be made sensible if the researcher does not ignore "wider social and political collectives" (Hopper and Powell, quoted in Humphrey and Scapens 1996, 87; see also Miller 1990). Thus, it is now well established by accounting researchers that accounting is an active agent in social processes, the implementation of political programmes and in the creation and maintenance of social structures (Tinker 1980; Tinker, Lehman and Neimark 1991). Accounting is no longer able to hide behind a disguise of neutrality and disinterested objectivity. Rather than accounting being mainly an instrument of calibration and description, in this chapter accounting has been shown to have been involved at all stages in the Holocaust to facilitate the efficient implementation of the Nazis' programme of firstly the exclusion of Jews and later their annihilation. In particular, accounting provided an unassuming and uncontested means to objectify Jews and to hallow the motives of the Nazis. Nor is there is evidence that the accounting profession during the Nazi reign provided any 'principled' moral leadership for accounting practitioners or was any different to the other professions in its sycophantic homage to the will of the state.

3 Accountants and the Holocaust

Ellen J. Lippman and Paula A. Wilson

INTRODUCTION

The world has known its share of genocide: in the USSR under Stalin; in Cambodia by the Khmer Rouge; and in Burundi, Rwanda, Sudan and Iraq, to name a few of the countries that endured such horrors just in the twentieth century alone. Each of the mass murders was country specific, where the struggle for power was confined within a country and resulted in the murder of the citizens in that country. In contrast, the Holocaust was an event unprecedented in the history of man. Never before had a country systematically and deliberately hunted a people, scattered in many different countries, for the sole purpose of annihilating them. This was not a disagreement of peoples within a country or even a disagreement between countries. This was organized hatred by one country against a people who lived disbursed among many nations. Germany's efficient Nazi Party was organized and focused to wipe Jews and other targeted groups from the earth.

The Holocaust occurred with the implied consent and participation of ordinary citizens. For instance, physicians participated in the euthanasia programme of the mentally and physically disabled (Glass 1997). Engineers designed gas chambers used to annihilate millions (Kipnis 1981). While some engineers claimed ignorance about their design, there was no mistaking the purpose for such facilities. The Holocaust could not, indeed would not, have occurred without the widespread complicity of businesspeople, lawyers, doctors, engineers, churchmen and women, public officials, military and police, as well as millions of others (Jones 1999). And included with these ordinary citizens were accountants.

When laying blame for the Holocaust, accountants probably do not come immediately to mind. As a group, accountants are not the type to elicit fear. After all, what decisions do they make? They provide the information to managers who make the decisions. Yet, accountants can be a critical component

---

This chapter draws on material from Ellen Lippman and Paula Wilson, *Accounting History* 12 (2007): 283–303. Reprinted by permission of SAGE.

in the efficient allocation of resources and in the quality of decisions made. By choosing the information to report and how to present it, accountants can deeply affect decisions made. Thus, ultimately accountants hold much power, a power they were reluctant to use during the Holocaust. This chapter considers the accountants' role and that of the accounting profession in the Holocaust to determine the extent to which their actions, or inactions, made them culpable in perpetuating the Holocaust.

SLAVE LABOUR OPERATIONS AND THE ROLE OF ACCOUNTING

During World War II, Germany expanded its grip on Europe. As it conquered each nation, Germany enacted anti-Jewish doctrines, and Jewish citizens of these conquered nations were transported to concentration camps that the Nazis had established. The Nazis developed a forced slave labour operation that used some of the camp prisoners in Nazi-run factories. The Nazis also leased prisoners to for-profit German corporations for use in the corporations' factories outside of the camps and, in some cases, in factories the corporations had established within the concentration camps. The corporations that used the slave labourers included the giants of German commerce, among them Bishmarchkhutte, Herman Goering Werke, I.G. Farbenindustries (IG Farben), Krupp, Oberschlesische Hyderwerkes, Siemens-Schuchert, Union Metallendustries and Volkswagen. While it was national policy to use slave labourers, German corporations also willingly used the cheap slave labour. The historian Mark Spoerer examined thirty-three known case histories of companies that employed concentration camp slave labour and found only one case where evidence exists that the state "forced a firm to use slavery against its will" (Allen 2002, 170).

The entire slave labour operation was run by a small group of engineers, accountants and managers who worked in the SS Wirtschaftsverwaltung-shauptamt (Business Administration Main Office, referred to as the WVHA). The WVHA controlled many economic enterprises that used concentration camp labour for the German state and also negotiated the contracts with private corporations for slave labourers, specifying pay and conditions. For instance, the WVHA negotiated a contract with IG Farben which agreed to pay between 1.5 and 3 Reichsmarks (RM) per day for each worker leased, with the price dependent upon the age and skill of the worker. This price was less than that paid to a free worker, as IG Farben management anticipated that the prison labourers would be one-third as efficient as the free workers due to the poor conditions of the concentration camp inmates (Borkin 1978). Krupp's contract specified the provisions provided to the camp inmates. Krupp gave each slave labourer one blanket, one set of eating utensils, one drinking cup and an allocation of food costing 70 pfennig per day (approximately 18 cents; see Muhlen 1959). Unlike ancient slaves who were given adequate food and housing as a means to protect their value to the slave owners, the contracts with the corporations limited the provisions provided to the prisoners. Neither state-owned and state-operated entities nor German corporations maintained reasonable working conditions, considered the health of the labourers or provided protective clothing, conditions often given to civilian workers. Thus, the prisoner slaves were not worth protecting. They became a disposable good. And a profitable one.

Employment of slave labourers was big business. In 1942, revenue to the SS from the lease of slave labourers totalled 13.2 million RM (Black 1991). Corporations and the Nazi enterprises used sophisticated accounting techniques to track the operations of the factories. Oswald Pohl, leader of the WVHA, developed standardized accounting systems capable of audit. IG Farben's accounting system provided board members with reports detailing company labour usage, with slave labour reported separately from other labour (Borkin 1978). The Gustloff Works, formerly a Jewish-owned business called the Suhler Weapons and Vehicle Works until it was taken over by the Nazis in 1935 (Allen 2002), maintained reports that catalogued each prisoner's output (Hacket 1995). The Textile and Leather Utilization GmbH (TexLed), a textile and garment company founded by the SS, tracked production statistics including "unit costs, labor costs, and depreciation rates on machinery and combined aggregate statistics to yield calculations of production minutes per unit product and unit labor costs" (Allen 2002, 73). Unlike many SS entities, TexLed maintained steady production from its employment of unskilled women of Ravensbrück, a women's concentration camp. Not common among state-run entities, it was a viable factory operation, run by management with business training and experience in textile production. The entity even generated real profits estimated at 18 per cent. However, management also relied on violence to succeed; women who failed to meet piece-rate quotas were beaten, with several women dying as a result of their beatings (Allen 2002).

WVHA accountants prepared statements to reflect the profit, and sometimes the violence, from the slave labour operations. Figure 3.1 contains an income statement from Buchenwald, a German prison camp in existence between 1937 until its liberation in 1945. (Figure 3.2 contains the original statement in German.) This statement reports the estimated revenue from the leasing of a single prisoner, less the costs to lease which were listed only as food and clothing amortization. Then, the net revenue per day is extrapolated for a period of nine months. The nine-month period represented the average life expectancy of a prisoner working in the factories, the result of the harsh working conditions and insufficient food allotment (Ferencz 1979). Even upon death, the prisoner still generated profit. The statement included estimated revenue from the value of the deceased's belongings, including personal clothing, valuables and currency. Further, it included estimated revenue from the prisoner's body, including sales of gold extracted from teeth, hair, fat for soap and ashes for fertilizer; it deducted the cost of cremation that was estimated, at a minimum, of two RM per person. Thus, the accounting information clearly stated the profit from the prisoners and clearly conveyed that the prisoners were killed unmercifully. The accountants, therefore, knew the object and consequences of their accounting.

Revenue	6.00 Reichmarks
Less food	.60
Less amortization for clothes	.10
Net revenue	5.30
Times – expected life span	
in months	9.00
- days worked per month	30.00
Total revenue for period	1,431.00
Plus revenue at death	200.00
Net profit per prisoner	1,631.00

This profit is based on efficient reutilization of prisoner corpses after 9 months from gold fillings; [privately-owned] individual articles of clothing which were mostly used as clothing for prisoners in other camps, so that costs related to acquiring new clothing was unnecessary, and as recycled fabric for SS uniforms; and items of value, which were left behind, only items of value and money owned by the minority of the prisoners, who were German citizens, were sent back to their families. These amounts were reduced by cremation costs on average by 2 Marks per corpse, so that there was a direct plus an indirect net profit per corpse of at least 200 Marks, but which in many cases resulted in thousands of Reichmarks.

The total profit of the turnover of prisoners per capita in a nine-month period on average amounted therefore to at least 1,630 Reichmarks. Through the reutilization of bones and ashes, usually additional special earnings resulted. (notes translated by Dr. Laura McLary 2010).

Figure 3.1   Income statement from Buchenwald.
Source: Kogon 1950 p. 269.

Unmerciful killing was also evident in a cost-benefit analysis performed during the Holocaust. While the cost-benefit analysis represents another common financial tool used to support decision-making, in Nazi Germany accountants used cost-benefit analysis to compare the cost of killing children with gas and then burning their bodies to the alternative of burning the children to death (Greenberg 1975). Both options incurred a cost for cremation, but the second option would use less gas, thereby reducing overall costs. For every fifteen hundred persons gassed, approximately 5.5 kilos of gas were required at a cost of 27.5 RM. By not gassing the children to death prior to cremation, the state could save two-fifths of a cent per child (Greenberg 1975). While death by gas was by no means humane, the pain from being burned alive was certainly worse. Nonetheless, the Nazis elected to burn the children alive, and their screams could be heard throughout the camp (Fleischner 1977).

The operating statement from Buchenwald included standard accounting concepts, such as estimates on life expectancy that are used today in determining post-retirement benefits and amortization used to report the systematic expensing of assets. The cost-benefit analysis used standard accounting concepts currently in practice. The operating statement also explicitly included the prison labourers' limited life expectancy due to the harsh working conditions. Estimating the useful life of the slave labourers

Täglicher Verleihlohn zwischen RM 6.— and RM 8. —.		
durchschnittlich	RM 6.—	
abzüglich 1. Ernährung	RM —.60	
2. Bekleidungsamortisation	RM—.10	—.70
Demnach bei durchschnittlich		
dreivierteljähriger Lebensdauer	mal 270 =	RM 1341. —
Dieser Gewinn erhöhte sich durch rationelle Verwertung der Häftlingsleiche nach 9 Monaten um den Erlös aus		
1. dem		Zahngold
2. den		Privatkleidern,
die teils der Häftlingsbekleidung in anderen Lagern zugeführt wurden, wodurch sich Neuanschaffungskosten erübrigten, teils der Spinnstofferwertung für SS-Uniformen		
3. den hinterlassenen		Wertsachen
4. dem hinterlassenen		Geld
Wertsachen und Geld wurden bis in die ersten Kriegsjahre hinein nur bei der reichsdeutschen Minderheit der Häftlinge den Angehörigen zurückgeschickt.		

Diese Beiträge verringerten sich je Leiche um die Verbrennungskosten von durchschnittlich	RM	2. —.
sodaß sich ein direkter plus indirekter Nettogewinn je Leiche von mindestens	RM	200. —.
ergab, der abe in vielen Fällen in die Tausende von Reichsmark ging.		
Der Gesamgewinn des Häftlingsumsatzes betrug daher in durchschnitlich 9 Monaten je Kopf wenigstens	RM 1630. —.	
Durch Knochen- und Aschenverwertung hat sich das eine oder andere KL noch Spezialeinnahmen veschafft.		

Published under Military Government Information Control Licence NR.US-W-2010

Figure 3.2   Income statement from Buchenwald (original).
Source: Kogon, 1946, pp.296–297.

at nine months was an accounting procedure that ignored the value of human life. Likewise, although a well-prepared cost-benefit analysis may be mathematically correct, it is not value neutral. Personally held values affect the information prepared, and, depending upon the values embedded in the task, the analysis may be flawed even when the computations are accurate. As Funnell (1998a) argued in his Holocaust research and as Fleischman and Tyson (2004) stated in their research on slavery, accounting can reduce individuals to numbers, masking the suffering of the victims who were worked to death. While the Buchenwald statement and the cost-benefit analysis did not highlight the suffering of the children and prisoners, such suffering could be inferred readily from an analysis of the statements. However, consideration of the suffering seemed not to matter.

Accountants prepared the financial statements that documented death through work and the cost-benefit analysis that considered how to cost effectively kill children. Initially, imprisoned Jews often were the accountants at individual factories, forced to record the transactions of the slave labour operations (*Trials of War Criminals* 1950). However, as the Jewish bookkeepers were exterminated, German accountants took their place. Some recorded transactions; others performed audits of the factory results. "I have examined the entries of the capital accounts and found these to be in order" (ibid., 520). The accountants doing this work, while sometimes SS officers, were often civilians (ibid.). Whether they worked directly for the state or for private corporations that leased slave labour from the state, accountants were aware of the slave labour operations and most likely had access to information about these operations and the mistreatment, and extermination, of the workers. They could not but have understood the magnitude of what they reported.

Although little documented evidence exists that accountants, as a group, formally opposed these policies, some accountants did protest the treatment of the Jews, although not always because of a concern for the prisoners. For instance, Dr. Max Horn, a university-educated accountant and SS officer, was the business manager of Ostindustrie GmbH (East Industries, abbreviated as OSTI), SS-run factories that used Jewish labour. Horn identified starvation as the key problem with low production and protested the conditions provided to the labourers. In a report, he had warned that "if the SS wished to exploit prisoners, some modicum of preservation of life had to take precedence over the denigration of the *work Jews* and—with the genocide in full swing—over their wholesale murder" (Allen 2002, 248). It is not clear whether Horn was concerned about Jews as humans or just as a source of labour since he could not maintain his factories without a healthy workforce. But he received no support for his request for better treatment for the prisoners. In November 1943 when OSTI was deprived of Jewish workers, Horn was placed in charge of liquidating the factories.

Yet, some accountants did perform individual, isolated efforts of resistance. For instance, one accountant protested when the Nazis took over the management of a previously Jewish-owned business for which she worked. She quit her job, stating that "she'd rather die" than work for the Nazis (Jones 1999, 219). Some individuals used accounting to sabotage the efforts of the Nazis. A district director of agricultural procurement altered bookkeeping records to increase the number of employees listed as employed at a factory. This allowed the factory to receive extra food, which was used to feed those starving in the ghetto of Zloczow (Paldiel 1993). Similarly, a candy factory added a number of Jews to the worker list, thereby saving the lives of these Jews from the gas chambers (Paldiel 1993).

While punishment for activism was severe, "contrary to popular assumption, those who decided to stop or not participate in atrocities were usually given other responsibilities. Quiet non-compliance was widely tolerated" (US Holocaust Memorial Museum; see http://www.ushmm.org/education/foreducators/question/#5). Thus, although accountants were not directly responsible for the killing, they did have ways to combat the status quo, and they have been called "desk-killers" for merely issuing reports that enhanced the efficiency of the killing machine (Rosenberg and Marcus 1988, 213). However, before applying a sweeping blame on accountants as killers and accomplices, it is important to consider the extent to which the profession of accountancy and the state of the professional accounting organization influenced accountants' actions during the Holocaust.

ACCOUNTANCY PROFESSION IN GERMANY

Prior to 1931, German accountants felt no compelling need to establish themselves as a profession. Instead, their status was obtained through education at commerce colleges or experience and recognition as technical experts. (Evans 2003; Harston 1993). Economic crises and political turmoil after World War I provided an impetus for business and accounting reform. Germany required significant capital investment as part of its recovery plan from World War I, and foreign investors would not accept the audits of German corporations that were performed by German accountants. The 1931 Company Law, however, significantly changed the German accounting profession. The law mandated audits of public corporations and specified report formats and valuation requirements for balance sheet and income statement accounts. Initially the law required audits of large firms with capital of at least 3,000,000 RM and, the following year, expanded the requirement to much smaller companies with capital of at least 500,000 RM. The audits were to be prepared by a new type of accountant, the publicly commissioned accountant. It was hoped that the newly established commissioned accountants would introduce professionalism to accounting and increase foreign acceptance of German audits.

The Institut der Wirtschaftsprüfer (IdW) became the comprehensive, self-contained professional organization of the publicly commissioned accountants. Initially, the IdW provided standardized protocols, uniform authorization and testing for publicly commissioned accountants called Wirtschaftsprüfers (WPs). To become certified as a WP, applicants needed to meet various requirements, including German residency, an orderly financial and personal life, a minimum age of thirty years, six years of professional practice including at least three years of auditing, successful completion of a written exam and demonstrated knowledge of the accounting discipline (Meisel 1992). While the certified accountants were to be commissioned only after passing an exam, a transition period from 1931 through 1935 existed when candidates with relevant experience and personal aptitude could become certified without testing. With these requirements, the profession of accountancy was elevated from discrete specialties into a new profession that had a monopoly on the examination of public entities and possessed credibility throughout the country. While the IdW established laws of professional practice, produced an official newspaper, provided professional assurance duties and worked with related professionals, it had not yet begun to consider ethical questions of professional practice. Indeed, the organization itself was only in its infancy when Hitler was appointed Chancellor of Reich in January 1933.

On 23 March 1933, the German government passed the Enabling Law (Ermachtigungsgesetz), which permitted dictatorial power by the National Socialists, of which Hitler was the leader. This began the systematic dehumanization and persecution of Jews. As Germany began to change under Hitler's leadership, so did the IdW. A general meeting of the IdW membership held in February 1933 became the last general meeting of the organization in its then present form until after the war. The IdW implemented Nazi policies which sought to exclude Jews from all parts of German society, notably the professions. Thus, on 4 April 1933, an advisory counsel of the IdW expressed support for the National Socialist government and two of the Jewish members of the council, previously elected at the February 1933 meeting, were asked to resign. Beginning 6 April 1933, Jews could no longer serve as authoritative tax representatives of the IdW (Meisel 1992). In September 1934 the IdW changed its statutes and adapted its professional requirements to ensure that they were consistent with the National Socialist principles Führerprinzip, the Institute of the Führer. The IdW became a professional accounting organization administered by loyal party members. Candidates and other professionals were required to produce proof of their Aryan heritage. A party member became the *führer* of the IdW, and administrative functions were performed by Dr. Otto Mönckmeier, a non-WP party member (Meisel 1992).

The National Socialist government prohibited Jews and others not friendly to the new regime from working as approved auditors, although exceptions were made for Jewish veterans of World War I or those Jews whose fathers or sons were killed during World War I. In the early 1930s, IdW members included fifty-five Jews. However, with the adoption of Führerprinzip in 1934 the hope was expressed that no additional Jews would be admitted to the IdW. In 1938, the IdW revoked the membership of any remaining Jewish IdW members, those who had neither dropped their membership nor emigrated from Germany (Markus 1997).

In 1937 when an oath of allegiance to Hitler was added to the WPs' certification requirements, the IdW no longer had independent oversight of WPs. The original oath: "I swear that I will fulfill the duties and obligation of a publicly commissioned accountant knowledgeably and impartially and that I will fulfill them with the desired expert opinion knowledgeably and impartially" (Meisel 1992, 186) was amended to read, "I swear by God that I will exercise absolute obedience to the Führer and Reichs-Chancellor Adolf Hitler and that I will carry out my duties and responsibilities of a publicly appointed Wirtschaftsprüfer conscientiously and impartially, that I will preserve professional secrecy and that all reports requested of me will be prepared conscientiously and impartially" (Markus 1997, 89). With a lack of independence came a shift in the focus of the WP from the needs of the corporation and the public for which it audited to become a mechanism for the advancement of the Nazi party.

Under the leadership of Dr. Otto Mönckmeier, the IdW used its official magazine to educate accountants about specific rules that discriminated against Jews. For instance, in 1939 the official accounting magazine outlined directives about Nazi regulations required of WPs in their interactions with Jews in business. Thus, accountants were forbidden from offering professional advice to Jews without expressed official permission in writing from appropriate Nazi officials. When representing Jews, accountants were to work for the good of the party over the personal benefit of a Jewish client. The magazine also reminded IdW members of business, including a law ordering Jewish businesses to sell or liquidate within an appointed time period as part of the process of Aryanization of Jewish companies (Reich Law Sheet Register RGBI, I 1938, in Genschel 1966). An article by Dr. H. Adler on New Business Laws in the accounting magazine describes this new order and the additional business for accountants who would be appointed as attestors of value in the dissolution of the Jewish businesses (Adler 1939). To add further to the injustice, the cost of the business audits which preceded any dissolutions were borne by the Jewish business. Thus, discrimination within Germany had become institutionalized, and the WPs, the German accountants, were actively engaged in the formation and implementation of the laws that discriminated against Jews.

The IdW relinquished its autonomy to the National Socialist Party without significant dissent. One possible explanation for the IdW's ready acceptance of Hitler's regime relates to the accounting organization itself. The IdW was a new organization without a professional history upon which to rely for guidance or a fully developed loyal membership that comes only with long-lived organizations. WPs could easily give up what they did not yet value. Additionally, consideration of ethical responsibilities of accountants had not become a part of accounting competency in Germany.

While German accountants acquiesced to Hitler and Nazi policies, accounting professionals from the international community supported Germany's accountants. The Fifth International Congress on Accounting was held in Germany in 1938; 315 representatives (Markus 1997) from thirty-three countries participated, with the largest number of delegates from Britain (Walker 2000). Walker argued that British delegates attended this conference, despite widespread knowledge of persecution of the Jews, in order to protect their business interests and the British chartered accountants who were already working in Germany. After the conference, accounting articles that appeared in the *Accounting Review* praised Germany and its efficient accounting methodology (Matz 1938, 1940). *Standardized Accountancy in Germany* (1943), published in England during the war, also touted Germany's regulatory system of standardized accounting, a result of the German "talent for organization" (Singer 1943, 10). Thus, accounting professionals from the international community, without any direct threat of retribution, still showed support for Germany's accounting body, even after the Nazis took office.

In countries such as the US, Great Britain and Canada, where self-imposed professionalism required a more active participation and where individual rights of citizens were paramount, accountants may have more actively opposed a state takeover of their accounting professional organization. However, in Germany the view of the state as guide was prevalent throughout society, where German communal responsibility was the primary focus and individual rights were secondary to societal goals (Harston 1993). German accounting emphasized compliance with laws and regulations, not representational faithfulness. Moreover, secrecy in German financial transactions was preferred over financial disclosure. These characteristics set a tone in financial reporting that discouraged the questioning of state actions, particularly since the state was the ultimate client as opposed to the corporation (Neal and Morgan 2002). It was state policy, articulated at the Wannsee Conference by Heydrich (second in command of the SS), to use slave labourers, to under-provide for the workers, to work some concentration camp inmates to death and to kill the remaining others who didn't die working (Shirer 1960). By the time the ghettoization and genocide began, the IdW had ceased acting as an independent organization to which concerned accountants could look for guidance. WPs were to serve the state, and if accountants disagreed with the state, they had no professional recourse, as their organization was controlled by the state.

CULPABILITY OF ACCOUNTANTS AND ACCOUNTING

Historically, accountants' responsibility has been to provide information that is clear and accurate. If accountants' responsibility ends at the point of information delivery, then accountants would not be responsible for any misconduct that resulted from the use of this information, regardless of what it reports or how it is used. However, accounting information does not exist independent of what it presents, and it is not a neutral tool when it depicts immoral events. Fleischman, Oldroyd and Tyson (2004) agree, stating that accounting contributed to slavery in the antebellum South in America and that accountants should be held accountable for the misdeeds of slave owners due to the severity of the slave mistreatment. Oldroyd, Fleischman and Tyson (2008, 766) state that a basic standard of justice exists for the "treatment of humans against which accounting and accounting practitioners can be judged culpable". In a similar manner, Fleischman, Tyson and Oldroyd (2004) believe that accountants are responsible for the consequences of slavery and guilty of "crimes against humanity" despite the wide use of slavery during that period. Using this standard of justice, German accountants are responsible for the consequences of their information.

Oldroyd, Fleischman and Tyson (2008) consider whether accountants are culpable for the support of slavery in the absence of a professional organization and code of professional ethics to guide accountants' behaviour. The authors argue that legality provides a framework for professional ethics in accounting. Applying this reasoning to the Holocaust, accountants would not be culpable, since discrimination, slave labour and annihilation were state authorized in Germany.

In the International Military Tribunal Trials held after the war, senior- and lower-level accountants were tried for war crimes and crimes against humanity. Many high-level SS accountants acknowledged their actions but argued that their actions were not wrong. They believed they were acting within the bounds of acceptable behaviour at the time. Further, they felt no additional responsibility for moral reflection. Some argued that they were made a scapegoat for others' transgressions. "Men like Himmler, Gluecks . . . these men are dead and I believe that I can say that if this dozen men would be sitting here in the defendants' dock today, then the bookkeepers of Amtsgruppe A would not be sitting in the first row of the defendants' dock" (*Trials of War Criminals* 1950, 761).

In the Tribunal's rulings, the court differentiated accountants' responsibility for the Holocaust depending on the ability of the accountant to affect change or obtain another job. "Mere knowledge of crime without the power to interfere carries no moral or legal condemnation. But knowledge of crime and participation in the system that makes that crime possible dissipates the concept of unblemished innocence" (*Trials of War Criminals* 1950, 1159). However, for all but higher-level accountants, the Tribunal did not find accountants responsible. The court convicted the top SS accountant, Dr. Hans Hohberg, of war crimes and crimes against humanity, holding him responsible for the information he and those who reported to him produced. He was sentenced to ten years imprisonment (UN War Crimes Commission 1948). The court exonerated some high-level accountants whose knowledge of war crimes and crimes against humanity was deemed remote or whose association with the concentration camps was only sporadic. Similarly, the court did not find lower-level accountants culpable for the genocide (*Trials of War Criminals* 1950).

IMPLICATIONS FOR FUTURE CONSIDERATION

Neither the practice of accounting nor accountants initiated the Holocaust. Yet, accounting practices involved in the slave labour operations contributed to the genocide. A weak professional accounting organization could not provide accountants with assistance and support to resist the Nazis. Additionally, the German accounting profession's emphasis on professional competence rather than moral considerations may have contributed to the accountants' lapse of moral judgment.

Few accountants today prepare accounting information detailing atrocities on the scale of that in Germany or are confronted with a government that has as its key strategy the elimination of a race of people. However, occasionally accountants encounter moral questions or conflicts with their values and the values of their organizations. Professional accounting organizations should assist accountants in these situations. In the US, well-established professional organizations, rich in tradition, provide professional guidance through codes of ethics that help define appropriate accountants' behaviour. Yet, in many respects, present codes are too general to be useful, since they rely upon the individual accountant's interpretation of ethical behaviour. For instance, the codes of the Institute of Management Accountants, the American Institute of Certified Public Accountants and the Institute of Financial Accountants all state that accountants need integrity to determine whether to engage in a behaviour or to provide information, but no specific guidance is provided. Without specific guidance, legal guidelines can become the minimum criteria. Indeed, at the International Military Tribunal in 1949, persons used legality as a defence of their actions. However, these behaviours were clearly illegal in other Western countries and did not conform to laws or values held in Germany either prior to or after the Holocaust.

A strong code of ethics and an equally strong accounting professional organization that takes an active role in managing accountant work may help accountants resist pressures to do work that supports illegal or immoral behaviours. Future research should consider the importance of accounting societies and codes of ethics for ensuring ethical behaviours of accountants. Additionally, work should consider the specificity of codes of ethics to determine whether the guidance provided is sufficient in situations of moral ambiguity or when laws of the country are counter to moral codes of ethics. Also, scripted training (Gentile 2010) can be considered as a technique for helping accountants give voice to their values when they conflict with those of their organizations.

Additionally, further development should occur of the International Tribunal's standard for accountant responsibility, which relinquished individual power to supervisors. This level of standard, however, is unsatisfying. Holding a few accountants responsible while absolving other accountants of culpability allows accountants to ignore questions of moral behaviour. Consideration of recent legal actions against accountants can be contrasted with that of the Tribunal to determine whether a more complete code that acknowledges personal responsibility can be developed.

If accounting is a profession and accountants are professional, then accountants must assume a level of responsibility that professionalism affords. As seen in this chapter, accounting information can have severe ramifications, and accountant responsibility for such information may change the way accountants work and, ultimately, the decisions made. When more accountants are liable for the illegal or immoral information they report, an elevation of responsibilities could increase the moral behaviour of society as a whole. In this way, individually and collectively, accountants can begin to understand their own culpability for the consequences of the information they provide.

Part II
Subjugation

4 Accounting and Canada's First Nations

Cameron Graham and Dean Neu

INTRODUCTION

From the earliest legislation in 1857 defining the Canadian government's relationship with the First Nations, funding relations have played an important role in encouraging certain behaviours on the part of First Nations peoples (Bartlett 1978, 583). Boldt (1993) suggests that federal government funding methods have been used to encourage institutional assimilation. Other writers refer to the use of money by-laws, taxation policies and so forth, tightly coupled with bureaucratic and political measures such as municipal forms of government, as "coercive tutelage" (Dyck 1991) aimed at colonizing First Nations peoples (Frideres 1990, 3). These quiet technologies of government stand in contrast, at least in the minds of many Canadians, to the violent methods of domination that characterize other countries' relations with their Aboriginal peoples. Yet a closer look at the mundane technologies of accounting employed by the Canadian government indicates a pervasive coercion lying at the heart of the bureaucratic, procedural approach.

This study examines how funding relations between the Canadian federal government and the First Nations were implemented during Canada's formative decades in the latter half of the nineteenth century. We suggest that putting federal legislation into practice involved the translation of legislative initiatives into an administrative bureaucracy, the Indian Department,[1] and from there into specific geographical and social spaces amongst the First Nations themselves. In some cases, federal legislation encouraged new forms of accounting and accountability. In other cases, it enlisted existing configurations of accounting technologies and agents. From legislature to local village, accounting practices and agents were central to the federal government's relations with indigenous peoples.

This chapter is based on the paper "Birth of a Nation: Accounting and Canada's First Nations, 1860–1900", *Accounting, Organizations and Society* 31, no. 1 (2006): 47–76. The authors would like to thank the publisher, Elsevier, for permission to use this material. Funding provided by the Canadian Academic Accounting Association and SSHRC is also gratefully acknowledged.

Drawing on legislative texts, Indian Department documents and archival materials from 1860 to 1900, our thesis is that this period institutionalized a particular form of governmentality in government–First Nations relations that increasingly relied on accounting technologies. The 1860–1890 period witnessed the great treaty-making processes that secured settler access to vast tracts of the prairies and led to the destruction of indigenous subsistence life-styles. This period also saw the federal government introduce a series of leg-islative initiatives within the *Indian Act* (Canada 1981), which continues to govern the lives of indigenous peoples in Canada. With this legislation came a variety of accounting practices and heterogeneous agents, both within and external to the Indian Department, translating the legislation into micro-practices. These policies and practices attempted to atomize the First Nations peoples, newly restricted to reserve lands, into individual economic citizens.

ACCOUNTING AND GOVERNANCE: DISTANCE, DIFFUSION AND AGENCY

Accounting can be defined as numerical, monetized calculations and tech-niques that mediate relations among individuals, groups and institutions (cf. Miller and Napier 1993, 632). Accounting is distributive in that it measures and rationalizes power relationships (Tinker 1980; Cooper and Sherer 1984). Through budgets, cost allocations and accounting inscriptions, account-ing translates abstract policy objectives into concrete field-specific practices (Robson 1992; Preston, Chua and Neu 1997; Edwards, Ezzamel and Robson 1999; Neu 2000a). Accounting represents distant knowledges by measuring and inscribing distant activities and transmitting the resulting information to centres of calculation (Said 1979; Latour 1987; Miller and Rose 1990, 9). Finally, accounting encourages action at a distance via incentive schemes and funding mechanisms (Thornton 1984; Preston, Chua and Neu 1997).

These conceptions of accounting are consistent with the notion of gov-ernmentality developed by Foucault (1991). Government, according to Fou-cault, refers to the "ensemble of institutions, calculations and tactics" (102) deployed to arrange things in such a way that certain ends are achieved. According to Miller and Rose (1990, 3), technologies of government such as accounting are among the mechanisms "through which authorities of various sorts have sought to shape, normalize and instrumentalize the con-duct, thought, decisions and aspirations of others in order to achieve the objectives they consider desirable". Instead of concentrating on a single site or mode of control exercised by the state, this notion of governance draws attention "to the diversity of forces and groups, that have, in heterogeneous ways, sought to regulate the lives of individuals" (ibid.).

In the current study, recognizing accounting as a technology of government draws our attention to the notions of distance, diffusion and agency within governance processes. *Distance*, in the context of the current study, includes both geographic and conceptual/cultural distance. Accounting attempts to minimize distance and enable the exercise of power by rendering distant behaviours into traces that can be mobilized and accumulated (Rose 1991, 676). Accounting then enables intervention in distant locales by propagating technical practices and introducing incentives. The ways of thinking and being implied in accounting practices efface conceptual and cultural distance by reconstituting the habits, customs and traditions of local populations.

Diffusion refers to the instantiation of accounting technologies at distant sites. As Miller and Rose (1990) suggest, techniques such as accounting often offer "ready-made" solutions. Furthermore, each solution has cascading effects, as one accounting technique often will not function in the absence of other accounting techniques (Neu 2000b). As Miller and Rose (1990, 4) comment, governmentality is inherently optimistic. This optimism encourages government bureaucrats to "improve" on prior governance attempts, reworking financial technologies that didn't engender the desired results and extending accounting technologies to more finely influence the minutiae of daily life (Neu 2000b). The end result is a web of financial technologies that seek to govern more and more aspects of distant sites.

Finally, *agency* refers to the notion that governmentality is accomplished via heterogeneous agents operating in heterogeneous sites (Miller and Rose 1990; Gordon 1991). These agents must be enlisted into the activities of governing, whether by direct incentives (cf. Milloy 1999, 269), appeals to professional expertise (cf. Puxty et al. 1987) or by a pedagogy of learning (cf. Oakes, Townley and Cooper 1998). Accounting technologies imply the presence of agents who are willing and able to undertake the activities of summarizing and recording costs, preparing budgets and constructing financial reports. These individual agents must adapt these technologies at the local level, completing the translation of policy into practice. As Miller (2001, 380) points out, accounting's specific role in government is the creation of individual agents who "act freely, yet in accordance with specified economic norms." The enlistment and enabling of such agents may, however, disable agency for other social groups.

In the present study, the organization of institutions of governance was both cause and consequence of conceptual, cultural and geographic distances. The bureaucracy administering Indian affairs had a central office in Ottawa, the capital of the country. The regions of the country each had an Indian Commissioner; the one for the North West Territories, for example, was located in Regina. Under the treaties that had been negotiated with the First Nations, some land in each region had been set aside for Aboriginal peoples and organized into reserves, where there typically lived a number of bands, each with its own chief. Each reserve was managed by a representative of the Indian Department, called the Indian Agent.[2] The department also typically employed one or more clerks and a number of farmers at each reserve.

This organizing and ordering of institutions and agents can be viewed as an institutional mapping of a particular configuration of geographic, conceptual and cultural distances. These distances provided the conditions of possibility for the use of accounting technologies. Local agents observed and measured indigenous lives and converted the observations into numerical traces. These traces were gathered at the regional and national levels, and then embedded in reports to politicians in Ottawa. The politicians considered these reports in light of government objectives and enacted further legislation. Subsequently, Indian Department bureaucrats in Ottawa and in regional offices interpreted the legislation, fashioning appropriate accounting policies. Finally, the Indian Agent in the field received memos respecting these policies and attempted to put them into practice, adapting the prescribed techniques to the local reserve. All these activities were crucial in acquiring land in the West and converting the Aboriginal populations to economic citizenship.

LAND ACQUISITION IN THE WEST

At the time of confederation in 1867, the political borders of Canada were very different from those of today. It was not until 1870 that the Hudson's Bay Company transferred its vast tracts in the north and the west to the government of Canada. Following this transfer, the government needed— for reasons of sovereignty and jurisdiction (*Royal Commission on Aboriginal Peoples* [*RCAP*] 1996, 1:35)—to claim these unexploited western lands for settlement. Commissioners were sent to negotiate with indigenous peoples. Treaties 1 through 7 (see Figure 4.1) were negotiated between 1871 and 1877, resulting in the cession of large tracts of land between the Great Lakes and the Rocky Mountains (Morris 1991, 25).

These treaties were negotiated entirely for the purposes of securing the cooperation of the Aboriginal peoples so that non-Aboriginal people could settle in the West. The report of the 1996 *RCAP* (vol. 1, chap. 6) argues that for a variety of historical reasons, Canada's expansion into the west required political and administrative solutions, rather than combative ones. The expansionist agenda of the federal government following Confederation, together with the Canadian Pacific Railway project and the general suitability of the prairies to European agricultural methods, opened up the prairies as a potential area for settlement by non-Aboriginals. For the government, the peaceful negotiation of treaties in the West was a symbol of the "justness" (Department of the Interior 1877, xvii) of Canadian government policies towards Aboriginal peoples.

The signing of the western treaties immediately implied the need for accounting. The First Nations ceded vast tracts of land in exchange for relatively tiny reserves plus a flow of annuity payments and agricultural implements or cattle. The initial accounting records of the Indian Department pertaining to the western territories thus focussed on flows of funds and goods from the government to the First Nations. The Indian Department also adopted accounting to represent activities at distant sites to the government. For example, the 1877 *Annual Report* (see Table 4.1)

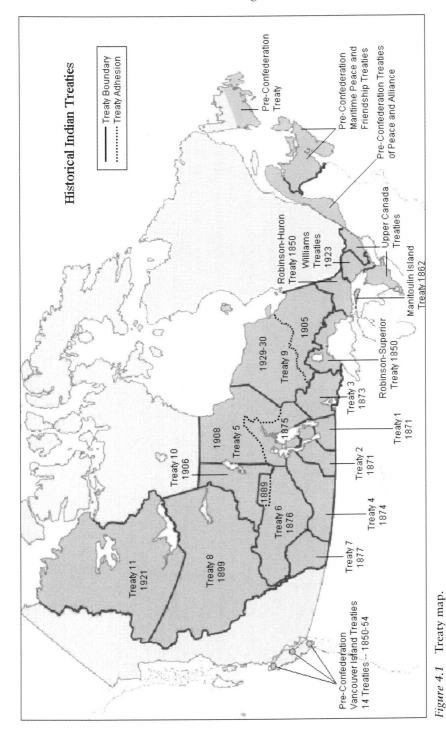

Figure 4.1 Treaty map.
Source: Report of the Royal Commission on Aboriginal Peoples, 1996.

Table 4.1   Summary of Property Held by Indians in Older Provinces

Province	Personal Property		Real Estate		Invested Capital		No. of Children	
	Total	Per Capita	Total	Per Capita	Total	Per Capita	Total	Attending School
	$ cts.	$ cts.	$ cts.	$ cts.	$ cts.	$ cts.		
Ontario	317,543 00	20 75	5,921,842 00	385 93	2,707,835 11	210 00	5,014	1,689
Quebec	146,375 00	13 54	1,344,055 00	124 35	176,017 65	27 28	1,219	334
Nova Scotia	15,442 00	8 03	32,300 00	17 47	—	—	381	82
N. Brunswick	8,676 00	5 56	329,475 00	211 07	1,119 68	00 79	486	—
P.E. Island	1,198 00	3 97	6,036 00	19 98	—	—	99	—
	489,234 00		7,633,708 00		2,884,972 44		7,199	2,105

Province	Stock						Grain, &c.					
	Horses	Cows	Sheep	Pigs	Oxen	Young Stock	Corn, Bushels	Wheat, Bushels	Peas, Bushels	Potatoes, Bushels	Oats, Bushels	Hay, Tons
Ontario	2,169	1,618	1,397	3,832	499	1,765	36,039	42,710	21,858	68,894	75,235	4,883
Quebec	530	709	82	636	9	113	3,145	1,739	3,292	18,885	11,397	2,951
Nova Scotia	18	27	11	22	16	42	33	115	17	5,120	490	915
N. Brunswick	25	31	78	50	5	12	22	210	2	2,720	2,125	210
P.E. Island	1	4	—	—	—	4	5	30	—	847	69	9

Source: Annual Report, Department of the Interior, 1875.

positioned indigenous adults in relation to things that interested Indian Department bureaucrats: the amount of personal property and real estate they possessed, their invested capital and the number of children they had. However, these reports could only be prepared for the older, eastern provinces, as the necessary information infrastructure did not yet exist in the western territories.

Commentary within these reports implies that the Indian Department did not realize that the complex of men and things to be governed in the West was different from the eastern provinces. Neither politicians nor department bureaucrats anticipated any problems confining formerly nomadic tribes in the West to small reserves of land. It was assumed that restricting the movement of indigenous peoples and giving them money and agricultural implements would transform them into farmers. As a consequence, the accounting reports of the day betray no concern with the results or effectiveness of the newly instituted annuity payments. Presented in broad ledger format (see Table 4.2), the reports simply show payments made for annuities and other provisions required under the treaties, set off against the legislative appropriations for these expenditures.

Accounting at this time was therefore used mainly to *represent* without any explicit attempt to use accounting to *intervene*. While local agents described in prose the activities of the Aboriginal people, no accounting record was kept of what happened to the annuity payments once they were made. This began to change with later legislative initiatives, beginning with the Indian Act of 1876. The 1877 *Annual Report* of the Department of the Interior stated the premise of the new act: "our Indian legislation rests on the principle, that aborigines are to be kept in a condition of tutelage and treated as wards or children of the state" (xiii). Through a series of financial regulations pertaining to land, the attempt was made to translate these sentiments into specific practices. For instance, the Indian Act (sections 25 and 26) granted the federal government a monopoly on the purchase of reserve lands and effectively circumscribed indigenous agency regarding the sale of such lands. An agent of the Indian Department had to supervise the procedure, and the decision had to be made by a majority vote, a practice that did not respect the tribal decision-making processes of the Aboriginal people.

Of the proceeds from any sale of reserve lands, only 10 per cent went directly to the band. Not surprisingly, First Nations resisted surrendering any more land than they already had under the treaty. Legislation governing the sale of reserve land was therefore "improved" in 1884, when the Indian Act was amended to give the Superintendent General the authority to lease indigenous lands to non-Indians (Tobias 1983, 47). At the end of the decade, the act was further amended to increase the band's direct share of proceeds from land sales from 10 per cent to 50 per cent. This dramatically increased the lands available for settlement (ibid., 49). In these ways,

Table 4.2   Portion of Report Showing Treaty Annuities

Return C (5)
Indians of Manitoba and the North-West

DR

	$cts.	$ cts.	$ cts.
To the following payments during the year ended 30th June, 1877:			
IN THE MANITOBA SUPERINTENDENCY.			
To Annuities, Treaties Nos. 1 and 2.			
13 Chiefs, each $25	325 00		
58 Headmen, each $15	870 00		
4,599 Indians, each $5	22,995 00		
Arrears of annuity due and paid to Portage and White Mud River Bands	1,975 00		
		26,165 00	
Annuities, Treaty No. 3.			
30 Chiefs, each $25	750 00		
84 Headmen, each $15	1,260 00		
2,532 Indians, each $5	12,660 00		
		14,670 00	
Annuities, Treaty No 5.			
9 Chiefs, each $25	225 00		
26 Headmen, each $15	390 00		
2,855 Indians, each $5	14,275 00		
			55,725 00

CR

	$ cts.	$ cts.	$ cts.
By Balance on 30th June, 1876			64,645 39
Legislative Appropriations for 1876-77, as follows:			
For Annuities, Treaties Nos. 1 and 2	22,926 00		
Annuities, Treaty, No.3	17,440 00		
Annuities, Treaty No.5	14,660 00		
		55,026 00	

[Report continues . . .]

financial legislation provided bureaucrats with leverage to transform the First Nations' relationship to the land.

This financial legislation was dependent on a complex of micro accounting practices—specifically, a system of trust accounting. Only a portion of the proceeds from land and timber sales went directly to the bands. This required the government to implement a system to track the remainder of the money, which still formally belonged to the Aboriginal people under the treaty terms. The trust fund set up for this purpose was referred to as the Indian Fund. To illustrate the vast amount of wealth at stake, the fund had a balance of just over $3 million in 1881 (Department of Indian Affairs 1881, lxi). This only pertained to land and timber sales from reserve land, and did not include the vast tracts of land originally ceded under the treaties. Thus it was a result of the signing of the treaties that a complex of land and men came to be constructed as a new domain of governance. This arbitrary bounding of the domain of governance (cf. Rose 1991) and the associated accounting implications—the costs of treaty annuities would be an expense of the Indian Department but the land sale proceeds would not be revenue—would continue to shape accounting representations and interventions for the remainder of the period.

Subdividing the Land

Because of the pattern of Canadian expansion from the East into the West and because of the great quantities of land received immediately by the government as a result of the western treaties, sales of reserve lands in the distant North West Territories were quite rare during the 1860–1900 period. We therefore found no evidence in the Battleford, Blood, Hobbema and Sarcee Indian Agents' correspondence pertaining to the sale of reservation lands. However, the correspondence does reveal other attempts to alter the relationship of these First Nations peoples to their land. This was done through individual incentives and the attempted introduction of the European[3] concept of private landownership. These initiatives originated in one of the final legislative acts of imperial administrators prior to Confederation, namely, the Gradual Civilization Act of 1857. This act was based upon the assumption that the full civilization of tribes could be achieved only when Indians were brought into contact with individualized property (Milloy 1983, 58). It stipulated that any Indian, adjudged by a special board of examiners to be educated, free from debt and of good moral character, could on application be awarded twenty hectares of land within the colony and the rights accompanying it (ibid.). In 1869 the government introduced a new and improved Act for the Gradual Enfranchisement of the Indians that updated enfranchisement provisions introduced in 1857. Finally, Section 86 of the 1876 Indian Act included the incentive of enfranchisement for Indian men and women by introducing the notion of a *location ticket*.[4] Under this provision, a band could allot to an individual band member a portion of reserve land. As a form of title, the Superintendent General would then give the band member a location ticket for this land.

This allotment of reserve lands required, of course, that they first be subdivided. The Indian Act specified that the band should make the allotment, subject to the approval of the Superintendent General. However, in the late 1880s the Indian Department attempted to encourage the use of location tickets by hiring surveyors to enter the reserves, measure the land and divide it into lots. This intrusion raised concerns amongst the native population, recognized by the Indian Commissioner in Regina as "misapprehension in the minds of the Indians regarding the object of the subdivision surveys" (1889c, para. 1). A hand-drawn diagram of the system for subdivision appended to this 1889 letter shows the use of rectilinear lots and the provision of a roadway for vehicular traffic, thereby illustrating how the softwares of governmentality (in this case surveying expertise and inventory control procedures for land management) sometimes lay the groundwork for the hardwares of governmentality (vehicular modes of transportation unknown to the native populations).

Despite the considerable effort embodied in these legislative and administrative measures, the enfranchisement policy was a failure in that it did not encourage assimilation. In fact, it actually undermined government–First Nations relations (*RCAP* 1996, 11). One of the sticking points for the First Nations was that land assigned to an enfranchised Indian through location tickets would be removed from tribal reserve forever. The 1996 Royal Commission report (11) points out that, as a result of the negative reaction of First Nations to these measures, only one person ever accepted enfranchisement.

ECONOMIC CITIZENSHIP

The attempt to individualize the First Nations was not limited to the surveying of lots and the use of location tickets. Even more comprehensive attempts were made by the Indian Department to change indigenous societies, through the introduction of economic relationships into Aboriginal societies. In these efforts, the Indian Department was somewhat more successful, partly due to the necessities imposed on Indian bands by the disappearance of the buffalo, but also due to administrative powers assigned to the department through legislation.

In 1860, seven years prior to Confederation, imperial legislators turned control of Indian affairs over to Canada through the Transfer to Canada of Indian Affairs & The Management of Indian Lands and Property Act (*Statutes of Canada* 1860). This act made the Chief Superintendent the *financial steward* for indigenous peoples. Viewed from our present-day vantage point, the paternalism inherent in appointing a government bureaucrat as steward over an entire race of people might seem shocking. But in the cultural milieu of the times, such paternalism was accepted. In the first annual report after responsibility for Indian affairs was transferred to his office, Secretary of State Hector Langevin expressed the pride of a parent: "I come now to Indian affairs, and I am happy to say that, thanks to the fatherly protection of the Government, the Indian tribes in general continue to be in a prosperous condition" (Department of Indian Affairs 1868, 4).

This explicit paternalism hints at the societal sentiments behind administrative actions. However, what remains unsaid in administrative accounts of this period is the manner in which government actions first stripped indigenous peoples of agency and then re-represented this lack of agency as evidence of the need for paternalism.

This circularity can be observed at the intersection of Indian Department policy directives and the activities of local Indian Agents. The Agents were exhorted by the Indian Department to encourage indigenous peoples to take up economic roles of employment, agriculture and the manufacture of farm goods. For example, in a letter dated 11 November 1889, Hayter Reed, the Indian Commissioner for the North West Territories and formerly the Battleford Agent (1881–1882), stated:

> Indians can be made to work by an exercise of firmness and kindness, and experience has already shown that in many instances they will do so as well as white men. They certainly may not be so constant nor so agreeable to manage, still they can be got to work, and it is our duty to put up with the annoyances connected with the employment of Indian labour. (Indian Commissioner 1889a, para. 6–7)

In this and other circular letters to the Agents of the North West Territories, the commissioner attempted to reform indigenous peoples as economic citizens. Correspondence between the Indian Commissioner and local Indian Agents shows how accounting forms, reports and methods were to be used to help convert the Aboriginal person into *homo economicus*. For example, the Indian Commissioner required regular reports on the employment status of Indians on the reserve. These reports were to indicate who had worked for what rate on which days and speculate on the reasons for Indians resigning from employment relationships (Indian Commissioner 1889a). These reports, prepared by the Indian Agents, made visible the employment activities on the reserves and allowed the commissioner to assess the success of his directives. This "success" was then described in detail in the department's annual reports to Parliament, in which the industriousness and "moral development" of each Indian band was described. For example:

> The Stoneys are said to be successful in raising cattle. They are also good hunters, and, being industrious, they readily obtain employment as herders of cattle or laborers. They have likewise plenty of wood

on their reserve which they cut and sell to settlers. The Sarcees are unfortunately not so favourably situated, nor are they industriously disposed. They spend much of their time about Calgarry [*sic*]. (Department of Indian Affairs 1882, xvii)

Annual reports closer to 1900 were more formal in representing the industriousness of Indians. They included detailed tabular reports listing the employment activities and earnings of individual Indians (e.g., Department of Indian Affairs 1896, 444).

The letter from Hayter Reed quoted in the preceding, which calls for the introduction of wage employment into First Nations society, conveys the expectation that Indians should engage in purposeful agriculture (as opposed to their prior subsistence relationship with the land) and the manufacture and trade of goods:

> They [the Indians] should be encouraged to take as [*sic*] hay and firewood, to be delivered to the purchaser, for by this means a market for their labor as well as for the raw material, is found. . . . No doubt however the mainstay of the great majority of Indians must be farming and it is therefore most important to teach this industry in the manner best calculated to render them self supporting when left to their own resources as well as at the present moment. (Indian Commissioner 1889b, para. 11)

In other words, the First Nations' subsistence way of life was to be replaced with industrial and mercantile activity, through the inculcation of a particular vision of economic citizenship.

Archival records and secondary accounts indicate that the Agents were central to these attempts to reform indigenous peoples (Carter 1990). However, it was necessary to enlist accounting practices because Agents had to account for the money the First Nations people had earned. Because money was foreign to indigenous culture (Price et al. 1975), the people had to be taught how to handle it. At the same time, the Indian Department had to develop procedures to account for the funds it distributed as payment for services provided by the First Nations people to the Agencies.

The solution devised by the Indian Department was not to distribute the earnings directly to the Indians, but to set up bank accounts at the nearest post office for each Indian who was to be paid. Procedures had to be developed for handling withdrawals on behalf of the Indians, since the post offices were located off the reserve, which the Indians could not leave without an official departmental permission slip. The Agent had to apply to the Indian Commissioner's Office for approval for each withdrawal and provide the Indian's signature or witnessed mark (Indian Commissioner 1895a), the Indian's number in the band and the name of the band (Indian Commissioner 1895b). Later the procedure required a receipt from the individual Indian for the expense being reimbursed, plus an "order" for it to be paid from his post office account (Indian Commissioner 1895c). Finally, a requirement was added for the application to be in duplicate and to state, "how the applicant proposes to expend the money withdrawn, in order that the Department may have some assurance that the money is to be spent for some useful purpose" (Indian Commissioner 1895d, para. 1). This elaborate protocol was then replaced by a new procedure, the desire for improvement being inherent in governmentality. The new procedure was apparently needed because "it is desired that, as far as possible, Indians be allowed to expend their moneys themselves" (Indian Commissioner 1895e, para. 2). The new procedure contained few provisions to enable this declared intent. The Indians' ability to spend their own money was to be "always of course under the advice of the Agent or Farmer" (para. 2). In addition, the new procedure was even more elaborate than the one it replaced, with nine points for the Agent to follow, including the requirement that the Indians endorse the cheques they received in front of an interpreter and turn them over to the Agent, who was to pay for implements and cattle he had purchased on the Indian's behalf. The balance of the funds were either to be remitted to the Indian or retained by the Agent to pay for supplies from merchants that the Indian "may have purchased, or may wish to purchase" (para. 5). The new procedure required signed receipts and balancing entries in Agency cash-books, appearing therefore to be very much intended to prevent misappropriation of the Indians' funds by the Agents. Such accounting practices enmeshed indigenous peoples and Agents in mutually sustaining webs of observation and discipline (cf. Hoskin and Macve 1986, 130).

The elaborate transactional protocol of these administrative processes cloaks coercion in banal procedure. Local records of life on the reserves indicate the Indian Department and its employees strove to maintain a peaceful, administrative posture, and that overt physical coercion was at odds with the image the department tried to project. A diary kept by an anonymous clerk at the Sarcee Agency during 1885 describes conflicting modes of governance being attempted over the First Nations peoples. On the one hand, apparently militaristic interventions were attempted by the North West Mounted Police. On the other hand, bureaucratic interventions were attempted by the Indian Department personnel. Handwritten diary entries reveal that the clerk who wrote them resented the activities of the police:

> *Sunday April 5th*
> *Dr Gerard left, also the Chinaman cook. Capt Cotton & Dewey paid a visit to the Reserve, they came to quiet the Indians as they said, but succeeded well in exciting them.*
> *In my opinion they had no business here without the Agents company & not interfere without they are asked so to do.*

Monday Apl 6th Issue at N Agency
Indians very much excited over the visit of yesterday, had a big talk
with them and quieted them down a great deal.

(Sarcee Indian Agency Clerk 1885)

The alleged conduct of the police officers contrasts not only with the bureaucratic mentality of the diary writer—who throughout his diary methodically records, almost in a debit-and-credit fashion, all arrivals and departures from the reserve—but with the need of the Indian Department to maintain the image of a just government. These diaries entries suggest that police officers agitated the Indian population, but they also imply that the population was unsettled before the police officers arrived. This is corroborated by an earlier entry in the diary, on 5 March, when the clerk wrote, "Indian troubles increasing with the mild weather." These "troubles" suggest why the police officers visited the reserve in April and call into question the benign nature of Indian Department routines and procedures.

It is important to recognize the genesis of dependency that was embedded in the accounting policies of the Indian Department. Paternalism echoed throughout the Indian Department, as Indian Agents were encouraged to think of the inhabitants of the reserves as "their Indians." Departmental accounting policies were propagated to the local Agencies, carrying with them not just the European imperatives of economy and efficiency, but also an explicit sense of the superiority of the "white" way of doing things. The goal of driving the Indians towards self-sufficiency is clearly stated by the Indian Department correspondents. However, such goals, based as they are on the sentiment that the Indians required "driving" by the government, undermined the very self-sufficiency they attempted to promote.

DISCUSSION AND CONCLUSION

Our analysis has emphasized how federal legislation presumes and requires what Miller and Rose (1990) refer to as technologies of government—that is, those "apparently humble and mundane mechanisms" such as "techniques of notation, computation and calculation" (8). We have observed how federal legislation implied, invoked and enlisted accounting technologies. The examples pertaining to land transactions illustrated how the signing of the western treaties constructed new domains of governance and how accounting was used to mediate new relations between the federal government and First Nations. Likewise, the examples regarding economic citizenship showed how it was necessary to enlist accounting practices to control and account for the wages indigenous peoples earned as participants in a market economy. Thus, accounting was used both to represent and to intervene.

Our analysis also examined distance, diffusion and agency associated with accounting technologies. Accounting was instrumental in extending political dominion over new geographical territory, overcoming the geographic distance between Ottawa and the new territories by selectively representing life on the reserves, documenting the "success" of departmental programmes and forming the basis for subsequent administrative and accounting interventions. Embedded within federal legislation and the resulting accounting practices, such as wage payment procedures, were mentalities consistent with the government's vision of acceptable habits, customs and cultural practices. The diffusion of accounting practices thus aided the implanting of these mentalities in the local population. However, despite being expected to take on "white man's" ways of industrious self-reliance, the Aboriginal people were effectively rendered passive objects of departmental programmes and procedures, a passivity that, at least with respect to inducements to surrender of pieces of reserve land, proved quite effective as a means of resistance.

This study provides a "history of the present" (Foucault 1984), giving us a vantage point for examining current government–indigenous peoples relations. As a field-specific case study, it provides detail on the ways that government policies and practices construct and govern populations as a complex assembly of people-and-things. The technologies of government introduced during the 1860–1900 period changed social relations among indigenous peoples, European settlers and government. The consequences of these changes continue to structure present-day relations. A legacy of the period examined was the disabling of indigenous agency. This rationalized both the government's paternal attitudes and the need for further government control of indigenous affairs. In this respect, the changes introduced in the 1880s foreshadowed the "new" indigenous management policies of the 1970s and 1980s (cf. Mercredi and Turpel 1993).

The study contributes to our understanding of how accounting underpins the implementation of financial legislation. This has interesting implications, not only for government–indigenous relations, but also for fields such as education, health care and social services, where financial legislation is tied to accounting in ever-more sophisticated and complex ways. This study demonstrates the functioning of agency within accounting-based governance processes, revealing accounting as a non-neutral technology that distributes agency unequally. The introduction of new accounting procedures at the local level confers agency on those with expertise to perform accounting and interpret its reports. While the relationship between accounting technologies and expertise has been well documented in prior studies of governance (e.g. Power 1996, 1997b), the present study demonstrates how the act of positioning and representing indigenous peoples via accounting numbers and calculations diminishes their agency, engendering their dependency on government.

These disabling effects in the case raise the question of how difficult it is to mount resistance in the face of the "humble and mundane" (Miller and Rose 1990, 8) technologies of accounting. Because accounting at the local level of the Indian Department was pervasive, decentralized and multilevel, as well as mundane to the point of appearing innocuous, it perhaps did not offer any clear points of purchase for those who would resist it. In this respect, it was more effective than armed aggression as a means to 'quiet the Indians'. Nonetheless, effective resistance was mounted: as mentioned, only one person ever took up enfranchisement, despite the elaborate intentions and interventions of governance. This suggests that the diffusion of mundane technologies such as accounting is not completely successful at disabling the agency of distant populations. Such observations, arising from the past, are salient today for relations between governments and indigenous peoples. Despite the vastness of the bureaucracy erected in an attempt to manage indigenous peoples, and the implacability of the mundane accounting procedures by which this goal of management is pursued, the objects of government policy retain their voice and will not be quieted.

NOTES

1. The Indian Department was a sub-department of the Department of the Interior.
2. We use the uncapitalized word 'agent' in the Foucauldian sense, and capitalize the 'Indian Agent'.
3. The archival records consistently use the term "white" to describe settlers and Indian Department staff. We often use "European" to describe them because their impact on Canada was cultural and political, not just racial. We occasionally use "white" to be consistent with the data and to recall the racial overtones of many Indian Department practices. Likewise, the archival material mainly uses "Indian" and sometimes "Aboriginal" or "Aborigine" to describe the First Nations. We use the word "Indian" when referring to the objects of specific Indian Department policies and practices, but prefer "First Nations" when referring to political matters and "indigenous" or "Aboriginal" when referring to cultural matters.
4. At the time, women did not have the right to vote in Canada. Therefore, "enfranchisement" here means Canadian citizenship.

5 Accounting and Pauperism

Stephen P. Walker

INTRODUCTION

At first sight the relief of poverty may seem an unlikely arena in which to discover anything sinister about accounting. However, its malevolent potential becomes apparent when it is recalled that accounting essentially involves the recording, processing, classification and disclosure of information. When these practices are deployed in state welfare systems (where, on occasion, they are explicitly described as 'accounting') they may operate in ways which adversely construct the identity of the poor, generate negative perceptions of self and serve to disrupt the social relationships of those in poverty. The recording, processing and classifying of data submitted by the claimant for relief can be understood as degradation ceremonies which inscribe stigmatizing labels and discourage applications for assistance. Where such processes individualize and include public disclosures of named welfare recipients they can compound the degraded status of the poor in local communities (Walker 2008a). Further, when stark asymmetries of power exist between those who finance relief and those who consume it, attempts by elites to reduce its cost may inspire attempts to correct the behaviour and morals of recipients. Such disciplining can involve the deployment of techniques of social control; accounting may feature among these.

In pre-industrial and early industrial Britain operating the system of poor relief was the principal function of local government. The statutes governing relief, the poor laws, "were a fundamental structure of the English state for 350 years" (Lees 1998, 7). These laws concerned "more than the relief of destitution" (Webb and Webb 1927, vi), they were "entwined in the fabric of society" (Poynter 1969, xi; Oxley 1974, 11). One such statute, the

---

This chapter is based on the paper "Expense, Social and Moral Control: Accounting and the Administration of the Old Poor Law in England and Wales", which originally appeared in *Journal of Accounting and Public Policy* 23, no. 2 (2004): 85–127. The author would like to thank the publisher, Elsevier, for permission to use this material.

Poor Law Amendment Act 1834, has been described as the most important piece of social legislation ever enacted in Britain. The report of the Royal Commission which preceded this act is a salient document in English social history (Englander 1998, 1; Fowle 1881, 75). The chronology of the Poor Law Amendment Act bisects the history of poor relief. A plethora of legislative changes before 1834 concern the 'old poor law'. The 1834 act ushered in the 'new poor law'. In this chapter the focus is on exploring the social implications of accounting in the closing years of the old poor law.

Numerous scholars have researched and written about the poor laws. Yet until recently few have explored the vast accounting exercise attending poor relief. This is surprising given the importance attached by contemporaries to the financing and administration of the system (Wood 1985). While parish accounts are recognized as "the staple of poor law records" (Oxley 1974, 56) and a key source for understanding the lives of the poor (Hitchcock, King and Sharpe 1997, 5–6), they are generally perceived as the mere canvas on which more compelling dimensions of poverty are painted. The canvas itself, the concepts underpinning its design and the techniques applied to it potentially illuminate contemporary perceptions of the poor, their management and the social and behavioural impacts of calculative inscriptions on the poor themselves. Although primarily advanced as a technique for pursuing economic imperatives such as expense control, accounting can seldom be detached from social objectives and consequences (Miller and Rose 1990).

THE ADMINISTRATION OF THE OLD POOR LAW

According to Eastwood (1994, 166) "The old poor law was the defining social and political institution in rural England". It enshrined and conditioned social structures and relationships. Further:

> In an economic system increasingly characterized by low wages and limited opportunities the receipt of poor relief, significantly dubbed being 'on the parish', was a pervasive experience amongst the rural labouring class. By thus defining a large dependent class and simultaneously according local employers significant political power, the old poor law mediated and reinforced patterns of authority and powerlessness which were embedded in economic function and sustained through the day-to-day politics of village life. (Eastwood 1994, 166)

The operation of the old poor law in England and Wales reflected a decentralized distribution of power and a culture of parochialism (Eastwood 1997, 9). It was administered in 15,500 parishes and townships (Oxley 1974, 34–40). The officers in the "petty kingdom" of the local parish (Fraser 1984, 34) tended to be drawn from the governing class of landowners, professionals, tradesmen and especially tenant farmers: that is, those who bore the burden of the local rates (Eastwood 1997, 42–48). The officers included the churchwardens, a constable and an overseer of the poor. Each of these produced accounts. Overseers were responsible for assessing the poor rate, collecting the rate, investigating claimants, calculating entitlement and disbursing relief (Oxley 1974, 43–45). Although the parochial officers exercised a good deal of autonomy in managing the local poor, they were accountable to Justices of the Peace, or county and borough magistrates, who monitored the administration of parishes.

The relief of the poor ranged from schemes of work creation to the care of the aged, sick and lunatic, to the placement of pauper apprentices (Horn 1980, 101–5). Paupers were classed as either 'able-bodied' or 'non-able bodied'. Those unable to work through age or infirmity, or who were unemployed, casual or underpaid labourers, received pensions or doles of money or essential goods (Oxley 1974, 62–78, 102–9; Poynter 1969, 13–17). Relief was classified as either indoor or outdoor. The assistance received by paupers who remained in their own homes was known as outdoor relief. This was the main form of poor relief (Boyer 1990, 10–23). Workhouses, erected as places where pauper labour could be expended in return for food and shelter, were the principal scenes of indoor relief (Oxley 1974, 79–82). In 1802–1803 there were 3,765 workhouses in England and Wales. These accommodated less than one-twelfth of the pauper population (Poynter 1969, 189; Wood 1991, 54–55).

The accounting obligations of parishes in relation to the poor were codified in statutes. Successive acts from the early sixteenth century required the keeping of books of accounts of monies gathered and disbursed for relief, books of the poor, registers of admissions to the poor roll and the examination of the records (Walker 2004a). During the eighteenth century increasing concerns about the misapplication of funds precipitated a strengthening of the accounting obligations on overseers and vested the magistrates with enhanced powers of inspection.

The Old Poor Law in Crisis

From the late eighteenth century there was "rising panic about the inadequacy, expense and potentially pernicious effects of the poor-relief system" (Hitchcock, King and Sharpe 1997, 9). Between 1795 and 1834 the burden of the poor resulted in a doubling of the rates. The poor law seemed unable to accommodate worsening poverty as a result of the cyclical and structural effects (especially on employment) of the shift towards an industrial economy and exceptionally high prices during the Napoleonic Wars. In 1750 poor relief accounted for 6 per cent of total expenditure by local and central government. By 1817–1818 this had risen to 11.6 per cent (quoted in Eastwood 1994, 127). Real expenditure on the poor increased by 23 per cent from 1817 to 1832 (Boyer 1990, 196). The poor law was implicated in the 'Swing Riots' of 1830–1831, provoked by harvest failure and the impact on agricultural labourers of the introduction of threshing machines (Brundage 1978, 15; Driver 1993, 26). It was also increasingly apparent that the administration and management of the poor was corrupt and inefficient (Wood 1991, 52).

Thus, the poor law became "the object of a vigorous attack, and the centre of a controversy in which new assumptions of social order challenged the old" (Poynter 1969, xi). In the context of mounting crisis a succession of official investigations were ordered into the system (Oxley 1974, 25). It is primarily through these sources that insights are offered to the perceived role(s) of accounting in the control of the poor.

Foremost among the official investigations was the Royal Commission into the Administration and Practical Operation of the Poor Laws, which commenced in 1832 (Brundage 1978, chap. 11). According to Marshall (1985, 18), the Royal Commission "set about the most detailed social investigation ever undertaken in these isles up to that time". Information was also gathered by twenty-six assistant commissioners who visited 20 per cent of all parishes and examined parish books and book-keeping systems (Wood 1991, 60–61; Marshall 1985, 20–21). The commissioners also sent questionnaires to all parishes in England and Wales (Brundage 1978, 22; Rose 1985, 4). Rural and urban parishes were asked for suggestions for improving the keeping, auditing and publishing of parish accounts. Urban parishes were also asked whether they provided for the auditing and publishing of accounts. Answers to these queries offer insights to the functioning of accounting under the old poor law (Answers to Rural Queries 1834; Answers to Town Queries 1834).

The reports, evidence and submissions of the Royal Commission and other committees on the poor law during the early nineteenth century suggest that accounting was perceived to have two main functions. First, systematic and uniform accounting would serve to control expenses and protect ratepayers' funds. There was considerable support for a common accounting system to be implemented in all parishes. This would ensure rigorous and accurate record keeping by competent staff and as well as effective audit and inspection. Such a system would prevent and detect defalcation and improper expenditure (Walker 2004a). The introduction of a uniform system of accounts was the foremost accounting recommendation of the Royal Commissioners in 1834 (Checkland and Checkland 1974, 444). The second set of themes relate to the governance and management of the pauper. In particular, the use of accounting as a technique of bureaucratic surveillance and the potential of accounting publicity in the social and moral control of the poor. These themes are the focus of the remainder of this chapter.

RENDERING THE PAUPER VISIBLE

There were two dimensions to rendering the poor visible and governable through accounting. The first concerned the collection and analysis of accounting information on the recipients of relief by those responsible for their management. The second related to the publication of accounts as a foundation for the community surveillance of the poor.

The keeping of detailed records to monitor paupers had long been necessary in relation to the laws of settlement. By defining the conditions under which a person had a right to relief from a particular parish the Settlement Act of 1662 sought to prevent individuals from moving to locations where relief was more generous (Fraser 1984, 34–35; Tate 1969, 198–205). The surveillance of the migratory poor was necessary to restrict the distribution of parish resources to those entitled to receive them (Landau 1988, 1990). During the late eighteenth century some reformers argued for a more comprehensive recording of the pauper population. Most prominent among these was Jeremy Bentham in his *Pauper Management Improved* (1797). Similarly, Sir Thomas Bernard of Stoke, conscious of the importance of knowledge about the recipients of relief, introduced "a detailed register of the poor, with all relevant points on their situation and relief tabulated" (Poynter 1969, 97).

The Royal Commission of 1832 applauded those systems which contained costs, prevented imposition and managed the pauper population by rendering individual recipients of relief visible. In Witham, Essex, it was proudly stated that an open account was kept for every pauper, such that the parish "can refer at once to the amount given to any individual, the time when and the cause for which it was granted, for many years back" (Answers to Rural Queries). The accounting records kept in Hartlip, Kent, ensured that "the expense of each pauper may be seen in a moment" (Answers to Rural Queries 1834). In Wisbech St. Mary, Cambridgeshire, it was reported that the Vestry Clerk kept accounts of "The paupers names . . . arranged alphabetically, with the several sums they may receive from the Overseer, in weekly columns; so that a parishioner may at one glance know what any pauper has had during the year" (ibid.).

Accounting systems which employed classifications were also deemed beneficial. These were invariably infused with, and often inscribed, the moral causes of poverty. They could ascribe an additional stigmatizing label on the recipient of relief. Taxonomies could distinguish bastards, aged, indigent, occasional, permanent, able-bodied and widowed paupers. Appropriate treatments could thus be applied to govern and manage the individual or class of poor. In Farnham, Surrey, a respondent advised, "The account of relief given should be kept and published according to the several classes, as it would more clearly show where the evil lies; say, Pay to large Families, to the Aged, Bastards, Casual, Labourers" (Answers to Rural Queries 1834). In Ford, Northumberland, a form of account which recorded the integrity of the claimant was advocated:

> Let a folio book be prepared with four columns; the first containing the name of the pauper and his parish, and whether he (or any other person)

was sworn to the circumstances of his case, or whether those circumstances were admitted by the Overseer on his personal knowledge; the
second containing his own account of the condition of his family, and of
the amount of his earnings; the agreement respecting it. (ibid.)

ACCOUNTING PUBLICITY AND THE
SURVEILLANCE OF THE POOR

In the local system of relief examined here accounting was a peripheral but
potent technique of community surveillance and governance of the poor.
Modern-day agencies for the prevention and detection of social security
fraud utilize the mass media and encourage the public to report on sus-
pected benefit cheats. In the early nineteenth century the publication of
poor law accounts assumed a similar function.

Early advocates of systematic approaches to poor relief acknowledged
the importance of identification and surveillance to effective pauper management. In 1528 Martin Luther advocated registration and licensing to
enable towns and villages to "keep an eye upon their paupers" (quoted in
de Schweinitz 1972, 37). Before the early nineteenth century, rendering
the pauper visible in England was achieved by physical identification in the
form of badging. From 1697 until its repeal in 1810 legislation required
that those in receipt of parish relief wear a badge on the shoulder of their
right sleeve emblazoned with a large *P* and the first letter of the parish. The
stigma associated with badging was perceived as a deterrent to claimants
and a means of reducing the rates (Eden 1797, 274, 343). Badging, however,
was often difficult to administer, especially in urban areas, and the practice
fell into disuse (Webb and Webb 1927, 160–61; Tate 1969, 207–08). It was
supplanted by another vehicle for giving visibility to the stigmatized pauper, accounting publicity. According to Oxley:

> This disappearance of badges mattered little because a new and more
> effective means of achieving the same end had now been discovered.
> This was the printed list of paupers distributed by the parish among
> the ratepayers, an idea which emerged in the towns where it was
> impossible for the overseers to keep track of all their numerous poor.
> They had to enlist the aid of all ratepayers in identifying the minority
> who would feign sickness or unemployment, collect their relief and
> then go off to remunerative employment, perhaps in another parish.
> (1974, 54–55)

Figure 5.1 contains an example of a printed list of paupers.

The function of accounting publicity should also be understood in the
context of rapid population growth, especially in urban parishes, and the
decline of the "intimate everybody-knowing-everybody-else atmosphere"

Paid to each					Weekly Relief			
£.	s.	d.	Names of Paupers	Age	No. of Children	s.	d.	Cause of Relief	Residence
-	10	-	Ayres, Thomas	47	6	2	-	Family	Cookham Deane
2	12	-	Aldridge, Charlotte	6	-	1	-	Bastard	Cookham
3	18	-	Blight, Mary	11	-	1	6	Bastard	Twyford Silk Mills
1	19	-	Beck, widow	67	-	1	-	Aged	Cookham
7	16	-	Bishop, widow	48	2	3	-	Family	Cookham Deane
2	12	-	Bristowe, Martha	31	1	1	-	Bastard	Pinkney's Green
-	10	-	Barker, William	37	6	2	-	Pay taken off	Cookham Deane
-	18	-	Brant, widow	-	2	2	-	Family	Maidenhead
2	18	6	Barrey's child	11	-	1	6	Father dead	North Town
1	12	6	Bolton's wife	72	-	2	6	Cripple	Pay taken off
4	16	-	Bradley, widow	31	3	6	-	Family	Pay taken off
12	10	-	Brown, widow	32	4	5	-	Family	Pigney's Green
4	12	-	Bowden, Ruth	24	-	2	-	Illness	Grays
3	18	-	Carter, Susanna	13	-	1	6	Bastard	Twyford Silk Mills
2	12	-	Cartland, -	32	1	1	-	Bastard	Cookham Deane
2	12	-	Carndice, Jane	30	1	1	-	Bastard	Cookham
2	12	-	Cattle, Jane	30	1	1	-	Bastard	Taplow
7	16	-	Charlton, John	72	2	3	-	Aged	Maidenhead
6	18	-	Collins, widow	41	3	6	-	Family	Bm. Pay taken off
2	10	-	Chapman, Sarah	40	-	2	6	Infirm	Bray
2	12	-	Cutter, widow	62	-	1	-	Aged	Cookham Deane
5	4	-	Chitts, widow	72	-	2	-	Aged	Cookham
2	-	-	Clift, widow	77	-	2	-	Aged	Pay taken off
2	12	-	Carter's child	10	-	1	-	Bastard	Cookham Deane
5	4	-	Cartland, Sarah	77	-	2	-	Aged	Cookham
4	10	-	Cannon, widow	31	2	4	-	Pay taken off	Staines
2	12	-	Cannon, widow	31	1	1	-	Bastard	Staines
3	18	-	Copas, Lydia	13	-	1	6	F. and M. dead	Twyford Silk Mills
3	18	-	Copas, Martha	14	-	1	6	Ditto	Twyford Silk Mills
2	12	-	Carter, Sarah	27	1	1	-	Bastard	Benson
5	4	-	Davis, widow	51	-	2	-	Infirm	Cookham
2	12	-	Dayley, widow	62	-	1	-	Aged	Pinkney's Green
2	12	-	Dayley, Joseph	9	-	1	-	Bastard	Battle
4	-	-	Dowding, James	11	-	2	-	Pay taken off	Cookham
3	18	-	Evans, widow	62	-	1	6	Infirm	Maidenhead
2	12	-	Fox's wife	37	1	1	-	Bastard	Cookham
4	12	-	Fryday, widow	74	-	1	-	Aged	North Town
5	4	-	Folley, widow R.	72	-	2	-	Aged	Cookham Deane
6	6	4	Folley, widow	36	6	6	-	Family	Pay taken off
2	12	-	Ford's child	-	-	1	-	Father dead	Cookham
1	7	-	Fowler, widow	72	-	1	6	Aged	Dead
-	18	-	Fry, widow	63	-	1	-	Illness	Dead

Figure 5.1 Excerpt from an annual list of paupers.

Source: Report from the Select Committee of the House of Lords (1831, Minutes, pp. 176–7).

associated with pre-industrial society (Oxley 1974, 47). Local inhabitants assumed greater anonymity. This was also "an underpoliced society" (Eastwood 1994, 191). Although a parish constable was appointed to keep the peace he had limited responsibility for crime detection (Tate 1969, 176–87). The latter depended heavily on the prevailing "communal self-regulation" of informers (Eastwood 1997, 140; Hay 1977, 34–37). Oral-centred devices of law enforcement were increasingly augmented by printed media. Newspaper advertisements and handbills encouraged information flows to assist the apprehension of criminals (Eastwood 1994, 230–31). Accounting publicity fell within this schema. It facilitated the citizen's capacity to identify those in the community who were undeserving recipients of poor relief (Lees 1998, 37).

Rendering the pauper visible via inscription and the public disclosure of claimants' identities through the medium of accounts was a component of the increasingly bureaucratized management of poverty. Surveillance thus shifted from symbolic labelling of the poor through dress (badging) on the corporeal subject to more calculable techniques. Alternatively, the pauper was definable by residence in the workhouse. Here direct supervision of the incarcerated subject offered greater opportunity for the imposition of bureaucratic and other techniques of social and moral discipline (Wood 1991, 57; Walker 2008a). When compared with workhouse inmates under the management of an institutional bureaucracy, the recipients of outdoor relief were more difficult to observe. Accounting publicity was a means of activating the local community as agents in the surveillance of claimants.

The Webbs found evidence of the increasing use of such publicity in towns as the cost of poor relief increased during the late eighteenth and early nineteenth centuries:

> Meanwhile a few parishes, in their new-born zeal for investigating the claims of the poor, invoked the aid of the public. For Chesterfield, Wolverhampton and Birmingham, for instance, printed lists are extant for various years between 1781 and 1796 "of those who receive pay", and sometimes also of the inmates of the workhouse. One for Nantwich (Cheshire) for 1816 gives also their ages. In 1833 we learn that "in St. Asaph, Holywell, Wrexham, and one or two other places in Flintshire and Denbighshire, a balance sheet of the yearly receipts and payments, and the names of those who have been relieved, with the amount granted to each, is printed and distributed amongst the ratepayers. This practice has been only of recent introduction; but of such advantage is it considered that the parishes adjoining those where it exists are beginning to adopt it. The printing and distributing a list of those receiving relief often brings to light cases of imposture which otherwise would have remained undetected; besides which the paupers seem to dislike the exposure, as in some instances they have given up a

part or the whole of their relief to prevent it. The printed accounts of St. Asaph contain the following entry: 'Sundry paupers who rather than be "classed" (that is, put in the printed list) pay part of their "rent"'. And in another parish a pauper ceased to apply for relief on learning that his name had been thus published. (1927, 165)

Similar disclosures with a view to encouraging the public to turn informer on those undeserving of relief were operated in cities such as Manchester and Plymouth during the 1810s and 1820s (Webb and Webb 1927, 165). Eastwood relates the case of Stow-on the-Wold where the vestry resolved in 1822 "that the names of Paupers and the several sums they receive be printed quarterly and put up in the public houses in this town and the names of parents of illegitimate children be also added and a request that any person knowing anything of the conduct or condition of said paupers be requested to communicate it to the Overseers" (1997, 129).

Demands for accounting publicity in poor law administration were likely to have been inspired by Jeremy Bentham's work but were not necessarily conceived or applied in a manner consistent with his notion of rendering management transparent (Gallhofer and Haslam 2003, 22–65). Other advocates included Samuel Whitbread, who, in the 1800s, proposed measures to achieve economy and check fraud through the greater publicity of parochial accounts (Eastwood 1994, 125). Having heard evidence of the circulation to parishioners of alphabetical lists of paupers and the amounts paid to them, the Report from the Select Committee of the House of Lords on the Poor Laws (hereafter, Report) referred to "the advantage of publicity in all accounts of public concern" (1818, 12). Reverend J.T. Becher informed the Lords Committee of 1831 that his 'Anti-Pauper System', a scheme of administration designed for the moral regeneration of the poor, included the quarterly disclosure of paupers and the allowances they received (Report 1831, 221). Becher reported that on the implementation of his system in Southwell, publication had checked extravagance, reduced applications for relief and enhanced social control by rendering the lower orders less 'insolent' towards their superiors (Report 1831, 223).

Accounting publicity was perhaps the subject most eagerly felt by respondents to the town and rural queries issued by the Royal Commission of 1832. References were made to the importance of publicity, its benefits, the details to be disclosed and the medium and frequency of publication. Some respondents argued that the accounts should be printed and circulated to all ratepayers. Others suggested the accounts should be publicly read or displayed in public places such as the church vestry, the churchyard and local inns, or printed in the local newspapers. The most common recommendation for posting the accounts was on the church door. The respondent of Letcombe Regis, Berkshire, was typical: "the disbursements of every Rate should be transcribed, setting forth the names of every person and family who have received relief, and the amount thereof; and a copy placed at the church door on the Sunday whenever a new Rate is published, and left there for the inspection of the whole Parish" (Answers to Rural Queries 1834). Most strikingly, the Churchwarden of Summertown, Oxfordshire, declared:

> Parish Accounts cannot be made too public. In extensive parishes the accounts should be printed every six months at least, on two sheets; one containing the names of all persons receiving permanent or temporary relief, divided into weekly columns, which sheet should be posted in some conspicuous part of every public-house and beer-shop in the parish by the Constable, and any person keeping such public-house or beer-shop suffering paupers to remain tippling in their houses to be subject to higher penalties than at present. (ibid.)

Although not all reported that accounting publicity had a beneficial impact, most assistant commissioners found that it was an effective means of community surveillance which served to cut poor expenditure and therefore the rates. They reported how the distribution of pauper lists rendered visible cases of imposition and acted as a disincentive to applying for relief (Reports of Assistant Commissioners 1834, 29:185) and could shame unworthy recipients. At Leamington, the overseer stated that on posting the names of the paupers on the church door "he was constantly being informed by the rate-payers of cases of imposture, either in paupers being at service or having other means of living" (ibid., 51). It was reported that in Bridgewater beneficial effects resulted from regularly printing a detailed account of those provided with relief, to which was appended the following:

> These lists are circulated monthly, that when instances occur of misapplied relief, notice may promptly reach the parish officers.
>
> If a person receiving parish pay *expend any part thereof in a public-house*, his relief will be at once stopped; and innkeepers are hereby cautioned against endangering the renewal of their licences by serving *any such person* with liquor. (ibid., 28:488–91; emphasis in original)

As well as being a deterrent to pauperism, accounting publicity was also considered beneficial in arresting one of its sources, the sexual immorality associated with bastardy (Tate 1969, 221). The putative father of an illegitimate child was obliged to provide financial support (Horn 1980, 99–101). Although extracting monies was often hopeless (due to death, absconding or poverty), the pursuit of putative fathers by overseers was considered "part of the punishment for a moral offence" (Webb and Webb 1927, 308). Almost all respondents reported to the Royal Commissioner that payments by the parish to support bastards exceeded amounts received from parents.

A number of suggestions were offered to the Royal Commission to address the problem of illegitimacy and its adverse financial consequences for parishes. These included the castration of offenders, imprisonment, forced emigration, financial penalties, public penance, improved moral education and the prevention of dancing in beer houses. Others noted the preventative effects of degrading the parents of illegitimate children by publishing their names on the church door. The Curate in Nayland, Suffolk, argued: "Relief given either to paupers or the parents of Bastard Children, should be made as public as possible; an account should be published, quarterly at least, of the names of each individual who has received relief, and of the sum received" (Answers to Rural Queries 1834).

ACCOUNTING PUBLICITY AND SOCIAL CONTROL

Accounting inscription and disclosure also assumed a social control function at a time when social structures and relationships were changing. The posting of the names of paupers on the church door symbolized and reinforced, through inscription and publicity, the dependent status of paupers. It confirmed their low status in communities acutely conscious of social placement and where individuals demonstrated their position in the local hierarchy through public display (Perkin 1969; Eastwood 1994, 24). In eighteenth-century plebeian culture anonymity offered scope for independent acts of defiance against the gentry (Thompson 1993, 66–67). Accounting publicity was the antithesis of this. Techniques of bureaucratic identification, such as the lists and accounts of paupers used in the early nineteenth century, were a confirmation of dependence and an instrument of social discipline. Publicity was a basis for stigmatization—for the identification of those deserving of moral condemnation in the local community. In these ways accounting for paupers was an instrument for conditioning social identity and affirming social placement. According to Eastwood (1997, 125), "The old poor law divided provincial society into four broad categories: those habitually dependent on public relief, those intermittently dependent on public relief, those who enjoyed genuine independence, and those who administered the poor".

The working of the old poor law traditionally reflected a pre-industrial society characterized by bonds of patronage and obligation between those at opposite extremities of the social scale (Perkin 1969). The manner in which many ratepayers resorted to accounting publicity during the early nineteenth century as their interests were threatened by the spiralling cost of poor relief is illustrative of the wider fracturing of the stratified but personalized structures of the 'old society' and the emergent anonymity of class (Poynter 1969, 22–24). The tendency to resort to publicity reflected shifting attitudes towards the poor and served to polarize the identities of the rate-paying and dependent classes.

Accounting publicity represented a manifestation of social distancing where the poor were less of the community and more an imposition on it, a class to be monitored and controlled. Publicity was antithetical to

traditional understandings of social citizenship (Lees 1998, 9)—it identified those who represented a burden on the local community. As ratepayers
in the early nineteenth century became increasingly clamorous for expense
reduction, the poor were no longer perceived as "neighbours in a face-to-
face society", but as "strangers who menaced the respectable through their
disorderly lives" (ibid., 113; Marshall 1985, 9–10). The administration of
relief on the basis of the 'common knowledge', oral tradition and public
memory was increasingly supplanted by an "impulse to define, to list, and
to fix the status and condition of the poor through a written record" (Lees
1998, 32). Oxley states, "it was difficult to feign poverty amongst one's
neighbours or to grind the faces of the poor if they lived next door" (1974,
42). It was easier when the claimant was dehumanized as an entry in an
account. Accounting disclosure placed distance between the poor and their
neighbours. The resort to inscription contributed to the alienation of the
dependent pauper, and it was more sinister in a context where the poor
were perceived less as unfortunates deserving of charity and more as a
costly burden emanating from idleness and vice.

CONCLUSIONS

By examining discourses on the relief of poverty in early nineteenth-century
England and Wales, a period of crisis in the old poor law, we have seen how
the problematizing of existing practices by government agencies exposed
the functioning and *raison d'être* of accounting techniques (Miller 1998,
606–7). Those techniques were largely motivated by the economic rationalism of expense reduction, but they also satisfied an aspiration to render
visible and control the objects of relief. Under the old poor law, accounting
functioned as a tool of social as well as financial management. Accounting
in the local administration of poverty was entwined with and reflected the
social structures in which it operated. In particular, it reflected the social
and cultural frameworks of a hierarchical, predominantly rural society.

Shifts in the practices of parish accounting reinforced the local distribution of power and the relationships between the rate-paying elite and the
dependent poor. Accounting was increasingly perceived as a device to assist
the preservation of the dominant interest, the propertied, from the financial imposition of maintaining the poor. The latter became more pressing
during the late eighteenth and early nineteenth centuries when population
increase and rural distress exerted pressure on the system of relief and
its financing. In a context where "contemporaries were apt to judge the
poor-law system by its cost rather than by its efficacy in providing relief or
employment" (Poynter 1969, 17), accounting featured among suggestions
for administrative reform to reduce the burden of the poor.

The causes of pauperism were also revisited. At a time when poverty
was increasingly perceived as a consequence of vice and improvidence

a harsher disciplinary regime was accepted for identifying and managing the recipients of relief. During the early nineteenth century bureaucracy and calculative techniques were increasingly applied as devices for the governance of personal conduct and morality (Driver 1993, 10–15). Administrative procedures such as accounting publicity were advocated to contain the expense of the poor law by discouraging claimants, arresting immorality and mobilizing local communities for the purposes of surveillance and social discipline. Accounts were a tool in the self-policing community designed to prevent and detect impositions by the pauper on the propertied ratepayer.

The social labelling which attended the accounting publicity implemented by the dominant class assisted the differentiation of the poor in local society: it detracted from the earlier "intimate connection between the parish and the poor" (Tate 1969, 189). Accounting publicity was a symbol of the power of the parochial elite over the dependent local poor, a confirmation of social placement and difference. Discourses on the role of accounting in the parish also tended to have the same subordinating effects.

The accounting publicity actuated during the early nineteenth century therefore fell short of the radical, empowering and benevolent variety envisaged by Bentham (Gallhofer and Haslam 2000, 13–14). In the case presented here, it was the powerful ratepayers and administrators of the poor law who discovered the enabling potential of accounting publicity. For the pauper publicity was divisive and oppressive, an attempt to discourage claims for relief through public degradation and social classification. Compulsory disclosure eliminated the capacity of the pauper to manage a discredited social identity. While accounting publicity was perceived as an instrument for checking frauds perpetrated on ratepayers and the poor, it was not a device for rendering the administrators accountable to those they were bound to support, or for ensuring relief was given to those entitled to it. Practicing the greatest happiness of the greatest number in poor law administration worked to the detriment of the minority poor, and to the advantage of those who financed their relief (Fraser 1984, 46–47).

6   Accounting for Famine and Empire

Philip O'Regan

INTRODUCTION

The Irish Famine (1845–1849) has been described as one of the worst demographic disasters to affect any Western European country in recent centuries (Kinealy 1994; Ó Gráda 1989, 1999). In absolute terms it resulted in the population of the island falling from 8.5 million to just over six million through a combination of starvation, disease and emigration. It precipitated a population decline that continued for over a century. It also proved the catalyst for major changes that shaped the economic, political, cultural and religious outlooks of the people of Ireland for generations (Ó Gráda 1999; Lyons 1973; Foster 1988; Lee 1989).

As one element of its response to the challenges posed by this crisis, the imperial government in London initiated a number of relief measures. These involved the introduction of relief payments based on task-work, an intervention informed by a desire to impact the moral habits of the Irish in relation to work. This policy committed the government to considerable expenditure, requiring the Treasury in London to introduce a range of accounting technologies and personnel intended to control this outlay. By 1847 the government had effectively established a vast accounting architecture underpinned by several hundred imported and native accountants and book-keepers.

ACCOUNTING AND CULTURAL IMPERIALISM DURING A PERIOD OF CRISIS

The work of Edward Said (1978, 1993) has been seminal in emphasizing the cultural aspects of the imperial project and the power of discourse in

This chapter is based on the paper "'A Dense Mass of Petty Accountability': Accounting in the Service of Cultural Imperialism during the Irish Famine, 1846–1847", which originally appeared in *Accounting, Organizations and Society* 35, no. 4 (2010): 416–30. The author would like to thank the publisher, Elsevier, for permission to use this material.

'constructing' the colony and its population. Defining imperialism as a process that involves "thinking about, settling on, controlling land that you do not possess," he has sought to articulate "the privileged role of culture in the modern imperial experience" (1993, 5, 7). While acknowledging the catalytic effect of economic and political impulses, this perspective locates a cultural imperialism at the centre of this expansionary dynamic (Said 1988, 1993; Neu 1999, 2000a; Ferguson 2003; Neu and Heincke 2004). In this context, the technologies available to the imperial power can be construed as cultural forces expressing certain values that encapsulate what it means to be 'civil' (Said 1988; Neu and Heincke 2004). They are deployed with a view to subverting those traditional mechanisms by which native societies have understood themselves in their interaction with their environments (Fanon 1963; Said 1978, 1993; Tilly 1994; Kalpagam 1999; Ballantyne 2005). From this viewpoint technologies such as those supplied by accountants can be interpreted as instruments of cultural imperialism capable of both mediating and enabling the transformation in moral values that natives must undergo in order to render them amenable to the imperial power (Said 1978; Kalpagam 1999; Davie 2000; Bush and Maltby 2004; Neu and Heincke 2004).

This process is facilitated by discourses that construct a particular image of the 'native' (Said 1978, 1993; Fanon 1963; Neu 1999, 2000a; Ferguson 2003; Neu and Heincke 2004). Thus, verbal and pictorial images of indigenous peoples are employed in such a way as to 'oblige' the imperial power to intervene (Said 1978, 1993; Foster 1993). As a result, "one has the shadowy discourse of colonial capitalism [in which] the indolent native again figures as someone whose natural depravity and loose character necessitate a European overlord" (Said 1993, 167). "What are striking in these discourses," according to Said, "are the rhetorical figures one keeps encountering . . . as well as the stereotypes about "the African (or Indian or Irish or Jamaican or Chinese) mind, the notions about bringing civilisation to primitive or barbaric peoples" (ibid., xi; Morrison 1998).

The racial stereotyping that underlies the construction of the 'Other' is crucial in providing focus and comfort for those involved in imperial projects (Foster 1993; Said 1993; Ferguson 2003). In particular, it allows those undertaking colonial endeavours to impute to themselves altruistic motives for initiatives intended to civilize natives whose all-too-obvious moral inadequacies 'require' such interventions. This had particular resonance in Ireland where such formulations had characterized the relationship between imperial power and native for centuries. Racial attitudes to the Irish were mixed. On the one hand, some writers and politicians viewed them as racially inferior: "though impeccably fair-skinned, [they] were Catholics and, in the eyes of many Englishmen, as racially inferior as if they had been the colour of coal" (Ferguson 2003, 252–53; Foster 1993; Gibbons 2000). In similar vein, Victorian polymath Charles Kingsley could describe Irish natives as "human chimpanzees" (Kingsley, quoted in Curtis 1968, 84).

For most imperialists, especially those imbued with a moralistic perspective, Irish natives were inferior not because of their Gaelic or Celtic blood but because of their moral inadequacies. And, importantly, these could be 'remedied' (Trevelyan 1848, 6; Foster 1988, 1993). This appealed strongly to those who believed that the famine, however tragic, afforded a God-given opportunity to challenge the "miserable apathy, the unmanageable doggedness . . . [the] listlessness and torpid stupidity" of the Irish labourer (Robert Traile to Peel, 18 November 1845, quoted in Lengel 2002, 66). The ambition of those charged with devising official policy, therefore, was not merely to ensure greater discipline via various accounting systems. Rather, it was to employ such technologies as a means of reforming the moral values of the native; to assist in replacing indolence with industry, passivity with endeavour (Gray 1999, 240–43; Neu 1999).

This cultural hegemony, with its importation of alien economic and cultural values, has as one of its ambitions the expression of imperial policies in the form of practices and media that impact the lives of those over whom the imperial power claims authority (Said 1978, 1993; Neu 1999, 2000a). Accounting assists in this by making available to empire an enabling culture, providing techniques for measuring and monitoring behaviour (Miller and Rose 1990). It provides mechanisms by means of which the authorities seek "to shape, normalise and instrumentalise the conduct, thought, decisions and aspirations of others in order to achieve the objectives they consider desirable" (ibid., 8). In so doing, accounting not only creates a basis for reward and punishment; it also introduces a frame of reference reflecting underlying hegemonic ambitions that subvert the cultural and moral world of the native (Neu 1999, 2000a; Bush and Maltby 2004).

"THE HEART OF A COLOSSAL ORGANISATION": ACCOUNTING SYSTEMS AND TASK-WORK

In the autumn of 1845 farmers in the southeast of Ireland began to notice a curious blight appearing in the potato crop, the staple diet of the bulk of the population (Ó Gráda 1994, 177). Within months, as an acute shortage of potatoes developed, workhouses capable of accommodating one hundred thousand persons established under Ireland's first poor law (1838) had been filled to capacity (Kinealy 1994, 106–8; Walker 2003a, 2004a, 2008b; Gray 2009). In addition, a further one hundred thousand persons were receiving relief under schemes coordinated by the Relief Commission, the Board of Works and the Poor Law Commission at a cumulative cost to the government of almost £1million (Kinealy 1994). By the summer of 1846 Sir Robert Peel's Tory government had been replaced by a Whig administration headed by Lord John Russell, which promised to tackle the abuses and overgenerous relief they believed had characterized Peel's approach to Ireland (Griffiths 1970; Lyons 1973; Foster 1988; Funnell 2001).

Members of the new government were strengthened in their resolve by those such as the Secretary to the Treasury, Charles Trevelyan; the Colonial Secretary, Earl Grey; and the Chancellor of the Exchequer, Charles Wood, who insisted that the hand of God was clearly discernible in unfolding events: "God grant that we may rightly perform our part and not turn into a curse what was intended for a blessing" (Trevelyan to Monteagle, 9 October 1846, quoted in Haines 2004, 5). The blessings intended by God would become a curse, Trevelyan believed, if the government intervened in such a way as to mitigate the effects of market forces (Trevelyan 1848; Gray 1995, 1999). In his opinion, the "false principle" of "free relief" was at the root of the moral malaise that characterized the Irish labourer (Trevelyan 1848, 183). Something must be done immediately, he insisted, to break this reliance on the government, which "eats like a cancer into the moral health and physical prosperity of the people" (ibid., 183–84; Haines 2004). In this he was fully supported by Prime Minister Russell as well as newspapers such as the *Times*, which denigrated "the national character, the national thoughtlessness, the national indolence" of the Irish, reckoning that "the Irish peasant had tasted of famine and found that it was good" (*Times*, 22 September 1846).

The Labour Rate Act (1846) introduced by Russell's government provided that the cost of public works to employ those most affected would be borne by the local 'cess' (or rates): Irish property would pay for Irish relief (Kinealy 1994, 90–92; Donnelly Jr. 1996). It also provided for local presentment sessions under the aegis of Grand Juries to initially assess applications for public utility works, such as roads. However, all decisions had to be confirmed by the Treasury, which retained the right of veto. If approved, the Office of Public Works (or 'Board of Works') automatically assumed administrative responsibility for the project, with local relief committees supplying lists of those considered suitable for employment, as well as generating funds from local rates and voluntary contributions (Griffiths 1970; Kinealy 1994; Ó Gráda 1994). These lists were closely monitored and those deemed incapable of work were removed by local relief committees or government officials— only those viewed as 'deserving' were to be issued with tickets entitling them to employment (Commissioners of Public Works to the Treasury, 10 October 1846, British Parliamentary Papers [hereafter, BPP] 1970, 6, 139–41; Extract from Journal of Captain Kennedy, 9 January 1847, BPP 1970, 7:112; Ó Gráda 1994, 1999; Kinealy 1994). One immediate impact of this classificatory regime was that it facilitated an analysis of poverty based on notions of utility. This problematization of the poor in a manner that emphasized individual agency had the additional effect of disrupting the communal approach to its management that had typically characterized local responses (Foucault 1980b, 167–69, 172; Kinealy 1994; Rabinow and Rose 2003).

The mechanism seized upon to help address the twin challenges of controlling costs while simultaneously assisting the Irish labourer to develop healthier moral attitudes to work and time, was 'task' (or 'piece') work. This was a method of organizing labour that linked payment to work actually done. Its proper application would ensure that the Irish labourer came to understand that relief should be earned and that there existed a direct relationship between wages, personal application and efficiency (Trevelyan 1848; Treasury Minute, 31 August 1846, BPP 1970, 6:103–5). If the accountability, greater transparency and discipline inherent in such a scheme encouraged the landlord class to participate more fully then it would also ensure that Irish property undertook the burden of Irish relief. If not, then the influence of Anglo-Irish landlords would be diluted further as the British body politic appropriated a greater level of control over the Irish economy and polity (Trevelyan 1848; Donnelly 1996).

To control this outlay on workers receiving relief, the Treasury insisted that a regime of accounting and financial management which was as efficient as possible be implemented. To this end Trevelyan recruited an Englishman, Thomas Stickney, as chief accountant. Stickney quickly established a scheme based on a comprehensive system of ledgers and daybooks. The primary source of information was to be data contained in labour sheets sent to Dublin weekly from every relief work in the country. These provided detailed information on individual labourers on every relief work throughout the country, including name, nature of tasks done, quantity of work performed, rate of payment and any incidental observations. As part of this process, labourers were required to inscribe their signature or mark, a practice that made a communal, semi-feudal population "susceptible to evaluation, calculation and intervention" (Miller and Rose 1990, 7), which prioritized notions of individual accountability. From the outset, therefore, accounting systems would be closely associated with a time-based process that temporalized native society in a manner alien to traditional ways of interacting with their environments (Tilly 1994; Kalpagam 1999, 2000).

The details of the task-work scheme were circulated in a Treasury Minute of 31 August 1846. This stipulated that persons employed on relief works should, "to the utmost possible extent, be paid in proportion to the work actually done by them" (BPP 1970, 6:100). This Minute was supplemented some time later by another four-page document entitled *Instructions for Engineers and Assistant Engineers* (BPP 1970, 7:93–97). Based principally on feedback received from superintendents of existing relief schemes, this outlined a set of national norms for various tasks that would allow some form of consistent national application of the terms of the Treasury Minute. It also confirmed the government's determination to introduce a system that would require extensive accounting controls and supports.

"A DENSE MASS OF PETTY ACCOUNTABILITY": IMPLEMENTING ACCOUNTING CONTROLS

By October 1846 the widespread failure of the potato harvest had been confirmed and demand for employment had very quickly exceeded expectations.

The Board of Works Report to the Treasury for that month provided a graphic description of the challenges being encountered in arranging payment for almost 115,000 labourers on several thousand relief works spread throughout the island. It also gave an insight into the "apparently humble and mundane mechanisms" (Miller and Rose 1990, 8) being deployed by empire: "the money cannot be paid without an assurance that the men have been employed on the particular Work on the days charged," the commissioners explained:

> This is ensured (in addition to the care of the overseer or gangsmen) by the visits from Work to Work at uncertain times of a Check Clerk, by whom the pay lists are made out for the certificate of the Engineer in charge, who has apportioned generally the tasks and is responsible for their execution. The pay list of each party so prepared and checked, must be ready on the day arranged by the Engineer for the Pay Clerk to attend on each Work, however far asunder the works may be, and the money paid to each individual must be vouched for by his signature or mark, and witnessed; and these vouchers are sent up to Dublin for examination, preparatory to their final audit, and there is no link of this chain which can be safely omitted. We have, in a word, to ascertain the amount to be paid, to remit the money, prepare the Pay Lists, and make the payments in small sums to every individual on more than 5,000 separate Works, widely distributed in almost every County, *within one week*, and to accomplish this with a staff hastily brought together, in great part new to their work—unaccustomed to act together or in concert. (Commissioners of Public Works to the Lords of the Treasury, 12 November 1846, BPP 1970, 6:229; emphasis in original)

Difficulties faced by the board encouraged those who opposed any such relief to lobby the Treasury for changes in its management and control procedures (Gray 1999). Stickney responded with accounts of the range of accounting, book-keeping and internal control practices he had introduced—consistent, significantly, with the modified system of double-entry book-keeping that the Treasury had adopted over recent years (Edwards, Coombs and Greener 2002):

> It is really some consolation to me to find that you are aware of the extent of this *centralized* business. I believe that the system of book-keeping by double entry is carried out here *most perfectly* and satisfactorily. But the *rendering of vouchers*, with their schedules, abstracts, etc., will be a difficult task. I find that we have 6,000 and upwards open accounts dispersed in 21 *sets of ledgers*, which form an interesting library of 54 ledgers, 27 journals and 4 cash books, and all these of large size. Of these there are: 20 ledgers for loans, 5 for grants, 12 for drainage, the other services being of minor extent, but all increasing

daily (Stickney to the Treasury, 4 January 1847, BPP 1970, 6:508, emphasis in original)

Commissioner Jones, empathizing with Stickney's difficulties, explained to Trevelyan that such was the workload, the accounting department in Dublin was now better imagined as "a great baza[a]r" than "a well-regulated London office" (Jones to Trevelyan, 14 November 1846, BPP 1970, 6:295; Griffiths 1970).

Reassured by Stickney's diligence, the Treasury was eventually persuaded to allow a further 276 book-keepers and clerks to be recruited to deal with the huge task of collating and auditing the returned labour sheets. In addition, the number of those specifically identified as 'accountant' was increased to ninety-nine (Commissioners of Public Works to Lord Lieutenant, 17 January 1847, BPP 1970, 7:35–37; Commissioners of Public Works to the Treasury, 4 March 1847, BPP 1970, 7:212). Despite this increase in personnel, by December 1846 the strain on the board and its officials was beginning to tell. Its report for that month recorded that on one day alone five thousand letters containing labour sheets had been received (Commissioners of Public Works to the Treasury, January 1847, BPP 1970, 6:518–29). In a private communication to the Treasury, Stickney was explicit in detailing the challenges this brought:

> We have 460 and upwards pay clerks; each pays weekly upon *many* separate lists for labour. We have the *debits* punctually recorded against them, but cannot at present get at the *credits* due to them upon vouchers. It is a dense mass of petty accountability, amounting *in the aggregate* to an enormous sum. Nearly 300,000 labourers sprinkled over Ireland in small squads, each squad chargeable against a separate road or work for which there is a separate account. But the accountant's branch is almost entirely taken up with reading hundreds of letters daily. (Stickney to the Treasury, 19 December 1846, BPP 1970, 6:508; emphasis in original)

With such a comprehensive set of "techniques of notation, computation and calculation" in place (Miller and Rose 1990, 8) the government remained confident that time and determination would ensure the gradual acceptance of task-work by the general population. Indeed, while acknowledging that difficulties existed, some officials eagerly reported early successes: according to one surveyor, wherever the system was "fully understood, the people are contented, happy, and cheerful at their work" (Report of Mr. John Benson, County Surveyor, Cork, 9 November 1846, BPP 1970, 6:302). Others even claimed to discern the desired civilizing effect that task-work was expected to have on native attitudes to work. One reported that he was "glad to be able to state that the Relief Works in this district have not tended to demoralise the working population by encouraging habits of indolence, of which we hear so much in all quarters" (Report of R.H. Frith, County Surveyor for the County of Dublin, 28 February 1847, BPP 1970, 7:210). The same official enclosed a private communication from another eager supporter: "[task-work] has done more good in teaching the labourer the value of time . . . and drawn a line of demarcation between the indolent and industrious," the author reported. "I wish all Ireland could be dealt with on the piece-work system, and I think we would soon see a different race of people" (John Potterton to Frith, 24 February 1847, BPP 1970, 7:189).

Those more familiar with the realities of the situation in Ireland were not, however, so sanguine. One senior official observed that "[a] great stand is making [*sic*] by the labourers against task work" (Commissary-General Hewetson to Trevelyan, 23 October 1846, BPP 1970, 5:607; Haines 2004, 265). In North Kerry an inspecting officer was surprised to find that, although task-work had been "partially introduced", and "it might have been supposed that every man employed would have wished to enjoy the increased pay," the fact was that "owing to some deep-rooted prejudices" this was not the case "and the majority still prefer being paid according to the old system" (Report of H.N. Greenwell, 14 November 1846, BPP 1970, 6:291). In the opinion of one engineer, the problem was more intractable: the natives had been "so utterly neglected, that numbers of them are little removed from savages, and any attempt at a new system begets a suspicion amongst them of some deception being practised against them" (Extract from Captain Sterling's Journal, Castlebar, 8 November 1846, BPP 1970, 6:219).

Notwithstanding the quasi-racist nature of many observations, resistance to task-work was compounded by serious problems in the operation of the scheme. Some works were badly organized and "tasks were not in many cases clearly defined, and the exact price to be given not stated" (Journal of Captain Farren, Mayo, 21 November 1846, BPP 1970, 6:306; Kinealy 1994). In addition, supervisors were often inefficient, inept or corrupt. Commissioner Dobree despaired of the "present class of gangsmen, with 'long-tailed coat and knee breeches, hands in pockets, and pipe in mouth.'" Wondering why Irish labourers were "so torpid and listless on their own dunghill," he recommended that overseers be brought in from England (Dobree to Trevelyan, 29 September 1846, BPP 1970, 5:522). The fact that task-work had not been successfully and uniformly introduced everywhere also meant that labourers on adjacent works could often be operating under different systems. Gradually this led to comparisons and discontent (Captain Sterling's Journal, Castlebar, 8 November 1846, BPP 1970, 6:219; Mr. King to Walker, 17 January 1847, BPP 1970, 7:38).

By early 1847, therefore, it was becoming apparent that the existing relief programme was unsustainable. On the one hand, there were questions about the capacity of the accounting system to continue to function in the face of the huge growth in numbers seeking assistance (Commissioners of Public Works to Lords of the Treasury, 7 January 1847, BPP 1970, 6:527; 4 March 1847, BPP 1970, 7:216) while other considerations were also contributing to a sense that a change in strategy was required. One of the most compelling was the dramatic escalation in cost (Commissioners of Public Works to Lords of the Treasury, 4 March 1847, BPP 1970, 7:211; Kinealy 1994). Of equal concern to the government was an expected shortage of labourers for spring farmwork. This would have disastrous consequences for the planting season that was about to commence. If this happened, Treasury officials noted, then "evils must ensue which . . . would produce calamities" (Treasury Minute, 10 March 1847, quoted in Kinealy 1994, 144). By early spring even Trevelyan had been persuaded that this was a critical consideration (Trevelyan 1848; Kinealy 1994, 100). The board's report for February, at which point over seven hundred thousand labourers were employed on the various works, argued strongly in favour of winding down the public relief schemes so that labourers could return to farmwork (Commissioners of Public Works to Lords of the Treasury, 4 March 1847, BPP 1970, 7:211–18; Haines 2004). By mid-March mass dismissals from the public works had begun (Kinealy 1994).

While seeking, on the one hand, to manage the relief schemes, government ministers and Treasury officials were also attempting to ensure that landlords shouldered the financial burden of relief (Donnelly 1996; Haines 2004). Like the attempt to introduce task-work, this was informed by an imperial economic philosophy that prioritized the needs of empire over those of land or labour. Landowners were reminded that, while some supports would be available, for example, in funding the clearance of over-populated estates, Irish property must bear the cost of relief (Kinealy 1994; Donnelly 1996; Gray 1999). Much of the financial management architecture put in place by the government in 1846 was specifically designed to achieve this. Thus, local rates were expected to bear the ultimate cost of relief, even if government grants and loans financed the initial outlay (Kinealy 1994; Gray 1999). Local Relief Committees were required to send detailed accounts of those who contributed to local relief funds, while the names of landowners who had not made charitable contributions or had failed to pay their rates were also forwarded to Dublin (O'Neill 1956, 217). Drainage schemes, which were intended to render previously unusable land productive, were particularly closely monitored since landlords stood to benefit directly from such improvements (Kinealy 1994; Donnelly 1996). Still, most commentators held out little hope that landlords would contribute appropriately: "The salvation of Ireland seems, under Providence, to rest in the hands of the proprietors and holders of land," Commissioner Dobree observed, before concluding that they could never be depended upon to be sufficiently "public-spirited" (Dobree to Trevelyan, 14 September 1846, BPP 1970, 5:495).

DISCUSSION

In the case of both landlords and labourers, a necessary prerequisite of the imperial power's attempt to exploit the potato crisis was a discourse that constructed a morally and culturally impoverished population in urgent need of intervention (Said 1978, 1993; Miller and Rose 1990; Ferguson 2003). Indeed, the assumptions of moral superiority implicit in the language with which this intervention was imagined and implemented were redolent of the cultural and racial tensions that had characterized the relationship between the English and native Irish for centuries (Foster 1993; Gibbons 2000; Canny 2001). Representations of illiterate, indolent and ungrateful Irish labourers barely capable of self-management, and of dissolute, irresponsible Anglo-Irish landlords unwilling to invest their rents in economic improvement of their estates, played an important role in informing the imperial power's understanding of the challenges it faced (Said 1993; Foster 1993; Gray 1995). They contributed to a situation in which the government felt "impelled by impressive ideological formations" (Said 1993, 9) to intervene in and dominate the Irish landscape and people by establishing systems of administration and instruction that placed accounting at the centre of imperial policy. By implementing a range of intrusive controls and reducing a human catastrophe to a series of numbers and reports, accountants actively assisted in this endeavour; they dehumanized a crisis, while simultaneously disseminating the disciplinary and calculative order of empire. At a time of compelling social and human tragedy, they made it possible for the imperial government to argue in favour of implementing policies dictated largely by considerations of cost (Miller and Rose 1990; Neu and Heincke 2004).

For a native population that had previously understood its relationship to both land and landlords in almost feudal terms, accounting information had become one critical means by which their lives were to be reconstituted in a manner that now included imported notions of morality and order. An environment that was previously less objectified was now subject to quantification and analysis; a cyclical, religious worldview was being supplanted (Tilly 1994; Thompson 1967; Kalpagam 2000). Significantly, reflecting the reduced military threat from Ireland, this intervention was being attempted at a time when "the "backward" structure of Irish society was becoming a primary concern of government (Gray 1999, 2; Ferguson 2003). Accounting was instrumental in this change of focus, enabling classifications and categorizations that accommodated these colonial goals and allowing the government to prioritize the gathering of information about the targeted population. This accounting intervention both reflected and facilitated the fundamental change in focus from territoriality to governmentality (Miller and Rose 1990; Tilly 1994; Ballantyne 2005).

Accounting information and its various classifications also made it possible for the colonial power to frame the discourse of poverty in terms of costs and efficiencies. This had the effect of privileging a conceptualization of poverty that problematized it in a manner intended to allow government "to lighten as much as possible the burden it imposes on the rest of society" (Foucault 1980b, 167). Supplemented by labour sheets and returns from local presentment sessions that were designed to distinguish the 'deserving' poor from others, this had the further effect of individualizing poverty. In a society in which poverty was typically perceived as a communal concern, accounting information and systems enabled the disruption of the natives' own conceptions of poverty and of 'being poor' (ibid., 169; Kinealy 1994; Gray 1995; Kalpagam 1999).

Accounting not only enabled representation and intervention, but by virtue of its accountability relationships, also allowed the transportation of alien imperial concepts, paradigms and measurement forms into the native universe. In the process it created new and intrusive accountability relations that undermined traditional familial and communal forms (Tilly 1994; Kalpagam 1999, 2000; Bush and Maltby 2004). It also disrupted traditional views of the world. Native Irish society attributed only a minimal role to measurable time in everyday life, drawing instead on internalized, circular ideas of time based on familiar patterns, "natural rhythms" as well as the "the logic of need" (Thompson 1967, 59). However, intervention prompted by the potato crisis was predicated on conceptions of time that were more characteristic of industrial capitalism and factories and which, in Ireland, had heretofore only—if ever—been associated with military campaigns (Thompson 1967; Ballantyne 2005). By allying itself closely in this manner to a time-based process of work measurement and discipline, accounting played a key role in the insinuation of particular and linear notions of time into a semi-feudal society.

This case suggests, therefore, that in a colonial context, where natives have no meaningful stake in government and where agents are increasingly marginalized by the centralizing tendencies of the imperial power, there may be little incentive for those targeted to adopt internalized knowledge discourses based on notions of 'efficiency'. This may point to a key feature of accounting when deployed in such suppressive contexts: its inability to translate efficiency-based discourse and techniques into meaningful expressions that connect with the needs or aspirations of the excluded. Furthermore, from the perspective of the native, accounting technologies employed in this manner constituted a particularly insidious and subtle form of aggression. Although ostensibly used as part of public relief schemes, accounting was essentially being deployed as a tool of empire. While new accounting systems, replete with notions of moral improvement, were capable of being presented as intended to assist relief, they had, in fact, the very profound consequence of partially obscuring the essentially imperial nature of these interventions. A native population that was proficient at identifying and combating more established forms of armed aggression now found itself confronting a more insidious, essentially power-backed, technology of colonial activity (Fanon 1963; Said 1993). On the one hand, therefore, accounting information imposed upon those targeted new means by which they were to understand themselves and their environment; on the other, its use in a colonial context required the development of innovative defensive strategies involving expressions of passive resistance and subversion.

CONCLUSION

The extent to which the imperial government's introduction of an extensive accounting infrastructure facilitated the embedding of accounting technologies and processes was confirmed by the operational provisions of the Temporary Relief Act (1847), which replaced the Labour Rate Act. This provided for the perpetuation of much of the accounting infrastructure that had already been put in place. This, officials believed, had already demonstrated "the value of the forms, rules and regulations . . . for the charge and accountability of money" and had "formed the groundwork for much future good" (Report of Relief Commissioners, Supplementary Appendix, 31 December 1847, BPP 1970, 8:10). Henceforth, it was to be a specific requirement of those appointed to coordinate relief that they "be able to keep accounts" (Poor Law Commission Circular, 1 July 1847, BPP 1970, 2:6). In this context, Relief Commissioners were instructed to circulate over ten thousand account books, eighty thousand work sheets and three million card tickets throughout the Irish countryside to ensure effective control and accountability during the next phase of imperial intervention. Testifying to the extent to which accounting information and new accountability relations had become now central to managing the crisis, the paperwork delivered to the Custom House in Dublin for distribution to officials in the late spring of 1847 weighed in excess of fourteen tonnes. The effect is to confirm how accounting had been recruited to assist in the cultural subordination of both agents and natives; how its coercive and disciplinary potential was now being deployed by an imperial power determined to exploit a socio-economic crisis for its own purposes.

Part III
Exploitation

7 Cost Accounting, Control and Capitalism

Trevor Hopper

MOTIVATION AND CONTEXT

This chapter relates the labour process theory history of management accounting articulated by Hopper and Armstrong (1991) and extends the analysis to more recent times. Its antecedents lay in a reaction to the triumphalist history of management accounting portrayed in Johnson and Kaplan's 1987 book, *Relevance Lost*. This castigated prevailing cost accounting practice and paved the way for Kaplan and associated consultants to propagate allegedly new cost accounting techniques such as activity-based costing (ABC). Cost accounting and financial accountants were cast as the villains and cause of US manufacturing woes in the face of Asian, especially Japanese, competition. However, despite widespread practitioner interest, *Relevance Lost* was essentially an historical account, based loosely on market and transaction cost theorizations, of how cost accounting developed (and allegedly stagnated) during the previous hundred years.

Like others, Hopper and Armstrong (1991) were critical of Johnson and Kaplan's theoretical and empirical claims. A book review of *Relevance Lost* intending, *inter alia*, to outline an alternative account of accounting transformation based on labour history grew into a book chapter (Hopper 1990), which Peter Armstrong reworked and extended, culminating in the Hopper and Armstrong (1991) article. From inception it was 'political'—being motivated by the authors' concerns about accounting's role within the ideologies of Thatcherism and Reaganism. Its deliberately critical edge was seen as unproblematic. All academic work is politically tinged—denials to the contrary are humbug: to occlude politics merely masks ideological reinforcement of the status quo. Nevertheless, political commitment does not override scholarship and reflection.

This chapter is based on the paper "Cost Accounting, Controlling Labour, and the Rise of Conglomerates", by T. Hopper and P. Armstrong, which originally appeared in *Accounting, Organizations and Society* 16, no. 5/6 (1991): 405–38. The author would like to thank the publisher, Elsevier, for permission to use this material.

The authors sought to encourage more accounting history research from the perspective of labour within the spirit of the then so-called 'New Accounting History' (Miller, Hopper and Laughlin 1991), which incorporated political economy and also Foucauldian approaches. The argument was that Johnson and Kaplan's theory was:

> Flawed, their history partial and some of their prescriptions neglectful of . . . socio-economic conditions . . . In contrast to the social harmony and self-equilibrating framework employed by Johnson and Kaplan, many of the historical events . . . are better understood through a 'labour process' approach to economic and industrial history . . . Recognising the need for a more critical, institutional analysis of capitalist development, the core presupposition . . . is that social and economic conflicts arising from the modes of control which characterise particular phases of capitalist development stimulate the creation of new forms of control intended to eliminate or accommodate resistance and to solve the associated problems of profitability. These new forms of control, in turn, decay, partly because their competitive advantage disappears as a consequence of their generalisation and partly because they give rise to new contradictions and forms of resistance. Thus a labour process approach, in contrast . . . stresses crisis rather than continuity; contradiction rather than internal consistency; social and political conflict rather than harmony; the monopoly power of corporations rather than self-equilibrating competitive markets; patterns of class formation in specific economies rather than an atomised view of the individual; and human agency in its cultural and institutional setting rather than economistic reductionism. (Hopper and Armstrong 1991, 406)

The desire was to link accounting's association with micro-processes of control at the point of production to macro socio-economic changes in capitalism, and to retheorize management accounting from a radical perspective. The authors endeavoured to be holistic and to establish historical patterns without denying local contingencies and agency. Labour process theory (then a major focal point for much European management research) was influential, especially the work of Braverman (1974) and labour historians such as Clawson (1980); Gordon, Edwards and Reich (1982); Littler (1982); Montgomery (1987); and Nelson (1959). The paper was rooted in conflicts over material interests, control, and resistance to the manufacture of consent. The empirical setting lay in the US—the focus of *Relevance Lost*. The findings may be pertinent elsewhere but they would require modification to accommodate local events and circumstances. The paper identified three major epochs of cost accounting development: circa 1820 to 1870, 1870 to 1920 and 1920 to 1970. It closed by cogitating whether a new epoch of controls was prescient.

INITIAL PROLETARIANIZATION OF LABOUR, 1820–1870

During early industrialization (pre-1820) owners were often relatively ignorant of manufacture and operational controls, including costs (though undoubtedly examples of experimentation and innovation occurred). This and the shortage of honest and sober managers meant owners had difficulties in directly controlling and expanding their firms. Consequently, much production relied on putting out and subcontracting within single product firms. However, circa post-1820 owners' increasingly sought to redress their difficulties in directly controlling labour and production and extracting a surplus from it. An *initial proletarianization* of the labour force occurred, *formally* subordinating labour to capital. Workers became employees reliant on employers and subject to the discipline of factory time and space. However, there was little *real* subordination whereby employers designed and controlled production processes.

Much knowledge of production lay with craftsmen rather than factory owners. Hence owners often relied on skilled artisans, who passed on their knowledge through apprenticeships, and/or heads of households to deliver production under various forms of internal subcontracting. This had the advantage of transferring the need to extract the most out of labour to others, and it mitigated problems arising from the owners' lack of knowledge of production, spread risk, tied costs to output and avoided large overheads associated with complex management controls. In short, craft knowledge acted "as a substitute for accounting" (Littler 1982, p. 67). However, given their lack of knowledge of production and detailed records of costs, owners found it difficult to ascertain prices and to control craftsmen and/or subcontractors, especially in times of labour shortage. Owners believed that undue profits were flowing to subcontractors (reinforced by the latter's ostentatious displays of wealth during periods of prosperity) and regretted that subcontractors, who often instigated innovations, reaped their benefits. Consequently firms increasingly turned to directly employing contractors. This necessitated detailed records of wages, which provided vital information for owners to renegotiate contracts, made subcontractors more reluctant to bid and induced them, albeit reluctantly and spasmodically, to enter direct employment.

Faced by increased competition, firms such as Lyman Mills, a textile factory in New England (a focal case in Johnson and Kaplan's study), sought to increase profitability by improving the efficiency of the conversion process and improving labour productivity. New systems for ascertaining prime cost enabled owners to monitor and compare the performance of workers and supervisors and induce them to pursue 'company goals' of reducing direct costs. Given single product factories, measures of return on capital or efficiency measures were of less concern (this is contentious, see Toms 2010a). However, this is not a story of socio-economic progress and enlightenment; owners colluded over wage rates and conditions of work, scrutinized costs to squeeze out efficiency gains and intensified labour by increasing quotas and/or lengthening the working day and/or cutting wages. Discipline was maintained by recruiting rural (often female) and immigrant labour dependent on employers for sustenance. The factory and associated institutions such as workers' dormitories bore the hallmark of 'total institutions'.

Rather than attributing productivity gains to mechanization and integration, and the growth of accounting to a costless reduction of 'slack', as in *Relevance Lost*, a labour process analysis draws attention to the need to contextualize the intensification of labour and distribution of rewards in terms of struggles to control labour. The suggestion is that the creation of internal cost records marks the beginning of a transfer of financial knowledge from the worker to the factory owner, which permitted rewards from innovation to flow in the same direction and helped make visible where returns might best be creamed off and labour be intensified and disciplined.

SCIENTIFIC MANAGEMENT AND THE HOMOGENIZATION OF LABOUR, 1870–1920

The period after 1870 was marked by heightened competition, and geographical expansion of markets due partly to railway developments and economic recessions. Firms responded in two ways: further assaults on internal subcontracting and craft labour controls and mergers to create more monopolistic conglomerates and/or achieve vertical integration. Whether this increased efficiency and drove accounting innovation is disputed. Historians such as Wells (1978) argue that the increased size, concentration and complexity of firms required more systematic means of labour control. This precipitated complex managerial hierarchies to administer the resultant paper bureaucracy, which increasingly replicated and controlled productive processes.

The destruction of internal contracting left "the employer facing the solidity of his own ignorance about shop-floor performance" (Littler 1982, 84). Initially employers sought to manage the labour process through cheaper, more dependent, salaried foremen who had replaced subcontractors. This solved the problem of relying on subcontractors but precipitated other problems, namely, how to control skilled craftsmen and their foremen. The latter's arbitrary and widespread powers were either a source of worker disputes or employers fretting that foremen's allegiance remained with the craftsmen under their jurisdiction. Whatever, their efforts at intensification were relatively unsystematic. Consequently, many functions of foremen were transferred to centralized staff departments. Rate-fixers and quality control inspectors appeared on the shop floor and personnel officers took over wage payment systems and hiring and firing. Accounting became integral to aligning foremen's behaviour with the goals of employers: cost

records revealed foremen's ability to cut costs and bonuses. Competition to minimize costs reinforced such behaviour.

The challenge of intensifying craft labour was of a different order. Experiments with piece-rates and time allowances from the 1880s failed to combat output restriction, partly through its association with rate cutting but especially because rates and allowances relied on observation, judgment or past experience and were prone to manipulation and conflict. Employers increasingly sought resolution by adopting 'scientific management' in factories. This had profound effects on the control of labour processes and beyond. Scientific management redesigned, fragmented and simplified production jobs so that semi-skilled labour rather than craftsmen could perform them in mass-production factories, often incorporating moving assembly lines. Planning and execution were separated—"All possible brain work [was] removed from the shop and centred in the planning or laying-out department" (Taylor 1903, pp. 98–99).

Taylor maintained that business could be controlled according to objective, repeatable and formally expressed management principles, and that people were self-interested rational economic agents motivated by individual financial rewards but reluctant to expend effort at work. He claimed that a clear, scientific and formal relation could be established between units of effort and financial rewards, reflected in bonuses and piece-rates. Workers would see that working harder would increase the size of the available pie, and through his payment system their earnings would grow (even if their proportion of the pie fell). Piece-rates based on allegedly scientific time and motion studies claimed to remove rate fixing from labour–capital conflicts and arbitrary judgments. Furthermore, those few who did not respond 'rationally' would be scientifically weeded out because their effort levels would be made visible through the supervisory element of scientific management. The result was a homogenized, deskilled and fragmented labour force concentrated in large factories controlled by production and planning control departments marking the growth of management in staff departments. This *real* subordination of labour to capital is a defining feature of a fully developed capitalist mode of production.

Taylor, consistent with his views on specializing labour, advocated allocating planning and control activities, including cost control, to various 'functional foremen'. There is little evidence that this was adopted in practice. Rather the tasks became the province of specialist staff departments, including cost offices, which monitored 'line' performance. This gave birth to the occupation of cost accountant. Scientific management pioneers like Emerson, Church and Harrison promulgated and helped develop standard costing (though its scale, timing of adoption and direct link to controlling labour remains disputed). Nevertheless, as Fleischman and Tyson (1998) note, "at the start of the industrial revolution, standard costing, in the form of past actual costs, aided managers in make-or-buy, pricing, outsourcing and other routine and special decisions. In the late nineteenth century, as the mass production of homogeneous products became more common, predetermined, norm-based standard costs were promoted as the means to control operations and reduce waste" (ibid, p. 92). However, their allegation that a labour process analysis fails because standard costing was not transmitted directly to operatives and foremen misses the point. The onus on cost control now shifted to line managers aided by labour and materials usage variances provided by staff cost departments. At the point of production it was sufficient to act on costs through physical rather than financial rates. Standard costing reflected Taylorism as it reinforced a separation of execution and control: standards derived from engineering redesign and analysis of the labour process were immune to influence by the workforce, which rendered them potent instruments of management control and work intensification.

FORDISM: COST ACCOUNTING WITHIN A
LABOUR–CAPITAL ACCORD, 1920–1970

The 'drive' system mechanized and deskilled production work, increased the power of foremen, made work more impersonal and alienating and created a mass labour market where individual workers became easily substitutable, especially by the 'reserve army of labour'. Up to the mid-1920s employers vigorously campaigned to extirpate unionism root and branch in the United States (Gordon, Edwards and Reich 1982). Trade union resistance reached a low ebb as trade union strength, indexed by membership and strikes, declined. There was widespread worker resentment of budgeting in the 1920s and 1930s due to its association with casualization. Labour bore the brunt of economic fluctuations through layoffs, shortened working weeks and/or the speed up of production lines. Practitioner reports of budgeting during this period reveal a preoccupation with smoothing production to counter seasonal and other cyclical fluctuations. Early flexible budgeting distinguished cost variations attributable to short-term output fluctuations from 'genuine' operating causes. Only by neutralizing union demands for employment security and their influence upon workloads could senior management in companies like General Motors secure the freedom to act on information from their accounting system.

Mergers that increased firm concentration and vertical integration helped stabilize mass production and the exploitation of economies of scale. Paradoxically, homogenization of labour in factories like Ford created common conditions of work amongst massive workforces and sowed the seeds of the 1930s upsurge of industrial unionism. More fundamentally, growing disparity between wages and labour productivity resulted in depression and mass unemployment, labour unrest and the questioning of capitalism. Despite the opposition of many leading firms, several mutually reinforcing developments laid the basis for 'Fordism' that changed the socio-political environment of cost accounting until the early 1970s.

National unionization of semi-skilled labour in large plants had important consequences. In the 1930s aggressive anti-trade unionism declined following firms and the state hammering out a labour–capital accord that recognized trades unions, addressed their demands and provided a modicum of secure employment. The government, believing that strong trade unionism would help revive the economy, passed the 1933 National Recovery Act with provisions for collective bargaining rights adjudicated by a National Labor Board (which imposed seniority conditions in layoffs and could hear claims of anti-unionism), and placed an upper limit on hours of work. The 1935 Wagner Act granted employer recognition of trade unions on a majority vote. Wage bargaining moved towards an industry and national level, with wages protected against inflation and tied to productivity gains. Complex seniority and local patronage based on internal labour markets (a shift from scientific control) began to motivate workers rather than the discipline of external labour markets. Rules for promotion, payment of bonuses and overtime and establishing standard units of work effort proliferated. In return for this labour–capital accord the new American Federation of Labor and Congress of Industrial Organizations (AFL-CIO) left unchallenged managerial prerogatives to plan and control work and introduce new machinery (Gordon, Edwards and Reich 1982). Apart from periodic renegotiations of labour contracts, trade union militancy was diverted from the firm to the state and social wages. This did not prevent the occasional well-anticipated contract strike, but it effectively ended violent conflict with official trade unions. Control was achieved on a political, rather than a scientific, basis.

However, these conditions only applied fully to oligopolistic sectors of the economy. Some industries (such as construction and retail services) remained highly competitive throughout the Fordist epoch. The rise in major bargaining centres, coupled on occasion to minimum wage legislation, tended to ripple out to non-Fordist sectors, thereby maintaining relativities and overall demand. But industries with an oligopolistic core always had a periphery of smaller-scale suppliers, distributors and niche market competitors that faced unstable market conditions. Large firms often placed the onus of adjustment to fluctuations upon subcontractors and small firms unable to afford the security of employment and high wages in dominant firms. Rather than merely representing impure variants of the dominant Fordism's reproduction process (that is, how activities within the production process are regulated to cope with differing interests—such as those of customers, suppliers, employees, trades unions and trade associations), this served to discipline workers in Fordist firms.

Ideologically, the working class was incorporated into a state, advancing the interests of industrial capital through an offer of modernization, social reform, equal opportunities and steady economic advance through methods justified as applied science. The labour–capital accord relied upon an interventionist, centralized, Keynesian, welfare-oriented nation-state, with a large bureaucracy to administer public provision of standardized welfare benefits such as national insurance and state pensions. Nuclear families living in conurbations, characterized by suburbs of mass housing, and universal education provision and welfare schemes experienced the growing private consumption of standardized mass-produced commodities. The state applied Keynesian demand management through bank credit controlled by a central bank to mitigate trade cycles that might threaten stabilized, high-capacity production runs and the attendant labour-capital accord within large firms. Thus Fordism created a virtuous circle of growth—mass production created mass consumption, which fed rising productivity from economies of scale anticipated in Fordist mass production. Rising incomes from these gains increased demand, increased firms' profitability and released funds to invest further in mass production devoted primarily, but not exclusively, to domestic markets.

The period 1900–1925 had been a 'golden age' of costing innovation. Many of its ideas were associated with Taylorism and the efficiency movements—but associated accounting innovations did not significantly ripple out to large firms until the 1930s. These included: centralized long-run strategy determined at headquarters; decentralized management based on divisionalization, especially return on investment (ROI) performance measures and market-based transfer pricing; functional management structures controlled through static negotiated budgets; operations controlled through flexible budgets and standard costing; and target ROI pricing based on standard volumes. These accounting innovations were crucial to the emergence of giant and otherwise unwieldy conglomerates of monopoly capitalism (Chandler 1966, 1977).

Divisionalization monitored the performance of managers and investments through delegated budgets. ROI and stock turnover ratios aligned managerial goals with capital accumulation. These and associated management accounting techniques created a vast shadow paper organization of periodic financial reports that mirrored the productive process, made it visible to managers, helped senior managers assess and compare the productivity of capital invested and reduced their need to continuously survey and intervene into operations, thereby leaving them free to concentrate on strategic issues. Separating planning from execution increased the number of managers devoted to planning and control within the elaborate functional bureaucracies that coordinated operations. As oligopolistic markets deepened in the 1950s, Fordist reproduction was increasingly pushed downward, into games and accommodations at lower levels. Paradoxically Tayloristic work measurement, standard costs and flexible budgets were not applied to specialist management functions like personnel, finance and marketing. Instead they were controlled by negotiated budgets, not linked directly to volumes. For such managers Fordist reproduction was based on professionalism and internal bureaucracy, legitimated by claims of expertise based on managerial science credentialed by the proliferation of formal qualifications from universities, colleges and various professional bodies.

Given the inflexible technology, the grudging acceptance of a large managerial bureaucracy for planning and control and the relatively fixed costs of supplies, financial gains through capacity utilization became the major variable affecting profits. Firms became preoccupied with sustaining a growing but predictable mass demand and smoothing production to maintain capacity utilization and reap economies of scale. Forward planning through flexible budgeting, coupled to advertising campaigns and special credit arrangements to regulate demand and inventory buffers to smooth production, helped counteract trade cycles. Given monopolistic markets, large firms could control accumulation at all stages, control barriers to entry and recover investments in products and processes free of fears of price competition from new producers. Competition increasingly relied on product differentiation and marketing—pricing was price-making rather than price-taking. Full cost plus pricing based on direct labour hours may have been adequate for this, especially if competitors set prices similarly. Moreover, recovering fixed costs through volume measures reinforced the economic benefits of scale: adverse volume variances identified failures of planned capacity utilization, material price variances encouraged bulk buying but de-emphasized inventory costs necessary for buffering and smoothing production, homogenous mass production simplified product costing by lessening problems of common costs and labour efficiency variances translated performance against time and motion standards into financial terms. Such systems were relatively neglectful of overhead cost control, possibly because they were a small proportion of total costs. The keys to unit cost reduction lay elsewhere in planning production and mass marketing to secure volume.

AFTER FORDISM: COSTING IN DEREGULATED GLOBAL CAPITALISM, POST-1970

Economic crises, peaking in the 1970s, heralded a new epoch marked by the Reagan regime that restricted trade union powers and cut back social programmes. Piore and Sabel (1984) attribute Fordisms decline to crises in final product markets. Mass markets became saturated and consumers demanded specialized and differentiated goods which mass-production systems were too inflexible to supply. Rates of exploitation and productivity growth declined and capital to output ratios increased due partly to Fordist production incurring high downtime costs when programmes changed. Neo-Schumpeterians like Freeman and Perez (1988) claimed that new computer technologies encouraged shifts to information-intensive products and processes utilizing flexible production systems. Related industries such as electronics, computers, telecommunications and the service sector experienced productivity growth, but elsewhere productivity gains slowed. Regulation theorists claim that Fordism hit technical and social limits as workers struggled to cope with the growing pace of semiautomatic equipment (Aglietta 1979).

Global demand and competition, accelerated by free trade agreements such as the North American Free Trade Agreement, increased, and a more consumerist society emerged. This derived its identity from products associated with a particular image or lifestyle, often espoused through the popular media. It meant that producers had to further differentiate products to meet more diverse and changing customer requirements—particularly nonmaterial factors like quality, brand, service, design and fashion. Product life cycles shortened, and manufacturing became more segmented nationally and internationally. Some fast-growing flexible production districts, such as North Carolina, grew whereas Fordist manufacturing areas like Detroit declined. Similarly, some increasingly demanded 'high-tech' services such as finance, design and consulting, often but not invariably supplied by small firms, developed as new growth areas. Some firms, however, maintained and extended Fordist production and marketing, often by subcontracting low-value-added activities (such as call centres) to poor countries (such as Mexico), where tax breaks, lower wages and lighter regulation prevailed, or to peripheral small firms unable to afford labour benefits offered by core firms. This deleteriously impacted upon the full employment policies central to Fordist regulation.

A more pronounced structure of 'core' and 'periphery' firms emerged. Some smaller firms survived by exploiting transnational market niches and joining networks around core firms, whereas others and certain industries (e.g., much of the retail and construction sectors) formed a growing periphery. Large core firms became increasingly 'hollowed out'—they developed reduced, less bureaucratic, flatter and less functional management hierarchies which concentrated on high-value-added activities such as design, network coordination and finance. Access and relationships to networks often rely on core firms' policies for grading suppliers and distributors. Favoured suppliers have long-term contracts and collaborate over matters like design and specifications, whereas those outside networks, unless they hold a scarce market niche, increasingly compete over low-value-added activities, which further polarized workers in core firms from the growing numbers employed in subcontracting and other peripheral activities.

Automation changed production, its planning and control, and reduced the numbers of production workers. Robotics (computer-controlled machines) has replaced direct production workers. Now 'factories of the future' working in the dark are envisaged; computer-aided design drastically reduces the need for draughting labour, shortens design periods and facilitates standardized parts; computer-aided manufacturing facilitates rapid machine changeovers for small batches and automatic control of machines and material flows; numerically controlled machines use computers to execute various metal-cutting jobs; computer-integrated manufacturing and flexible manufacturing systems link such machines and control movement of parts; material requirement planning systems ensure materials and products are available for production and customers by due dates, minimize inventory levels and determine manufacturing, purchasing and delivery schedules. Later versions linked to enterprise resource planning systems integrate and automate the provision of internal and external management information, including finance/accounting, manufacturing, sales and service dates, across the organization. In essence these changes extended Fordist principles of central planning and technological design to enhance control, not least of labour.

In contrast, just-in-time (JIT) systems were a major disjuncture to Fordism. JIT accommodates small batch sizes, short lead times and flexibility to quickly meet customer requirements. This has increased inter- and intra-organizational dependencies. For example, purchasing must not merely shop for better prices, but should also monitor delivery times and the quality of goods from suppliers. JIT is preoccupied with eliminating waste through continuous improvement and product simplification; eliminating material handling costs by redesigning shop-floor layouts and standardizing containers; eliminating scrap and rework by emphasizing zero defects in design, operations and materials; and seeking near zero inventories of work-in-progress (by reduced batch sizes, short set-up times, greater flexibility and improved workflows), raw materials (by suppliers delivering directly to the shop floor immediately to use) and finished goods (by producing to order). In contrast to Fordist assembly lines manned by specialized semi-skilled workers, JIT lines are U-shaped or parallel; have balanced capacity; have stable rates; and employ more flexible and multiskilled workers responsible for aspects of maintenance, short-run planning, quality, continuous improvement and costs.

The effects of all this on labour have been marked. Trade union membership, militancy and concentration, especially in mass industrial unions, have declined as corporations shifted to plant-based bargaining and more individualized rewards. Trade unions, under the threat of globalization and fears of impending employee bankruptcy or relocation of jobs to low-cost regions, often abroad, have increasingly become 'partners' of employers. The 'foot-loose' location of activities, employer anti-union campaigns and legislation unfavourable to trade unions reflecting ideologies of individualism, free markets and deregulation, such as right to work statutes, have mitigated worker resistance to management changes. Indeed, as unemployment and welfare expenditure increased, the state has cut the social wage. Manufacturing jobs have declined and service jobs have grown, not least in financial services, which developed increasingly esoteric and ultimately toxic financial products. The rise of skilled 'knowledge' workers has been accompanied by an increase in low-wage workers—often employed part-time and reflecting gender and racial divides. The intensity and insecurity of work has risen, especially amongst workers in the growing periphery. The decline of mass labour unions in urban areas and a rise in individualism, consumerism and self-identity, often stemming from popular culture propagated or reinforced by the media and cultural industries, have brought a declining identification with class, especially the working class. Consequently, politics have de-emphasized class issues despite declining social mobility, more pronounced wealth differentials and the few productivity gains which filter down to the lower and middle classes.

If there was a crisis in Fordism then one would expect a similar crisis and experimentation in cost accounting. Since the 1980s there has been a plethora of accounting innovations, including strategic management accounting, quality costing, balanced scorecards, target costing, throughput accounting and economic value added (see Bromwich and Bhimani 1989, 1994). Their uptake, persistence, practice and effectiveness are contentious, but, *prima facie*, they represent attempts to create forms of costing and cost management apposite to the epoch. This is apparent in accounting innovations relating to demand. These include costing product characteristics perceived by customers; customer-based performance measures covering quality, delivery and a product's lifetime costs to consumers (product life cycle costing); competitive position, cumulative production and learning; competitor and customer cost analysis; accounting control policies related to generic strategies; and value-added accounting and benchmarking against competitors' costs. These resonate with product market changes within post-Fordist accumulation regimes such as greater awareness of shorter product life cycles; the importance of innovation for increasing high-value-added activities; increased international competition and market volatility; and rising consumerism and more differentiated and changing patterns of demand bringing non-price issues like services, quality and design to the fore.

Automation has provoked increased concerns with conventional cost accounting. For example, investment evaluation procedures, especially discounted cash flow, may neglect less tangible benefits such as quality and improved customer satisfaction. Given the increased scale of capital investment and the importance of pre-production activities like product design upon operational costs, automation has become a strategic issue. Similar problems occur with short-run cost controls. Overhead recovery rates based on direct labour hours can produce arbitrary, distorted and volatile product costs in automated settings incurring large depreciation charges, especially if direct labour forms a small proportion of manufacturing cost. Automation of information processing has also had consequences. Reduced inventories render departments more interdependent and supplier relations more important, thus variance reports premised on independent departments responsible for local cost control can give misleading signals on the causes of failure and priorities such as due dates over budgets. Considerably more physical data associated with production such as waste, flexibility, inventory, maintenance, machine utilization, delivery/throughput times, quality and human resources can now be generated, leading to some non-financial statistics becoming more important for operational control than financial ones. Like production automation, automation of planning and control, alongside communication innovations like video-conferencing and email, represent neo-Fordism extending centralized staff planning and control, reshaping technology to control, intensify and reduce labour.

On the other hand, traditional production cost controls have diminished in significance. Now controlling the costs of indirect labour and activities and product and service attributes are the main concerns. The nomenclature of managerial overheads as 'burden' succinctly expresses their position in Fordist firms—costly, relatively immune from cost-benefit analysis but seemingly unavoidable and thus to be grudgingly shouldered. Given overheads were a growing proportion of costs, and the difficulty of associating them with small batch flexible manufacturing, ABC appeared to offer a superior solution to Fordist cost recovery methods. Its claim that all overhead costs are potentially variable but not necessarily with production volume resonated with the problems of bloated managerial bureaucracies in firms during Fordism—a major concern of chief executives in the US in the early 1980s. Viewed in this context, and despite evidence that it could give misleading information, ABC's cult status amongst cost accountants facing a diminished role with declining influence following the introduction of automated and integrated information processing systems is understandable. It offered a neo-Fordist cost accounting solution to neo-Fordist problems, by making visible the drivers and value of many service activities, and thence rendering them amenable to elimination or intensification by activity-based management or subcontracting to peripheral sectors domestically or abroad (Armstrong 2002). In brief, ABC appeared to render overhead activities visible and construct them as economic entities susceptible to new forms of market discipline.

In contrast, JIT espouses a different management philosophy. Fordist costing directed at short-run cost savings may frustrate aims of reduced lead-times and wastage and increased flexibility. Increased throughput speeds and small batch sizes have heightened interdependencies between departments, and increased labour flexibility has rendered formal detailed monitoring of production costs difficult and possibly redundant. Hence the switch to real-time physical controls based on kanbans, traffic lights and line stops for quality defects and production bottlenecks. Minimal inventories and regular small batch deliveries from subcontractors and zero defects render cost pools such as quality and goods inwards unnecessary and precipitate moves towards process and/or backflush costing and factory-wide overhead pools. This compounds problems of tracing costs to products. Standard cost variance reporting may no longer be apposite as it de-emphasizes quality concerns. For example, low labour usage variances might disguise a neglect of maintenance; material price variances might encourage bulk buying and inventory building; utilization and efficiency variances are irrelevant to balanced workflows and inventory reduction; constant standards run counter to learning and continuous improvement; and zero defects eliminates tolerance of planned defect rates. In short, standard costing derived from Taylorism fails to meet the needs of flexible production. Like automation, it calls for more cost control within engineering and design, procurement and scheduling.

Accounting changes associated with flexible manufacture have often been justified within a rhetoric of new forms of governance that empowers workers through devolved and broader responsibilities. The most intensive US-centred research on this is the Foucauldian study of Caterpillar by Miller and O'Leary (1994). They claim the shift to flexible manufacture involving, *inter alia*, team-working, benchmarking and cellular manufacturing, constitutes workers as docile 'economic citizens'. Potentially this could contribute to understanding how accounting reproduces managerial ideologies and manufactures consent in new times, and how and why collective identities and action have declined. However, their explanation is non-teleological and concentrates on management rhetoric rather than empirical observation of behaviour. This has raised a barrage of criticism, including their neglect of worker resistance, material issues, trade union militancy, workers' construction of meaning, the impact of national policies and contextualizing events within changes in capitalism (see McKinlay and Pezet 2010). The result is an ahistorical study.

CONCLUSIONS

The central argument presented in this chapter is that management accounting is shaped by and shapes various epochs of capitalism. Transitions are rooted, at least partly, by political struggles, manifest in corporations by attempts to control labour processes. Problems of converting labour power into effort and conflicts over any ensuing surplus are seen as inevitable. Material issues and consideration of economic exploitation have become unfashionable in accounting history circles. Yet economic approaches, often incorporating transaction cost theory and interpretations of Chandler's work (which fail to recognize his acknowledgement that his work neglects labour history), such as in Johnson and Kaplan (1987), and agency theory explicitly recognize control problems deriving from conflicting interests of agents and principals. However, they depict problems that arise as essentially local and portray drives for efficiency as self-equilibrating and in the public interest. In contrast, labour process theory relates such struggles to class formation; the subjugation of labour; and political, ideological and economic arrangements that extend to the state and forms of regulation.

The denial of Foucauldians of labour process issues is equally odd, for Foucault often refers to these or notes that they are beyond his purview in specific texts. A common criticism of labour process approaches is their neglect of subjectivity, as Braverman (1974) acknowledges. However, this has been debated substantially since Burawoy's (1979) study of why workers consent. Foucauldian studies of how accounting knowledge constitutes and disciplines subjects can significantly help understand the ideological role of accounting, but their neglect of industrial relations, material interest, and worker resistance remains puzzling, especially as they are significant factors in sites they study (Armstrong 1994, 2006; Arnold 1998). Moreover, it risks ignoring how management accounting practices have involved struggles and choices, and that more humane and egalitarian alternatives have and can exist.

Undoubtedly, subjective class allegiances have changed and possibly diminished since the Fordist epoch. However, this does not warrant writing class issues from the script, especially as material inequality, insecurity of employment and work intensification has grown for many US subjects according to economic dimensions of class. Management accounting has played a part in this. But whilst labour has been weakened, its institutions remain intact and resistance remains. To ignore material factors and how management accounting seeks to control labour risks missing important motors for contemporary changes in capitalism and thence accounting, and in so doing it risks propounding relativism and an acceptance of the status quo.

8 Somebody Knows the Trouble I've Seen

Moral Issues of New World Slavery and Accounting Practitioners

David Oldroyd, Richard K. Fleischman and Thomas N. Tyson

INTRODUCTION

In a recent series of papers, we have argued that accounting practice played a key role in sustaining slavery in the US and the British West Indies (BWI) in the eighteenth and nineteenth centuries. In the US, it was instrumental in commodifying, objectifying and dehumanizing an entire class of people through practices such as valuing slaves and maintaining data on their daily whereabouts and productivity. The valuations are an interesting case in point. In both the US and the BWI, slaves were valued alongside livestock as economic commodities, obscuring their humanity and reinforcing the commonly expressed view of planters that slavery was essentially about business, not exploitation. Similarly, the popularization of a scientific approach to plantation accounting in the US in the 1850s, at a time when the continued existence of slavery was seriously under threat, suggests that accounting was used to legitimize the institution as a normal, scientific, business activity. The majority of plantations in the BWI were owned by absentee gentry in Britain for whom a regular flow of accounting data was necessary to control their agents in the Caribbean.

Accounting also played an important role in sustaining slavery once it was threatened with abolition. From 1807, for example, it was no longer possible to replenish the wasting slave population with new imports from Africa given the abolition of the slave trade. Planters in both venues responded by switching from ganging to tasking to reduce the wear and tear on slaves. Tasking involved monitoring slave performance either individually or in gangs against preset standards while ganging, which

This chapter is based on the paper "The Culpability of Accounting Practice in Promoting Slavery in the British Empire and Antebellum United States", which originally appeared in *Critical Perspectives on Accounting* 19, no. 5 (2008): 764–84. The authors would like to thank the publisher, Elsevier, for permission to use this material.

depended on close supervision and physical coercion, was typically more exacting on the slaves.

The abolition of slavery in the BWI in 1834 was followed by a four-year period of transition in which the "freed" slaves, now termed "apprentices," were obliged to work for their former masters while they were taught how to behave like responsible wage-workers. The British government created a complex synthesis of punishments, incentives and indoctrination to effect this change. The system functioned only because accounting measured apprentices' work effort and recorded punishments for shortfalls. That accounting served as an instrument of coercion is illustrated by the fact that corporal punishment meted out on the basis of accounting evidence remained the ultimate deterrent for non-compliant workers. In the US, accounting played a less prominent role following emancipation in the mid-1860s because of the absence of a central agency comparable to Britain's Colonial Office, which formulated a set of codified and institutionalized record-keeping practices.

Thus, accounting practices were complicit in facilitating slavery in the US and BWI and in helping to sustain it even after its abolition. Demonstrating complicity, however, is not the same as saying that those who prepared or used reports deserve to be castigated for their support of slavery. However, it can be argued that a transcendent standard of justice exists relating to the treatment of humans against which accounting practitioners can be judged culpable. They contributed to genocide since slavery, with its high mortality rates, created a perilous demographic situation, rendering its collaborators guilty of crimes against humanity. The notion of a transcendent standard of justice for humankind, either derived through religion or moral philosophy, was well known to contemporaries. This issue suggests two key questions that should be addressed:

1. To what degree can personalities of the past be held responsible for actions that were not necessarily immoral in the environment in which they operated?
2. Did accountants have the power to influence managers toward more moral action and decision-making?

The first question speaks of judging the morality of slavery both from modern-day and contemporary perspectives. We will argue that virtue in accounting is a philosophical construct that is historically contingent on the social context and practice of the time. Therefore, to deem accounting practices opprobrious becomes primarily a matter for contemporaries to judge. The second question raises the possibility of accounting being deployed in society in order to reduce oppression. Such a situation would provide an interesting foil to previous studies which have tended to emphasize the repressive use of accounting by social elites as an implement of social and moral control over disadvantaged classes (e.g., Neu 1999; Funnell 2001;

Walker 2004a). We consider that accounting's role with regard to slavery was ambiguous in this respect, serving not just to facilitate slavery, but also to regulate the health and safety of slaves and eventually to promote their emancipation. If wider implications regarding the social potential of accounting practice can be drawn from the study, it will be mainly from this last point because it demonstrates accounting being successfully deployed to help engineer a fundamental change in social policy through promotion of alternate incentives.

The present study proceeds first by reflecting on the notion of an inherent virtue in accounting practice, and, second, on eighteenth- and nineteenth-century political opinion regarding the relationship between humanity, justice and property rights. The chapter then examines the antithetical proposition that accounting practice also served as a force for *good* in moderating the treatment of slaves and in facilitating their emancipation.

VIRTUE IN ACCOUNTING FOR SLAVERY

The first question posed in the preceding section as to the degree to which personalities of the past can be held responsible for actions that were not necessarily judged immoral in their environment suggests that ethics may be contingent on particular historical situations and raises the issue of moral judgments in history. Looking at the question of historical contingency first, Lovell (1995) considered the possibilities of an inner moral base to the practice of accounting and the accounting profession, following Kohlberg's six-step taxonomy of the stages of moral reasoning. He argued that while accounting practice exists in a wider social, economic and political context, it is inadequate to excuse its moral base on the grounds that it "reflects the prevailing values and beliefs of modernity" (61). According to Lovell (74), the accounting profession currently stands at the lowest self-interested level of Kohlberg's table—fear of antagonizing the business community and the state causes it to leave its members "to resolve ethical dilemmas as private issues"—whereas it should be aiming towards the higher levels where "the notion of living within a community assumes increasing significance" (61). The ultimate aim, which few persons or organizations attain, would be "a universalistic, principled notion of reasoning," going beyond "legally defined laws" or even "notions of a social contract," and assuming a quasi-spiritual dimension (61, 64). However, accounting behaviour is regarded by Lovell (68) as a function of the prevailing "moral atmosphere" and is therefore very much contingent on the historical situation. The same is true of T. Jones's (1991) model of ethical decision-making employed by Lippman and Wilson (2007) to theorize the behaviour of Nazi accountants in the Holocaust. Here the key factor was the "moral intensity" of the issue in question, which depends on such variables as social consensus and the psychological closeness of perpetrator and oppressed.

By contrast, Francis (1990) recognized accounting's potential to be used as an agent for improvement in society, arguing that particular virtues can be derived from performing accounting excellently. He held that accountants realize virtue by personal development and the attainment of internal rewards peculiar to the practice of accounting. These he identified as honesty, concern for the economic status of others, sensitivity to the value of cooperation and conflict, the communicative character of accounting practice and the dissemination of accounting information. Concern for the economic status of others implies reflection on the part of the accountant on "how accounting is used to effect economic relations between people" (9). This is certainly relevant to accounting for slavery which directly impinged on economic relations between planters and slaves. Honesty, too, was a virtue for attorneys and overseers, where the presumption on behalf of plantation owners was that their agents would act dishonestly without an elaborate system of reporting requirements. Francis never claimed his list of internal rewards leading to virtue from the practice of accounting to be comprehensive. But the point is, they stem from the practice of accounting, which is dynamic, and are thus themselves subject to change. Lovell (1995, 74) also recognized the difficulties of examining the moral base of a practice within a broader social context which spans millennia.

How, therefore, can one judge virtue in accounting historically if it is contingent as a philosophical concept on the social context or practice of the time? Wiencek (2003, 135) maintained that "the obvious objection to many modern inquiries into the morality of slaveholding is that they apply modern standards of ethics to the people of the past in a way that is manifestly unfair, illogical, and futile. To conduct a just inquiry, we would need an advocate of moral law from that time."

Most historians in fact eschew explicit moral judgments primarily because they are "extraneous" to the "theory and methodology of history," which seeks to uncover and understand the past rather than to judge it in moral terms (Evans 1997, 49). In this respect, one could argue that even to question accountants' culpability in the practice of slavery may be improper, notwithstanding the reality that moral judgments in history abound, even among leading proponents of an explicitly impartial approach. Indeed, the preclusion of contemporary biases and agendas from the analysis is probably not realistic. There is a tendency in history to use the past to justify the historian's view of the present, which is especially relevant to the history of slavery given its emotive nature when viewed against a background of racism and race relations in the modern world. Atoning for the past is a current issue for those private companies in the US being sued for their misdeeds by the descendants of slaves some 150 years on. Much of the furore that was engendered by Conrad and Meyer's (1958) and Fogel and Engerman's (1974) perceived justification of slavery arose not simply through opposition to slavery *per se*, but through concern over the place of African Americans in the history of the US and their place in society in the post–civil rights era.

Slavery reached maturity in the *Age of Enlightenment*, when it became the subject of moral debate. As the eighteenth century progressed, it was increasingly judged immoral by a ground-swell of popular opinion. The legacy is a mass of documentary evidence relating to the ethics of slavery. To an extent, therefore, judging the past through the eyes of the present is not relevant, notwithstanding the existence of certain basic issues of humanity that transcend time and become fully justified in evaluating past historical epochs.

HUMANITY, JUSTICE AND PROPERTY RIGHTS

The most emotive issue in the abolition debate was the magnitude of cruelty inflicted on slaves. Indeed, it is difficult to gain a true picture from contemporary tracts alone because while the abolitionist propaganda emphasized slavery's cruelty (e.g., Clarkson 1808; Wilberforce 1792), the charge was disputed by the plantation lobby (e.g., Francklyn 1789). B. Edwards (1798, 195), for instance, while not denying that some of the accounts of "whippings, mutilations, &c." were true, asserted that "in general terms . . . the treatment of West Indian slaves is mild and indulgent." Here there is a case for arguing that the agents who prepared the accounts were culpable for hiding the severity of the punishments that were being inflicted on the slaves. We know, for instance, that the punishments implemented in the BWI by post-emancipation laws were extremely cruel, albeit intended to protect the apprentices from the excesses they had formerly endured. Yet, the reports we have seen submitted by agents in the Caribbean to absentee owners in Britain made little mention of punishments. Narrative and literary evidence, such as the eyewitness testimony of Prince (1831) and Clarkson (1808), suggests a far higher level of disciplinary violence against slaves. Whiteley (1833), who visited Jamaica in 1832, found that all of the slaves on a pimento plantation had at some time been lashed for failing to achieve their picking quotas.

Whether or not slavery was inhumane in the minds of contemporaries depended to a large extent on whether they believed Africans fully human. Writing a century before the modern eugenics movement was born, the argument that Africans were "a distinct and inferior species" was seen by one abolitionist as the best defence available to the pro-slavery lobby, could it be proven (Anon. 1790, 128). In commenting on "the dull stupidity of the Negroe" compared to the "quick sagacity of the [American] Indian," Knox (1789, 14) speculated on whether this was because "the Creator [had] originally formed these black people a little lower than other men." This was not just prejudice, but reflected a lack of scientific knowledge about Africa and Africans. A House of Commons Select Committee (1791) took evidence in the 1790s on whether Africans were capable of feelings, affection and moral behaviour. The myth that slaves were not as human as Europeans was one that the abolition lobby had to dispel. Gisborne (1792, 28), for example, affirmed with a hint of irony that the Negro "is a human creature. He has some powers of understanding; he has organs of articulation; he has a language not altogether unintelligible to European ears." His purpose was to answer a section of the pro-slavery propaganda which had "reasoned Negroes down to a level with the Ourang-Outangs; or rather the Ourangs up to, or above the Negroes" (Gentleman Long Resident in Jamaica 1792, 5).

The religious lobby was particularly vehement in emphasizing that slaves shared a common humanity with the rest of mankind. Thus, Niel (1792, 3–4) stressed that "the swarthy sons of Africa, and the savage tribes of America in their native wilds" had all been created in the image of God alongside "the fair and ruddy European, and the proudly pompous Asiatic." Slaves were "equally the objects" of God's "paternal care," and "were entitled to the same immortality and salvation" (Knox 1790, 2).

The myth that slaves were less than human was one which agents and book-keepers helped to perpetuate through commonly classifying them with the mules and cattle in inventories and valuations of livestock. Slaves in both venues were annually subjected to a parade before appraisers in which superficial characteristics served as the basis for evaluation since no individual productivity records were in evidence.

Meanwhile in the US, the three-fifths compromise of the Constitution provided that each Negro count as three-fifths of a white person for determining seats in the House of Representatives, thus institutionalizing their inferiority. It remained in effect until the 1860s, changed only as the verdict of war.

Plantation owners were unable to capture the moral high ground from the abolitionists by justifying themselves on the grounds that property should be protected (e.g., Adair 1790). For Innes (1789), private property was "sacred," and the planters had equal rights to its protection as other British subjects. Protection of property was fundamental to the dominant code of ethics in Britain and America originating from Biblical theology. Blackburn (1997) argued that Christian theology gives tacit support to slavery, notwithstanding the leading role played in the abolition movement by Christian sects such as the Baptists, Methodists, Quakers and Anglicans in particular. However, the numbers of church writers who used Scripture to justify slavery were probably in the minority. More typical were the views of Reverend Randolph (1788, 15), who argued that such use of the Bible was "adding blasphemy to our iniquity."

Protection of property is achieved implicitly through accounting. Funnell (2001) considered the triangular relationship between accounting, justice and property, drawing on the writings of contemporary political-economists such as Smith, Hume, Locke and Bentham. Funnell argued that in capitalist societies, accounting is concerned with justice on the basis of entitlements derived from property, and that the preservation of property is enshrined in law as the ultimate end of justice. The periodic reports sent by Caribbean agents were commissioned by plantation owners and designed to protect their interests. Notions of need and fairness to the slaves were therefore irrelevant to these accounts, which provided "justice" to the property owners. In this respect, one could argue that these agents were not morally opprobrious. Opponents in the House of Commons of the 1792 abolition bill stressed the link between "justice" and the "preservation" of the planters' "property" (Gisborne 1792, 24).

The relationship between property and justice was also seized upon by the abolitionists. Slavery was not necessarily adjudged immoral because of the conditions under which slaves laboured. First, they did have some rights in law, notwithstanding that the law failed to safeguard them from abuse (e.g., Wilberforce 1792); second, their living conditions were not unfavourable compared with those of the labouring classes in Britain as was frequently argued. That said, statistical analysis of mortality and fertility rates in fact suggest that living conditions were harder in the BWI than in the US (Blackburn 1997; Fogel and Engerman 1974; Higman 1976; J. Ward 1991). What distinguished slavery as unjust from a political perspective was that the slaves were denied their innate property rights over their own persons. Hence, Roscoe (1788, 8) could argue that "no title to perpetual servitude of another can be supported by purchase; for the origin being unjust, the right cannot be validated by transfer."

The theme of contract law was argued by Tucker (1796), a professor of law. Quoting directly from Blackstone (1826, 422–23), the foremost eighteenth-century commentator on English common law, he urged that selling slaves offended the laws of property because the slaves themselves received nothing in exchange for the value given. This implied that slavery was incompatible with the principles of liberty on which the revolutionary American government had been founded. Blackstone (ibid., 422–24) himself, while arguing that "pure and proper slavery . . . cannot subsist in England . . . whereby an absolute and unlimited power is given to the master over the life and fortune of the slave," stopped short of concluding that slavery contracts should be forfeit. Although the law would protect a slave in England "in the enjoyment of his person and property," it would not free him from the property rights of his master to his service, providing they had been lawfully acquired.

Blackstone's work was especially influential in the drafting of the American Constitution. However, the debate on slavery at the Constitutional Convention of 1787 centred on practical issues of taxation and representation rather than ethics. Contemporaries were not unaware of the inconsistencies between the political aspirations of the Declaration of Independence and the practice of slavery. According to Ramsay (1789, 38), the case for liberating "the poor African" was "much stronger" than that of the American colonies in their secession from Britain, applying the logic that had been espoused during the revolution. Some one hundred years post-Blackstone, Bagehot (2001, 153), the leading Victorian commentator on the English constitution, used the property argument in reverse to show the dangers slaves faced following their emancipation. Writing at the end of the American Civil War, he maintained that slaves had been "formerly protected" because they were "articles of value," whereas now no one had an interest in their preservation but themselves.

The notion that only individuals had property rights over their own persons was not new and had been developed extensively by Locke. He argued that protection of self was the rationale for humans in a "state of nature" to form themselves into societies. Locke's definition of property, therefore, was the "preservation of lives, liberties and estates," and he regarded men's lives and liberties as the chief parts of their property (Locke 1764, chap. 9, S.123–24). Furthermore, he referred to slavery explicitly as being incompatible with the concept of property. This is what was understood by "Africanus" (1788, 79, 85) when he spoke of slavery as contravening the "laws of Nature" or "the rights of man," which he defined in terms of "the privileges . . . of protection." Even Dundas (1796, 24), who opposed the 1796 abolition bill on pragmatic grounds, accepted the moral argument that the slave trade was "contrary to the principles of justice and humanity." Slavery activists attempted to subvert Locke's argument by maintaining that slavery was more conducive to "the preservation of the lives" of the slaves than life in Africa (Planter 1789, 4). Locke's (1764, chap. 4, S.23) assertion that liberty was so integral a part of the nature of man that it was not in his power to part with it "by compact, or his own consent" was picked up by the abolitionists (e.g., Roscoe 1788; Anon. 1790). Locke's proposition that slavery could only be acceptable as a substitute for execution enabled abolitionists to argue further that slavery was "unjust" because its victims had "not forfeited their right to freedom by committing felony" (Gentleman Long Resident in Jamaica 1792, 6). It also helps explain the emphasis in the abolitionist literature and evidence presented to Parliament that slaves were first procured in Africa through "unjust wars" or kidnapping by local despots (e.g., Wilberforce 1792).

To sum up, judging the past in relation to the present may be questionable from a philosophical or historiographical perspective. However, the personalities of the past who engaged in slavery or generated accounts that protected their interests can still be seen to have acted unethically when weighed against a standard of justice linked to accounting's protection of property entitlements, entitlements which were soundly critiqued and widely understood by leading thinkers and social critics of the time.

ACCOUNTING AND EMANCIPATION

The other question posed about whether accountants have the power to influence managers towards more moral action and decision-making suggests a more positive role for accounting practice historically as well as in the present. Work has already been undertaken relating accounting to "emancipation" by Gallhofer and Haslam (2003), who cite cases where labour activists utilized accounting data to fight repression. Champion, for example, used published accounting data in the 1880s to campaign for better wages at a match manufacturer by contrasting the workers' terms with returns to shareholders. Reducing social exclusivity is a related issue, and Brackenborough (2003) similarly demonstrated how the annual income and expenditure accounts published by the Newcastle Corporation in the nineteenth century were employed by ship-owners and traders on the Tyne to wrest control away from the narrow oligarchy which controlled the city. Whether the outcome could be regarded as social progress would depend on the perspective of the interests served, but it does illustrate accounting being deployed effectively by interest groups as an agent of social change.

Accounting data were likewise used for lobbying purposes in the debate over the abolition of slavery. As the issue of abolition gathered force in Britain in the later eighteenth century, a range of accounting statistics was presented to the various parliamentary committees which, once in the public domain, were seized upon by the protagonists to support their arguments. In 1789, for example, a tract made use of "accounts laid before Parliament" on imports, exports and British and East Indian "manufactures" in order "to prove to the conviction of every rational British subject, that the abolition of the British trade with Africa for negroes, would be a measure as unjust as impolitic, fatal to the interest of this nation, and ruinous to its sugar colonies" (Anon. 1789, 10–17).

The moral import of the plantation accounts themselves is not clear-cut. In the first place, the question of whether the agents and book-keepers who kept the accounts on the Caribbean plantations had the power to influence the owners towards more moral action towards the slaves—better conditions, greater freedoms, more humane treatment, etc.—does not wholly apply because it was the self-same attorneys, overseers and book-keepers who had power over the slaves' daily lives. Similarly, in the US where plantations were generally smaller, the owners tended to keep the books. Most surviving BWI accounts were returns submitted to absentee owners, who used them in an attempt to control the actions of officials they could not monitor firsthand. While we have suggested that there was some concealment in these returns of the brutal nature of the treatment meted out to slaves, it is probably also the case that their situation would have been worse had the agents not been compelled to account regularly for the increases or decreases in numbers of slaves with explanations for lives lost. The first priority of the absentee owners was to avoid punishments that would have incapacitated slaves or made females less fertile. Therefore, the accounts were intended to align the economic interests of the agents with the health and safety of the slaves. If the agents maintained the value of the stock of slaves, it would help secure their positions and even attract rewards; if it declined, they risked punishment. Thus, although accounting practices helped sustain slavery, plantation accounts also served to protect the lives of slaves by providing managers with appropriate incentives, albeit from the purely self-interested motive of preserving the value of the plantations' most important productive resource. Accounting served a similar unintended positive role in the movement to abolish slavery.

In the British colonies, accounting served as an emancipatory force in a more direct way because without it the slaves could not have been emancipated. Accounting was employed to regulate the transition from slavery to waged-labour. Although the reality of the situation may have been to maintain the oppression of the so-called "apprentices," neither the owners nor the local judiciary were allowed by the Colonial Office to act with impunity. Apprentices now received more protection under the law against abuse. Incidents in Jamaica in 1834 and British Guiana in 1842 reveal them confident enough to appeal to the law for redress when their rights had been transgressed. The whole process was built on a hierarchy of accountability stretching upwards from the workers, planters and judiciary to the British government.

Accounting played a more significant role still in facilitating emancipation in the British colonies. Plantation owners would not have agreed to emancipation without compensation. The "sacredness" of private property in the British constitution meant that it would have been morally unjust, as well as politically inexpedient, for the government to have withheld compensation. To suggest otherwise was "absurd" and "absolutely contrary to the Faith of all Charters and Acts of Parliament, granted for the Protection of the Colonies, and for the general Benefit of this Country" (Innes 1789, 6–7).

The alternative of freeing the slaves without compensating the owners was only tenable in the US because of the Civil War. Compensating BWI planters was also considered vital by the British government to ensure the continued survival of the local plantation economies. If the planters, many of whom were heavily in debt, were not adequately compensated, it was feared they would emigrate and cultivation in the BWI would cease.

Accounting was actively deployed by the British government in the negotiations over compensation, as well as in the administration of the actual process during the transition from slave to wage-workers. It was used by the Treasury in the negotiation of a £15 million loan from Rothschild to fund the bulk of the compensation. Slave owners were required to classify the slaves they held on 1 August 1834 into designated categories, each of which was assigned a standard value. Knowing that the slaves would be rated according to their economic value again created an incentive for the owners to maintain their health. Claims had to be attested by two disinterested parties or government officials. It follows that accounting was fully integrated in the compensation process.

CONCLUSION

The chapter has considered whether it is justifiable to hold accounts' users and preparers culpable for their involvement in slavery. On the one hand, previous studies demonstrate the complicity of accounting in promoting slavery, and that the agents and owners who were involved in this process transgressed the dominant code of ethics at the time. Justice stemmed from the protection of property entitlements, to which accounting was key. However, by the eighteenth century, the notion of property had been developed to embrace property rights over one's own person and was therefore incompatible with slavery. On the other hand, slavery was eventually abolished, and accounting was actively deployed by the British government to gain the acquiescence of planters in facilitating emancipation. Moreover, while slavery lasted, accounting protected the value of the owners' stock of slaves, and thereby contributed indirectly to promoting their health and well-being. Thus, accountings were working in opposite directions, the one to oppress, the other to sustain life or liberate.

There are perhaps two general inferences that can be drawn from this dichotomy about the social agency of accounting practice, notwithstanding the danger this creates of imposing present beliefs on the past (Miller and Napier 1993). The first concerns the role of accounting as a lobbying tool. Once information enters the public domain, it becomes available for lobbying purposes by interest groups. This was particularly true of the campaign for the abolition of slavery, described by G. Trevelyan (1966, 599) as "the first successful propagandist agitation of the modern type." From an accounting perspective, exposing organizations to greater public scrutiny, obliging them to be more open in their disclosures about the effects of their activities, increases the likelihood that the status quo will be challenged by pressure groups. As in the case of slavery, a shift in public opinion can be used by government to justify direct political action that once would have been deemed unacceptable, whatever the underlying causes.[1] Manipulating the *demos* for political ends is certainly not new and would have been well known to Julius Caesar or Demosthenes.

The second inference concerns the relationship between accounting and economic incentives. Maintaining a healthy workforce that was capable of reproducing itself organically was not incompatible with slavery in the US or the BWI given the costs of procuring and transporting new slaves from Africa. It was in the interests of investors to maintain the economic value of the workforce, and they utilized accounts to translate this incentive to their agents. The need to preserve the workforce became especially critical after 1807 when new imports of slaves were banned by the British and American governments. Some slave owners responded by switching from "ganging" to "tasking" production systems, the latter relying less on physical coercion and more on economic incentives to elicit satisfactory performance. During apprenticeship in the BWI, slaves were given the opportunity to purchase their freedom in advance of full emancipation. However, planters used accounting valuations to inflate the price they would have had to pay, thereby discouraging them from trying. Conversely, the apprenticeship regulations attempted to give workers the incentive to work hard for their former masters by paying them for any labour provided in excess of their basic quota. Finally, accounting was employed by the British government to create the incentive for the owners to agree to abolition by compensating them for the resulting loss of value. Accounting was instrumental in all of these initiatives (imposing rewards and punishments, setting targets and monitoring efforts, valuing slaves) and, thus, revealed itself capable of being used to promote different incentives for slaves, agents and owners as the economic and political circumstances changed.

In the 1990s, a dispute arose over the renovation of the frieze above St. George's Hall in Liverpool which depicted a grateful Negro kneeling with shackles broken beneath the figure of Britannia who had liberated her slaves. The revisionists argued that the image should be torn down and replaced as it misrepresented history. It was deemed wholly inappropriate for modern multicultural Liverpool; it was Britannia, after all, who had enslaved the Negroes in the first place.[2] Should accounting practitioners be lauded for facilitating the emancipation or should they be condemned for supporting slavery during the previous two hundred years of its existence? The fact that accounting could serve both ends illustrates its flexibility as an instrument of both social control and social change.

NOTES

1. Blackburn (1997) argues that the abolition of slavery in the BWI was linked to a relative decline in its economic importance compared to new markets opening up elsewhere for manufactured goods.
2. Hammond (2002, 124–25) relates another interesting case of symbolism relating to slavery. The social attitudes which excluded African Americans from the role of CPA were encapsulated on the Mississippi certificate until the mid-1980s by their portrayal in the corner of the document picking cotton.

9 Accounting and Colonial Liberalism

Keith Hooper and Kate Kearins

INTRODUCTION

The period 1885–1911 was a significant one in the development of New Zealand, and particularly so when one considers the means and effects of colonial public finance policies in New Zealand with regard to the distribution of property rights and wealth. As signalled by Gallhofer and Chew (2000), there is important work to be done in explicating accounting's role in Western domination as part of an attempt to address injustices to indigenous peoples. The chapter is thus positioned to contribute to literature in post-colonial studies in accounting, following the authors' earlier work in the New Zealand context, and studies by Neu (2000a, 2000b); Neu and Graham (2004, 2006) in Canada; Gibson (2000) in Australia; and Davie (2000) in Fiji.

The chapter makes an explicit contribution to discussion on Liberal reformism—a common context for colonial development in the antipodes—and the role of accounting in Maori land transactions within that context. In spite of the socialistic aspect of New Zealand colonial Liberalism, the government remained committed to market philosophies. More tellingly, given the tribal nature of Maori land holdings, there was a commitment by the government to individual property ownership. Inevitably, such a philosophy would be in conflict with Maori—as the historical case study in this chapter shows.

The chapter first explains Liberal reformism and expertocracy. The character of hypocrisy in politics is briefly touched upon. The historical case study comprises relevant background to the development of colonial New Zealand from its foundation in 1840, followed by consideration of

This chapter is based on the paper "The Walrus, Carpenter and Oysters: Liberal Reform, Hypocrisy and Expertocracy in Maori Land Loss in New Zealand 1885–1911", which originally appeared in *Critical Perspectives on Accounting* 19, no. 8 (2008): 1239–62. The authors would like to thank the publisher, Elsevier, for permission to use this material. Funding by the Crown Forestry Rental Trust for a larger project, a history of Maori and taxation 1840–2001, is also acknowledged.

aspects of the period of Liberal governance during which Maori dispro-portionately financed Liberal policies, and discussion which integrates the aforementioned theory.

Evidence for the case study is drawn from *Appendices to the Journals of the House of Representatives* (*AJHR*), which record specific land trans-fers, government revenues from territories acquired, land and survey fees, ledger accounts and other official information. Use is also made of the *New Zealand Parliamentary Debates* (*NZPD*), where arguments of legislating politicians are shown to make the case for Maori land sales. The research also drew upon histories of New Zealand and its politics.

LIBERAL REFORMISM AND EXPERTOCRACY

Liberalism is variously described as an ideology, a philosophy and a politi-cal tradition. Its diverse strands generally emphasize liberty and individual rights. An intrinsic mediating principle is that of 'doing no harm'. As a political movement, Liberalism became popular in the late nineteenth cen-tury in many Western countries. Liberal ideas were also in the ascendancy in most developed countries during the late twentieth century (Rosenblum 1989; Catley 2005).

In broad terms, traditional forms of Liberal governance were character-ized by the promotion of individual freedoms, respect for the rule of law, a market economy that supported relatively free private enterprise and a transparent system of government in which the rights of all citizens were to be protected (Mill 1859/1946; Hall 1988). The application of Liberal ideals thus requires public policy to be shaped in accordance with the wishes of the citizenry (Dewey 1963).

Proponents of Liberalism differ notably on the appropriate degree of gov-ernment interference—particularly in relation to the market. They differ as to the extent to which the proceeds of market regulation should support government provision of general welfare, with European use of the term 'Liberal' more likely to apply to a defender of the free market and North American use mostly indicating a defender of the welfare state (Honderich 1995, 483). Both J.S. Mill (1859/1946) and (Lord) Keynes (1936) argued that some form of interference by governments was necessary to offset injustices and inefficiencies that occur, not least economic injustices and inefficiencies. Indeed, similar arguments were apparent in the Liberal reformism of the early twentieth century—although social welfare reforms generally "were relatively minor and had limited coverage" (Barr 2004, 13).

Liberal reformism is premised on particular sorts of changes that are not without their own problems. According to Burchell (1993, 271), early forms of Liberalism regarded the market, as a kind of "economic nature reserve" marked off, secured and supervised by the state. "That is to say, the rational conduct of government must be intrinsically linked to natural, private interest motivated conduct of free market exchanging individuals". Such intrinsic linking was disastrous for those communities not comprising "free market exchanging individuals", because no matter what was promised by Liberal politicians by way of protection from free market pressures, such promises could always be reneged upon. Burchell (1993) identifies Liberal government as "cheap government" geared to securing the conditions for optimum economic performance. His analysis reveals how communistic systems of land tenure based on self-sufficiency would be doomed by Liberal governance and that promises of protection to the contrary would be worthless.

The mechanism by which condemnation of communistic self-sufficiency is generally achieved is through various state agencies employing 'experts' to reach conclusions based on economic rationalities. Preston, Chua and Neu (1997), citing N. Rose (1993), suggest that the tactics of arranging and disposing of things under advanced Liberalism place the expert, a foundation stone of Liberal government, in a new relationship with the apparatus of political rule. However, even early Liberal governments employed experts to distance themselves from the process of management (Rose 1993). Preston, Chua and Neu (1997, 148) continue: "The process of government may also be indirect, mediated and decentralised through the use of multiple intermediaries". Such intermediaries might also include technologies and bodies of knowledge such as accounting and statistics. Accounting can function as a macro-pricing mechanism embedded in micro-allocation decisions, as Preston, Chua and Neu (1997, 157) point out, "albeit in a variety of localized transactions and interpretations". What is more, Power (1992, 487) observes, "it does not take much reflection on the practices of 'creative accounting' to argue that this supposed neutrality of quantification is a myth which conceals a capacity for partisan representations."

Political power is thus exercised through a multitude of agencies and technologies. Like N. Rose (1993), Gorz (1989, 108) argues that the concept of economic rationality may colonize Liberal governments, excluding wider social considerations. Moreover, "Economic rationality itself is formalized into calculations, procedures and formulae inaccessible either to debate or reflection. We are left with debates between experts, quibbling over technicalities of method not with the substance of the debate" (122). Thus if, as Burchell alleges, economic rationality is intrinsic to Liberal government, then Gorz is correct to argue that 'experts' of economic rationality may well colonize government. The consequences of such penetration are such that "the reduction to technique allows economic calculation to emerge as a substitute for value judgement" (Power 1992, 479). Power (ibid., 482) summarizes the change which occurs under Liberalism as incorporating "the emergence of an expert occupational class of organizers who increasingly colonize the sphere of civil society in the sense of defining the way 'functional' problems are perceived and addressed".

Accountants and accounting expertise are an important element of this 'expertocracy'—a term Leonard (2006, 7) defines as "statism joined to expertise". This joining is not meant to imply equal status between, or a hierarchy of, governments and their agents. Expertocracy also includes non-human actors such as bodies of expert knowledge and relevant technologies like accounting. It attempts to embrace expert interaction in hierarchical and non-hierarchical situations (Heipertz and Verdun 2005). Thus it implies multidirectional rather than simply top-down or state-directed influence. Seen in this light, accountants should not be considered mere agents of governmental masters; they make decisions, and they provide information as a basis for others to make decisions, which can drive direction and, on occasion, determine the fate of those who depend on these decisions.

According to Neu (2000b), accounting operated as "the software of imperialism", facilitating action at a distance, and helping to translate imperial objectives into practice. Miller and Rose (1990, 1) note that accounting "functioned as an indirect mechanism—aligning economic, social and personal conduct with the socio-political objectives of colonial powers". Though the focus in this chapter is not squarely on imperialism, which featured in the authors' previous work (Hooper and Kearins 2003, 2004), the notion of accounting facilitating action at a distance is important here, as in Neu (2000b; Neu and Graham 2004). Liberal reformism relied on accounting technologies for its implementation:

> These formulae for a state of welfare sought to maintain a certain distance between the knowledges and allegiances of experts and the calculations of politicians. The truth claims of expertise were highly significant here: through the powers of truth, distant events and persons could be governed 'at arms length': political rule would not set itself the norms of individual conduct, but would install and empower a variety of 'professionals' who would, investing them with authority to act as experts in the devices of social rule. (Rose 1993, 285)

Moreover, these experts worked as intermediaries without substantive identification beyond the actual accounts produced and retained in the archives. Their work remains at once integral to the implementation of government policy and yet 'at a distance'.

That the work of accounting experts is part of a potent colonization formulation is not in doubt. Neu (2000b, 167) found that "accounting facilitated solutions that were 'convenient' for bureaucrats and settlers". Accounting is argued to have enlisted and worked with and on indigenous people to serve complex processes of empire building (Davie 2000). And it has been "instrumental in extending political dominion over new territory" (Neu and Graham 2006, 73). In New Zealand (see Hooper and Kearins 2003, 2004), as in Canada, accounting techniques have been shown to provide "a tentative method of reconciling the goals of colonial self-sufficiency, cost-containment and the 'civilizing' of indigenous peoples" (Neu 2000b, 170). Miller and Rose (1990, 7) observe, "The events and phenomena to which government is to be applied must be rendered into information—written reports, drawings, pictures, numbers, charts, graphs, statistics . . . to be literally re-presented in the place where decisions are to made about them". Neu (2000b, 176), referring to Canada, claims:

> We observe accounting numbers representing not only the amount indigenous people received for their land but perhaps more importantly the value that colonial officials placed on the indigenous people themselves . . . the colonial government's desire to save money and the desperate position of the indigenous peoples encouraged colonial officials to not only minimize purchase prices wherever possible but also to structure the transactions in such a way that a capital payment for the land was not required.

As illustrated in this chapter, similar techniques of monopoly land acquisition were followed in colonial New Zealand with the added feature of deducting from the purchase price significant transaction costs. Expertocracy worked at a distance from the political realm and became the purveyor of a supposedly objective truth. It is by removing the mechanisms of dispossession from the realm of political decision-making that Liberal politicians in New Zealand were able to maintain a façade of sympathy.

Hypocrisy, commonly defined as saying one thing while doing another, is shown to be implicated in the practice of Liberal governance in New Zealand. Brunsson (2002, xiii) argues that "hypocrisy is a way of handling several conflicting values simultaneously". Hypocrisy, he suggests, operates as a solution seemingly possessing moral advantages rather than posing as a problem. Hypocrisy works because most people believe that talk pointing in a certain direction increases the likelihood of action occurring in that direction. Hypocrisy may be seen as a solution to the dilemma of handling inconsistent norms and at the same time wishing to avoid conflict. Liberal governments which are generally multi-ideological can win legitimacy not by fighting for a single interest, but by being associated with several interests and incorporating those interests into their values. Such a situation invites colonization by experts.

ACCOUNTING AND MAORI LAND LOSS

Background

New Zealand was annexed by Great Britain in 1840 with the ensuing establishment of colonial rule, European-style law and regulation. Increased settler demand for land fuelled Maori resistance to land sales, setting the scene for the New Zealand Land Wars of the 1860s and 1870s. A confiscation policy was then introduced, though not all rebel tribes were punished.

The government took land in an arbitrary fashion. Requisitions of Maori lands for public works purposes followed, often with meagre or no compensation. Maori tribes were also subjected to a host of other government fees and taxes. By the 1880s, Maori held nearly one-third of New Zealand as Native Reserves and, with the progressive Liberal Party emerging as a political force, had reason to expect to retain control of their remaining lands. The Liberal Party won the general election of 1890, formed a government in 1891 and remained in power until 1912.

Liberal leaders, though imbued in the doctrines of individualism and *laissez-faire*, also believed that state intervention was needed to address problems (Sinclair 1991). An official summary notes: "The Liberal government reinforced an established pattern of state involvement in the economy and regulation of society. Its old age pensions and workers' dwellings anticipated the welfare state" (Te Ara 2006). Liberal leaders "hoped not for the destruction of capitalism but for "reconciliation between capital and labour on a fair and equitable basis" (Sinclair 1991, 175). With the aspirations of many settlers unrealized, the Liberals saw it as necessary to legislate for the desired social and economic order (ibid.). It has been said that "if the Liberals had one common and dominant preoccupation, it was how to best use land, widely recognised as the country's richest resource" (King 2003, 260).

The 1890 election saw the return of twenty Liberal members endorsed by labour groups. Maori votes were a lesser consideration for the Liberal Party as Maori had their own representatives in parliament and many Maori were not registered to vote. Implementing the Liberal government vision of welfare and state regulation meant uncovering additional sources of revenues preferably, from the Liberals' point of view, without alienating the majority of European voters. Maori land was the politically expedient choice which matched Liberal's plans for closer settlement and the establishment of small farms (Te Ara 1966a). With refrigeration opening up export markets for meat and dairy products, smaller farms became viable. Land settlement policy was "based on the principle of 'one man, one farm', and land legislation . . . [was] directed towards closer settlement of farm land and the prevention of undue aggregation" (Te Ara 1966b). Even more Maori land was set to pass into European hands.

Fine Promises

When the Liberals came to power in 1891, Maori made up 10 per cent of the population and retained 30 per cent of the land (King 2003). Given the Liberal's pre-election promises, Maori expected better control over their remaining lands. "He had heard it stated that this government above all others was the government that would redress the wrongs" (H. Tapua, Member of Parliament [MP], Western Maori, *NZPD*, 74:161). Indeed, as this MP reminded Parliament, Liberal leader, John Ballance, had toured the remaining Maori lands, assuring the tribes of his party's good intentions:

> I say it deliberately—and I say it in the presence of the fact that I am criticized severely in some parts of the colony for expressing this senti- ment—that it is not the desire of the government to strip the Native of their lands. On the other hand, it is the desire of the government to assist the Natives in preserving a portion of their territory, in order that their prosperity and their existence and their happiness may be maintained in the future. (Ballance to Arawa Tribe, *AJHR*, 1885, G-1, p. 42)

In government, Premier Ballance continued to repeat his claim of pro- moting Maori well-being: "It is our sincere desire to promote in every pos- sible way the happiness and prosperity of the Native people" (Ballance to Waikato Tribe, *AJHR*, 1885, G-1, p. 13). Perhaps most reassuring was the promise that from then on, Maori would receive equal consideration. "The government of which I am a member propose to treat the Native people just the same as they would Europeans" (Ballance to Wanganui Maori, *AJHR*, 1885, G-1, p. 4). What he did not mention was that 17 per cent of the gov- ernment's revenue was coming from the sale or lease of Maori land and was helping to pay for an expanding programme of European immigration and farm settlement.

Experts employed by the government recognized, facilitated and reported on the potential for government gain from sales of Maori land. In a report on land at Taheke, Thomas McDonnell writes of Maori wanting 12s an acre, while he offered 2s. 6d. and admitted, "private individuals might be inclined to give more." He concludes, "The Government are in every way gainers by the present arrangement" (*AJHR*, 1873, Vol. 3, G-8).

Taxation by Survey, Public Works and Commissions

In order to open up land for settlement, boundaries of Native Reserves had to be defined. Surveys were expedited, with Maori responsible for paying survey charges. The West Coast Commission Report (cited in *AJHR*, 1882, G-5, Appendix II, No. 2, pp. 9–10) is illustrative of the costs involved. One instance concerns the 18,000-acre Stony River block returned to Maori after the war of 1865. The report claims Maori were anxious to have the block surveyed so that they could lease it to Europeans and divide owner- ship among six or seven sub-tribes. With four survey parties, the work was estimated to take two years and cost £9,500. To facilitate "the occupation of the country by European settlers which is certain to follow", the report recommended doubling the number of survey parties, claiming an addi- tional reason for speeding up was that "the Natives at present are in an excellent humour and very desirous to have the work done" (cited in *AJHR*, 1882, G-5, Appendix II, No. 2, p. 10).

By 1885, Maori were recorded as protesting against the exorbitant survey fees (*AJHR*, 1885, G-1, p. 45). Maori claimed that in some cases the survey fees were greater than the value of the land. Premier Ballance concurred: "I agree you have a very solid grievance and I shall see at once that it is remedied" (*AJHR*, 1885, G-1, p. 45). He promised that in the future Maori would pay no more for surveys than the government rate. But Maori had already surrendered land to pay the exorbitant government survey charges and, in the process, had provided another source of government revenue. Six years later, survey costs remained an ongoing debt burden for Maori— even if they did not plan to sell their land:

> The above amounts [totalling to £28,817] represent liens on Native lands for survey performed by the Government either for purposes of the Native Land Court or in expectation of purchase of land by the Government. In the case of the former liens are recovered when the Native Land Court finally deals with the land, and in the latter case the liens are written off when the land is finally purchased by the Government. (*AJHR*, 1891, Session II, G-10, p. 55)

Under The Native Land Act 1873 (section 106), the governor was entitled to "take and lay off for public purposes one or more line or lines of road or railway through said lands". Sometimes compensation was granted for land acquired for public works, but not always. For example, the construction of one road (from Kaihu to Maunganui Bluff) was delayed "owing to difficulties with the Natives". The difficulty consisted "in the demand for payment for the land taken by the road". The Chief Surveyor's Report (cited in *AJHR*, 1881, C-4, p. 31) concludes: "It would be wrong in principle to pay for this road which has been taken under rights secured by the Native Lands Act". The need for the road, adduced in the report, was "for the number of settlers [that] will be ready to locate themselves there."

With control of Maori Lands vested in the Public Trustee, successive Liberal governments remained figuratively at a distance from land-holding tribes, while various 'experts' made decisions about Maori rental accounts as to commission, interest, salaries and disbursements. From time to time Native Reserves were sold to meet expenses. Orange (1987, 274) observes, "Reserves did not give Maori the expected benefits". By way of example, she relates how the "Dunedin reserve was lost to Maori use through judicial and administrative manipulation".

The records of the Native Reserves Accounts in the late 1880s illustrate such calculative manipulation. They disclose the extent to which rents received from leasing Maori reserves were controlled for the government through the Public Trustee (Butterworth and Butterworth 1991) and subjected to management commissions. A typical excerpt from the Native Reserves Ledger is provided here:

No 132, Mungaroa Account

Receipts	£	s	d	Disbursements	£	s	d
Balance at 31st December 1883	6	15	0	To Erin Turoa, share of rent	7	17	6
Rent	20	0	0	Hemi Kuti, share of rent	7	17	6
				Public Trust Office, commission	1	0	0
				Public Trust Agent, commission	1	0	0
				Balance (since paid)	9	0	0
	26	15	0		26	15	0

(*AJHR*, 1885, G-5, p. 1)

The account reveals Public Trust commission on rents of around 10 per cent and a holding balance in each account totalling £3,350, or 30 per cent of the rental income. This represents monies not disbursed, and was a source of interest for the government. Such accumulated undistributed balances became a source of credit for European settlers developing leased Maori land. There is evidence on occasion of government agencies consuming over one-quarter of the rent monies, while enjoying the undistributed balances.

Maori protested the levies on their lands, but in spite of Liberal parliamentary promises to remedy exorbitant charges, nothing was done at an administrative level (*AJHR*, 1885, G-1, p. 45). The levies on Maori land incomes managed by the government were subject only to bureaucratic approval. The extra charges applied meant it was little wonder that "Maori felt themselves to be steadily impoverished" (*NZPD*, 29 September 1893, 82:865–66).

Allocation of Development Funds and Improving Returns

Maori were also shut out from government sources of funding available to others to buy and develop small farms. In 1907, a Commission on Native Lands and on Native Land Tenure articulated the problem:

> It is difficult for the Maori owner to acquire his own land be he ever so ambitious and capable of using it. His energy is dissipated in Land Courts in a protracted struggle, first, to establish his own right to it, and secondly, to detach himself from numerous other owners to whom he is genealogically bound in the title. And when he has succeeded he is handicapped by want of capital, by lack of training—he is under the ban as one of a spendthrift, easy-going, improvident people. (*AJHR*, 1907, G-1c, p. 15)

The difficulties faced by Maori working their land were raised in the Petition of Te Wherowhero, which was presented to the Native Affairs Committee in 1905. "There is no channel open to us whereby we can get hold of any money to enable us to work the lands and raise money on the lands. Pakeha settlers may be absolutely without any money at all but they are placed on Government lands, and the Government immediately provides for them with the cash to work the thing to a success" (*AJHR*, 1905, I-3B, p. 4).

The Liberals' policy to increase the supply of, and improve the returns from, land was reinforced by reports from 'experts'. A Government Lands Royal Commission Report in 1905 noted that much unoccupied Native Land in the North Island was producing nothing and paying no rates, but benefitted from the road and rail networks that surrounded it. Some six million acres were deemed suitable for settlement. The report claimed: "The Natives show no disposition to undertake this work [sheep farming] so far as they are concerned, it will probably remain for many years a wilderness" (*AJHR*, 1905, C-4, p. xviii). The report recommended that these lands be acquired for settlement.

While the Liberals justified the selling of Maori land as a means to increase the prosperity of all by developing dormant assets, Maori continued to object to the government's profiteering. One tribe complained in a petition: "Within the Ngatimaniapoto many lands have been sold to the Government, sold from 1s 6d. up to 4s. and 5s. per acre, 7s. per acre being the largest price ever given, and these lands have been resold by the Government to settlers from £1 to £2 10s. per acre. How many millions of pounds have the Government received of profit when the purchased land was from Maoris?" (*AJHR*, 1905, I-3B, p. 17). However, in spite of such protests, The Native Land Act 1909 specifically stated that Maori customary title was not to prevail over the government (Ward 1974, 306).

Liberal rule in New Zealand ended in 1912. The Liberals had endeavoured to ensure a continuous flow of future revenues by leasing to settlers over 750,000 acres of land acquired (*AJHR*, 1920, G-9, pp. 2–3). The Reform Party had come to power, with leader William Massey promising state leaseholders that they could freehold their land (Te Ara 2006). The estimated area of land held by Maori up to World War I was 4,787 million acres (Report of Secretary of Native Affairs, *AJHR*, 1920, G-9, pp. 2–3). Maori landownership had decreased from 30 per cent of New Zealand's land area in the 1890s to 7 per cent in just over thirty years of mostly Liberal government. Grievances remain and despite some restoration efforts by recent governments, Maori are still seeking redress today.

DISCUSSION

The historical case study reveals how Liberal governments and their agents affected the transfer of much remaining Maori land into mostly European ownership. This loss of Maori land occurred at a time of a growing awareness of Maori discontent and expressions of sympathy by the Liberals. Having electioneered by calling for justice to Maori, promising future protection and maintaining a façade of sympathy, successive Liberal governments systematically extracted revenue from Maori at a disproportionate rate. Maori, it proved, were not part of the Liberal's vision of landownership. Although there were few explicit statements to the effect, the plan was to steadily reduce the options of Maori to labour or welfare. Their communistically held land was not considered productive in an economic sense.

The Liberals' policies clearly favoured European settlers. To stay in power, and to sustain their development and welfare policies, the Liberals needed revenue. Maori land was a readily available source with low political risk as most Maori were disenfranchised. Liberal voters tended to be European migrants with ambitions to establish their own farms. With an eye to developing export markets, and an ideology of support for facilitating enterprise and welfare, Liberal governments concurred with settler wishes for low-interest government loans and cheap land. The enactment of these policies did not occur 'without harm' to Maori.

The Liberals appeared as moral but behaved in a ruthless way—through the enactment of expertocracy. Hypocrisy enabled the simultaneous handling of conflicting values—the appearance of serving all interests without presenting the actual doing so as problematic. The three elements—Liberal reformism, hypocrisy and expertocracy—worked together. The politicians professed high-sounding ideals and sympathy for Maori while enacting laws and empowering experts to undertake tasks that contributed to the impoverishment of Maori. For Maori, fighting was no longer a good option, and the 'civilized' political debate was geographically distant and scarcely penetrable to those whose votes did not really count. When their representatives raised issues in Parliament, Maori were 'caressed' while elsewhere being crushed.

Distance between those in parliament and those involved in the actual transfer of land from Maori to mostly European hands is a key element of expertocracy, as evident too in Neu's (Neu and Graham 2004, 2006) studies. Within the legal framework set by successive Liberal governments in New Zealand, accountants can be seen to have utilized both rational methods and discretion. These experts fixed rents for Maori land vested in the Public Trustee but under inactive management and deducted expenses. Incomes and distributions for each tribal block of land were recorded. It could thus be shown that Native assets were yielding very low returns. This is not surprising given that the land was leased at very low rents and extortionate management expenses had to be borne. On the other hand, with demand for land so strong, it was surprising in a market context that the rents should have been set so low. The case was nevertheless made for selling land due to its low returns and the need to increase general prosperity. Expertocracy worked through a legal framework which allowed the undervaluing of Native land, exploited the government's position as a monopoly purchaser, raised transaction costs and utilized the agency of local land boards. By such means, settler demand for land could be satisfied and government revenues augmented. Whatever Maori might have felt about these local experts, the Liberals themselves were able to maintain the appearance of working for the greater prosperity and happiness of Maori while expressing regret for their losses.

CONCLUSION

This chapter has illustrated the implications of accounting in colonial Liberalism. It reveals expertocracy as an important element in implementing the Liberal government reformist agenda which, in this case, was mediated by hypocrisy.

What can be said of the experts who served their colonial masters and of the technologies they employed? First, these experts are less visible and often ignored in conventional histories. Any retrospective blame comes down on whole societies or on governments who can be shown to have acted hypocritically, rather than on experts such as accountants. But these experts were almost certainly interested in and benefitted from the performance of their role. It cannot be said that the accountants were hypocritical although it is likely that they would have known hypocrisy to have been part of the formula of appeasement.

Second, while accounts may convey a sense of facticity and neutrality, both these attributes are suspect. The early accounts in this study did not recognize the contribution made by Maori to government revenues we have outlined. The aggregate figures they present belie the disgruntlement on the part of those Maori forced to disproportionately pay various levies and charges—often associated with works that served to dispossess them of their land. Accounting acts as a key technology in achieving a redistribution of assets, particularly where accounts can be shown to reveal a poor return. Such a result has a narrow focus but presents a distinctive 'objectivity' and a kind of technical fairness.

Third, and finally, accounting experts are an important feature in systems of government. They are shown in this case to have facilitated the generation of more efficient returns through a range of mechanisms, ultimately often by changing ownership of operational assets, as part of a wider governmental programme. Expertocracy fragments responsibility, with hypocrisy shown to be a key element in the New Zealand Liberal formulation of that fragmentation. Hypocrisy functions as a supposedly more humane solution to the problems engendered by conflicting values and an unfair system of redistribution, allowing those in power to be seen to publicly comfort their victims with smooth utterances. The evidence in this chapter shows that hypocrisy can, however, engender more far-reaching and enduring problems than those it seeks to solve.

a monopoly purchaser, raised transaction costs and utilized the agency of local land boards. By such means, settler demand for land could be satisfied and government revenues augmented. Whatever Maori might have felt about these local experts, the Liberals themselves were able to maintain the appearance of working for the greater prosperity and happiness of Maori while expressing regret for their losses.

CONCLUSION

This chapter has illustrated the implications of accounting in colonial Liberalism. It reveals expertocracy as an important element in implementing the Liberal government reformist agenda which, in this case, was mediated by hypocrisy.

What can be said of the experts who served their colonial masters and of the technologies they employed? First, these experts are less visible and often ignored in conventional histories. Any retrospective blame comes down on whole societies or on governments who can be shown to have acted hypocritically, rather than on experts such as accountants. But these experts were almost certainly interested in and benefitted from the performance of their role. It cannot be said that the accountants were hypocritical although it is likely that they would have known hypocrisy to have been part of the formula of appeasement.

Second, while accounts may convey a sense of facticity and neutrality, both these attributes are suspect. The early accounts in this study did not recognize the contribution made by Maori to government revenues we have outlined. The aggregate figures they present belie the disgruntlement on the part of those Maori forced to disproportionately pay various levies and charges—often associated with works that served to dispossess them of their land. Accounting acts as a key technology in achieving a redistribution of assets, particularly where accounts can be shown to reveal a poor return. Such a result has a narrow focus but presents a distinctive 'objectivity' and a kind of technical fairness.

Third, and finally, accounting experts are an important feature in systems of government. They are shown in this case to have facilitated the generation of more efficient returns through a range of mechanisms, ultimately often by changing ownership of operational assets, as part of a wider governmental programme. Expertocracy fragments responsibility, with hypocrisy shown to be a key element in the New Zealand Liberal formulation of that fragmentation. Hypocrisy functions as a supposedly more humane solution to the problems engendered by conflicting values and an unfair system of redistribution, allowing those in power to be seen to publicly comfort their victims with smooth utterances. The evidence in this chapter shows that hypocrisy can, however, engender more far-reaching and enduring problems than those it seeks to solve.

Part IV
Exclusion

10 Women and the Accountancy Profession in England and Wales

Linda M. Kirkham and Anne Loft

INTRODUCTION

This chapter analyses the nature and causes of the exclusion of women from the established accounting profession in England and Wales over the sixty years from 1871 to 1931. The formal processes of professionalization in English accountancy began in the 1870s with the establishment of various local professional associations. In 1880 these merged as the Institute of Chartered Accountants in England and Wales (ICAEW). In 1885 a Society of Incorporated Accountants and Auditors (SIAA) was also formed.[1] The ICAEW and the SIAA were the principal professional organizations during the period studied. Neither of them initially admitted women, who were simply excluded by virtue of their sex. This situation was common among the established professions at the time. But the exclusion of women did not go unchallenged. The activities of organizations such as the Society for Promoting the Employment of Women (established in 1859), female suffrage societies and individual campaigning women ensured that the admission (or not) of women to the accountancy profession was a recurring issue and one which was periodically discussed in the most influential accounting journal of the time, the *Accountant*.

For decades the admission of women was not seriously contemplated by the profession, but by the start of the First World War in 1914 there was extensive pressure from suffrage campaigners for the right of women to enter the professions, including accountancy. During the war millions of men entered the armed forces (Taylor 1970) and many of their jobs were taken over by women, including work in the offices of professional accountants. After the war the Sex Disqualification (Removal) Act, 1919 was passed and the fight for women to enter the professional organizations

This chapter is based on the paper "Gender and the Construction of the Professional Accountant", which originally appeared in *Accounting, Organizations and Society* 18, no. 6 (1993): 507–58. The authors would like to thank the publisher, Elsevier, for permission to use this material.

seemed to have been won. But in accountancy this turned out to be hollow victory; even though women now had the opportunity to join the professional organizations, few did so. In fact by 1931 the census of population identified only 119 women accountants. In that year less than one in a hundred professional accountants were women.

Although this chapter is primarily concerned with women in the accountancy profession, it is also important to consider occupations associated with the accounting function as a whole (Loft 1992). For while women were excluded from the profession many began to work as office clerks and book-keepers during this period—occupations previously dominated by men. Consequentially the discussion of women's exclusion from professional accountancy in the focal period will be accompanied by an analysis of the seemingly parallel development of the rapid rise in the number and proportion of female clerks—from 1 per cent of all clerks in 1871 to 42 per cent in 1931. What was the relationship between the exclusion of women from professional accountancy and their inclusion in offices as clerks and book-keepers?[2] It is argued here that the gendering of these occupations—accountancy as masculine and, increasingly, clerking as feminine—was an important factor in explaining the lack of women professional accountants.

The start and end dates for the study, 1871 and 1931, not only concern a formative period in the professionalization of accounting; they also represent years of the decennial census of population. From the mid-nineteenth century the census in England and Wales[3] recorded information about occupation, and this makes it useful for exploring the occupations of 'accountant' and 'clerk' over time. There are some problems in using these data, the main one being that the system used to classify occupations changed somewhat over time. There could also be potential gender bias in the process of enumeration. For example, enumerators may have assumed that accountancy was a masculine occupation and any woman who reported her occupation as 'accountant' might instead be counted as a clerk or book-keeper (as Strom [1992] suggests for the US).[4] Despite such limitations the published census data represent an important source for tracking the growth and gendering of occupations, as is revealed in Table 10.1 for clerks and accountants.

The focus of this chapter is on public accountancy work in practicing offices[5]—the base for the professionalization of the occupation. In the period up to the First World War it appears that few qualified public accountants worked as employees in commerce and industry. Matthews, Anderson and Edwards (1998, 137–38) estimate that only around 7 per cent of professional accountants worked 'outside' the profession in 1911. The figure was less than 1 per cent for the membership of the ICAEW, which had implicitly proscribed such activity because it was not considered to be 'professional' work. This situation was to change. By 1931 12 per cent of ICAEW members were occupied outside public practice. The figure for

Table 10.1 Number of Women Accountants and Clerks in England and Wales, 1861–1931

Year	Clerks			Accountants		
	Total	Number of women	Women %	Total	Number of women	Women %
1861	92,012	279	0.3	6,239	–	0
1871	130,717	1,446	1.1	9,832	–	0
1881	236,125	6,375	2.7	11,606	89	0.8
1891	370,433	18,892	5.1	7,980	50	0.6
1901	518,900	57,598	11.1	9,028	2	0.02
1911	685,998	124,843	18.2	9,499	19	0.2
1921	998,226	429,921	43.1	7,260	43	0.6
1931	1,375,431	579,945	42.1	13,944	119	0.9

Source: Decennial censuses for England and Wales.

the other major organization in England and Wales, the SIAA, was higher at 38 per cent (ibid.). While the work of the 'professional' accountant was initially closely defined as 'in practice' the growing numbers of clerks were involved in a broad range of activities. By far the majority of clerks worked in industry and commerce. In the profession itself 'clerk work' was done mainly by male articled clerks, though, as we will see, this was to change during the First World War.

The remainder of the chapter will proceed as follows. We begin with a short section on gender and professionalization. Then follows a history of the exclusion of women from the accountancy profession and the attempts to secure their inclusion. This history is organized on a chronological basis. Sections will cover the early to mid-Victorian age, the late-Victorian and Edwardian years, the First World War and the post-war period.

GENDER AND THE PROFESSIONALIZATION OF ACCOUNTANCY

In this chapter the term 'gender' is used to signify more than biological sex, it also refers to the social construction of what it means to be female or male (Oakes and Hammond 1995; Kirkham 1992; Lehman 1992). Scott (1988, 25) goes further, defining gender as "the multiple and contradictory meanings attributed to sexual difference", and uses the term to mean "knowledge about sexual difference" (2). Knowledge in this case is taken to mean more than the social roles designated to men and women; it refers to the understandings produced by societies and cultures of the relationships between men and women. Gender, then, is used to articulate social understandings of sexual difference in specific contexts. It follows from this definition that occupations and activities, as well as people, have gender identities. Moreover, these identities are not dependent on (though they may be related to) the physical persons who practice them, but are produced and reproduced in relation to a wide range of activities, social institutions and organizations, at all levels of society (Scott 1987).

Scott (1988) provides an example of this use of gender when she argues that the Chartist Movement in Britain during the mid-nineteenth century was a 'masculine' movement, and further, that the gendered representation of class that Chartism offered probably contributed to the meaning of class which endured long after the decline of the movement. In the case of the professionalization of accounting, such an approach suggests that we need to examine if the profession was gendered masculine from the start or if it became so under specific circumstances, and if and how this was maintained over the course of the period under investigation. The concept of gender, as used by Scott, also points to a need to address when and how gendered identities of occupations such as accountant and clerk were constituted and reconstituted. It requires an appreciation of the ways in which gender was both a factor in how these occupations developed and in the ways in which women participated in them. An important part of Scott's approach is the connection she makes between the study of language and gender, in particular the creation of meaning through differentiation. She argues that if meaning is constructed in terms of difference by distinguishing implicitly or explicitly what something is from what it is not, then sexual difference becomes an important way of specifying or establishing meaning (Scott 1988, 55).

A good example of this is a comment made in the *Accountant* on 21 April 1917: "There is as much difference between a bookkeeper and an accountant as there is between a nurse and a doctor, or between a dental mechanic and a dentist". Nurses were gendered feminine, and the commentator uses this fact to convince the reader that book-keepers are feminine, and also compares the dental mechanic, who was not a professional like the dentist (who in this case was almost certainly male).

To summarize, in this chapter we are concerned as much with the definition and meaning of the label 'accountant' as with the organization and practice of professional work. We do not assume that the gender of accountants or other categories of worker (in particular clerks), was, or is, fixed.[6] Rather we seek to explore some of the ways in which gender processes contributed to the shifting meaning of the 'accountant' during the period 1871–1931: how it came to be gendered masculine, and how clerking and book-keeping work, became feminine.

THE EARLY AND MID-VICTORIAN PERIOD, 1837–1870

During early industrialization in England and Wales there was a transformation in the nature of employment as many tasks moved out of the home and into factories and workshops. As industry and commerce expanded, the occupation of accountant developed. At first the occupational identity of the accountant was unclear. Chatfield (1977) wrote that a self-styled "expert in accounts" might be a book-keeper, appraiser, attorney, actuary, bankruptcy auditor, executor of estates, a winder-up of dissolved companies or a combination of these. He was, however, "invariably a man" (113). As shown in Table 10.1, the 1861 census reported 6,239 accountants, all of whom were men. This was a motley group. It appears that while some accountants were held in high esteem for their expertise and legal knowledge (Howitt 1966, 4), others using the title "acted merely as clerks" (Chatfield 1977, 113).[7] Established professions at this time did not admit women to their ranks. However, some women were beginning to campaign for this right. One of the most well-known cases of challenges to exclusion was that of Elizabeth Garrett. Not allowed to attend university, she studied privately to become an apothecary. Having passed its examinations the Society of Apothecaries gave Garrett a license to practice in 1865 but then changed its constitution to prevent any other women from becoming members (Hollis 1979, 49).

The white-collar occupation of clerk was held in high regard during this period. Until the second half of the nineteenth century the occupation was still fairly limited in number, with 92,012 clerks identified in the 1861 census. The typical clerk started work as an apprentice, performing menial tasks on a very low salary. However, he might gradually work his way up through the office hierarchy (Anderson 1976). In the mid-nineteenth century there were very few women clerks. The 1851 census counted only nineteen, rising to 279 ten years later. It was difficult for women to enter clerkdom. Few working-class women received an adequate education for such work. Middle-class women may have received sufficient education but as 'ladies' were considered too delicate and sensitive for the public world of work. The contemporary assumption was that their skills would be deployed in the domestic realm. So although some women's rights campaigners saw clerking as potentially a good job for an unmarried woman, it was almost impossible to enter, a situation that male clerks were anxious to maintain. The occupations of both accountancy and clerking were therefore gendered masculine in this period.

THE LATE VICTORIAN AND EDWARDIAN PERIOD, 1871–1913

As indicated earlier, from 1870 the elite accountants in England and Wales began to form local associations and these were consolidated as a national body, the ICAEW, in 1880. In 1885 a second national body was established, the SIAA. Both organizations were only open to men. A number of closure devices were instigated. Once the founders had been admitted future aspirant members had to jump a series of hurdles to join. First a premium had to be paid for taking articles (copying long-established professions such as the law), and examinations had to be passed. The cost of becoming a member of the profession *de facto* (if not *de jure*) made it virtually impossible for working-class men to obtain admission.

The Education Act of 1870 ensured that a basic elementary education was available to all children. Along with the growth of secondary education and the rapid growth in commercial courses at various institutions these developments provided greater access to the knowledge required of the Victorian clerk—literacy, numeracy and business skills. During this period, characterized by the maturing of the industrial economy and the growing size and complexity of businesses, the number of clerks recorded in the decennial census grew from 130,717 in 1871 to 685,998 in 1911 (see Table 10.1). The growth in the number of clerks during these forty years was far greater than that of the occupied population as a whole. The social status of the clerk fell slowly but surely during this period, and women, who were attractive to employers because they could be paid less than men, entered the occupation in increasing numbers. In 1871 only 1.1 per cent of clerks were women, but by 1911 the figure had risen to 18.2 per cent (see Table 10.1). Detailed study of the census reveals that virtually all the female commercial and business clerks in 1911 were single, and 95 per cent of them were under the age of thirty-five (Anderson 1988, 10). A gender hierarchy in clerical work was being established; the woman clerk was young and single, paid less than her male counterparts and expected to leave the labour market when she married. A process was occurring where clerking, especially at its lowest levels, was gradually becoming gendered feminine. The first typewriters were operated by men, but this job in particular rapidly became women's work.

It was during this period that the issue of the admission of women to the accountancy profession first arose. The SIAA discussed the matter at its annual meetings in 1889 and 1891. During these debates, speakers argued in terms of the difference between women's 'natural' abilities and the qualities of an accountant. It was suggested that: "accountancy was amongst those professions which required for their proper fulfilment those masculine qualities and experience of the world and intellectual capacity and courage which were rarely to be found in members of the weaker sex" (quoted in Garrett 1961, 7). Women were not physically or psychologically equipped for the rigours of public accountancy. Not surprisingly, the exclusively male membership voted against the admission of women. When the issue was publicly discussed by the ICAEW in 1895 it was treated with a lack of seriousness and was summarily dismissed. The response of the president was to claim that "it would be so embarrassing to manage a staff composed partly of women, that he would rather retire from the profession than contemplate such a position". His comments were greeted with "loud laughter" (Howitt 1966, 54).

Another indication of contemporary male opinion is offered by Richard Brown in his *History of Accounting and Accountants* published in 1905. On the subject of the role of women in public accountant's offices he observed: "with all respect for the undoubted genius of women, it may be questioned if their faculties are at all specially adapted for accountants' work at large . . . Of course, hundreds of women find employment as typists—and to a less extent as clerks in accountant's offices, and their patience and manual dexterity seem to fit them admirably for routine and mechanical work" (1905/1968, 331). Clearly, 'patience' and 'manual dexterity' were being discursively connected to the occupation of clerk, and at the same time identified as feminine characteristics. No longer was the clerk purely gendered masculine.

What were the faculties required of a professional accountant? An answer to this was given in 1909 by the Earl of Chichester when he introduced the 'Professional Accountants Bill' to Parliament. This measure aimed to close the profession by the registration of ICAEW and SIAA members. The Earl suggested that it was necessary for accountants to be "men of great integrity and force of character". In the same speech he noted that provision had been made in the bill for the admission of women, but suggested that "it does not appear that the profession of accountancy would be particularly attractive to members of the opposite sex" (House of Lords, 15 July 1909, s.561–65). For members of the ICAEW and SIAA the provision in the bill for the admission of women was a small price to pay for achieving the greater goal of statutory registration of the profession. However, the measure did not succeed. Neither did another bill put forward in 1911.

Gendered discourse thus did not only serve to legitimate the exclusion of women; it was part of the process of constructing the meaning of professional accountancy vis-à-vis other occupations, in particular that of clerk. Gender was thus discursively implicated in the construction of the professional accountant on at least two, interrelated levels. First, it was used to establish the meaning of accountancy work and signify its importance and nature. Second, by reinforcing and utilizing prevailing concepts of gender, such discourse served as legitimation for excluding or limiting the participation of women, and some men, in the profession.

As the ICAEW and SIAA pursued social closure and erected barriers to entry, such as premiums (and very low or no pay during articles) and fees for admission, those unable to gain access looked to the formation of new professional bodies with a more meritocratic basis of entry. One such organization was the London Association of Accountants, founded in 1904 (LAA[8]). Such organizations, perceived as 'lesser', 'outside bodies' by the established professional elite, provided an opportunity for prospective women accountants to further their claims. In May 1909, at the time when the Professional Accountants Bill was being introduced by the Earl of Chichester, the LAA admitted Ethel Ayres Purdie, a "lady in public practice" to membership. Two years previously she had been refused admission to the ICAEW (ACCA 1954, 11). Ethel Ayres Purdie was a suffragist and an active member of the Women's Freedom League, which at the time was pressing hard for women to gain access to the accounting profession. There was a clear coincidence of interests between the LAA and suffragists in that both wanted to challenge the established accounting profession represented by the ICAEW and the SIAA. Ethel Ayres Purdie was later described as having "not infrequently rendered useful service to the LAA" as she "attracted the attention of the national press and did not hesitate on each and every occasion to give her candid opinion of the other two accountancy bodies" (*Certified Accountants Journal*, February 1919, 14; ACCA 1954, 11).

A characteristic of this period was that while women's organizations fought to gain the admission of women to the profession, the response of the ICAEW and SIAA was that their 'natural' qualities did not fit with those required of a professional accountant. At the same time more and more women were employed in commerce and industry as clerks and book-keepers, even in the offices of accountants themselves. By the eve of the First World War, the 'professional accountant' had consolidated a distinctively masculine identity. The 'clerk', however, was an ambiguous construct; its previous masculine gender was being contested and its feminine elements were becoming more prominent.

THE FIRST WORLD WAR, 1914–1918

During this period of national trauma the foundations of the exclusion of women came into question. When women were employed to fill the places vacated by accountants and articled clerks who had gone to fight, they revealed their capacity to do work previously denied to them. But the story is more complex than that, and a new range of discourses about work and the women who performed it were articulated in ways which acted to keep them outside of the profession.

The First World War brought major changes to British society and institutions. In the four years of conflict, the mass of British people became, in the words of the eminent historian A.J.P. Taylor, "active citizens" whose lives were shaped by orders from above (1970, 26). In January 1915 recruiting posters appeared with the message "Women of England! Do your duty! Send your man *Today* to Join our Glorious Army" (Stevenson 1984, 62). But far more was to be asked of women than just sending their men off to fight. As five million men entered the armed forces many of their places in factories and offices were taken by women. Over the period from July 1914 to July 1918 the number of women identified as working in commerce rose from just over 500,000 to 930,000 (Davidoff and Westover 1986, 20).

In October 1915, a letter of advice was sent to the associations of employers of clerical labour (including the ICAEW and SIAA). The government's Clerical and Commercial Employments Committee stressed "the desirability of giving preference in employment to the women relations of enlisted men" (Cd. 8110, 1915, 11). Not only did such a strategy provide an economic role for women; it was also a means of creating the conditions for their return to the home once the emergency had passed. The committee was anxious to emphasize that women's employment was to be only temporary and, in the case of a wife replacing her husband, his return might be expected to cause no resistance (ibid., 5). Under the conditions of war, lower-level clerks' work was not only becoming work which women might perform, but also 'women's work'. The committee also recognized, though, that relatives and friends of servicemen could not supply all the skills required and that it would be necessary to attract women "of superior education". It advised that "every effort should be made to attract this kind of woman into the work", but that the "temporary character of the work, that is for the duration of the war only, should be made quite clear" (Cd. 8110, 1915, 8).

War changed accountancy. It gave it a new importance as the government tried to prevent profiteering by manufacturers and the distributors of items needed for the war. Regulations from 1915 onwards brought production increasingly under the control of the war ministries, new pricing structures for war production were implemented and new taxes were introduced to curb burgeoning war profits and bolster government finances (Loft 1986). All these measures created work for accountants and their clerks, but many had already volunteered to fight and others went to work in government departments. In November 1915 the *Accountant* reported that about 25 per cent of ICAEW members of military age had "joined the colours" and about two-thirds of articled clerks had enlisted along with "a very considerable number" of the rest of the staff (20 November 1915, 601). There was a 'manpower' shortage in accountants' offices. Before the war women were only employed in the offices of practicing public accountants in a limited capacity, mainly as typists, and in some cases as clerks (*Accountant*, 22 January 1916, 114–16; Brown 1905/1968). This was to change.

The employment of women in accounting firms was already an issue by August 1915 when the *Incorporated Accountants' Journal* published an article entitled "War and the Accountancy Profession". Here it was noted that women were "being employed to do work other than that with which they have usually been associated". While this was recognized as a temporary expedient, the author was of the view that these developments seemed to raise: "a wider question as to whether accountancy had a permanent place for women in its work, not, we believe, to displace the men who are serving the country nor even the younger men who are still to come on, but if at all, alongside and with them" (249).

Similar discussions about women potentially joining the profession surfaced elsewhere, but during the ensuing years the discourse shifted. While women were indeed encouraged to take on accountancy work, in doing so they were not referred to as accountants, but rather as 'lady clerks', 'women clerks', 'women working in accountants' offices', 'lady assistants' or 'lady audit clerks'. They were discursively signified first and foremost by their sex and also identified as a separate category of employee. This separateness may well have been reinforced through their conditions of work. For example, a Miss Catherine Conlin was described as having entered a chartered accountant's office in early 1917 with four years' experience as a secretary, four as a book-keeper and one as senior lady clerk in a tax office. She was placed in charge of a staff of about a dozen "young ladies" (*Accountant*, 16 January 1918, 75). The construction of women working in accountants' offices as 'lady clerks' singled them out as different from men doing the same work. This, despite the fact that there is evidence that women were doing the sorts of jobs which male articled clerks and accountants had performed before the war. In Manchester, for example, it was reported that "several well known firms of accountants have appointed women as audit clerks, and intend sending them out to commercial houses and business establishments for the auditing of their books" (*Accountant*, 18 March 1916). Further enquiries by the *Accountant* revealed that in one case the employment of women had enabled the firm to undertake an enormous amount of government work in addition to its usual business, and that the clients were very satisfied with the work performed (20 May 1916).

Training became a sensitive issue. While the profession managed to recruit well-educated women, these women needed knowledge and skills in accounting. The problem was articulated by the *Accountant* in May 1916 when it observed that "outside professional circles" there existed practically "no education schemes whatsoever" (13 May 1916, 545–47; Lehman 1992, 269). It was suggested that the various chartered accountants students' societies in England and Wales should consider "extending their educational facilities to non-articled clerks, irrespective of sex". This would have two benefits—fill up half-empty classes (many articled clerks had left for the war) and enable young women employed in accountants' offices to be made "really efficient for the purposes for which they have been engaged". It was noted that such classes had been opened to women in Scotland (*Accountant*, 13 May 1916, 545–47). However, this issue remained unresolved at the end of 1917 when the *Accountant* noted that none of the Students' Societies in England had opened their doors to women. The London Students' Society in particular was heavily criticized as "it was supported by members in practice who would benefit if women could attend classes", and all that was required by the Society was an announcement that the classes would be "open to non-articled clerks, as well as articled clerks of Chartered Accountants, irrespective of sex" (29 December 1917, 493–95). The London Students' Society insisted that this was not possible as it would require a change to its constitution and this would require consulting all the members, many of whom were on active service (9 February 1918). The *Accountant* responded that such objections were unfounded and what was required was only a "special concession to meet a special urgency", referring to it as a "small matter" (16 February 1918, 139–40). The London Student's Society obviously did not think that this was a "small matter", perceiving that such a move would imply that women clerks would gain levels of competence resembling that of male articled clerks.

Despite such resistance by the next generation of chartered accountants, a wider debate about the entry of women to the professions had commenced. In 1917 the Chartered Institute of Secretaries rescinded an earlier resolution not to admit women, and a series of letters in the accountancy press reported the progress of women solicitors, women barristers, women stockbrokers and women accountants in 'outside societies' (i.e., not the ICAEW or SIAA). The *Accountant* suggested to readers a "careful perusal" of an article reprinted from the *Times* in which it was argued that while women should have the possibility of admission to the legal profession "the bulk of womankind are less well equipped by nature than a corresponding number of men with the logical qualities of mind and the great physical strength demanded by the highest work in the legal profession" (3 February 1917, 105, 121). So, despite the advances in women's employment during the war, gendered discourse continued to be invoked in ways which signified women's 'natural weaknesses', and the accountancy profession's similarity to the legal profession where traditional views remained.

Little seemed to have changed on the question of the admission of women to the established accountancy organizations in England and Wales, but in the last years of the war developments were taking place beyond the control of the profession. Legislative changes were being proposed which would extend the franchise to women and various organizations were advocating strongly that women should be allowed to enter all professions. Examples were given of women gaining some of the highest places in mathematical and medical degree courses and thereby demonstrating their abilities in numerical, masculine disciplines. This made it difficult to argue that they were incapable of becoming accountants. Confronted with the inevitable, in autumn 1918 the SIAA voted to amend its constitution to permit the admission of women to membership (Lehman 1992, 296; Garrett 1961, 112–13). Ethel Ayres Purdie reported this decision in an article in the *Vote* entitled "Why Be Grateful? Women and the Society of Incorporated Accountants". Here she pointed out that because Liberal and Labour Party leaders had adopted a policy of the admission of women to all professions on equal terms, the Society could never hope to carry any measures relating to the protection of the profession through Parliament whilst excluding women. Hence, she described the decision to admit women as a matter of expediency (*Vote*, 24 January 1919, 62). The ICAEW was not to admit women until forced to do so by the passage of the Sex Disqualification (Removal) Act in 1919.

During the First World War gender boundaries in accounting were restructured, women began to enter the citadel—the offices of professional accountants—to do more than typing and simple clerical work. However, their contribution had been discursively defined as different and temporary, and structural barriers to gaining access to professional training reinforced this definition. One consequence was that the conditions had been created in which it was possible to dispute whether women had been involved in "accountancy work" at all (*Accountant*, 26 October 1918, 231). Just nine days before the Armistice on 11 November 1918, when peace talks were in progress, the *Accountant* asked what was to happen to the "somewhat large" class of women who had, during the previous four years:

> Been actively engaged in professional accountancy, some of whom doubtless have already acquired a considerable amount of experience and knowledge of professional subjects, without having gone through, or having been through, the formality of articles. Are these now going to be asked to go back to the beginning, and take their articles from the present time, or will they be given credit for their past service as service under articles? (2 November 1918, 234)

No answer was forthcoming, and in the turmoil of post-war reconstruction the issue was not revisited by the *Accountant*.

THE POST-WAR PERIOD, 1919–1930

In 1918 the Representation of the People Act enfranchised women aged over thirty and in 1919 the Sex Disqualification (Removal) Act secured women's right to become members of the ICAEW, SIAA or any other accounting professional association. The statute provided that no person should be disqualified from the exercise of any public function or appointment by virtue of their sex or marriage. Women could now even enter the highest ranks of the civil service (Stevenson 1984, 85). Despite this there were still men in the accountancy profession who argued that women should not be admitted. For example in a letter published in the *Accountant* it was argued that admitting women would "not tend to raise the dignity of our profession" and that "the Institute has no place for feminism" (10 May 1919, 384).

When the war ended there was jubilation and hope for a better future, but the ambitious plans for post-war reconstruction rapidly ran into difficulties. After a short post-war economic boom in the economy, there was a slump (Johnson 1968). Zimmeck (1988b, 4–5) writes that following the Armistice ex-servicemen "campaigned for employment in the battlefield style to which they were accustomed". Their goal was to achieve full employment for themselves as soon as possible, and one of their major targets were those 'selfish' women who preferred "to wield a pencil when [they] might have wheeled a pram" (ibid.). The gendered rhetoric which portrayed ex-servicemen as the epitome of masculine warriors, waiting for 'homes fit for heroes' had a powerful impact. Zimmeck describes demobilization as "not so much a relaxation into normalcy as an attempt to recreate it by main force" (1988, 89).

While the plight of women who had worked in accounting during the war was being ignored, the discussion began to focus on the special exemptions to be given to ex-servicemen who had been, or wanted to become, articled clerks. A discourse emerged which linked male military service with new routes to professional qualification. "Soldier accountants" (*Accountant*, 17 May 1919, 410) were considered to be deserving of favourable conditions in order to encourage and facilitate their return to the profession. The state was actively involved in the process of privileging soldier accountants through its training grants, and in 1921 it was noted that nearly half of the successful candidates at the Final Examination of the ICAEW were trained under this scheme. Many soldier accountants had less accountancy experience than the women who had worked in accounting firms during the war. However, having been discursively constructed as "lady clerks" (and not articled clerks) it was easy to dismiss their skills. While they had gained the right to become professional accountants, no special allowances were made for the 'ladies' on the basis of their contribution to the war. If they were able to gain a position as an articled clerk (which was not certain), then they, or rather their parents, would have to pay the full premium to train.

Little seems to have been written about what happened to the 'lady clerks' who worked in accounting firms during the war. The 'ladies' disappeared from the discussion. An exception is a remark contained in the history of Touche Ross. Here it is related that in the firm's London office: "during the war women had carried out 'international office duties'" and that after the war "women were retained as shorthand writers, typists, and telephonists, but the remainder were gradually replaced by men returning from the Forces" (Swanson 1972, 27).

By the end of the war the accountancy profession was firmly established as a profession (and received official recognition as such during the war). Its status was no doubt enhanced by the important work its members had performed for the government during the war. The profession of 'accountant' in England and Wales had come to be defined around the membership of the two dominant organizations, the ICAEW and SIAA. In preparation for the 1921 census the classification of occupations was revised extensively. Accountants were now classified as members of the highest group, 'social class 1', and the number of accountants thus enumerated was 7,260.[9] In this period the number of clerks rose tenfold, and while they were defined as in social class 1 in 1911, in 1921 they went down to class 2 and in 1931 to class 3. In 1921 only 0.6 per cent of accountants enumerated by the census were female. By contrast, the proportion of clerks who were women had increased from 18.2 per cent in 1911 to 43.1 per cent.

Beyond the profession, in commerce and industry, although many women clerks were expelled from their positions to make room for men, according to Walby (1986, 164–70), they did not suffer the total expulsion experienced by women in some fields, notably engineering. An interview with a clerk working at the time throws light on the role of women in factory offices during the 1920s. Ernest Laidler started work at the age of sixteen in the office at Armstrong Whitworth and Co. (Iron Founders) in 1924, remaining there until 1930. On arrival he received low wages while being trained to do a variety of office jobs. His salary was increased by small increments until he reached adulthood. On "becoming a man" he received "the large sum of about £2 10s 0d". Laidler commented how he was later: "put in charge of wages; I had about five girls under me. Most of the clerks in the office were girls. Incidentally they weren't moved around like I was to get experience; they normally stayed at what they were doing. Usually they left when they got married" (interview with Loft, 1984, quoted in Loft 1990, 134–35). The gendered discourse here suggests not only limited career mobility for women and the operation of the marriage bar, but also that becoming a 'man' discursively prevented a woman from obtaining a more senior position. The description also fits well with others of the time. Women's work in the office was generally of a menial nature and becoming increasingly routinized.

As Table 10.1 shows, the Sex Discrimination (Removal) Act, 1919 had little impact on opening the accountancy profession to women by 1931. Women represented less than 1 per cent of accountants enumerated in the census of that year. While the act outlawed the exclusion of women from membership of professional organizations, it did little to facilitate their access to systems of vocational preparation such as articled clerkship. The profession was still gendered masculine, and informal barriers to entry operated in ways which effectively excluded most women. It is notable that a number of the women who did become professional accountants at this time had fathers or other male relatives who were chartered or incorporated accountants, or could boast other close connections to the profession. Some women accountants began to practice on their own account rather than work in established, male-dominated firms. By 1931 it was much more common to find a woman typist in an accounting firm than a woman accountant.

CONCLUSION

The period from 1871 to 1931 witnessed major changes in society and in the occupation of accountant. At the beginning of the period the accountancy profession in England and Wales began to organize, and, in common with other professions at the time, it did not admit women to its ranks. In fact it was not until after the First World War that women gained the right to become professional accountants. Despite this victory, few were able to take up the opportunity. The word 'exclusion' summarized most women's experiences of the accounting profession throughout the focal period. Where women did advance and secure 'inclusion' was in the menial branches of accounting work performed by clerks and book-keepers. In this chapter we have analysed how this gendered exclusion/inclusion in the accounting sphere developed from the late nineteenth to the early twentieth century.

Our study has shown that the professionalization of accountancy was not only furthered through the use of a discourse which gendered the profession masculine, but also one which gendered clerks and book-keepers feminine. In this way professional accountants were situated discursively at the head of occupational and gender hierarchies. As clerking and book-keeping became increasingly feminized and downgraded in social status, the principal qualifying associations were given the discursive 'ammunition' to define women and lower-class men as unsuitable for the profession of accounting.

By 1931 accountancy had become firmly established as a profession in England and Wales. We have shown that a key factor in the success of the professionalization project was the creation and maintenance of a masculine identity for the professional accountant. The discursive construction of types of accounting work and the classes of people performing them in terms of equivalences and non-equivalences were important ways in which accountancy came to be constituted as both professional and men's work. The rise of the accounting profession and its exclusion of women became connected to the inclusion of women and declining status of clerical work. The professional accountant had become constituted, in part, as someone who was not a clerk or book-keeper and very rarely a woman. Indeed, it was not until after the late 1970s that women entered the accountancy profession in large numbers, and this was at least partly related to the passing of sex discrimination legislation. Both of the authors of this chapter entered the profession at this time, when women were relatively rare in accounting firms, and when managers might be heard ringing clients to ask whether they had any objection to their audit being carried out by a woman. As late as 1978 a woman was not quite the same as a man when it came to being a professional accountant!

NOTES

1. The SIAA (by this time the Society of Incorporated Accountants [SIA]) was merged with the ICAEW in 1957.
2. Book-keepers are of particular interest here as being, in a sense, 'more' than a clerk, but 'less' than an accountant. Before the Great War the occupation had an ambiguous gender. For a detailed study see Walker (2003b). For accounting work performed by women in the private sphere see Walker (1998); Walker and Llewellyn (2000); Kirkham and Loft (2001).
3. The history of women in the Scottish or Irish accounting professions is not within the scope of the current study. For Scotland, see Shackleton (1999).
4. The nature and role of the census is dealt with in more detail in Kirkham and Loft (2004).
5. Some of the accountancy firms became quite large and sophisticated in this period, one of the most prominent of these being Cooper Brothers and Co. (1954/1986).

6. For further discussion of the concept of gender and its usage, see Khalifa and Kirkham (2009).
7. For more on the formation of the profession in this era, see Walker (2004b).
8. Following several mergers the LAA eventually became what is known today as the Association of Chartered Certified Accountants (ACCA).
9. Once members working abroad or retired are taken into account this figure was close to the total membership of the ICAEW (5,640) and SIAA (3,300).

11 African Americans and Certified Public Accounting

Theresa Hammond and Denise W. Streeter

INTRODUCTION

While there has been little attention to the shortage of African Americans in the profession (for exceptions, see Mitchell 1969; Hammond 2002), those studies that do exist indicate that, throughout the history of certified public accountancy, racial discrimination has prevented African Americans from full participation in the field and, despite some progress since the 1960s, the percentage of CPAs who are African American has never exceeded 1 per cent.

When studying exclusion, the accounting literature has not adequately addressed the importance of examining *individual* experiences to understanding the field. It should be recognized that history is most often told by the dominant group, and that group generally elides or ignores the experiences of the less powerful (Gates Jr. 1989; Hammond and Oakes 1992; Hammond and Preston 1992; b. hooks 1981; Kirkham 1992; Kondo 1990). While the history of subordinate groups cannot be eradicated, eliding this history serves many purposes. One such purpose is to lend legitimacy to the group whose history is being told. Given the ideology of equality that has been a major tenet of US history, occupations have an interest in appearing to grant equality of access (Abbott 1988; Bledstein 1976; Davis 1949). This is particularly true of those occupations with government sanctions. Federal and state governments have provided CPAs with a monopoly of audit services. Certified *public* accountants are perceived as serving the public interest and are charged with protecting community members from mismanagement. In order to maintain legitimacy and their government mandate, CPAs must appear to fulfil their altruistic role, which precludes restricting entry (Roberts and Coutts 1992, 382). In order to maintain this

This chapter is based on the paper "Overcoming Barriers: Early African American Certified Public Accountants", which appeared in *Accounting, Organizations and Society* 19, no. 3 (1994): 271–88. The authors would like to thank the publisher, Elsevier, for permission to use this material.

appearance, the barriers to entering the public accounting field have been obscured in most histories of accounting.

Just as it is a mistake to treat public accountants as a homogeneous group, ignoring the experiences of white women and people of colour, it is also in error to treat African-American CPAs as a unified whole. Gathering individual experiences is critical to furthering our understanding of accounting, but this type of particularistic history is lacking in the accounting literature. Inviting informants to voice their own experiences is especially important to documenting the history of dispossessed groups.

The term 'white-collar occupation' may derive from the hue of someone's shirt, but it also indicates the skin colour of the typical occupant of the occupation. Throughout US history, a distinction has been drawn between the type of work considered appropriate for whites and that considered appropriate for blacks. The typical distinction is between physical and mental labour, with arduous physical labour often being termed "Negro work" (Johnson 1938, 251). This interpretation has trenchant roots: enslaved Africans and their descendants were not allowed to read or write, and they typically performed labour considered unfit for white workers.

In order to best determine the impact of racism in public accounting as well as respond to the need for more particularistic research, our main data source is interviews with African Americans who earned their CPA qualification prior to 1965. We build on a 1990 study conducted by the National Association of Black Accountants that identified the first one hundred African-American CPAs (Streeter 1990). We contacted most of those who were still living and performed extensive in-person or telephone interviews. We supplemented this information with literature on African American accountants contemporaneous with the period under study.

EARLY AFRICAN-AMERICAN ACCOUNTANTS

The years prior to the passage of the Civil Rights Act of 1964, which outlawed racial discrimination in employment, included some dramatic periods for African-American progress in education and vocational opportunity. In 1947, as a result of massive political pressure, President Harry Truman desegregated the armed forces (Hamilton 1991). In 1954, with *Brown v. Board of Education*, the US Supreme Court struck down the 1896 'separate but equal' decision in *Plessy v. Ferguson*, which had paved the way for the Jim Crow laws that promoted racial segregation and discrimination.

However, progress in these areas apparently did not have a discernable impact on certified public accountancy. While public-sector occupations could begin to be desegregated with an executive order or Supreme Court decision, entrance to the field of certified public accountancy was controlled by state societies of CPAs. Individual CPAs had unusual power in controlling ingress to the field, because most states required prospective CPAs to serve a one- to three-year apprenticeship supervised by a certified public accountant. This, in conjunction with the federal requirement that publicly traded firms be audited annually by a CPA, gave certified public accountants a monopoly over lucrative accounting practices and effectively excluded African Americans as well as other minority group members and women of all races (Lehman 1992). This chapter now turns to an exploration of the ways these restrictions affected aspiring African-American CPAs by sharing their individual stories.

1914–1940

The first African-American CPA, John Cromwell, Jr., earned his certificate in 1921 (interview with Cromwell, 1992; Previts and Merino 1979; Streeter 1990). Other African Americans had attempted to earn the CPA before this time, but to no avail, as indicated by this response to a 1933 survey of African-American public accountants:

> Immediately after graduation from university in 1914, I applied to take the C.P.A. examination . . . However I could not meet the requirement of the law which provided that all applicants must have three years of practical experience with a firm of certified public accountants. You can realize the fact that it was impossible for me to meet this provision because white firms would not employ me and there were no negro firms of certified public accountants. (Martin 1933, 116)

Similar conditions persisted for several decades. By 1935, there were only five African-American CPAs; by 1945, there were only nine (Hammond 2002). The few who earned their certificates before World War II, including John Cromwell, overcame the barriers to becoming CPAs through extraordinary means.

Cromwell's background was not typical for an African American. His father, though born a slave, had become unusually wealthy; he was a lawyer and newspaper publisher in Washington DC (Simmons 1887). John Cromwell Jr.'s older sister was the first black graduate of Smith College, an exclusive women's college, and she became an English professor (Levy 1971). This family background provided Cromwell with contacts and financial resources available to few other African Americans.

In addition to the prestige and wealth of his family, Cromwell was also an exceptional student. He graduated Phi Beta Kappa from Dartmouth College in 1906 and earned a master's degree in 1907. However, despite these advantages, he was apparently unable to sit for the CPA examination in Washington DC. Instead, he took the CPA exam in New Hampshire in 1921, the first year it was offered in that state. Due to the newness of the certification, there was no experience requirement. Now in his late thirties,

Cromwell decided to take the examination, even though he returned to Washington DC after completing his education. His daughter surmised that he had connections in New Hampshire from his days at Dartmouth who facilitated his efforts to become a CPA (interview with Cromwell, 1992).

From the beginning, Cromwell's race dramatically affected his career. Like most African-American professionals, Cromwell worked within the African-American community in Washington DC. He handled accounts for churches, lawyers, restaurants and funeral homes, and, in 1930, became comptroller of Howard University (Streeter 1990, 20). His wealthy background, exceptional ability and opportunity in New Hampshire enabled him to overcome impediments others found insurmountable.

The experience of Chauncey Christian in 1926, the third African American to earn the CPA qualification, also indicates the unusual characteristics the profession required of African Americans. Although he did not have the advantage of family wealth, Christian's fair skin colour made him appear to be white. When he wanted to take the CPA examination in Kentucky, he was advised to "submit his application to a specific person as late as possible on the last day of registration so as to preclude the background check which would have resulted in his exclusion due to race" (Streeter 1990, p. 21).

The person to whom he submitted his application was a white man for whom Chauncey Christian had worked. Christian, whose father was white and mother was of African descent, did not attract notice at the examination site. However, because according to Kentucky law he was a 'Negro' (most Southern and some Northern states defined anyone with a 'drop' of black blood as a 'Negro'[Davis 1991]), a background check of his educational credentials would have revealed his "race" because he had gone to segregated schools (interview with Christian, 1992; for discussions of skin colour, see Davis 1991; Lawrence-Lightfoot 1988).

Like John Cromwell, Chauncey Christian also worked within the African-American community. He moved his family to Harlem, where he was a tax consultant to many African-American entertainers (interview with Christian, 1992).

Theodora Rutherford, a contemporary of John W. Cromwell and Chauncey Christian, took a longer road in reaching her goal to become a CPA. She attended Howard University in Washington DC, the historically black college where John Cromwell would later work. There, she was inspired and mentored by the instructor who taught all her accounting classes, O.C. Thornton. Although Thornton had found it impossible to meet the requirements to become a CPA, he held the certification out as the highest achievement in the profession and strongly encouraged his students to pursue the qualification. As she said in an interview, "I wanted to be a CPA from the moment I met O.C. Thornton" (interview with Rutherford, 1992). In 1923, she graduated from Howard with highest honours at the age of nineteen. She graduated from Columbia University in New York City the following year, the first African American to earn a master's degree in business at the university. However, she was unable to find a position with a CPA firm, which was necessary to become a CPA in New York. Instead, she taught at a black college in West Virginia. After decades of teaching, West Virginia amended its CPA requirements so that those with master's degrees did not need to meet an experience requirement. Theodora Rutherford earned her CPA in 1960, thirty-six years after finishing her formal education. Despite the delay, she was the first African-American CPA in West Virginia (interview with Rutherford, 1992; Streeter 1990).

In 1933 I.M. Martin, an African-American businessman and leader in Philadelphia, conducted a survey of black accountants for an article in the *Journal of Accountancy*. The survey revealed that while many of them had some white clients, the vast majority worked for African American–owned firms. Martin recognized that the paucity of African-American public accountants and the curriculum at historically African-American colleges were linked. He noted that although there were fifty-four African-American colleges in the US in 1933, only twenty of them offered any accounting courses, and few offered courses in auditing, cost accounting or income tax. Since 97 per cent of African Americans in college at this time attended African-American institutions (Blackwell 1987), the number of qualified African-American accounting graduates was unlikely to increase.

Martin recognized the special problems African Americans faced in attempting to enter the public accounting field. He acknowledged that obtaining a CPA was a prerequisite for establishing a lucrative practice. He also realized that African Americans faced problems gaining the experience that was often necessary to sit for the CPA examination:

> It is very difficult for the colored man to gain employment with a reputable firm of public accountants. This difficulty is caused by the belief of accounting firms that their clients' employees will object to having a colored man come into their office to examine their books.
>
> One finds a growing tendency on the part of various states to restrict the practice of accountancy. In many instances where the colored accountant could not obtain employment with an accounting firm he has been able to open up an office and practise [*sic*] for himself. The restrictive laws prevent him from doing this unless he is certified. Most states require the applicant to obtain a certain amount of experience with a C.P.A. in order to qualify for the examination. Unless there is a colored C.P.A. in that state or a white accountant who will give him the opportunity to meet these requirements, the young colored accountant is practically excluded from the practice of his profession. (Martin 1933, 114–115)

Although he clearly recognized the inequities facing African-American accountants, Martin's recommendations for mitigating this problem barely hinted that action was needed on the part of the white accountants who comprised the majority of *Journal of Accountancy* readers. Instead, he concluded:

> The field of public accounting will continue to be the most difficult one for colored men for some time to come. The colored public accountant today is in the same position as the colored doctor or lawyer was twenty-five years ago. He must do a great deal of pioneer work before he is properly recognized. However, the information gathered during this survey indicated that the field of public accounting is practically untouched as far as the colored man is concerned. The real development of businesses among negroes is just beginning and a wonderful opportunity to be of real service in the guidance and advising of these enterprises awaits the colored accountant. (Martin 1933, 116)

Another early article on African-American accountants also advocated looking for opportunities among 'Negro businesses'. Jesse B. Blayton (1939), the fourth African-American CPA, recommended several African American–owned businesses, such as insurance companies, churches, African-American colleges and black fraternal orders, as clientele and sources of income for African-American accountants. He indicated that African Americans' exclusion from the practice of public accountancy had the potential to open up opportunities in the public sector:

> It would seem logical to anticipate that Negroes might enter the government service as accountants, actuaries, and the like at a rapid rate in the near future. Private business and industry among white people of the larger type pay more for the services of accounting experts than governments. As a result, the better white accountants are often found in private business, and not in the government. It would follow, therefore, if the governments are to keep their departments up to the level of efficiency maintained by private industry, it will be necessary to engage the services of the best prepared experts obtainable regardless of race. Many of these would likely be found among the Negro race, since the minority status of no other group seems to work against its members as the Negro's does. (Blayton 1939, 24)

Despite Blayton's argument that government might provide better opportunities for black accountants than the private sector, the federal government and most states did not hire African Americans as accountants until after World War II (interview with Davenport, 1992; Whiting 1992).

1940–1965

While it may not be surprising that so few African Americans entered public accounting during the Great Depression, it might be expected that opportunities would have been extended during World War II. During the war there was a severe shortage of accountants. Only approximately 50 per cent of the demand for accountants was being met (Wootton and Spruill 1994). However, while opportunities were extended to white women during this period (Lehman 1992; Wootton and Spruill 1994), the status of African Americans in the profession remained virtually unchanged. Only five African Americans received their CPAs during the war.

After the war, opportunities opened in the federal government for African-American accountants. However, change was imperceptible in the field of public accounting, as another five African Americans struggled to earn their CPAs in the late 1940s.

One of these was Ernest Davenport, who had graduated from high school in Ohio, worked in the Civilian Conservation Corps, a federal programme, during the Depression and then went to university at Morris Brown, historically an African-American college in Atlanta. Jesse B. Blayton, the fourth African-American CPA, was his accounting instructor. Davenport received his degree in 1940, and was offered a job in Georgia with an African-American insurance company. However, he found the open racism of the South oppressive and returned to Ohio in the hope of attaining a position with a CPA firm and thus satisfy the experience requirement. To his consternation, he found that no white firm (and there were no African-American firms in Ohio) would hire him:

> I was looking for an accounting job, because I had not taken the examination. At that time, of course, almost the only way to become a CPA was to work under a CPA for three years and get your experience. You could not get it by attending school, and you could not get it by working for government or anything like that; you had to work under a CPA. I, of course, inquired discreetly around about working for accounting firms and the answers were "No". So I finally . . . realized that I had to try to get whatever I could. (interview with Davenport, 1992)

Davenport worked for the National Youth Administration, another federal agency, until he was drafted into the army. At the end of the war, he resumed his search for a position with a CPA firm, but to no avail. Eventually he heard that there was an African-American CPA in Michigan, Richard Austin, and he moved to Michigan to gain experience by working for Austin, who later became Michigan's secretary of state. When asked if opportunities for blacks had changed during the war, Ernest Davenport responded:

> After I became a CPA in Michigan, I was very active with the Michigan Association of CPAs and I joined the American Association. I was co-chairman of the Michigan Association graduate study conference. In the mid-50s I had heard that there was a black with one of the major

CPA firms. . . . So it just happened at that graduate study conference that year we had invited as one of the speakers the managing partner of one of the major firms. . . . I said I understood they had a black in their firm. His answer to me was, *quote:* "Not that we're aware of". So, that was many years after the war, and it was a major firm. Consequently, it didn't happen during the war; it didn't happen in the following ten years. (interview with Davenport, 1992)

In 1946, Lincoln Harrison became the first African American to become a CPA in the state of Louisiana. Like Ernest Davenport, he had studied at Atlanta University with Professor Blayton, who inspired him to attain the CPA qualification and provided the necessary experience. However, the CPA examination in Louisiana was taken at the Roosevelt Hotel, which, in the era of the Jim Crow South, did not admit African Americans. At his own request, Harrison took the examination in Illinois and had the results transferred to Louisiana. Despite his status as a CPA, Harrison found that none of the major firms in Louisiana would hire him once they discovered his race. In addition, the Louisiana State Society of Certified Public Accountants denied him membership until 1970 (interview with Harrison, 1992).

While earlier pioneers were more likely to succeed through unique characteristics and individual effort, in the 1950s many African Americans who earned their CPAs worked together to overcome barriers. In this period virtually the only route to attaining a CPA for an African American was to gain a position with one of the few African-American certified public accountants operating their own firms. Wilmer Lucas and Alfred Tucker, the first (i.e., 1929 certification) and third (i.e., 1938 certification) African-American CPAs in New York, respectively, started their own firm, Lucas, Tucker and Company, which then provided opportunities to other African Americans interested in becoming CPAs.

Unlike the many African-American men who met their experience requirement by working for Lucas, Tucker and Company, the first African-American woman to earn a CPA in the state of New York, Bernadine Gines, had to overcome barriers based on both race *and* sex. Raised in Virginia, she went to Virginia State University, where her mentor, Professor Singleton, encouraged her to pursue further education as well as the CPA. She moved hundreds of miles to New York City to attend New York University, Singleton's alma mater, for her MBA, because of the complete segregation of Southern education:

At that time, where I lived was about a mile from the University of Virginia. But I could not go to the University of Virginia. So the state of Virginia paid my tuition to New York University because in the state of Virginia they did not have a graduate school programme in business administration for blacks. (interview with Gines, 1992).

After graduation, Bernadine Gines stayed in New York because she thought there were more opportunities there than in Virginia. When she looked for a position in the late 1940s she did not have an easy time:

> The greatest challenge was to obtain the requisite three years experience to take the CPA examination. Most of my job applications were completely ignored. This may have been related to the fact that my address was in Harlem. The only Black CPA firm in the City at that time did not employ female accountants. After I moved to Queens, where my address did not immediately suggest my ethnicity, I was invited for interviews. To this day, I remember the name of the first firm to interview me. One of the partners advised that he would not give me a job, but that his wife was looking for a maid if I knew anyone who wanted that job.
>
> Finally I was interviewed by two young men who had never considered the possibility that a Black person might apply. I later learned that one partner polled his clients to determine whether they would object to my working with them. When only one client responded that he would have a problem, that client was dropped. The second partner never said a word to his clients. He just showed up with me and there were no problems. Prior to being hired, I was called in for one final interview at which time only one question was asked, "Are you a communist?" (Streeter 1990, 45)

Having passed this political litmus test Bernadine Gines took the job with the young men and earned her CPA before working for the city of New York. She never applied to Lucas, Tucker and Company, the only African American–owned CPA firm in New York, because she had heard that the firm did not hire women (interview with Gines, 1992; interview with Coulthurst, 1992).

One of Gines's contemporaries, Milton Wilson, also had to move in order to earn his CPA. Although Wilson had attained his CPA certificate (and PhD) in Indiana in 1951, when he moved to Texas to teach he faced another barrier—membership of the Texas State Society of Certified Public Accountants. The state society required that two members recommend any candidate for membership. Dr. Wilson was dean of the business school at Texas State College for Negroes (now Texas Southern University). In that position, he did not encounter many members of the state society. However, a Jewish professor who worked for Wilson got the necessary signatures to nominate him and two other African-American professors at the university, Evelyn Henderson and Calvin Cooke. Wilson recalled that the Society expressed concern about blacks attending the group's socials:

> I do remember there was something about dancing; they had social affairs. That was about the least interest of mine, and I know Cooke,

two, and Evelyn, three. They had three ideal people because we wouldn't have been interested in dancing. . . . I'm positive none of us *could* dance. (interview with Wilson, 1991)

The history of the Texas Society of CPAs is unapologetic about the episode, despite its post–civil rights movement publication date:

> The first Constitution of the Texas Society restricted membership to whites only, though there were not black CPAs in Texas in 1915 and for nearly four decades to come. The formal wording prohibiting black members was soon deleted, but informal opposition remained into the late 1960s. Meanwhile, in March, 1952, the Texas State Board issued, by reciprocity from Indiana, the first Texas certificate to a black accountant, Professor Milton Wilson of Texas Southern University. Wilson made application for membership in the Texas Society soon thereafter, but his application was pigeon-holed in deference to the argument that the Society was, in part, a private organization entitled to select its members according to social as well as professional criteria. (Tinsley 1983, 172)

Like Professors Cooke, Henderson and Wilson in Texas, and the (albeit all-male) Lucas, Tucker and Co. contingent in New York, four men in Washington DC worked together in the 1950s to overcome the barriers to becoming CPAs (interviews with Broadus, Lee and Reynolds, 1992). The four men met at American University in Washington DC, where they were pursuing accounting degrees. As suggested by Martin (1933) and Blayton (1939) and because of changes in government policy (Hill 1977), it is not surprising that all four men worked for the federal government. Jerome Broadus worked for the army and the Internal Revenue Service. Carroll Lee worked for the Veterans Administration. Arthur Reynolds worked for the Air Force Auditor General, and Benjamin King worked for the army. The men all noted that opportunities for African Americans in the government had expanded with the desegregation of the military in 1947, and three of them returned from military service and attended school with the financial aid under the GI Bill. The four men studied together, and all decided to become CPAs. With the guidance of some helpful instructors, and having met the educational requirements, they sought jobs where they could meet the one year of experience required by the District of Columbia. Their experiences were very similar to those in other states:

> So, I went to every CPA firm in the District to get that one year's experience. And of course at that time, being a minority, it was always, "I'm not prejudiced, but you'll have to go into my clients' offices, and my clients . . .", or "I'm not prejudiced, but my partner . . ." So . . . it was impossible to get an apprenticeship. (interview with Lee, 1992)
>
> [Mr. King and I] started looking at the requirements for the CPA exam. We tried to get work for firms here in Washington but nobody,

and I mean *nobody,* would hire a black as an accountant. (interview with Reynolds, 1992)

Having exhausted the avenues their white classmates had pursued, the men took the unusual step of offering to work for free:

They had a [white] accountant teaching at Howard [the prestigious, historically black college, which several people in this study attended] . . . and he had a firm, and I asked him if I could work, and told him I would work for free and he hemmed and hawed and hemmed and hawed, and I'm still waiting for something positive to happen from that. He worked at Howard; he was earning his livelihood from our tuition; and he wasn't hiring any of the students who were coming out of that programme, [not even to get] the time requirement to take the examination. (interview with Reynolds, 1992)

There was one African-American CPA practicing in Washington DC at the time—John Cromwell, Jr., the first African-American CPA in the US The American University group heard about him, and they approached him to ask for jobs. Once again, they all offered to work for free in order to get the experience to take the examination. However, Cromwell would not or could not meet their request. Cromwell's clientele was limited because he served only African-American businesses, and he did not believe there was enough work in the District of Columbia to support more African-American CPAs (interviews with Reynolds and Lee, 1992).

Persistent in their desire to obtain the CPA qualification, the American University group took the only alternative available. They learned that Maryland, a neighbouring state, had no experience requirement. So they all moved their families to Maryland for the requisite residency period. Several complications still remained. If a prospective CPA had not attended the University of Maryland, the education requirements went up "to the point where you had to have taken just about every known accounting course" (interview with Lee, 1992). These men did not attend the University of Maryland, despite its proximity to Washington DC, because it was a segregated university and did not admit African-American students. In addition, they were circumscribed in their choice of where to live because there were very few neighbourhoods that allowed African Americans (ibid.).

Despite these adversities, Benjamin King became the first black CPA in the state of Maryland when he passed the examination in 1957. The others soon followed. Each of the men kept his government job, but they also formed two CPA firms, King and Reynolds and Lee-Broadus, where they worked part-time. Not surprisingly, virtually all of their clients were from the black community. Their experiences of trying to attain the CPA is reflected in their attitude towards other young African Americans who desired to become CPAs:

Our experience was such that we pretty much had an open office. If someone was interested in accounting and wanted to work and adhere to the discipline that we required, then they could come work with us to get whatever experience they needed to qualify for the examination. (interview with Reynolds, 1992)

With the exception of the growth of firms like King and Reynolds, who offered opportunities to African-American accountants, the conditions for African-American CPAs remained limited even in 1962, when an article appearing in the *Journal of Negro Education* estimated that there were no more than seventy-five African-American CPAs in the country (Harrison 1962). A survey of African-American public accountants revealed that they, like those in the 1933 study by Martin, were generally self employed or employed by African American–owned firms. Other themes in the article showed that there had been little change in the previous three decades:

> Among the problems mentioned frequently by others was the limitation of their practice to members of the Negro race, whose businesses generally are very small and which may not require or cannot afford the specialized services of a certified public accountant. Also mentioned was the restriction of membership on the part of some state societies, which prevents the Negro accountant from receiving the benefits of their organized professional activities. [As noted earlier, Harrison himself was denied membership in the Louisiana society until 1970.]
>
> As for future prospects, the majority of the Negro CPAs surveyed seem to think that there are rapidly expanding opportunities for qualified accountants, due in part to the increased development of business enterprises owned and operated by Negroes and greater integration of Negroes into the general economic and business life of the nation. (Harrison 1962, 505)

This article, which appeared eight years after the Supreme Court's landmark *Brown v. Board of Education* decision, revealed that African-American accountants' major source of revenue was still African American–owned businesses. However, the final words of the quotation do indicate some change in aspirations. African American hopes were rising as the incipient civil rights movement made its way into white America's consciousness.

CONCLUDING COMMENTS

Although the number of African American CPAs doubled between 1959 and 1965 it continued to represent a miniscule proportion of the CPA population. Even by the late 1960s, the presence of minority group members in the accounting profession was lower than their meagre representation in the medical and legal professions (American Institute of Certified Public Accountants 1980). Only 150 African-American CPAs were practicing in the US in 1968 (Mitchell 1969). This represented just 0.15 per cent of the total number of CPAs in the country. While genuine changes have occurred since the passage of the Civil Rights Act of 1964, perhaps due to the threat of legal sanction (Hammond 1990), African Americans continue to constitute less than 1 per cent of all certified public accountants, despite the fact that they comprise more than 12 per cent of the US population (Hammond 2002).

The oral histories of the earliest African-American certified public accountants clearly indicate that blacks who desired to become CPAs faced many barriers to entering the field. Unlike white women, whose exclusion was mitigated during periods of extreme labour shortage (Lehman 1992), it was virtually impossible for an African American to become a CPA prior to 1960. The stories shared by those we interviewed indicate the variety of obstacles that faced prospective CPAs and the multiple ways in which these exclusionary obstacles could be overcome by a small number of extraordinary men and women.

12 Racialization in Accountancy

Marcia Annisette

If "race" is a manner of dividing and ranking human beings by reference to selected embodied properties (real or imputed) so as to subordinate, exclude and exploit them, then we must study those *practices of division* and the institutions that both buttress and result from them. (Wacquant 1997, 229)

INTRODUCTION

This chapter illustrates the various ways in which racial practices of division have occurred in the organization of accountancy in Trinidad and Tobago (T&T). Unlike the UK and US contexts where 'blacks' and 'Asians' are considered ethnic minorities, in T&T these two groups constitute 80 per cent of the population. Thus whereas the chapter by Hammond and Streeter illustrates minority exclusion and under-representation in the US profession, this chapter focuses on the multiple ways in which race has been deployed to bring about majority under-representation and exclusion. The chapter will first show how the practice of accountancy came to be initially raced 'British' in T&T. It will then illustrate the consequences of this racing on the evolution of the profession in the country. In particular, it shows that underlying every later development would be an unmistakable racial component: either an attempt to destroy its British racialization or alternatively an attempt to (re)assert it.

COLONIALISM: 'WHITES ONLY PLEASE'

In T&T's colonial society, accountancy was always associated with whiteness or more accurately 'Britishness'. From the final decade of the nineteenth century, the colony's embryonic corporate sector had established a

This chapter is based on the paper "The Colour of Accountancy: Examining the Salience of Race in a Professionalisation Project", which appeared in *Accounting, Organizations and Society* 28, no. 7/8 (2003): 639–74. The author would like to thank the publisher, Elsevier, for permission to use this material.

practice of importing accounting labour from Britain—a product of the island's economic history. As a plantation economy, the prevailing principles of mercantilism confined industry to the metropolis and the production of primary goods to the colony. T&T's economy in the nineteenth century was therefore completely agricultural. Sugar accounted for the bulk of the colony's revenues and employed most of its labour force (Brereton 1981, 199). By the early decades of the twentieth century the colony had switched production from sugar to oil. The import of accounting labour became the established practice in the dominant oil sector and amongst the country's two practicing accounting firms—Fitzpatrick Graham (which became Pannell Fitzpatrick in 1966, then Ernst and Young in the early 1990s); and Hunter Smith and Earl (which became Price Waterhouse in 1960)—branches of London-based Chartered Accountant firms. In 1938 there were six professionally qualified accountants resident in T&T, all of whom were British nationals.

As the corporate sector developed in T&T, the race-based division of accounting labour became more refined. Accountants from Britain were imported to perform 'expert' accountancy work, whilst lower-level book-keeping tasks were conducted by the 'intermediate' races—in particular those representing the Coloured/Mixed category (Karch 1985). The African and East Indian segments of the population—considered the 'subordinate' races in the colony's racial hierarchy—were strictly excluded from accountancy, professional or otherwise. Indeed, way into the late 1930s it was felt that the place for the African was the oilfields and the Indian, the plantation. Thus English doctor Vincent Tothill writing about his visit to Trinidad noted that:

> The manual work entailed in the oil fields is of a very heavy nature . . . The Negro has a magnificent physique and is eminently suited to manual labour in the tropics. His cherry [*sic*] disposition and devil-may care outlook on life are a great asset, and make it more easy for him to do heavy work in gangs than the Indian . . . The Negro will sing songs and chants when doing an extra piece of manual gang work. . . .
> The Indian is more adapted to working alone or in sparsely scattered groups where he can carry on a mild and desultory conversation. Also, he does not have the physique of the Negro, and is ill adapted for heavy work. (Tothill, quoted in Ryan 1991a, 175)

This discursive practice of linking social categories to their most 'appropriate' kind of work is an important aspect of occupational closure. Indeed, as vividly depicted in Naipaul's 1970 novel *A Flag on the Island*, part of the commonsense of T&T society was that "every race have to do special things" (Naipaul 1970, 67). This commonsense manifested itself in what came to be known in T&T as the 'white bias', characterized by a marked under-representation of the country's numerically major racial groups in the highest or most preferred occupations (Harewood 1971).

By the 1950s very little had changed with respect to accountancy. As Table 12.1 demonstrates, twenty of the twenty-six professionally qualified accountants in the country were British expatriates. Of the six nationals who held an accountancy credential, three were from the Coloured/Mixed racial group, two were Chinese and one was White (French Creole). No persons of the Negro/Black or East Indian racial groups had succeeded in receiving a professional accountancy credential.

Although race was the foundation for the commonsense of colonial T&T society, having a deterministic effect on occupational choice (Crichlow 1991, 193), there were also tangible mechanisms which served to exclude the Afro and Indo population from obtaining a professional accountancy credential. The prestigious Chartered Accountant credential (CA), granted by the Institute of Chartered Accountants in England and Wales (ICAEW) required articles to be taken in Britain. But, as disclosed in a letter addressed to ICAEW member firms highlighting the plight of West African students, "The principal obstacle in the way of satisfying their aspirations [of becoming Chartered Accountants] is the difficulty in finding, at short notice, members in the profession who would be willing to accept them as articled clerks" (*Accountant*, 27 August 1949, 228).

The ICAEW was not unaware of the difficulties that its requirements for articles imposed on non-British residents. Indeed as early as 1927 when they considered removing this restrictive clause from its Charter, it was noted that that such a development would "have the effect of commencing

Table 12.1   Professionally Qualified Accountants in Trinidad and Tobago, 1950

'Race'[1]	Professional Credential		Total
	ACCA	CA	
Negro	0	0	0
East Indian	0	0	0
Mixed	3	0	3
Chinese	2	0	2
White			
French Creole	1	0	1
British Expatriate	1	19	20
Total	7	19	26

[1]   'Race' defined in terms of census classifications 1950.

Sources: ICAEW Topographical list of Members 1950, Burke (1995), Smith (1950).

the dilution of the profession with Orientals, and possibly in 100 years' time we shall see a coloured gentleman taking this [the president's] chair" (*Accountant*, 7 May 1927, 710).

While the ICAEW might have been closed to persons of colour, pursuing the qualification of the British-based Association of Certified and Corporate Accountants (ACCA) locally was another option. Unlike the ICAEW, the ACCA—currently known as the Association of Chartered Certified Accountants—permitted non-British residents to sit its exams. However, the ACCA required that its students be engaged in 'approved' accountancy work. For Afro- and Indo-Trinidadians, options for such engagement were limited. The two local professional firms were closed to all but British expatriates, and whereas obtaining the requisite experience with the colonial government was always an option, this too posed some difficulties. An ACCA aspirant of East Indian descent recalled that:

> In 1947 . . . I registered with the ACCA. . . . and was prepared for the examinations in December 1950. . . . I got leave from the office to do the final preparations . . . I was reading for Mercantile Law and the postman brought an air letter form from the ACCA. When I opened it all the air letter form said was with respect to your application for sitting the examination we regret to inform you that you are not engaged in work of an approved accountancy nature. They said you are working in the Prisons as a clerk and therefore we can't let you sit the examination . . . So I wrote to the Colonial Secretary indicating what had happened . . . asking that I be transferred to the audit department . . . I got a letter stating that in order to consider your transfer to the audit department you must be the holder of an approved accountancy qualification. . . . So all the doors were closed. (interview #4, 1995)

There was, however, promise of change. The colony would be granted responsible self-government in 1956 and independence in 1962. As part of the process of preparing nationals to take over the bureaucratic machinery which it would leave behind, the colonial state in 1952 introduced an Accountancy Training Scheme (ATS), which provided funding to government employees wishing to pursue accountancy studies (letter to author from Maharaj, 15 September 1995). The experience of an Afro-Trinidadian reveals that such support may not have been open to all eligibles:

> When I went to the Department of Education and told them that I wanted to do accountancy they said—the Director of Education in the Colonial Government in 1954—'You've won a Government Scholarship . . . you could become a doctor or a lawyer and be self employed.

You are wasting your time'. So I was very conscious that I was the first non-white person going in that direction. (interview #8, 1995)

In the 1950s whilst it seemed acceptable for 'non-whites' to enter the medical and legal profession, it was still felt by the soon-to-be-dismantled colonial state (or certainly some functionaries thereof), that accountancy was not an appropriate profession for those so defined.

The manifest exclusion of Afro- and Indo-Trinidadians from accountancy only reflects one aspect of its racialization in the 1950s. Table 12.1 also discloses the incipient racialization of accountancy credentials. The nineteen holders of the prestigious CA qualification were all British expatriates, whilst five of the seven ACCAs were 'Non-White'. This close correspondence between 'race/colour' and accountancy credential, meant that in keeping with the wider structures of society, the two accountancy credentials could also be 'raced/coloured'. Thus the CA had emerged as raced 'White-British' whereas the ACCA was beginning to be raced 'Non-White'.

Racialization in the practice of accountancy was also evident in the employment sites of the twenty-six practitioners in T&T in 1950. Table 12.2 discloses two distinct tendencies. British expatriates were confined to professional practices and the British-owned private sector whereas the non-whites were confined to the state sector, thus establishing a strong link between 'race/colour', work site and accountancy credential.

The country's first black CA recalled that "in the early 1950s . . . Chartered Accountants were either employed in the oil fields or one of the practicing firms . . . and it was a non-black thing" (interview with John Hunt, 1995).

Table 12.2 Employment Distribution of Professionally Qualified Accountants in Trinidad and Tobago, 1950

'Race'[1]	Practice Elite Firm	Foreign Private Sector	Local Private Sector	State	Self-employed	Total
Mixed				3		3
Chinese				1	1	2
White						
French Creole			1			1
British Expatriate	5	15				20
Total	5	15	1	4	1	26

[1] 'Race' defined in terms of census classifications 1950.

Sources: ICAEW Topographical list of Members 1950, Burke (1995), Smith (1950).

The tight coupling of 'race-colour', work site and accountancy credentials widened pre-existing status gaps between the dichotomous groups. As one contemporary recalled:

> the Chartered Accountants always felt that we were inferior people all the time . . . The Chartereds felt that we did not have the practical experience . . . They were right up to a point . . . When I qualified I had virtually never seen a cash book . . . you don't see a double entry in the Public Service. (Sookh Supersad, 1995, retired chairman of the Board of Inland Revenue, First East Indian accountant)

During the 1950s therefore, the organization of accountancy in T&T could be summed up in the following shorthand:

Chartered Accountant (CA) = White/British, Experienced, Private Sector = High Status

Certified Accountant (ACCA) = Non-White, Inexperienced, Public Sector = Low Status

In short, race/colour was emerging as a powerful marker of status differentials *within* the practice of accountancy. As the following section will show, some of these patterns were reinforced by the county's changeover to independence, while others were significantly changed. Of the latter, the most significant was the creation of opportunities for members of 'subordinate' groups to obtain a professional accountancy credential. This materialized with the emergence of Eric Williams and the People's National Movement (PNM).

INDEPENDENCE: CHANGING THE FACE OF ACCOUNTANCY

By 1948, when he returned to Trinidad, Eric Williams was already a highly acclaimed international scholar, Black Nationalist and spokesman for colonial peoples (Williams 1969, 84, 100). Almost immediately he became a dominant figure in political groups whose memberships constituted T&T's coloured intellectual elite occupying the middle stratum of society (Ryan 1972, 107). Through a series of public lectures, Williams with fiery, anti-imperialist rhetoric also began to build up a strong following among the disillusioned black working-class masses who were convinced that this was the kind of educated and sophisticated leadership needed to confront the "the white imperialist class" (Craig 1982). The coloured middle-class elite, well aware of William's appeal to the black working class and unemployed masses, formulated the idea of an essentially coloured middle-class party, with black working-class grassroots support. This idea came to fruition as the PNM.

In January 1956, with Williams at the helm, the PNM was officially launched to fight the forthcoming election. This was an important election. Britain had agreed that responsible self-government would be fully instituted by 1956, and that the victors of the 1956 election would be the government which would lead T&T to full political independence scheduled for 1962.

The PNM won. And it did so again in the 1961 election. Immediately after its success at the polls in 1961, Williams implemented the first phase of his social revolution. The major target was the reform of the country's education system. A number of policies were implemented including free secondary and tertiary education. This significantly undermined the basis of the old social order and contributed to the growth of the predominantly Afro-Trinidadian educated elite who replaced the whites who had previously occupied strategic positions in the political, educational and bureaucratic arenas (Ryan 1991b, 61–62).

Almost simultaneously, Williams implemented measures which ultimately changed the face of accountancy. First was a massive programme of public-sector reform underpinned by the theme of financial rectitude (Annisette 1999). A number of new accounting roles were established in the state bureaucracy; the ATS was expanded and several state employees were granted scholarships to pursue studies in accountancy. Later, such scholarships and low-interest loans for professional accountancy education were made widely available. Then a ban was imposed on the import of accounting labour. Work permits were only granted to those firms which had established that appropriate steps were being taken to train nationals. The practicing firms were thus forced to install measures to train locals in accountancy. The firms turned to the ACCA. That is, now banned from importing British accountants, the practicing firms switched to importing a British examining body to train and examine locals (ibid.). Critically, the locals that they trained occupied the next available rung on the pre-existing racial pecking order—local whites and Chinese.

Thus by 1975, 142 nationals held professional accountancy credentials. In Braithwaite's (1980) study of the country's occupational elite, just over 32 per cent of the professionally qualified accountants were from T&T's two major racial groups (see Table 12.3). Whilst these two groups remained seriously under-represented, the picture had changed markedly to that presented in 1950.

Braithwaite's survey results are insightful for two other reasons. Firstly, they show accountancy's closure vis-à-vis other high-status professions. While the law mirrored accountancy with respect to East Indian under-representation, Africans were better represented in the law although they were still under-represented. The picture presented for medicine was quite different. Here there was East Indian *over-representation*. Thus Afro- and Indo-Trinidadian combined entry into

Table 12.3   Race Distribution of Occupational Elite in Trinidad and Tobago, 1975

'Race'[1]	Doctors %	Lawyers %	Accountants %	Racial Distribution of non-institutional population at 1970 census %
African	14.8	29.6	16.7	42.8
Indian	47.7	15.2	15.5	40.1
Mixed	16.8	31.2	44.0	14.2
Other[2]	20.1	24.0	23.8	2.9
Total	99.4	100.0	100.0	100.0
N	149	125	84	

[1] 'Race' defined in terms of census classifications 1970.
[2] Other in Braithwaite's survey referred to persons defined as White, Off-White and Chinese.

Source: Braithwaite (1980).

accountancy (32.2 per cent) lagged behind their combined entry into medicine and the law (62.5 per cent and 44.8 per cent). This paralleled observations in the US, which indicated that accountancy has persistently lagged behind law and medicine with respect to minority representation in the profession (Paige 1991). Secondly, Braithwaite's study provides insights to changes in the racial bases of the professions over time (see Table 12.4).

Most striking is the study's revelation that law and medicine followed a similar pattern of change with respect to individual racial groups, whilst in every instance the trend in accountancy appears anomalous. For both

Table 12.4   Age Distribution of Occupational Elite in Trinidad and Tobago, 1975

'Race'[1]	% Doctors born		% of Lawyers born		% Accountants born	
	Pre 1937	1937– 1958	Pre 1937	1937– 1958	Pre 1937	1937– 1958
African	17	10	31	26	12	29
Indian	43	56	10	33	16	12
Mixed	20	12	36	15	57	13
Other	20	22	23	26	15	46
Total	100	100	100	100	100	100

[1]'Race' defined in terms of census classifications

Source: adapted from Braithwaite (1980).

medicine and law there was a *decline* in African representation over time (7 per cent and 5 per cent, respectively). With respect to accountancy there was *increased* representation (17 per cent). Indians, on the other hand, experienced large *increases* in representation in medicine and law over time (13 per cent and 23 per cent, respectively), but a slight *decline* with respect to accountancy (4 per cent). The Mixed group experienced declines in all professions over time but the decline in accountancy (44 per cent) was substantial when compared to that of law and medicine (21 per cent and 8 per cent, respectively). Finally, the 'Other' group experienced marginal increases over time with respect to medicine and law (2 per cent and 3 per cent, respectively), but with respect to accountancy the increase was substantial (31 per cent). The general picture one can glean about accountancy is that the emerging trend in 1975 was one in which new entrants to the profession were dominated by racial groups defined as 'African' (29 per cent) and Other (46 per cent)—the latter comprising (numerical) minority racial groups of White and Chinese.

Other important changes had also occurred in the post-independence period. Major government accountancy posts (such as Accountant General and Auditor General) were filled by non-whites, and, in 1964, the country's first national association of accountants—the Trinidad and Tobago Association of Chartered Accountants and Certified Accountants (TTA-CACA), a body dominated by state-employed accountants—was formed. Immediately after its formation the TTACACA embarked on a number of initiatives aimed at indigenizing professional accountancy education (see Annisette 1999, 119–21; 2000, 642–44). These initiatives came to fruition in 1970 with the establishment of the Institute of Chartered Accountants of Trinidad and Tobago (ICATT). This organization was created with two objectives. The first was to indigenize professional accountancy education (Annisette 2000). The second was to increase the supply of expert accounting labour in the country. Despite the state's initiatives in the previous decade, by 1970 there remained a dire shortage of accountants in the country. Indeed, on 16 August 1970 the conservative white-owned *Sunday Guardian* newspaper reported that there were "some 100 qualified accountants in the country and . . . the demand was for about three times that number". It further noted that "opportunities for local non-whites to study . . . are just not there". The shortage meant that reliance on British expatriate accountancy labour—which was anathema to the Black Nationalist T&T state—could be expected to continue.

Thus the state perceived the ICATT as the means for correcting these ills. From inception therefore, state presence—and by extension Afro-Trinidadian presence—in the governance of the ICATT was high—63 per cent in both cases. But by 1974, state presence in the governing council had dropped to 25 per cent while the British-linked practicing firms had increased their presence to 50 per cent (from 13 per cent). In a similar trend Afro-Trinidadian presence declined to 13 per cent and whites increased from 13 per cent to 38 per cent. And to make matters worse, the Institute's president was a British expatriate. The leadership and management of the ICATT had been transferred to the white chartered, practicing firms and coinciding with this was the ICATT's abandonment of its founding objective of indigenization (see Annisette 2000). By 1974 the ICATT had forged close links with a number of overseas professional bodies, the most important of which was its examination link with the ACCA. Thus, rather than becoming an association which designed its curriculum and examinations, by 1974, the ICATT had evolved into a body which accepted for membership, graduates of other accounting associations which ICATT designated as 'registered societies'. In 1974 all of the ICATT's 'registered societies' were British-based bodies except for one, which was Canadian based.

1974 was a momentous year for T&T's Black Nationalist state. Oil prices increased and T&T benefitted from this windfall. Endowed with its new-found oil wealth, the government embarked on its policy of state capitalism and initiated a series of mega-projects, which included cement, fertilizers, nitrogen and iron and steel products. Accountants were needed for the control and surveillance of these newly created state enterprises. Although the state had already spent vast sums of money financing scholarships for persons to pursue the ACCA qualification, there still remained an acute shortage of accountants in the country and in the state service in particular (Joseph 1976) since the ACCA pass rate was notoriously low (Montano 1978). Thus by the mid-1970s the T&T state had the incentive and the means to frustrate the ICATT's anti-indigenization professional strategy.

It was against this background that Prime Minister Williams turned to the University of the West Indies. He provided the newly created Department of Management Studies with funding to establish an MSc Accounting degree—a programme designed "to equip graduates with the training necessary to become professional accountants" (University of the West Indies 1991).

A RACE WAR IN ACCOUNTANCY

> There are no races . . . There is only a belief that there are such things, a belief which is used by some social groups to construct an Other (and therefore the Self) in thought as a prelude to exclusion and domination, and by other social groups to define Self (and so to construct an Other) as a means of resisting that exclusion. Hence, if used at all, the idea of race should be used only to refer descriptively to such uses of the idea of race. (Miles 2000, 135)

The MSc Accounting degree was introduced at the University of the West Indies in October 1975. The development of the degree did not sit well with the now elite-controlled ICATT. Indeed as early as the mid-1960s there had been strong feelings amongst the professional elite that the University of the

West Indies was not the proper institution for the training of accountants (Annisette 2000, 643–44). There was much contemporaneous support for the view that at the University of the West Indies "there might be too great a bias towards USA thinking whereas it is necessary, in accounting matters at least, that the link with U.K tradition . . . should be preserved" (Desmond Davis 1965, Partner Fitzpatrick Graham).

Moreover, it was felt that the MSc might pose a long-run threat to the ICATT's professional monopoly. Indeed, in a 1974 memo ICATT President Richard Hobday warned council members that this was perhaps an unconscious attempt "by UWI to get control of our examinations and education process".

The University of the West Indies, though set up in 1948 as a university college of the University of London, had by the 1970s become a West Indian institution with campuses in Jamaica (Mona), Barbados (Cave Hill) and Trinidad (St. Augustine). Significantly, the University of the West Indies was seen as the minting ground of the Afro-Caribbean intelligentsia (Ryan 1992b) and more significantly, the St. Augustine campus was closely associated with the 'Black Power' race revolts, which rocked Trinidad during the first half of 1970.

In December 1974, therefore, the ICATT Council granted membership qualification rights to the proposed MSc Accounting degree very hesitatingly. However, it did not perceive that it would be yielding too much since "UWI had given an undertaking that people coming into that Masters Degree would have to be the cream of the crop . . . of the BSc degree. We did not therefore envisage a large number of entrants" (interview #16, ICATT Council Member, 1974–1975).

But the status of the MSc Accounting degree within the ICATT was always very tenuous, and a number of mechanisms ensured *de facto* exclusion of its graduates. First the ICATT imposed a thirty-month 'approved post qualification' requirement for graduates of the programme. This was considered onerous in the light of the twelve months required for ACCA graduates. Then there were the exclusionary hiring practices of private sector and practicing firms, which resulted in 85 per cent of the graduates working in state enterprises in finance rather than in accounting roles (MSc Accounting Association 1990). As a result, by 1979 none of the forty MSc graduates in accounting had met the post-qualification requirement set by the ICATT.

It was also the case that the very basis of the degree's acceptance by the ICATT was questionable. That is, it was accepted under the discretionary powers of the Council rather than by membership vote. This provoked later arguments that its acceptance by the Institute was unconstitutional (interview with Mark, 1995).

The final assault on the MSc qualification was a damaging critique of the programme published in the Institute's newsletter by Alwin Chow—a partner of the prestigious practicing firm, Pannell Fitzpatrick.

The syllabus was criticized for its lack of "consideration of the IASC Standards and Exposure drafts", whilst aspects of the course were said to "border on the ridiculous" (Chow 1974, pp. 12). Following Chow's critique, there were a series of repeated charges about the "poor quality of the MSc graduates" (Minutes ICATT AGM, 1981). Thus in March 1981 the ICATT withdrew eligibility to membership for persons graduating from the programme after 1984, arguing that the MSc qualification was sub-professional.

While the fate of the MSc Accounting in the ICATT could easily be read as the case of a young professional body attempting to define and redefine entry requirements in the light of changes in the minimum range of skills expected of a professional accountant, in some quarters it was seen as a race war, played out in technical accounting terms. The problem lay with the fact that at all levels the protagonists were perceived to represent two historically opposing racial groups in T&T. At the institutional level, the University of the West Indies was seen as an Afro-Caribbean institution. This, after all, was the institution that had produced the black revolutionaries who had rioted in 1970 with their slogans of 'Black Power' and calls for black enfranchisement (Craig 1982). On the other hand, the ICATT, despite its historic origins, was seen as an institution which had come to represent the interests of the white-chartered accounting firms. Thus the president of the MSc Association would conclude:

> You had this elite group of people who were in charge of the accounting firms. The majority was white people and I feel that they had a problem with these little black pygmy [sic] people getting into their club. The power of ICATT was in the hands of a particular caste. (interview with Le Hunte, 1995)

At the individual level, the early battle was fought between the president of the ICATT, David Law, and the director of the MSc programme, Ainsley Mark. Law, who was white, of British parentage and a senior partner of one of the elite practicing firms, had, as early as 1965, strenuously resisted the profession's attempts to collaborate with the University of the West Indies:

> I am considering the present worth of the profession in Trinidad and do not wish it to be *debased* any further. . . . I do not believe that a university grind will produce the type of individual that Trinidad needs or that should be welcomed into the fraternity. (letter to Desmond Davis, 14 June 1965; emphasis added)

Mark, on the other hand, was of African descent, had trained in Canada in the late 1960s and had close links with protagonists in the Black Power riots. He would describe himself as "militant, cocky and abrasive" (interview with Mark, 1995). Thus on a personal level, the battle was seen in racial terms. An MSc accounting graduate viewed the impasse this way:

> Remember we are also talking about two . . . different types of people. One of the key players here in addition to being black had a lot of beard on his face . . . so everything in Trinidad has to do with politics and ethnicity. (interview #7, 1995)

In discussing the impasse with key players, while the ICATT used technical arguments to support its decision to withdraw its recognition of the MSc Accounting, those so excluded saw their situation as intimately related to race. The president of the MSc Association explained it as "colonialism . . . It is an emotional issue because it is a typical apartheid situation with this MSc" (interview with Le Hunte, 1995).

For those who were connected with the MSc degree it seemed difficult to escape the conclusion that there was a racial factor involved. The technical arguments advanced by the ICATT seemed not to stand up to scrutiny. For instance, the Chow critique which formed the basis for ICATT's arguments pointed out, "Neither the undergraduate nor postgraduate syllabus includes specifically the consideration of the IASC Standards and exposure drafts although these are the working tools of the profession in Trinidad and Tobago" (*ICAN*, Vol. 4 [1], April, pp. 12–15).

Yet at that time, the ACCA credential which the ICATT had endorsed gave little emphasis to IASC accounting standards and exposure drafts. Its focus was on the UK standards. The Chow critique also asserted, "Financial Accounting II, a compulsory subject in the MSc program, includes comprehensive coverage of *believe it or not* Soviet Accounting" (*ICAN*, Vol. 4 [1], April, pp. 12–15; emphasis in original).

But the defenders of the MSc pointed out that the programme gave extensive coverage of accounting in other non–Anglo Saxon contexts (interview with Le Hunte, 1995). Moreover, they added, unlike any of the other credentials recognized by the ICATT (all of which were foreign based), theirs gave extensive coverage of Trinidad tax and company law (interviews with Le Hunte and Mark, 1995). But this seemed to count for very little at the ICATT. Ainsley Mark commented:

> So . . . we have . . . gone right back to where we were in the 1970s. I can come out of Canada with my Canadian Law and Canadian Tax and I can get into ICATT. You can come out with your English Tax and your English Law and you can get into ICATT, and somebody who . . . has done Trinidad Tax and Trinidad Law can't get in. (interview, 1995)

The MSc defenders' belief in a racial explanation for the ICATT's rejection of the qualification was further strengthened by a comparison with ICATT's posture towards the Canadian-based Certified Management Accountant degree (the CMA)—then considered a second-tier accountancy qualification in Canada (Richardson 1987b, 598). The CMA credential had won the favour of Pannell Fitzpatrick—which had installed a CMA training scheme for its audit trainees (interview with Hobday, 1995). The credential was so popular in T&T that by 1985 the ICATT had estimated that there were about four hundred students studying for it locally and another one hundred in Canada (report of the Committee set up to consider the CMA and CGA, 1985). Although the ICATT seemed to have greater grounds for denying membership to holders of the CMA credential, it was nonetheless accepted with strong Council support—a decision described elsewhere as "anomalous" (Annisette 1999, 124). Whilst it could be argued that this anomaly is consistent with ICATT's strategy of internationalization (ibid., 126), in the view of the MSc accountants, as well as some accountants within the ICATT, the anomaly could easily be explained in racial terms. Thus the president of the MSc Accounting Association described the ICATT's acceptance of the CMA as about "white people. All that they [the local CMA representatives] did was to come down with some white people and talk and they [the ICATT] just accepted it" (interview with Le Hunte, 1995).

A member of the ICATT 'Special Committee to Evaluate the CMA Degree' stated that despite the committee's poor evaluation of the degree and its recommendation that it not be recognized, the CMA succeeded where the MSc had failed because "at that time Richard Young was the President [of the ICATT], Terry Chang was the Vice President [of the ICATT], and Leslie Chang was at the head of the CMA body here. So the Chinese made a deal" (interview with John, 1995). To this practitioner, racialism again appeared as the only explanation for the "CMA anomaly".

ICATT's exclusion of the MSc degree and its simultaneous inclusion of the CMA credential might have been the outcome of non-racial social processes. But in an occupational system where race so strongly coincided with credentials, work site and professional status, the role of race in occupational dynamics can be overly or spuriously attributed. Thus in the view of those excluded, what was *solely* at play was racialism. While the evidence suggests that much of the support for the CMA credential came from social actors defined in T&T society as white and Chinese, and the support for the MSc emanated from social actors defined as black, it can never be confidently asserted that these outcomes were on the grounds of race. But that has not been the purpose here. In Rex's view, one of the possible sources of racial and ethnic conflict in societies that start from a colonial base, is "the maintenance of social order in the absence of a legal basis in an estate system" (1986, 57). Certainly from the standpoint of some of the major protagonists in the MSc impasse, the colonial social order had been maintained, and *race* served as a powerful mobilizing force.

CONCLUSION

The chapter has attempted to illustrate the shifting terrain over which racial practices in accountancy are undertaken and achieved. It has revealed that with each shift, different mechanisms of racial exclusion can emerge, giving rise to varied patterns of racialization. For instance, while some US accounting societies instituted explicit racial barriers to the profession, the elite arm of the UK profession achieved the same effect by insisting on articles in Britain. Such overt exclusionary practices are now things of the past. Yet with the opening-up of the profession to previously excluded groups, more subtle genres of racial exclusion have emerged. For instance, the establishment of alternative routes to the profession can facilitate new patterns of exclusion as more accessible routes themselves become racialized. Where, for instance, alternative routes involve new accounting credentials, racial practices of exclusion may become manifest in status differentials around qualification systems. Here both race and credentials play mutually reinforcing roles in maintaining pre-existing status gaps, which in turn can lead to a fragmented profession.

In addition, different types of accounting work can become racialized in response to measures designed to increase access to practice. The T&T case illustrates that specific accounting work sites, such as public practice or government accounting, can become racialized, mirroring and reinforcing existing status differentials between, say, public accountants and state accountants. Even where the racialization of accounting work *between* work sites does not emerge, it may exist *within* specific work sites in the form of glass ceilings— freer entry at the lower levels and restricted or no access to the top. Thus within specific work sites the lower echelons of the accounting hierarchy may be populated by racial 'Others' and the upper echelons remain reserved for a select racial group. Data for 1990 on T&T's two elite practices—Price Waterhouse and Ernst and Young—provide some preliminary evidence of this phenomenon. Of note here is the over-representation of Chinese (25 per cent) and whites (60 per cent) at the partnership level at a time when Chinese and whites represented merely 0.4 per cent and 0.8 per cent of the island's population, respectively. The case of the Chinese in the accounting profession in T&T is particularly interesting from a comparative point of view. Whereas this chapter has shown that in post-independence T&T this group has been consistently over-represented in the profession and has seemingly encountered no glass ceiling, in other sites, evidence suggests that they have faced formidable barriers in advancing to the top of the profession (Kim 2004a). This instance of differing experiences of persons of similar ancestral backgrounds in two different contexts serves to reinforce a point made by theorists of race. That is, racial practices are dynamic and assume different logics in different times and in different sites.

With respect to our understanding of racial logics as they apply to accountancy, the chapter has made another contribution. The evidence for

T&T is consistent with US findings which suggest that accountancy has consistently lagged behind medicine and the law with respect to access to the profession by persons socially defined as 'black'. The key may lay in the corporate patronage basis of accountancy (Johnson 1972). Unlike law and medicine, which have a heterogeneous source of demand, the prime source of demand for accounting services is large corporate organizations (ibid.). This drives accountancy's recruitment practices, for as Johnson points out, "under corporate patronage . . . the practitioner is expected to be socially acceptable" (ibid., 66–67). That the management and control of contemporary corporations has been, and continues to be, largely the domain of white males may therefore help explain accountancy's racial imperviousness over time when compared to other high-status professions.

Contributors

Marcia Annisette is Associate Professor of Accounting at the Schulich School of Business, York University. She has published on the history of professional accountancy in Trinidad and Tobago. Her research interests include accounting and its interface with race, colonialism, imperialism and globalization. She is currently conducting research on accounting and its effects on the immigrant and refugee populations in Canada and Australia.

Richard K. Fleischman is Professor Emeritus from John Carroll University. He has published extensively on British Industrial Revolution accounting, US standard costing and slave plantation accounting. He has served three terms as editor of the *Accounting Historians Journal* and as president of the Academy of Accounting Historians. He has been honoured as Ohio's Outstanding Accounting Educator and the Academy's Hourglass Award.

Warwick Funnell is Professor of Accounting at the University of Kent. He has published widely on the history of public-sector accounting. The contributions of his writing to the history of accounting and the Holocaust have been recognized by Yad Vashem, the Jewish Holocaust Memorial in Jerusalem. He has held appointments as Professor of Accounting at both British and Australian universities and received the Hourglass Award from the Academy of Accounting Historians.

Cameron Graham is Associate Professor of Accounting at the Schulich School of Business, York University, Toronto. He draws on social theory to examine the roles of accounting in society, particularly how it affects the poor. The accounting policies, procedures and reporting mechanisms of Canada's Department of Indian Affairs have been a focus of his work.

Theresa Hammond is Professor and Ernst & Young Diversity Fellow in the Department of Accounting at San Francisco State University. Her primary research is on the under-representation of African Americans in the public accounting profession, including the book, *A White-Collar Profession: African-American Certified Public Accountants*, published by the University of North Carolina Press in 2002.

Trevor Hopper is Professor of Management Accounting at Sussex University, Visiting Professor at Stockholm School of Economics and Adjunct Professor at Victoria University of Wellington. His major contributions have lain in developing social theories of management control and change, often through intensive case studies. Currently he is researching accounting in developing countries and the evaluation of innovations. He has received a Lifetime Achievement Award from the British Accounting Association.

Keith Hooper is Professor of Financial Accounting and Head of Accounting at Auckland University of Technology. He has published on colonial accounting history and on corporate collapse in the New Zealand context. His research interests include financial reporting, asset valuation and accounting in international contexts.

Kate Kearins is Professor of Management and Associate Dean Research for Business and Law at Auckland University of Technology. Her publications range from those on accountability and corporate collapse through to a more focused interest in business and sustainability. In the latter areas she has published on conceptions of sustainability and on stakeholder engagement and reporting practices, as well as on business education for sustainability. She has won several awards for case research.

Linda M. Kirkham is Professor of Accounting at the Robert Gordon University, Aberdeen. She has written extensively on the accounting profession, gender and accounting history. Her publications include a number of key articles examining the interface of accounting history and gender processes.

Ellen J. Lippman is an Associate Professor of Accounting at the Pamplin School of Business, University of Portland. Her research interests include analysing the ethical responsibilities of accountants. A case based upon her research on accountants during the Holocaust earned her the Innovation in Accounting History Education Award from the Academy of Accounting Historians.

Anne Loft is Professor of Accounting at Lund University in Sweden, but originally from England. She is a former editor of the *European Accounting Review* and has been awarded the Hourglass Award from the Academy of Accounting Historians for work on the history of management accounting. Her current research focuses on the history of the International Federation of Accountants 1977–2011.

David Oldroyd is a Professor of Accounting at Durham University. He has published on the Industrial Revolution and plantation economies of the British Caribbean and American South. He is particularly interested in the role played by landowners and their stewards in formative industrial enterprise in the eighteenth century.

Dean Neu is Professor of Accounting at the Schulich School of Business, York University, Toronto. His research examines the relationship between accounting and the public interest. He has published widely on Canada's indigenous peoples, including *Accounting for Genocide: Canada's Bureaucratic Assault on Indigenous Peoples.*

Philip O'Regan is Dean of the Kemmy Business School at the University of Limerick. He has published a number of articles on the accounting profession in Ireland and accounting in an imperial context. He is currently researching the role of the church in the development and dissemination of accounting practices.

Denise W. Streeter is a Certified Public Accountant and PhD candidate at Old Dominion University. She has published her research on the first one hundred black CPAs for the National Association of Black Accountants and in *Accounting, Organizations and Society*. Her other research interests include accounting and its intersections with corporate finance, financial institutions and social welfare.

Thomas N. Tyson is Professor of Accounting at Rochester, New York. He has served as visiting professor at universities in Australia, Denmark, Ireland and the UK and has numerous peer-reviewed publications and presentations in accounting history. In 2010 he was the recipient of the 2010 Academy of Accounting Historians Hourglass and Innovation in Accounting History Education Awards.

Stephen P. Walker is Professor of Accounting, Cardiff Business School, Cardiff University. He is currently editor of *Accounting History Review*, is a former editor of *Accounting Historians Journal*, a past president of the Academy of Accounting Historians and a recipient of the Academy's Hourglass Award. His research focuses on the history of the accounting profession and accounting histories of gender, social control and identity construction.

Paula A. Wilson is Associate Professor of Accounting at the School of Business and Leadership, University of Puget Sound. She has published research on the role of accounting during the Holocaust and on public interest issues related to mining operators and their environmental liabilities. Her research focuses on accounting ethics, accountability and environmental accounting.

Bibliography

Abbott, A. (1988). *The System of Professions: An Essay on the Division of Expert Labor.* Chicago: University of Chicago Press.

ACCA (Association of Certified and Corporate Accountants) *Fifty years: The story of the Association of Certified and Corporate Accountants 1904–54.* London: ACCA.

Adair, J.M. (1790). *Unanswerable Arguments against the Abolition of the Slave Trade. With a Defence of the Proprietors of the British Sugar Colonies.* London: J.P. Bateman.

Adams, C. (2004). "The Ethical, Social and Environmental Reporting-Performance Expectations Gap". *Accounting, Auditing & Accountability Journal* 17 (5): 731–57.

Adams, C., and C. Larrinaga-González. (2007). "Engaging with Organisations in Pursuit of Improved Sustainability Accounting and Performance". *Accounting, Auditing & Accountability Journal* 20 (3): 333–55.

Adler, H. (1939). "Neues Wirtschaftsrecht: VO. über den Einsatz des jüdischen Vermögens vom 3.12.38". In *Der Wirtschaftstreuhänder, Zeitschrift für deutsches Prüfungs- und Treuhandswesen. VIII, no. 1,* edited by O. Mönckmeier, 31.

Aerts, W., and D. Cormier. (2009). "Media Legitimacy and Corporate Environmental Communication". *Accounting, Organizations and Society* 34 (1): 1–27.

Africanus. (1788). *Remarks on the Slave Trade, and the Slavery of the Negroes. In a Series of Letters.* London: James Phillips.

Aglietta, M. (1979). *A Theory of Capitalist Regulation: The US Experience.* London: New Left Books.

Ahrens, T. (2008). "Overcoming the Subjective-Objective Divide in Interpretive Management Accounting Research". *Accounting, Organizations and Society* 33 (2/3): 292–97.

Albrecht, S., and R. Sack. (2000). *Accounting Education: Charting a Course through a Perilous Future.* Sarasota, FL: American Accounting Association.

Allen, M. (2002). *The Business of Genocide: The SS, Slave Labor and the Concentration Camps.* Chapel Hill: University of North Carolina Press.

American Institute of Certified Public Accountants. (1980). *The First Decade. Minority Recruitment and Equal Opportunity Committee.* New York: AICPA.

Amernic, J. (1992). "A Case Study in Corporate Financial Reporting: Massey-Ferguson's Visible Accounting Decisions 1970–1987". *Critical Perspectives on Accounting* 3 (1): 1–43.

———. (1996). "The Rhetoric versus the Reality or Is the Reality 'Mere' Rhetoric? A Case Study of Public Accounting Firms' Responses to a Company's Invitation for Alternative Opinions on an Accounting Matter". *Critical Perspectives on Accounting* 7 (1): 57–75.

———. (1998). "'Close Readings' of Internet Corporate Financial Reporting: Towards a More Critical Pedagogy on the Information". *Internet and Higher Education* 1 (2): 87–112.

Amernic, J., and R. Craig. (2000a). "Accounting and Rhetoric during a Crisis: Walt Disney's 1940 Letter to Stockholders". *Accounting Historians Journal* 27 (2): 49–86.

———. (2000b). "The Rhetoric of Teaching Financial Accounting on the Corporate Web: A Critical Review of Content and Metaphor in IBM's Internet Webpage Guide to Understanding Financials". *Critical Perspectives on Accounting* 11 (3): 259–87.

———. (2001). "Three Tenors in Perfect Harmony: 'Close Readings' of the Joint Letter by the Heads of Aluminum Giants Alcan, Pechiney, and Alusuisse Announcing Their Mega-Merger Plan". *Critical Perspectives on Accounting* 12 (6): 763–95.

———. (2009). "Understanding Accounting through Conceptual Metaphor: Accounting Is an Instrument?" *Critical Perspectives on Accounting* 20 (8): 875–83.

Anderson, G. (1976) *Victorian clerks*. Manchester: Manchester University Press.

———."The White Blouse Revolution". In *The White Blouse Revolution: Female Office Workers since 1870*, edited by G. Anderson, 2–30. Manchester: Manchester University Press.

Anderson, M., and S.P. Walker. (2009). "'All Sorts and Conditions of Men'. The Social Origins of the Founders of the ICAEW". *British Accounting Review* 41 (1): 31–45.

Andrew, J. (2007). "Prisons, the Profit Motive and Other Challenges to Accountability". *Critical Perspectives on Accounting* 18 (8): 877–904.

Annisette, M. (1999). "Importing Accounting: The Case of Trinidad and Tobago". *Accounting, Business & Financial History* 9 (1): 103–33.

———. (2000). "Imperialism in the Professions: The Education and Certification of Accountants in Trinidad and Tobago". *Accounting, Organizations and Society* 25 (7/8): 631–59.

———. (2003). "The Colour of Accountancy. Examining the Salience of Race in a Professionalisation Project". *Accounting, Organizations and Society* 28 (7/8): 639–74.

Annisette, M., and P. O'Regan. (2007). "Joined for the Common Purpose: The Establishment of the Institute of Chartered Accountants in Ireland as an All-Ireland Institution". *Qualitative Research in Accounting and Management*, 4 (1): 4–25.

Anon. (1789). *No Abolition; or, an Attempt to Prove to the Conviction of Every Rational British Subject. That the Abolition of the British Trade with Africa for Negroes Would Be a Measure as Unjust as Impolitic, Fatal to the Interests of this Nation, and Ruinous to Its Sugar Colonies*. London: J. Debrett.

Anon. (1790). *A Short Journey in the West Indies, in which Are Interspersed, Curious Anecdotes and Characters*. Vol. 1. London: J. Murray.

Answers to Rural Queries, Report from His Majesty's Commissioners for Inquiry into the Administration and Practical Operation of the Poor Laws. (1834). *British Parliamentary Papers*. Vol. 34, Appendix B1.

Answers to Town Queries, Report from His Majesty's Commissioners for Inquiry into the Administration and Practical Operation of the Poor Laws. (1834). *British Parliamentary Papers*. Vol. 36, Appendix B2.

Arad, Y., Y. Gutman and A. Margarliot. (1981). *Documents on the Holocaust: Selected Sources on the Destruction of European Jewry*. Jerusalem: Yad Vashem.

Aras, G., and D. Crowther. (2008). "Developing Sustainable Reporting Standards". *Journal of Applied Accounting Research* 9 (1): 4–16.

Armstrong, P. (1985). "Changing Management Control Strategies: The Role of Competition between Accountancy and Other Organisational Professions". *Accounting, Organizations and Society* 10 (2): 129–48.

———. (1991). "Contradiction and Social Dynamics in the Capitalist Agency Relationship". *Critical Perspectives on Accounting* 16 (1): 1–25.

———. (1994). "The Influence of Michel Foucault on Accounting Research". *Critical Perspectives on Accounting* 5 (1): 25–55.

———. (2002). "The Costs of Activity-based Management". *Accounting, Organizations and Society* 27 (1): 99–120.

———. (2005), "The Flight of the Accountant: A Romance of Air and Credit". *Critical Perspectives on Accounting* 16 (3): 165–183.

———. (2006). "Ideology and the Grammar of Idealism: the Caterpillar Controversy Revisited". *Critical Perspectives on Accounting* 17 (5): 529–48.

Arnold, A., and S. McCartney. (2003). "'It May be Earlier than You Think': Evidence, Myths and Informed Debate in Accounting History". *Critical Perspectives on Accounting* 14 (3): 227–53.

Arnold, P. (1998). "The Limits of Postmodernism in Accounting History: the Decatur Experience". *Accounting, Organizations and Society* 23 (7): 665–84.

Arnold, P., and C. Cooper. (1999). "A Tale of Two Classes: The Privatisation of Medway Ports". *Critical Perspectives on Accounting* 10 (2): 127–52.

Arnold, P., and T. Hammond. (1994). "The Role of Accounting in Ideological Conflict: Lessons from the South Africa Divestment Movement". *Accounting, Organizations and Society* 19 (2): 111–16.

Arnold, P., T. Hammond and L. Oakes. (1994). "The Contemporary Discourse on Health Care Cost: Conflicting Meanings and Meaningful Conflicts". *Accounting, Auditing & Accountability Journal* 7 (3): 50–67.

Arnold, P., and P. Sikka. (2001). "Globalization and the State-profession Relationship: the Case the Bank of Credit and Commerce International". *Accounting, Organizations and Society* 26 (6): 475–99.

Arrington, E. (1997). "Tightening One's Belt: Some Questions about Accounting, Modernity, and the Postmodern". *Critical Perspectives on Accounting* 8 (1/2): 3–13.

Arrington, E., and J. Francis. (1989). "Letting the Chat out of the Bag: Deconstruction, Privilege and Accounting Research". *Accounting, Organizations and Society* 14 (1/2): 1–28.

Arrington, E., and T. Puxty. (1991). "Accounting, Interests and Rationality: A Communicative Relation". *Critical Perspectives on Accounting* 2 (1): 31–58.

Bagehot, W. (2001). *The English Constitution*. Cambridge: Cambridge University Press.

Baker, R., and M. Bettner. (1997). "Interpretive and Critical Research in Accounting: A Commentary on its Absence from Mainstream Accounting Research". *Critical Perspectives on Accounting* 8 (4): 293–310.

Baker, R., and R. Hayes. (2004). "Reflecting Form over Substance: The Case of Enron Corp.". *Critical Perspectives on Accounting* 15 (6/7): 767–85.

Bakre, O. (2005). "First Attempt at Localising Imperial Accountancy: The Case of the Institute of Chartered Accountants of Jamaica (ICAJ) 1950s–1970s". *Critical Perspectives on Accounting* 16 (8): 995–1018.

———. (2006). "Second Attempt at Localising Imperial Accountancy: The Case of the Institute of Chartered Accountants of Jamaica (ICAJ) 1970s–1980s". *Critical Perspectives on Accounting* 17 (1): 1–28.

Ball, A. (2007). "Environmental Accounting as Workplace Activism". *Critical Perspectives on Accounting* 18 (7): 759–78.

Ballantyne, T. (2005). "The Sinews of Empire: Ireland, India and the Construction of British Colonial Knowledge". In *Was Ireland a Colony?: Economics, Politics and Culture in Nineteenth-Century Ireland*, edited by T. McDonough, 145–61. Dublin: Irish Academic Press.

Barney, D., and D. Flesher. (1994). "Early Nineteenth-Century Productivity Accounting: The Locust Grove Plantation Slave Ledger". *Accounting, Business & Financial History* 4 (2): 275–94.

Barr, N. (2004). *The Economics of the Welfare State*. Oxford: Oxford University Press.

Bartlett, R. (1978). "The Indian Act of Canada". *Buffalo Law Review* 27:581–615.

Baskerville, R. (2006). "Professional Closure by Proxy: The Impact of Changing Educational Requirements on Class Mobility for a Cohort of Big 8 Partners". *Accounting History* 11 (3): 289–317.

Basu, S., and G. Waymire. (2010). "Sprouse's What-You-May-Call-Its: Fundamental Insight or Monumental Error". *Accounting Historians Journal* 37 (1): 121–48.

Bauer, Y. (1989a). "Genocide: Was It the Nazis' Original Plan". In *The Nazi Holocaust: Historical Articles on the Destruction of the European Jews*, Book 3, Vol. 1, edited by M. Marrus. Westport, CT: Meckler.

———. (1986b). *Remembering the Future: The Impact of the Holocaust on the Contemporary World*. Oxford: Pergamon.

Baxter, J., and W. Chua. (2003). "Alternative Management Accounting Research— Whence and Whither". *Accounting, Organizations and Society* 28 (2/3): 97–126.

Bebbington, J. (1997). "Engagement, Education and Sustainability: A Review Essay on Environmental Accounting". *Accounting, Auditing & Accountability Journal* 10 (3): 365–81.

Bebbington, J., J. Brown, B. Frame and I. Thomson. (2007). "Theorizing Engagement: The Potential of a Critical Dialogic Approach". *Accounting, Auditing & Accountability Journal* 20 (3): 356–81.

Bebbington, J., and R. Gray. (2001). "An Account of Sustainability: Failure, Success and a Reconceptualization". *Critical Perspectives on Accounting* 12 (5): 557–88.

Bebbington, J., R. Gray and D. Owen. (1999). "Seeing the Wood for the Trees: Taking the Pulse of Social and Environmental Accounting". *Accounting, Auditing & Accountability Journal* 12 (1): 47–52.

Bebbington, J., C. Larrinaga and J. Moneva. (2008). "Corporate Social Reporting and Reputation Risk Management". *Accounting, Auditing & Accountability Journal* 21 (3): 337–61.

Bebbington, J., and I. Thomson. (2001). "Commentary on Some Thoughts on Economic and Environmental Accounting Education". *Accounting Education* 10 (4): 353–55.

Bentham, J. (1797) Pauper Management Improved. Reprinted in P. Schofield (ed) (2010) *The Collected Works of Jeremy Bentham. Writings on the Poor Laws Volume II*. Oxford: Oxford University Press.

Berland, N., and E. Chiapello. (2009). "Criticisms of Capitalism, Budgeting and the Double Enrolment: Budgetary Control Rhetoric and Social Reform in France in the 1930s and 1950s". *Accounting, Organizations and Society* 34 (1): 28–57.

Berlant, J.I. (1975). *Profession and Monopoly*. Berkeley: University of California Press.

Berry, A., T. Capps, D. Cooper, P. Ferguson, T. Hopper and E. Low. (1985). "Management Control in an Area of the NCB: Rationales of Past Practices in a Public Enterprise". *Accounting, Organizations and Society* 10 (1): 3–28.

Birkin, F. (2000). "The Art of Accounting for Science: A Prerequisite for Sustainable Development". *Critical Perspectives on Accounting* 11 (3): 289–309.

Black, E. (1991). *IBM and the Holocaust: the strategic alliance between Nazi Germany and America's most powerful corporation*. New York: Crown Publishers.

Black, J. (2006). "War, Women and Accounting. Female Staff in the UK Army Pay Department Offices, 1914–1920". *Accounting, Business & Financial History* 16 (2): 195–218.

Black, J., H. Blustein, K. Johnson and D. McMorris. (1976). *Area Handbook of Trinidad and Tobago*. Washington, DC: American University Press.

Blackburn, R. (1997). *The Making of New World Slavery from the Baroque to the Modern 1492–1800*. London: Verso.

Blackstone, W. (1826). *Commentaries on the Laws of England*, vol. 1, *Rights of Persons*. London: William Walker.

Blackwell, J. (1987). *Mainstreaming Outsiders: The Production of Black Professionals*. New York: General Hall.

Blanco, I., and D. de la Rosa. (2008). "Hispanics in Business Education: An Under-Represented Segment of the U.S. Population". *Critical Perspectives on Accounting* 19 (1): 17–39.

Blayton, J. (1939). *Bulletin #11*. Atlanta: National Youth Council, Colored Division.

Bledstein, B. (1976). *The Culture of Professionalism: The Middle Class and the Development of Higher Education in America*. New York: W.W. Norton.

Boldt, M. (1993). *Surviving as Indians: The Challenge of Self-government*. Buffalo: University of Toronto Press.

Booth, C., P. Clark, A. Delahaye, S. Procter and M. Rawlinson. (2007). "Accounting for the Dark Side of Corporate History: Organizational Perspectives and the Bertlesmann Case". *Critical Perspectives on Accounting* 18 (6): 625–44.

Borkin, J. (1978). *The Crime and Punishment of IG Farben*. New York: Free Press.

Bowman, C., and S. Toms. (2010). "Accounting for Competitive Advantage: The Resource-Based View of the Firm and the Labour Theory of Value". *Critical Perspectives on Accounting* 21(3): 183–94.

Boyce, G. (2000). "Valuing Customers and Loyalty: The Rhetoric of Customer Focus versus the Reality of Alienation and Exclusion of (Devalued) Customers". *Critical Perspectives on Accounting* 11 (6): 649–89.

———. (2004). "Critical Accounting Education: Teaching and Learning outside the Circle". *Critical Perspectives on Accounting* 15 (4/5): 565–85.

———. (2008). "The Social Relevance of Ethics Education in a Global(ising) Era: From Individual Dilemmas to Systemic Crises". *Critical Perspectives on Accounting* 19 (2): 255–90.

Boyer, G.R. (1990). *An Economic History of the English Poor Law 1750–1850*. Cambridge: Cambridge University Press.

Boyns, T., and J. Edwards. (1996). "The Development of Accounting in Mid-Nineteenth Century Britain: A Non-Disciplinary View". *Accounting, Auditing & Accountability Journal* 9 (3): 40–60.

———. (2000): "Pluralistic Approaches to Knowing More: A Comment on Hoskin and Macve". *Accounting Historians Journal* 27 (1): 151–58.

Brackenborough, S.J. (2003). "Pound Foolish Penny Wise System: The Role of Accounting in the Improvement of the River Tyne, 1800–1850". *Accounting Historians Journal* 30 (1): 45–72.

Braithwaite, F. (1980). "Race, Social Class and the Origins of Occupational Elites in Trinidad and Tobago". *Bulletin de Estudios Latin Americano* 28:13–30.

Braverman, H. (1974). *Labor and Monopoly Capital*. New York: Monthly Review Press.

Brennan, N., and J. Solomon. (2008). "Corporate Governance, Accountability and Mechanisms of Accountability: An Overview". *Accounting, Auditing & Accountability Journal* 21 (7): 885–906.

Brereton, B. (1981). *A History of Modern Trinidad 1783–1962*. London: Heinemann Press.

Bricker, R., and K. Brown. (1997). "The Use of Historical Data in Accounting Research: The Case of the American Sugar Refining Company". *Accounting Historians Journal* 24 (2): 1–24.

Bricker, R., and N. Chandar. (2003). "On Integrating Empirical and Historical Accounting Research". In *Doing Accounting History*, edited by R. Fleischman, V. Radcliffe and P. Shoemaker, 147–62. New York: JAI.

Briloff, A. (1981). *The Truth about Corporate Accounting*. New York: Harper and Row.

———. (1990). "Accountancy and Society: A Covenant Desecrated". *Critical Perspectives on Accounting* 1 (1): 5–30.

———. (1993a). "The Accountancy Regulatory Process: The United States Experience". *Critical Perspectives on Accounting* 4 (1): 73–83.

———. (1993b). "Unaccountable Accounting Revisited". *Critical Perspectives on Accounting* 4 (4): 301–35.

———. (2001). "Garbage In/Garbage Out: A Critique of Fraudulent Financial Reporting 1987–1997 (the Coso Report) and the SEC Accounting Regulatory Process". *Critical Perspectives on Accounting* 12 (2): 125–48.

British Parliamentary Papers. (1970). *Famine Series Vols. 5–8, 1846–48*. Shannon: Irish University Press.

Broadbent, J. (1995). "The Values of Accounting and Education: Some Implications of the Creation of Visibilities and Invisibilities in Schools". *Advances in Public Interest Accounting* 6:69–98.

———. (2002). "Critical Accounting Research: A View from England". *Critical Perspectives on Accounting* 13 (4): 433–49.

Broadbent, J., C. Gallop and R. Laughlin. (2010). "Analysing Societal Regulatory Control Systems with Specific Reference to Higher Education in England". *Accounting, Auditing & Accountability Journal* 23 (4): 506–31.

Broadbent, J., J. Gill and R. Laughlin. (2008). "Identifying and Controlling Risk: The Problem of Uncertainty in the Private Finance Initiative in the UK's National Health Service". *Critical Perspectives on Accounting* 19 (1): 40–78.

Broadbent, J., and J. Guthrie. (1992). "Changes in the Public Sector: A Review of Recent 'Alternative' Research". *Accounting, Auditing & Accountability Journal* 5 (2): 3–31.

Broadbent, J., and R. Laughlin. (1994). "Moving towards an Accounting that Will Be Enabling: Accounting, Habermas and Issues of Gender". Seminar paper, Department of Accounting and Finance, University of Wollongong.

———. (1997). "Developing Empirical Research in Accounting: An Example Informed by a Habermasian Approach". *Accounting, Auditing & Accountability Journal* 10 (5): 622–48.

Broadbent, J., R. Laughlin and S. Read. (1991). "Recent Financial Administrative Changes in the NHS: A Critical Theory Analysis". *Critical Perspectives on Accounting* 2 (1): 1–29.

Bromwich, M., and A. Bhimani. (1989). *Management Accounting: Evolution not Revolution*. London: CIMA.

———. (1994). *Management Accounting: Pathways to Progress*. London: CIMA.

Brown, R. (1905/1968). *A History of Accounting and Accountants*. London: Frank Cass.

Browning, C. (1980). "The Government Experts". In *The Holocaust: Ideology, Bureaucracy, and Genocide*, edited by H. Friedlander and S. Milton. Millwood: Kraus International Publications.

———. (1985). *Fateful Months*. New York: Holmes and Meier.

———. (1988). "Bureaucracy and Mass Murder: The German Administrator's Comprehension of the Final Solution". In *Comprehending the Holocaust*, edited by A. Cohen, Y. Gelber and C. Wardi. Frankfurt am Main: Verlad Peter Lang.

Brundage, A. (1978). *The Making of the New Poor Law*. London: Hutchinson and Co.

Brunsson, N. (2002). *The Organization of Hypocrisy*. Copenhagen: Copenhagen Business School Press.

Bryer, R. (1994). "Why Marx's Labour Theory Is Superior to the Marginalist Theory of Value: The Case from Modern Financial Accounting". *Critical Perspectives on Accounting* 5 (4): 313–40.

———. (1998). "The Struggle to Maturity in Writing the History of Accounting, and the Promise—Some Reflections on Keenan's Defence of 'Traditional' Methodology". *Critical Perspectives on Accounting* 9 (6): 669–81.

———. (1999). "A Marxist Critique of the FASB's Conceptual Framework". *Critical Perspectives on Accounting* 10 (5): 551–89.

———. (2000a). "The History of Accounting and the Transition to Capitalism in England: Part One: Theory". *Accounting, Organizations and Society* 25 (2): 131–62.

———. (2000b). "The History of Accounting and the Transition to Capitalism in England: Part Two: Evidence". *Accounting, Organizations and Society* 25 (4/5): 327–81.

———. (2006). "Accounting and Control of the Labour Process". *Critical Perspectives on Accounting* 17 (5): 551–98.

Buhr, N. (1998). "Environmental Performance, Legislation and Annual Report Disclosure: The Case of Acid Rain and Falconbridge". *Accounting, Auditing & Accountability Journal* 11 (2): 163–90.

Buhr, N., and M. Freedman. (2001). "Culture, Institutional Factors, and Differences in Environmental Disclosure between Canada and the United States". *Critical Perspectives on Accounting* 12 (3): 293–322.

Bullock, A. (1973). *Hitler: A Study in Tyranny*. London: Book Club Associates.

Burawoy, M. (1979). *Manufacturing Consent*. Chicago: Chicago University Press.

———. (1985). *The Politics of Production*. London: Verso.

Burchardt, T., J. Le Grand and D. Piachaud. (2002). "Introduction". In *Understanding Social Exclusion*, edited by J. Hills, J. Le Grand and D. Piachaud, 1–12. Oxford: Oxford University Press.

Burchell, G. (1993). "Liberal Government and Techniques of Self". *Economy and Society*, 22 (3): 267–82.

Burchell, S., C. Clubb, A. Hopwood, J. Hughes and Nahapiet. (1980). "The Roles of Accounting in Organizations and Society". *Accounting, Organizations and Society* 5 (1): 5–27.

Burchell, S., C. Gordon and P. Miller, eds. (1991). *The Foucault Effect: Studies in Governmentality*. Chicago: University of Chicago Press.

Burke, P. B. (1995). Interview with M. Annisette. February 1995.

Burnett, R., and D. Hansen. (2008). "Defining a Role for Environmental Cost Management". *Accounting, Organizations and Society* 33 (6): 551–81.

Burritt, R., and S. Schaltegger. (2010). "Sustainability Accounting and Reporting: Fad or Trend?" *Accounting, Auditing & Accountability Journal* 23 (7): 829–46.

Burrows, G. (2002). "The Interface of Race and Accounting: A Comment and Extension". *Accounting History* 7 (1): 101–13.

Bush, B., and J. Maltby. (2004). "Taxation in West Africa: Transforming the Colonial Subject into the 'Governable Person,'" *Critical Perspectives on Accounting* 15 (1): 2–34.

Butterworth, G., and S. Butterworth. (1991). *The Maori Trustee*. Wellington: Butterworth.

Byington, R., and S. Sutton. (1991). "The Self-Regulating Profession: An Analysis of the Political Monopoly Tendencies of the Audit Profession". *Critical Perspectives on Accounting* 2 (4): 315–30.

Byrne, D.S. (2005). *Social Exclusion*. Buckingham: Open University Press.

Camfferman, K., and S. Zeff. (2009). "The Formation and Early Years of the Union Européenne des Experts Comptable Economiques et Financiers (UEC). 1951–63: Or How the Dutch Tried to Bring Down the UEC". *Accounting, Business & Financial History* 19 (3): 215–57.

Canada, V.S.H. (1981). *Indian Acts and Amendments, 1868–1975: An Indexed Collection*. Saskatoon: University of Saskatchewan Native Law Centre.

Canny, N. (2001). *Making Ireland British, 1580–1650*. Oxford: Oxford University Press.

Carmona, S. (2004). "Accounting History Research and Its Diffusion in an International Context". *Accounting History* 9 (3): 7–23.

Carmona, S., and M. Ezzamel. (2007). "Accounting and Accountability in Ancient Civilizations: Mesopotamia and Ancient Egypt". *Accounting Historians Journal* 22 (2): 177–209.

Carmona, S., M. Ezzamel and F. Gutiérrez. (1998). "Towards an Institutional Analysis of Accounting Change in the Royal Tobacco Factory of Seville". *Accounting Historians Journal* 25 (1): 115–47.

———. (2004). "Accounting History Research: Traditional and New Accounting History Perspectives". *De Computis* 1 (1): 111–22.

Carmona, S., and F. Gutiérrez. (2005). "Outsourcing as Compassion? The Case of Cigarette Manufacturing by Poor Catholic Nuns (1817–1819)". *Critical Perspectives on Accounting* 16 (7): 875–903.

Carmona, S., and L. Zan. (2002). "Mapping Variety in the History and Accounting of Management Practices". *European Accounting Review* 11 (2): 291–304.

Carnegie, G., and C. Napier. (1996). "Critical and Interpretive Histories: Insight into Accounting's Present and Future through Its Past". *Accounting, Auditing & Accountability Journal* 9 (3): 7–39.

———. (2010). "Traditional Accountants and Business Professionals after Enron: Portraying the Accounting Profession". *Accounting, Organizations and Society* 35 (3): 360–76.

Carrera, N., I. Gutiérrez and S. Carmona. (2001). "Gender, the State and the Audit Profession: Evidence from Spain (1942–88)". *European Accounting Review* 10 (4): 803–15.

Carter, C., A. McKinlay and M. Rawlinson. (2002). "Introduction: Foucault, Management and History". *Organization* 9 (4): 515–26.

Carter, C., and T. Tinker. (2005). "It May Well Be that Briloff Is the Nearest U.S. Equivalent to Sikka". *Accounting, Auditing & Accountability Journal* 18 (1): 150–54.

Carter, C., and S. Toms. (2010). "The Contours of Critical Accounting". *Critical Perspectives on Accounting* 21 (3): 171–82.

Carter, S. (1990). *Lost Harvests: Prairie Indian Reserve Farmers and Government Policy*. Montreal: McGill-Queen's Press.

Catchpowle, L., and C. Cooper. (1999). "No Escaping the Financial: The Economic Referent in South Africa". *Critical Perspectives on Accounting* 10 (6): 711–46.

Catley, B. (2005). *The (Strange but Understandable) Triumph of Liberalism in Australia*. Sydney: McLeay Press.

Chandler, A. (1966). *Strategy and Structure: Chapters in the History of the American Industrial Enterprise*. Boston, MA: MIT Press.

———. (1977). *The Visible Hand: The Managerial Revolution in American Business*. Boston, MA: Harvard University Press.

Chandler, R. (1991). "Guardians of Knowledge and Public Interest: A Reply". *Accounting, Auditing & Accountability Journal* 4 (4): 5–13.

Chapman, C., A. Hopwood and M. Shields, eds. (2006). *Handbook of Management Accounting Research*. 2 vols. Oxford: Elsevier.

Chatfield, M. (1977). *A History of Accounting Thought*. New York: Robert E. Kreiger.

Chatfield, M., and R. Vangermeersch, eds. (1996). *The History of Accounting: An International Encyclopedia*. New York: Garland Publishing.

Checkland, S.G., and O.A. Checkland, eds. (1974). *The Poor Law Report of 1834*. Harmondsworth: Penguin Books.

Chew, A., and S. Greer. (1997). "Contrasting World Views on Accounting: Accountability and Aboriginal Culture". *Accounting, Auditing & Accountability Journal* 10 (3): 276–98.

Cho, C., and D. Patten. (2007). "The Role of Environmental Disclosures as Tools of Legitimacy: A Research Note". *Accounting, Organizations and Society* 32 (7/8): 639–47.

Cho, C., J. Phillips, A. Hageman and D. Patten. (2009). "Media Richness, User Trust and Perceptions of Corporate Social Responsibility: An Experimental Investigation of Visual Web Site Disclosures". *Accounting, Auditing & Accountability Journal* 22 (6): 933–52.

Chomsky, N. (1999a). *Latin America: From Colonisation to Globalisation*. Melbourne: Ocean.

———. (1999b). *Profits over People: Neoliberalism and Global Order*. New York: Seven Stories Press.

———. (2004). *Hegemony or Survival? America's Quest for Global Dominance*. London: Penguin.

———. (2006). *Imperial Ambitions: Conversations with Noam Chomsky on the Post-9/11 World*. London: Penguin.

Chow, A. (1974). The MSc Accounting. *ICAN: The Institute of Chartered Accountants Newsletter* Vol. 4 (1), p. 12–15.

Christensen, M. (2004). "Accounting by Word Not Numbers: The Handmaiden of Power in the Academy". *Critical Perspectives on Accounting* 15 (4/5): 485–512.

Chua, W. (1988). "Interpretive Sociology and Management Accounting Research: A Critical Review". *Accounting, Auditing & Accountability Journal* 1 (2): 59–79.

———. (1998). "Historical Allegories: Let Us Have Diversity". *Critical Perspectives on Accounting* 9 (6): 617–28.

Chua, W., and P. Degeling. (1993). "Interrogating an Accounting-Based Intervention on Three Axes: Instrumental, Moral and Aesthetic". *Accounting, Organizations and Society* 18 (4): 291–318.

Chua, W., and C. Poullaos. (1998). "The Dynamics of 'Closure' amidst the Construction of Market, Profession, Empire and Nationhood: An Historical Analysis of an Australian Accounting Association 1886–1903". *Accounting, Organizations and Society* 23 (2): 155–87.

Chua, W., and A. Preston. (1994). "Worrying about Accounting in Health Care". *Accounting, Auditing & Accountability Journal* 7 (3): 4–17.

Chwastiak, M. (2001). "Taming the Untamable: Planning, Programming and Budgeting and the Normalization of War". *Accounting, Organizations and Society* 26 (6): 501–19.

———. (2006). "Rationality, Performance Measures and Representations of Reality: Planning, Programming and Budgeting and the Vietnam War". *Critical Perspectives on Accounting* 17 (1): 29–55.

———. (2008). "Rendering Death and Destruction Visible: Counting the Costs of War". *Critical Perspectives on Accounting* 19 (5): 573–90.

Chwastiak, M., and J. Young. (2003). "Silences in Annual Reports". *Critical Perspectives on Accounting* 14 (5): 533–52.

Ciancanelli, P., S. Gallhofer, C. Humphrey and L. Kirkham. (1990). "Gender and Accountancy: Some Evidence from the UK". *Critical Perspectives on Accounting* 1 (2): 117–44.

Cinquini, L. (2007). "Fascist Corporative Economy and Accounting in Italy during the Thirties: Exploring the Relations between a Totalitarian Ideology and Business Studies". *Accounting, Business & Financial History* 17 (2): 209–40.

Clarke, F., R. Craig and J. Amernic. (1999). "Theatre and Intolerance in Financial Accounting Research". *Critical Perspectives on Accounting* 10 (1): 65–88.

Clarkson, P., Y. Li, D. Richardson and P. Vasvari. (2008). "Revisiting the Relation between Environmental Performance and Environmental Disclosure: An Empirical Analysis". *Accounting, Organizations and Society* 33 (4/5): 303–27.

Clarkson, T. (1808). *History of the Rise, Progress and Accomplishment of the Abolition of the African Slave Trade*. London: Longman, Hurst, Rees, and Orme.

Clawson, D. (1980). *Bureaucracy and the Labor Process: The Transformation of U.S. Industry, 1860–1920*. New York: Monthly Review Press.

Clegg, S. (2006). "The Bounds of Rationality: Power/History/Rationality". *Critical Perspectives on Accounting* 17 (7): 847–63.

Colignon, R., and M. Covaleski. (1991). "A Weberian Framework in the Study of Accounting". *Accounting, Organizations and Society* 16 (2): 141–57.

Collier, P. (2006). "Costing Police Services: The Politicalization of Accounting". *Critical Perspectives on Accounting* 17 (1): 57–86.

Collins, M., and R. Bloom. (1991). "The Role of Oral History in Accounting". *Accounting, Auditing & Accountability Journal* 4 (4): 23–31.

Collins, R. (1990). "Market Closure and the Conflict Theory of the Professions". In *Professions in Theory and History. Rethinking the Study of the Professions*, edited by M. Burrage and R. Torstendahl, 24–43. London: Routledge.

Collison, D., R. Gray, D. Owen, D. Sinclair and L. Stephenson. (2000). "Social and Environmental Accounting and Student Choice: An Exploratory Research Note". *Accounting Forum* 24 (2): 170–86.

Committe, B. (1990). "The Delegation and Privatization of Financial Accounting Rulemaking Authority in the United States of America". *Critical Perspectives on Accounting* 1 (2): 145–66.

Conrad, A., and J. Meyer. (1958). "The Economics of Slavery in the Antebellum South". *Journal of Political Economy* 64 (2): 95–130.

Cooper Brothers and Co. (1954/1986). *A History of Cooper Brothers and Co., 1854 to 1954*. London: B.T. Batsford.

Cooper, C. (1992). "The Non and Nom of Accounting for (M)other Nature". *Accounting, Auditing & Accountability Journal* 5 (3): 16–39.

———. (1997). "Against Postmodernism: Class Oriented Questions for Critical Accounting". *Critical Perspectives on Accounting* 8 (1/2): 15–41.

———. (2002). "Critical Accounting in Scotland". *Critical Perspectives on Accounting* 13 (4): 451–62.

Cooper, C., and L. Catchpowle. (2009). "US Imperialism in Action: An Audit-Based Appraisal of the Coalition Provisional Authority in Iraq". *Critical Perspectives on Accounting* 20 (6): 716–34.

Cooper, C., and P. Taylor. (2000). "From Taylorism to Mrs Taylor: The Transformation of the Accounting Craft". *Accounting, Organizations and Society* 25 (6): 555–78.

Cooper, C., P. Taylor, N. Smith and L. Catchpowle. (2005). "A Discussion of the Political Potential of Social Accounting". *Critical Perspectives on Accounting* 16 (7): 951–74.

Cooper, D., and S. Essex. (1977). "Accounting Information and Employee Decision Making". *Accounting, Organizations and Society* 2 (3): 201–17.

Cooper, D. and T. Hopper (eds). (1988). *Debating Coal Closures: Economic Calculation in the Coal Dispute 1984–5*. Cambridge: Cambridge University Press.

Cooper, D., A. Puxty, K. Robson and H. Willmott. (1996). "Changes in International Regulation of Auditors: (In)stalling the Eighth Directive in the UK". *Critical Perspectives on Accounting* 7 (6): 589–613.

Cooper, D., and K. Robson. (2006). "Accounting, Professions and Regulation: Locating the Sites of Professionalization". *Accounting, Organizations and Society* 31 (4): 415–44.

Cooper, D., and M. Sherer. (1984). "The Value of Corporate Accounting Reports: Arguments for a Political Economy of Accounting". *Accounting, Organizations and Society* 9 (3/4): 207–32.

Cooper, D., and T. Tinker. (1990). "Editorial". *Critical Perspectives on Accounting* 1 (1): 1–3.

Cooper, K. (2010). "Accounting by Women: Fear, Favour and the Path to Professional Recognition for Australian Women Accountants". *Accounting History* 15 (3): 309–36.

Cooper, S., and D. Owen. (2007). "Corporate Social Reporting and Stakeholder Accountability: The Missing Link". *Accounting, Organizations and Society* 32 (7/8): 649–67.

Cousins, J., and P. Sikka. (1993). "Accounting for Change: Facilitating Power and Accountability". *Critical Perspectives on Accounting* 4 (1): 53–72.

Covaleski, M., and M. Aiken. (1986). "Accounting and Theories of Organizations: Some Preliminary Considerations". *Accounting, Organizations and Society* 11 (4/5): 297–319.

Covaleski, M., and M. Dirsmith. (1995). "The Preservation and Use of Public Resources: Transforming the Immoral into the Merely Factual". *Accounting, Organisations and Society* 20 (2/3): 147–73.

Covaleski, M., M. Dirsmith and S. Samuel. (2003). "Changes in the Institutional Environment and the Institutions of Governance: Extending the Contributions of Transaction Cost Economics within the Management Control Literature". *Accounting, Organizations and Society* 28 (5): 417–41.

Cowton, C., and A. O'Shaughnessy. (1991). "Absentee Control on Sugar Plantations in the British West Indies". *Accounting and Business Research* 22 (85): 33–45.

Craig, R., and J. Amernic. (2004). "Enron Discourse: The Rhetoric of a Resilient Capitalism". *Critical Perspectives on Accounting* 15 (6/7): 813–52.

Craig, R. and L. Rodrigues. (2007). "Assessing International Accounting Harmonization using Hegelian Dialectic, Isomorphism, and Foucault". *Critical Perspectives on Accounting* 18 (6): 739–57.

Craig, S. (1982). "Background to the 1970 Confrontation in Trinidad and Tobago". In *Contemporary Caribbean: A Sociological Reader: Vol. 2*, edited by S. Craig, 385–423. Trinidad: College Press.

Crichlow, M. (1991). "Stratification and the Small Business Sector in Trinidad and Tobago". In *Social & Occupational Stratification in Contemporary Trinidad and Tobago*, edited by S. Ryan, 191–209. St. Augustine: Institute of Social and Economic Research.

Cromwell, A. (1992) Daughter of John W. Cromwell. Interview with Theresa Hammond 17 June.

Cullinan, C., and Sutton, S. (2002). "Defrauding the Public Interest: A Critical Examination of Reengineered Audit Processes and the Likelihood of Detecting Fraud". *Critical Perspectives on Accounting* 13 (3): 297–310.

Curtis, L.P. (1968). *Anglo-Saxons and Celts: A Study of Anti-Irish Prejudice in Victorian England*. New York: New York University Press.

Cushing, B. (1984). "A Kuhnian Interpretation of the Historical Evolution of Accounting". *Accounting Historians Journal* 16 (2): 1–41.

Czarniawska, B. (2008). "Accounting and Gender across Times and Places: An Excursion into Fiction". *Accounting, Organizations and Society* 33 (1): 33–47.

Dambrin, C., and C. Lambert. (2008). "Mothering or Auditing? The Case of Two Big Four in France". *Accounting, Auditing & Accountability Journal* 21 (4): 474–506.

Darnall, N., I. Seol and J. Sarkis. (2009). "Perceived Stakeholder Influence on Organizations' Use of Environmental Audits". *Accounting, Organizations and Society* 34 (2): 170–87.

Davenport, E. (1992) Interview with Theresa Hammond and Denise Streeter, 11 January.

Davidoff, L., and B. Westover. (1986). "From Queen Victoria to the Jazz Age: Women's World in England, 1880–1939". In *Our Work, Our Lives, Our Words*, edited by L. Davidoff and B. Westover, 3–35. London: McMillan Educational.

Davie, S. (2000). "Accounting for Imperialism: A Case of British Imposed Indigenous Collaboration". *Accounting, Auditing & Accountability Journal* 13 (3): 330–59.

———. (2005a). "Accounting's Uses in Exploitative Human Engineering: Theorizing Citizenship, Indirect Rule and Britain's Imperial Expansion". *Accounting Historians Journal* 32 (2): 55–80.

———. (2005b). "The Politics of Accounting, Race, and Ethnicity: A Story of a Chiefly-Based Preferencing". *Critical Perspectives on Accounting* 16 (5): 551–77.

Davila, T., and D. Oyon. (2008). "Cross-Paradigm Collaboration and the Advancement of Management Accounting Knowledge". *Critical Perspectives on Accounting* 19 (6): 887–93.

Davis, F.J. (1991). *Who Is Black? One Nation's Definition*. University Park: Pennsylvania State University Press.

Davis, K. (1949). *Human Society*. New York: Macmillan.

Davis, S., and R. Sherman. (1996). "The Accounting Education Change Commission: A Critical Perspective". *Critical Perspectives on Accounting* 7 (1): 159–89.

Davison, J. (2008). "Rhetoric, Repetition, Reporting and the 'Dot-Com' Era: Words, Pictures, Intangibles". *Accounting, Auditing & Accountability Journal* 21 (6): 791–826.

Dawidowicz, L. (1975). *The War against the Jews 1933–1945*. London: Weidenfeld and Nicholson.

———. (1976). *A Holocaust Reader*. New York: Behrman House.

Deegan, C. (2002). "Introduction: The Legitimising Effect of Social and Environmental Disclosures—A Theoretical Foundation". *Accounting, Auditing & Accountability Journal* 15 (3): 282–311.

Deegan, C., and M. Rankin. (1996). "Do Australian Companies Report Environmental News Objectively?: An Analysis of Environmental Disclosure by Firms Prosecuted Successfully by the Environmental Protection Authority". *Accounting, Auditing & Accountability Journal* 9 (2): 50–67.

De Lange, P., and B. Howieson. (2006). "International Accounting Standards Setting and U.S. Exceptionalism". *Critical Perspectives on Accounting* 17 (8): 1007–32.

Dellaportas, S., and L. Davenport. (2008). "Reflections on the Public Interest in Accounting". *Critical Perspectives on Accounting* 19 (7): 1080–98.

Department of Indian Affairs. (1868–1900). *Annual Reports*. Ottawa: Government of Canada.

Department of the Interior. (1877). *Annual Report*. Ottawa: Government of Canada.

de Schweinitz, K. (1972). *England's Road to Social Security*. New York: A.S. Barnes and Company.

Dewey, J. (1963). *Liberalism and Social Action*. New York: Capricorn Books.

Dillard, J. (2002). "Dialectical Possibilities and Thwarted Responsibilities". *Critical Perspectives on Accounting* 13 (5/6): 621–41.

———. (2008). "A Political Base of a Polyphonic Debate". *Critical Perspectives on Accounting* 19 (6): 894–900.

Dillard, J., and M. Reynolds. (2008). "Green Owl and the Corn Maiden". *Accounting, Auditing & Accountability Journal* 21 (4): 556–79.

Donnelly, J., Jr. (1996). "Irish Property Must Pay for Irish Poverty: British Public Opinion and the Great Irish Famine". In *Fearful Realities: New Perspectives on the Famine*, edited by C. Morash and R. Hayes, 60–76. Dublin: Irish Academic Press.

Donoso-Anes, R. (2002). "Accounting and Slavery: The Accounts of the South Sea Company 1713–1732". *European Accounting Review* 11 (2): 441–52.

Driver, F. (1993). *Power and Pauperism. The Workhouse System, 1834–1884*. Cambridge: Cambridge University Press.

Duff, A., and J. Ferguson. (2007). "Disability and Accounting Firms: Evidence from the UK". *Critical Perspectives on Accounting* 18 (2): 139–57.

Dundas, H. (1796). *Speech of the Right Hon. Henry Dundas, Delivered in the House of Commons, 15 March 1796, on the Farther Consideration of the Report of the Committee upon the Bill for the Abolition of the Slave-Trade*. London.

Dwyer, P., and R. Roberts. (2004a). "The Contemporary Gender Agenda of the U.S. Public Accounting Profession: Embracing Feminism or Maintaining Empire?" *Critical Perspectives on Accounting* 15 (1): 159–77.

———. (2004b). "Known by the Company They Keep: A Study of Political Campaign Contributions made by the United States Public Accounting Profession". *Critical Perspectives on Accounting* 15 (6/7): 865–83.

Dyball, M., W. Chua and C. Poullaos. (2006). "Mediating between Colonizer and Colonized in the American Empire: Accounting for Government Money in the Philippines". *Accounting, Auditing & Accountability Journal* 15 (1): 47–81.

Dyball, M., C. Poullaos and W. Chua. (2007). "Accounting and Empire: Professionalisation-as-Resistance: The Case of Philippines". *Critical Perspectives on Accounting* 19 (1): 47–81.

Dyck, N. (1991). *What is the Indian "Problem": Tutelage and Resistance in Canadian Indian Administration*. St. John's.: Institute of Social and Economic Research, Memorial University of Newfoundland.

Eastwood, D. (1994). *Governing Rural England. Tradition and Transformation in Local Government 1780–1840*. Oxford: Clarendon Press.

———. (1997). *Government and Community in the English Provinces, 1700–1870*. Basingstoke: Macmillan Press.

Eden, Sir F.M. (1797). *The State of the Poor*. Edited by A.G.L. Rogers. London: George Routledge and Sons.

Edgley, C., M. Jones and J. Solomon. (2010). "Stakeholder Inclusivity in Social and Environmental Reporting Assurance". *Accounting, Auditing & Accountability Journal* 23 (4): 532–57.

Edwards, B. (1798). *The History Civil and Commercial, of the British Colonies in the West Indies*. London: B. Crosby.

Edwards, J.R., ed. (2000). *The History of Accounting*. 4 vols. London: Routledge.

Edwards J.R., T. Boyns and M. Anderson. (1995). "British Cost Accounting Development, Continuity and Change". *Accounting Historians Journal* 22 (2): 1–41.

Edwards, J.R., H.M. Coombs and H.T. Greener. (2002). "British Central Government and the Mercantile System of Double Entry Bookkeeping: A Study of Ideological Conflict". *Accounting, Organisations and Society* 27 (7): 637–58.

Edwards, J.R., and S.P. Walker. (2008). "Occupation Differentiation and Exclusion in Early Canadian Accountancy". *Accounting and Business Research* 28 (5): 373–91.

———, eds. (2009). *The Routledge Companion to Accounting History*. London: Routledge.

Edwards, P., M. Ezzamel and K. Robson. (1999). "Connecting Accounting and Education in the UK: Discourses and Rationalities of Education Reform". *Critical Perspectives on Accounting* 10 (4): 469–500.

Eisner, J. (1983). "The Genocide Bomb". In *Perspectives on the Holocaust*, edited by R. Braham. Boston, MA: Kluwer-Nijhoff Publishing.

Elad, C. (1998). "Corporate Disclosure Regulation and Practice in the Developing Countries of Central Africa". *Advances in Public Interest Accounting* 7:51–106.

Elkington, J. (1998). *Cannibals with Forks: The Triple Bottom Line of 21st Century Business*. Stony Creek, CT: New Society Publishers.

Elster, J. (1986). *Karl Marx: A Reader*. Cambridge: Cambridge University Press.

Emery, M., J. Hooks and P. Stewart. (2002). "Born at the Wrong Time? An Oral History of Women Professional Accountants in New Zealand". *Accounting History* 7 (2): 7–34.

Englander, D. (1998). *Poverty and Poor Law Reform in Britain, from Chadwick to Booth, 1834–1914*. London: Longman.

Epstein, M. (1996). *Measuring Corporate Environmental Performance*. Chicago: Irwin.

Evans, L. (2003). "Auditing and Audit Firms in Germany Before 1931". *Accounting Historians Journal* 30 (2): 29–64.

Evans, R.J. (1997). *In Defence of History*. London: Granta Books.

Ezzamel, M., K. Hoskin and R. Macve. (1990). "Managing It All by Numbers: A Review of Johnson and Kaplan's *Relevance Lost*". *Accounting and Business Research* 20 (78): 153–66.

Ezzamel, M., and H. Willmott. (1993). "Corporate Governance and Financial Accountability: Recent Reforms in the UK Public Sector". *Accounting, Auditing & Accountability Journal* 6 (3): 109–32.

Ezzamel, M., H. Willmott and F. Worthington. (2004). "Accounting and Management Labour-Relations: The Politics of Production in the 'Factory with a Problem'". *Accounting, Organizations and Society* 29 (3/4): 269–302.

———. (2008). "Manufacturing Stockholder Value: The Role of Accounting in Organizational Transformation". *Critical Perspectives on Accounting* 33 (2/3): 107–40.

Ezzamel, M., J.Z. Xiao and A. Pan. (2007). "Political Ideology and Accounting Regulation in China". *Accounting, Organizations and Society* 32 (7/8): 669–700.

Fanon, F. (1963). *The Wretched of the Earth*. New York: Grove Press.

Fearfull, A., C. Carter, A Sy and T. Tinker. (2008). "Invisible Influence, Tangible Trap: The Clerical Conundrum". *Critical Perspectives on Accounting* 19 (8): 1177–96.

Fearfull, A., and N. Kamenou. (2007). "How Do You Account for It? A Critical Exploration of Career Opportunities for and Experiences of Ethnic Minority Women". *Critical Perspectives on Accounting* 17 (7): 883–901.

Ferencz, B. (1979). *Less than Slaves: Jewish Forced Labor and the Quest for Compensation*. Cambridge, MA: Harvard University Press.

Ferguson, N. (2003). *Empire: How Britain Made the Modern World*. London: Penguin.

Fielden, K. (1968). "Samuel Smiles and Self-Help". *Victorian Studies* 12 (1): 155–76.

Fleischman, R. (2000). "Completing the Triangle: Taylorism and the Paradigms". *Accounting, Auditing & Accountability Journal* 13 (5): 597–624.

———. (2004). "Confronting Moral Issues from Accounting's Dark Side". *Accounting History* 9 (1): 7–23.

———, ed. (2006). *Accounting History*. 3 vols. London: Sage Publishing.

Fleischman, R., K. Hoskin and R. Macve. (1995). "The Boulton and Watt Case: The Crux of Alternative Approaches to Accounting History?" *Accounting and Business Research* 25 (99): 162–76.

Fleischman, R., L. Kalbers and L. Parker. (1996). "Expanding the Dialogue: Industrial Revolution Costing Historiography". *Critical Perspectives on Accounting* 7 (13): 315–37.

Fleischman, R., and R. Macve. (2002). "Coals from Newcastle: An Evaluation of Alternative Frameworks for Interpreting the Development of Theories of Cost and Management Accounting in Northeast Coal Mining during the British Industrial Revolution". *Accounting and Business Research* 32 (3): 133–52.

Fleischman, R., P. Mills and T. Tyson. (1996). "A Theoretical Primer for Evaluating and Conducting Historical Research in Accounting". *Accounting History* 1 (1): 55–75.

Fleischman, R., D. Oldroyd and T. Tyson. (2004). "Monetising Human Life: Slave Valuations on U.S. and British West Indian Plantations". *Accounting History* 9 (2): 35–62.

Fleischman, R., and V. Radcliffe. (2005). "The Roaring Nineties: History Comes of Age". *Accounting Historians Journal* 32 (2): 51–109.

Fleischman, R., V. Radcliffe and P. Shoemaker, eds. (2003). *Doing Accounting History: Contributions to the Development of Accounting Thought*. Amsterdam: JAI.

Fleischman, R., and K. Schuele. (2006). "Green Accounting: A Primer". *Journal of Accounting Education* 24 (1): 33–56.

Fleischman, R. and T. Tyson. (1997). "Archival Researchers: An Endangered Species". *Accounting Historians Journal* 19(2): 167–202.

———. (1998). "The Evolution of Standard Costing in the U.K. and U.S.: From Decision Making to Control". *Abacus* 34 (1): 92–119.

———. (2000). "The Interface of Race and Accounting: The Case of the Hawaiian Sugar Plantations, 1835–1920". *Accounting History* 5 (1): 7–32.

———. (2004). "Accounting in Service to Racism: Monetizing Slave Property in the Antebellum South". *Critical Perspectives on Accounting* 15 (3): 376–99.

———. (2006). "Accounting for Interned Japanese-American Civilians during World War II: Creating Incentives and Establishing Controls for Captive Workers". *Accounting Historians Journal* 32 (1): 167–202.

Fleischman, R.K., T.N. Tyson and D. Oldroyd. (2004). "Somebody Knows the Trouble I've Seen: A Critical and Comparative Analysis of Racial Aspects of Slave Plantation Accounting in the U.S. and the British West Indies". Paper presented at the Tenth World Congress of Accounting Historians.

Fleischner, E. (1977). *Auschwitz. Beginning of a New Era*. New York: Cathedral Church of St. John the Divine.

Fleming, G. (1985). *Hitler and the Final Solution*. London: Hamish Hamilton.

Fleming, R., S. Graci and J. Thompson. (2000). "The Dawning of the Age of Quantitative/Empirical Methods in Accounting Research: Evidence from the Leading Authors of the *Accounting Review*". *Accounting Historians Journal* 27(1): 43–72.

Flesher, D., and T. Flesher. (1981). "Human Resource Accounting in Mississippi before 1865". *Accounting and Business Research* 10:S124–S29.

Fogarty, T. (1994). "Structural-Functionalism and Financial Accounting: Standard- Setting in the US". *Critical Perspectives on Accounting* 5 (3): 205–26.

———. (1996). "The Imagery and Reality of Peer Review in the U.S.: Insights from Institutional Theory". *Accounting, Organizations and Society* 21 (2/3): 243–67.

———. (1997). "The Education of Accountants in the U.S.: Reason and Its Limits at the Turn of the Century". *Critical Perspectives on Accounting* 8 (1/2): 45–68.

———. (1998). "Accounting Standard-Setting: A Challenge for Critical Accounting Researchers". *Critical Perspectives on Accounting* 9 (5): 515–23.

Fogarty, T., J. Helan and D. Knutson. (1991). "The Rationality of Doing 'Nothing': Auditors' Responses to Legal Liability in an Institutionalized Environment". *Critical Perspectives on Accounting* 2 (3): 201–26.

Fogarty, T., M. Hussein and J. Ketz. (1994). "Political Aspects of Financial Accounting Standard Setting in the USA". *Accounting, Auditing & Accountability Journal* 7 (4): 24–46.

Fogarty, T., J. Ketz and M. Hussein. (1992). "A Critical Assessment of FASB Due Process and Agenda Setting". *Research in Accounting Regulation* 6:25–38.

Fogarty, T., V. Radcliffe and D. Campbell. (2006). "Accountancy before the Fall: The AICPA Critical Perspectives on Accounting Vision Project and Related Professional Enterprises". *Accounting, Organizations and Society* 31 (1): 1–25.

Fogel, R., and S. Engerman. (1974). *Time on the Cross*. 2 vols. Boston, MA: Little, Brown and Company.

Foster, R.F. (1988). *Modern Ireland, 1600–1972*. London: Penguin.

———. (1993). *Paddy and Mr. Punch: Connections in Irish and English History*. London: Penguin.

Foucault, M. (1979). *Discipline and Punish*. New York: Vintage Books.

———. (1980a). *Language, Counter-Memory, Practice*. Ithaca, NY: Cornell University Press.

———. (1980b). "The Politics of Health in the Eighteenth Century". In *Michel Foucault, Power/Knowledge: Selected Interviews and Other Writings, 1972–1977*, edited by C. Gordon, 166–82. Brighton: Harvester Press.

———. (1984). "Panopticism". In *Foucault Reader*, edited by P. Rabinow, 206–13. New York: Pantheon.

———. (1991). "Governmentality". In *The Foucault Effect*, edited by G. Burchell, C. Gordon and P. Miller, 87–104. Chicago: University of Chicago Press.

Fowle, T.W. (1881). *The Poor Law*. London: Macmillan and Co.

Francis, J. (1990). "After Virtue? Accounting as a Moral and Discursive Practice". *Accounting, Auditing & Accountability Journal* 3 (3): 5–17.

———. (1994). "Auditing, Hermeneutics, and Subjectivity". *Accounting, Organizations and Society* 19 (3): 235–69.

Francklyn, G. (1789). *Observations Occasioned by the Attempts Made in England to Effect the Abolition of the Slave Trade; Showing the Manner in which Negroes Are Treated in the British Colonies in the West Indies*. London: Logographic Press.

Fraser, D. (1984). *The Evolution of the British Welfare State*. London: Macmillan Press.

Freedman, M., and B. Jaggi. (1988). "An Analysis of the Association between Pollution Disclosure and Economic Performance". *Accounting, Auditing & Accountability Journal* 1 (2): 43–58.

Freeman, C., and C. Perez. (1988). "Structural Crises of Adjustment, Business Cycles and Investment Behaviour". In *Technical Change and Economic Theory*, edited by G.C. Dosi, R. Freeman, G. Nelson, L. Silverberg and L. Soete, 38–66. London: Pinter Publishers.

French, S., and V. Meredith. (1994). "Women in Public Accounting, Growth and Advancement". *Critical Perspectives on Accounting* 5 (3): 227–41.

Frideres, J. (1990). "Native Rights and the 21st Century: The Making of Red Power". *Canadian Ethnic Studies* 22 (3): 1–7.

Froud, J., C. Haslam, S. Johal, J. Shaoul and K. Williams. (1998). "Persuasion without Numbers?: Public Policy and the Justification of Capital Charging in NHS Trust Hospitals". *Accounting, Auditing & Accountability Journal* 11 (1): 99–125.

Funnell, W. (1990). "Pathological Responses to Accounting Controls: The British Commissariat in the Crimea 1854–1856". *Critical Perspectives on Accounting* 1 (4): 319–35.

———. (1994). "Independence and the State Auditor in Britain: A Constitutional Keystone or a Case of Reified Imagery". *Abacus* 30 (2): 175–95.

———. (1996). "Preserving History in Accounting: Seeking Common Ground between 'New' and 'Old' Accounting History". *Accounting, Auditing & Accountability Journal* 9 (4): 38–64.

———. (1997). "Military Influences on the Evolution of Public Sector Audit and Accounting, 1830–1880". *Accounting History* 2 (2): 9–29.

———. (1998a). "Accounting in the Service of the Holocaust". *Critical Perspectives on Accounting* 9 (4): 435–64.

———. (1998b). "The Narrative and its Place in the New Accounting History: The Rise of the Counternarrative". *Accounting, Auditing & Accountability Journal* 11 (2): 142–62.

———. (2001). "Accounting for Justice: Entitlement, Want and the Irish Famine of 1845–7". *Accounting Historians Journal* 28 (2): 187–206.

———. (2004). "Victorian Parsimony and the Early Champions of Modern Public Sector Audit". *Accounting History* 9 (1): 25–60.

———. (2006). "National Efficiency, Military Accounting and the Business of War". *Critical Perspectives on Accounting* 17 (6): 719–51.

———. (2008). "The 'Proper Trust of Liberty': The American War of Independence, Economical Reform, the English Constitution and the Protections of Accounting". *Accounting History* 13 (1): 7–32.

———. (2010). "On His Majesty's Secret Service: Accounting for the Secret Service in a Time of National Peril 1782–1806". *Accounting Historians Journal* 37 (1): 29–52.

Funnell, W. and Williams, R. (2005). *Critical and Historical Studies in Accounting*. Sydney: Prentice Hall.

Gaffikin, M. (1998). "History is Dead, Long Live History". *Critical Perspectives on Accounting* 9 (6): 631–39.

Gallhofer, S. (1998). "The Silences of Mainstream Feminist Accounting Research". *Critical Perspectives on Accounting* 9 (3): 355–75.

Gallhofer, S., and A. Chew (2000). "Introduction: Accounting and Indigenous Peoples". *Accounting, Auditing & Accountability Journal* 13 (3): 256–67.

Gallhofer, S., K. Gibson, J. Haslam, P. McNicholas and B. Takiari. (2000). "Developing Environmental Accounting: Insights from Indigenous Cultures". *Accounting, Auditing & Accountability Journal* 13 (3): 381–409.

Gallhofer, S., and Haslam, J. (1997a). "Beyond Accounting: The Possibilities of Accounting and Critical Accounting Research". *Critical Perspectives on Accounting* 8 (1): 71–95.

———. (1997b). "The Direction of Green Accounting Policy: Critical Reflections". *Accounting, Auditing & Accountability Journal* 10 (2): 148–74.

———. (2000). "Bentham, Accounting and Critical Theory: Encounters in a Critical Theoretical Reading". Paper presented at the Sixth Interdisciplinary Perspectives on Accounting Conference, Manchester.

———. (2003). *Accounting and Emancipation. Some Critical Interventions*. London: Routledge.

Gallhofer, S., J. Haslam, S. Kim and S. Mariu. (1999). "Attracting and Retaining Maori Students in Accounting: Issues, Experiences and Ways Forward". *Critical Perspectives on Accounting* 10 (6): 773–802.

Garrett, A.A. (1961). *History of the Society of Incorporated Accountants 1885–1957*. Oxford: Oxford University Press.

Gates, H., Jr. (1989). "Canon-Formation, Literary History, and the Afro-American Tradition: From the Seen to the Told". In *Afro-American Literary Study in the 1990s*, edited by H. Baker and P. Redmond, 14–39. Chicago: University of Chicago Press.

Genschel, H. (1966). *Die Verdrangung der Juden aus der Wirtschaft im Dritten Reich*. Göttingen: Meisterschmidt-Verlag.

Gentile, M. (2010). *Giving Voice to Values, How to Speak Your Mind When You Know What's Right*. New Haven, CT: Yale University Press.

Gentleman Long Resident in Jamaica. (1792). *A Letter on the Greater Necessity of an Abolition of the African Slave Trade*. Bath: R. Cruttwell.

Gibbons, L. (2000). "Race against Time: Racial Discourse and Irish History". In *Cultures of Empire: A Reader*, edited by C. Hall, 207–23. London: Routledge.

Gibson, K. (2000). "Accounting as a Tool for Aboriginal Dispossession: Then and Now". *Accounting, Auditing & Accountability Journal* 13 (3): 289–306.

Gilbert, M. (1986). *The Holocaust: The Jewish Tragedy*. London: Collins.

Gisborne, T. (1792). *Remarks on the Late Decision of the House of Commons Respecting the Abolition of the Slave Trade*. London: R. White and Sons.

Glass, J. (1997). *Life Unworthy of Life: Racial Phobia and Mass Murder in Hitler's Germany*. New York: Basic Books.

Glover, H., P. Mynatt and R. Schroeder. (2000). "The Personality, Job Satisfaction and Turnover Intentions of African-American Male and Female Accountants: An Examination of Human Capital and Structural Class Theories". *Critical Perspectives on Accounting* 11 (2): 173–92.

Godfrey, A., and K. Hooper. (1996). "Accounting and Decision-Making in Feudal England: Domesday Book Revisited". *Accounting History* 1 (1): 35–54.

Goebbels, J. (1942). *Diaries*. London: Weidenfeld and Nicolson.

Goldhagen, D. (1996). *Hitler's Willing Executioners, Ordinary Germans and the Holocaust*. London: Little, Brown and Company.

Gomes, D. (2008). "The Interplay of Conceptions of Accounting and Schools of Thought in Accounting History". *Accounting History* 13 (4): 479–509.

Gordon, C. (1991). "Government Rationality: An Introduction". In *The Foucault Effect: Studies in Governmentality*, edited by G. Burchell, C. Gordon and P. Miller, 1–52. Chicago: University of Chicago Press.

Gordon, D.M., R. Edwards and M. Reich. (1982). *Segmented Work, Divided Workers*. Cambridge: Cambridge University Press.

Gorz, A. (1989). *Critique of Economic Reason*. Translated by G. Handyside and C. Turner. London: Verso.

Gotlob, D., and D.A. Dilts. (1996). "Accounting Images and the Reality of Collective Bargaining". *Journal of Collective Negotiations* 25 (2): 83–88.

Gray, A., and B. Jenkins. (1993). "Codes of Accountability in the New Public Sector". *Accounting, Auditing & Accountability Journal* 6 (3): 52–67.

Gray, P. (1995). "The Triumph of Dogma: The Ideology of Famine Relief". *History Ireland* 3:31–36.

———. (1999). *Famine, Land and Politics: British Government and Irish Society 1843–50*. Dublin: Irish Academic Press.

———. (2009). *The Making of the Irish Poor Law, 1815–1843*. Manchester: Manchester University Press.

Gray, R. (1992). "Accounting and Environmental Nationalism: An Exploration of the Challenge of Gently Accounting for Accountability, Transparency and Sustainability". *Accounting, Organizations and Society* 17 (5): 399–425.

———. (1993). *Accounting for the Environment*. London: PCP Publishers.

———. (2010). "Complexities of Sustainability: Pitfalls and Unrealistic Claims". *Accounting, Organizations and Society* 10 (1): 47–62.

Gray, R., and D. Collison. (2002). "Can't See the Wood for the Trees. Can't See the Trees for the Numbers? Accounting Education, Sustainability and the Public Interest". *Critical Perspectives on Accounting* 13 (5/6): 797–836.

Gray, R., R. Kouhy and S. Lavers. (1995a). "Constructing a Research Database of Social and Environmental Reporting in UK Companies". *Accounting, Auditing & Accountability Journal* 8 (2): 78–101.

———. (1995b). "Corporate Social and Environmental Reporting: A Review of the Literature and a Longitudinal Study of UK Disclosure". *Accounting, Auditing & Accountability Journal* 8 (2): 47–77.

Gray, R., and M. Milne. (2004). "Toward Reporting on the Triple Bottom Line: Mirages Methods, and Myths". In *The Triple Bottom Line: Does It All Add Up?*, edited by A. Henriques and J. Richardson. Sterling, VA: Earthscan.

Gray, R., D. Walters, J. Bebbington and I. Thompson. (1995). "The Greening of Enterprise: An Exploration of the (NON) Role of Environmental Accounting and Environmental Accountants in Organizational Change". *Critical Perspectives on Accounting* 6 (3): 211–39.

Green, D. (1999). "Litigation Risk for Auditors and the Risk Society". *Critical Perspectives on Accounting* 10 (3): 339–53.

Greenberg, I. (1975). "Confronting the Holocaust and Israel". Speech given to UJA Study Conference.

Greer, S. (2009). "In the Interests of the Children: Accounting in the Control of the Aboriginal Family Endowment Payments". *Accounting History* 14 (1/2): 166–91.

Greer, S., and C. Patel. (2000). "The Issue of Australian Indigenous World-Views and Accounting". *Accounting, Auditing & Accountability Journal*, 13(3): 307–29.

Grey, C. (1994). "Debating Foucault: A Critical Reply to Neimark". *Critical Perspectives on Accounting* 5(1): 5–24.

Griffiths, A. (1970). "The Irish Board of Works in the Famine Years". *The Historical Journal*, 13: 634–52.

Guénin-Paracini, and Y. Gendron. (2010). "Auditors as Modern Pharmakoi: Legitimacy Paradoxes and the Production of Economic Order". *Critical Perspectives on Accounting* 21 (2): 134–58.

Hacket, D. (1995). *The Buchenwald Report*. Boulder, CO: Westview Press.

Hackston, D,. and M. Milne. (1996). "Some Determinants of Social and Environmental Disclosure in New Zealand Companies". *Accounting, Auditing & Accountability Journal* 9 (1): 77–108.

Haines, R. (2004). *Charles Trevelyan and the Great Irish Famine*. Dublin: Four Courts Press.

Hall, J.A. (1988). *Liberalism: Politics, Ideology, and the Market*. London: Paladin Grafton.

Hamilton, C. (1991). *Adam Clayton Powell, Jr.: The Political Biography of an American Dilemma*. New York: Atheneum.

Hamilton, G., and C. Ó hÓgartaigh. (2009). "The Third Policeman: 'The True and Fair View,' Language and the Habitus of Accounting". *Critical Perspectives on Accounting* 20 (8): 910–20.

Hammond, T. (1990). "The Minority Recruitment Efforts of the Major Public Accounting Firms in New York City: A Sociological Analysis". PhD diss., University of Wisconsin.

———. (1997a). "From Complete Exclusion to Minimal Inclusion: African-Americans and the Public Accounting Industry, 1965–1988". *Accounting, Organizations and Society* 22 (1): 29–53.

———. (1997b). "Sexual Harassment and the Public Accounting Industry: The Need for Critical Examination". *Critical Perspectives on Accounting* 8 (3): 267–71.

———. (2002). *A White Collar Profession: African-American Critical Perspectives on Accountings since 1921*. Chapel Hill: University of North Carolina Press.

———. (2003a). "Histories outside the Mainstream: Oral History and Non-Traditional Approaches". In *Doing Accounting History: Contributions to the Development of Accounting Thought*, edited by R. Fleischman, V. Radcliffe and P. Shoemaker, 81–96. Amsterdam: JAI.

———. (2003b). "History from Accounting's Margins: International Research on Race and Gender". *Accounting History* 8 (1): 9–24.

Hammond, T., P. Arnold and B. Clayton. (2007). "Recounting a Difficult Past: A South African Accounting Firm's Experiences in Transformation". *Accounting History* 12 (3): 253–81.

Hammond, T., B. Clayton and P. Arnold. (2009). "South Africa's Transition from Apartheid: The Role of Professional Closure in the Experience of Black Chartered Accountants". *Accounting, Organizations and Society* 34 (6/7): 705–21.

Hammond, T., and L. Oakes. (1992). "Some Feminisms and Their Implications for Accounting Practice". *Accounting, Auditing & Accountability Journal* 5 (3): 52–70.

Hammond, T., and A. Preston. (1992). "Culture, Gender and Corporate Control: Japan as 'Other'". *Accounting, Organizations and Society* 17 (8): 795–808.

Hammond, T., and P. Sikka. (1996). "Radicalizing Accounting History: The Potential of Oral History". *Accounting, Auditing & Accountability Journal* 9 (3): 79–97.

Hammond, T., and D. Streeter. (1994). "Overcoming Barriers: Early African-American Certified Public Accountants". *Accounting, Organizations and Society* 19 (3): 271–88.

Harewood, J. (1971). "Racial Discrimination in Employment in Trinidad and Tobago (Based on Data from the 1960 Census)". *Social and Economic Studies* 20 (3): 267–93.

Harris, B. (2004). *The Origins of the British Welfare State: Society, State and Social Welfare in England and Wales, 1800–1945*. London: Palgrave.

Harrison, J. (1957). "The Victorian Gospel of Success". *Victorian Studies* 1 (1): 155–64.

Harrison, L. (1962). "The Status of the Negro CPA in the United States". *Journal of Negro Education* 31 (4): 503–6.

Harston, M.E. (1993). "The German Accounting Profession—1931 and Before: A Reflection of National Ideologies". *Accounting Historians Journal* 20 (2): 139–62.

Hay, D. (1977). "Property, Authority and the Criminal Law". In *Albion's Fatal Tree. Crime and Society in Eighteenth-Century England*, edited by D. Hay, P. Linebaugh and E.P. Thompson, 17–64. Harmondsworth: Penguin Books.

Haynes, K. (2000). "Transforming Identities: Accounting Professionals and the Transition to Motherhood". *Critical Perspectives on Accounting* 19 (5): 620–42.

———. (2008). "Moving the Gender Agenda or Stirring Chicken's Entrails?: Where Next for Feminist Methodologies in Accounting?" *Accounting, Auditing & Accountability Journal* 21 (4): 539–55.

———. (2010). "Other Lives in Accounting: Critical Reflections on Oral History Methodology in Action". *Critical Perspectives on Accounting* 21 (3): 221–31.

Heck, J., and R. Jensen. (2007). "An Analysis of the Evolution of Research Contributions by the *Accounting Review*, 1926–2005". *Accounting Historians Journal* 34 (2): 109–41.

Heier, J. (1988). "A Content Comparison of *Ante Bellum* Plantation Records and Thomas Affleck's Accounting Principles". *Accounting Historians Journal* 15 (2): 131–50.

Heier, J., and Leach-López. (2010). "Development of Modern Auditing Standards: The Strange Case of Raymond Marien and the Fraud at Interstate Hosiery Mills, 1934–1937". *Accounting Historians Journal* 37 (2): 67–93.

Heipertz, M. and Verdun, A. (2005) The stability and growth pact: Theorising a case in European integration. Paper presented at North Biennial International European Union Studies Association Conference, Austin Texas, 31 March-2 April.

Hendrickson, H. (1998). "Relevant Financial Reporting Questions Not Asked by the Accounting Profession". *Critical Perspectives on Accounting* 9 (5): 489–505.

Higman, B.W. (1976). *Slave Population and Economy in Jamaica, 1807–1834*. Cambridge: Cambridge University Press.

Hilberg, R. (1972). *Documents of Destruction*. London: W.H. Allen.

———. (1980). "The Significance of the Holocaust". In *The Holocaust: Ideology, Bureaucracy, and Genocide*, edited by H. Friedlander and S. Milton. Millwood: Kraus International Publications.

———. (1985). *The Destruction of the European Jews*. New York: Holmes and Meir.

———. (1988). "Developments in the Historiography of the Holocaust". In *Comprehending the Holocaust*, edited by A. Cohen, Y. Gelber and C. Wardi. Frankfurt am Main: Verlad Peter Lang.

———. (1989). "German Railroads/Jewish Souls". In *The Nazi Holocaust: Historical Articles on the Destruction of the European Jews*, Book 3, Vol.1, edited by M. Marrus. Westport: Meckler.

———. (1993). *Perpetrators, Victims, Bystanders: The Jewish Catastrophe*. New York: HarperCollins.

Hill, H. (1977). *Black Labor and the American Legal System: Race, Work, and the Law*. Madison: University of Wisconsin Press.

Hill, W., I. Fraser and P. Cotton. (2001). "On Patients' Interests and Accountability: Reflecting on Some Dilemmas in Social Audit in Primary Health Care". *Critical Perspectives on Accounting* 12 (4): 453–69.

Himmelfarb, G. (1984). *The Idea of Poverty*. London: Faber and Faber.

Hines, R. (1989a). "Financial Accounting Knowledge, Conceptual Framework Projects and the Social Construction of the of the Accounting Profession". *Accounting, Auditing & Accountability Journal* 2 (2): 72–92.

———. (1989b). "The Sociopolitical Paradigm in Financial Accounting Research". *Accounting, Auditing & Accountability Journal* 2 (1): 52–76.

———. (1991). "The FASB's Conceptual Framework, Financial Accounting and the Maintenance of the Social World". *Critical Perspectives on Accounting* 16 (4): 313–31.

Hitchcock, T., P. King and P. Sharpe. (1997). "Introduction". In *Chronicling Poverty. The Voices and Strategies of the English Poor, 1640–1840*, edited by T. Hitchcock, P. King and P. Sharpe, 1–18. Basingstoke: Macmillan Press.

Holden, A., W. Funnell and D. Oldroyd. (2009). "Accounting and the Moral Economy of Illness in Victorian England: The Newcastle Infirmary". *Accounting, Auditing & Accountability Journal* 22 (4): 525–52.

Hollis, P. (1979). *Women in Public: The Women's Movement 1850–1900*. London: George Allen and Unwin.

Hollister, T., and S. Schultz. (2010). "Slavery and Emancipation in New York: Evidence from Nineteenth-Century Accounting Records". *Accounting History* 15 (3): 371–405.

Holmes, S., S. Welch and L. Knudson. (2005). "The Role of Accounting Practices in the Disempowerment of the Coahuiltecan Indians". *Accounting Historians Journal* 32 (2): 105–43.

Honderich, T., ed. (1995). *The Oxford Companion to Philosophy*. Oxford: Oxford University Press.

Hoogvelt, A., and T. Tinker. (1977). "The Sierra Leone Development Company: A Case Study of Imperialism". *Critique of Anthropology* (June): 10–27.

———. (1978). "The Role of the Colonial and Post-Colonial State in Imperialism". *Journal of Modern African Studies* 16 (1): 1–13.

Hooks, B. (1981). *Ain't I a Woman: Black Women and Feminism*. Boston, MA: South End Press.

Hooks, J., and R. Stewart. (2007). "The Geography and Ideology of Accounting: A Case Study of Domination and Accounting in a Sugar Refinery in Australasia, 1900–1920". *Accounting Historians Journal* 34 (2): 143–68.

Hooks, K. (1992a). "Gender Effects and Labor Supply in Public Accounting: An Agenda of Research Issues". *Accounting, Organizations and Society* 17 (3/4): 343–66.

———. (1992b). "Professionalism and Self-Interest: A Critical View of the Expectations Gap". *Critical Perspectives on Accounting* 3 (2): 109–36.

Hooks, K., and S. Cheramy. (1994). "Facts and Myths about Women". *Journal of Accountancy* 178 (4): 79–85.

Hooks, K., and J. Moon. (1993). "Management Discussion and Analysis: An Examination of the Tensions". *Critical Perspectives on Accounting* 4 (3): 225–46.

Hooper, K., and K. Kearins. (1997). "The Excited and Dangerous State of the Natives at Hawkes Bay: A Particular Study of Nineteenth Century Financial Management". *Accounting, Organizations and Society* 22 (3/4): 269–92.

———. (2003). "Substance Not Form: Capital Taxation and Public Finance in New Zealand 1840–59". *Accounting History* 8 (2): 101–19.

———. (2004). "Financing New Zealand 1860–1880: Maori Land and the Wealth Tax Effect". *Accounting History* 9 (2): 87–105.

———. (2008). "The Walrus, Carpenter and Oysters: Liberal Reform, Hypocrisy, and Expertocracy in Maori Land Loss in New Zealand 1885–1911". *Critical Perspectives on Accounting* 19 (8): 1239–62.

Hooper, K., and M. Pratt. (1995). "Discourse and Rhetoric: The Case of the New Zealand Native Land Company". *Accounting, Auditing & Accountability Journal* 8 (1): 10–37.

———. (2003). "The Growth of Agricultural Capitalism and the Power of Accounting: A New Zealand Study". *Critical Perspectives on Accounting* 4 (3): 247–74.

Hooper, K., M. Pratt and K. Kearins. (1993). "Accounting, Auditing and the Business Establishment in Colonial Auckland, 1880–1895". *Accounting, Auditing & Accountability Journal* 6 (1): 79–98.

Hopper, T. (1990). "Social Transformation and Management Accounting: Finding Relevance in History". In *Accounting and Organizational Action*, edited by C. Gustafson and L. Hassel, 111–48. Turku: Abo Academy Press.

———. (1999). "Postcard from Japan: A Management Accounting View". *Accounting, Auditing & Accountability Journal* 12 (1): 58–69.

Hopper, T., and P. Armstrong. (1991). "Cost Accounting, Controlling Labour and the Rise of Conglomerates". *Accounting, Organizations and Society* 16 (5/6): 405–38.

Hopper, T., D. Cooper, A. Lowe, T. Capps and J. Mouritsen. (1986). "Management Control and Worker Resistance in the National Coal Board: Financial

Controls in the Labour Process". In *Managing the Labour Process*, edited by D. Knights and H. Willmott, 109–41. Aldershot: Gower.

Hopper, T., D. Northcott and R. Scapens, eds. (2007). *Issues in Management Accounting*. 3rd. ed. London: Prentice Hall.

Hopper, T., J. Storey and H. Willmott. (1987). "Accounting for Accounting: Towards the Development of a Dialectical View". *Accounting, Organizations and Society* 12 (5): 437–56.

Hopwood, A. (1987). "The Archaeology of Accounting Systems". *Accounting, Organizations and Society* 12 (3): 207–34.

Horn, P. (1980). *The Rural World, 1780–1850*. London: Hutchinson.

Hoskin, K. (1994). "Boxing Clever: For, Against and Beyond Foucault in the Battle for Accounting Theory". *Critical Perspectives on Accounting* 5 (1): 57–85.

Hoskin, K., and R. Macve. (1986). "Accounting and the Examination: A Genealogy of Disciplinary Power". *Accounting, Organizations and Society* 11 (2): 105–36.

———. (1988). "The Genesis of Accountability: The West Point Connections". *Accounting, Organizations and Society* 13 (1): 37–73.

———. (1994). "Reappraising the Genesis of Managerialism: A Re-Examination of the Role of Accounting at the Springfield Armory 1815–45". *Accounting, Auditing & Accountability Journal* 7 (2): 4–29.

———. (1996). "The Lawrence Manufacturing Co.: A Note on Early Cost Accounting in US Textile Mills". *Accounting, Business & Financial History* 6 (3): 337–61.

———. (2000). "Knowing More as Knowing Less? Alternative Histories of Cost and Management Accounting in the U.S. and the U.K". *Accounting Historians Journal* 27 (1): 91–149.

Howitt, H. (1966). *The History of the Institute of Chartered Accountants in England and Wales and Its Founder Bodies, 1870–1965*. London: ICAEW.

Hull, R., and P. Umansky. (1997). "An Examination of Gender Stereotyping as an Explanation for Vertical Job Segregation in Public Accounting". *Accounting, Organizations and Society* 22 (6): 507–28.

Humphrey, C., L. Lewis and D. Owen. (1996). "Still too Distant Voices: Conversations and Reflections on the Social Relevance of Accounting Education". *Critical Perspectives on Accounting* 7 (1/2): 77–99.

Humphrey, C., P. Miller and R. Scapens. (1993). "Accountability and Accountable Management in the UK Public Sector". *Accounting, Auditing & Accountability Journal* 6 (3): 7–29.

Humphrey, C., and P. Mozier. (1990). "From Techniques to Ideologies: An Alternative Prospective on the Audit Function". *Critical Perspectives on Accounting* 1 (3): 217–38.

Humphrey, C., P. Mozier and S. Turley. (1992). "The Audit Expectations Gap— *Plus ca Change, Plus c'est la Meme Chose?*" *Critical Perspectives on Accounting* 3 (2): 137–61.

Humphrey, C., and R. Scapens. (1996). "Methodological Themes: Theories and Case Studies of Organizational Accounting Practices: Limitation or Liberation?" *Accounting, Auditing & Accountability Journal* 9 (4): 86–106.

Inanga, E., and W. Schneider. (2005). "The Failure of Accounting Research to Improve Accounting Practice: A Problem of Theory and Lack of Communication". *Critical Perspectives on Accounting* 16 (3): 227–48.

Indian Commissioner. (1889a). *Circular Letter from the Office of the Indian Commissioner for the North West Territories, Regina, to the Battleford Agency, Battleford, Saskatchewan, 1889/11/11*. Calgary: Glenbow Archives.

———. (1889b). *Circular Letter from the Office of the Indian Commissioner for the North West Territories, Regina, to the Battleford Agency, Battleford, Saskatchewan, 1889/11/19*. Calgary: Glenbow Archives.

———. (1889c). *Circular Letter from the Office of the Indian Commissioner for the North West Territories, Regina, to the Battleford Agency, Battleford, Saskatchewan, 1889/11/21.* Calgary: Glenbow Archives.

———. (1895a). *Circular Letter from the Office of the Indian Commissioner for Manitoba and the North West Territories, Regina, to the Battleford Agency, Battleford, Saskatchewan, 1895/03/30.* Calgary: Glenbow Archives.

———. (1895b). *Circular Letter from the Office of the Indian Commissioner for Manitoba and the North West Territories, Regina, to the Battleford Agency, Battleford, Saskatchewan, 1895/04/25.* Calgary: Glenbow Archives.

———. (1895c). *Circular Letter from the Office of the Indian Commissioner for Manitoba and the North West Territories, Regina, to the Battleford Agency, Battleford, Saskatchewan, 1895/05/13.* Calgary: Glenbow Archives.

———. (1895d). *Circular Letter from the Office of the Indian Commissioner for Manitoba and the North West Territories, Regina, to the Battleford Agency, Battleford, Saskatchewan, 1895/09/10.* Calgary: Glenbow Archives.

———. (1895e). *Circular Letter from the Office of the Indian Commissioner for Manitoba and the North West Territories, Regina, to the Battleford Agency, Battleford, Saskatchewan, 1895/12/31.* Calgary: Glenbow Archives.

Innes, W. (1789). *The Slave Trade Indispensable: In Answer to the Speech of William Wilberforce, Esq. on the 13th May, 1789.* London: W. Richardson.

Institute of Chartred Accountants in England and Wales (1950). *Topographical List of Members 1950.* London, ICAEW

Institute of Chartered Accountants of Trinidad and Tobago. (1979). *ICATT List of Members 1978/1979.* Port of Spain: Institute of Chartered Accountants of Trinidad and Tobago.

International Military Tribunal. (1949). *Trial of Major War Criminals Vol. 11.* Nuremberg: Secretariat of the Tribunal under Jurisdiction of the Allied Control Authority for Germany.

Jacobs, K. (2003). "Class Reproduction in Professional Recruitment: Examining the Accounting Profession". *Critical Perspectives on Accounting* 14 (5): 569–96.

James, K. (2008). "A Critical Theory Perspective on the Pressures, Contradictions and Dilemmas Faced by Entry-Level Accounting Academics". *Critical Perspectives on Accounting* 19 (8): 1263–95.

James, K., and S. Otsuka. (2009). "Racial Biases in Recruitment by Accounting Firms: The Case of International Chinese Applicants in Australia". *Critical Perspectives on Accounting* 20 (4): 469–91.

Jeppesen, K. (2010). "Strategies for Dealing with Standard Setting Resistance". *Accounting, Auditing & Accountability Journal* 23 (2): 175–200.

John, A., ed. (1986). *Unequal Opportunities: Women's Employment in England 1800–1918.* Oxford: Blackwell.

Johnson, C. S. (1938) *The Negro college graduate.* Chapel Hill, NC: The University of North Carolina Press.

Johnson, P. (1968). *Land Fit for Heroes: The Planning of British Reconstruction 1916–1919.* Chicago: University of Chicago Press.

Johnson, T. (1972). *Professions and Power.* London: Macmillan.

Johnson, T., and R. Kaplan. (1987). *Relevance Lost: The Rise and Fall of Management Accounting.* Boston, MA: Harvard University Press.

Jones, D. (1999). *Moral Responsibility in the Holocaust: A Study in the Ethics of Character.* Oxford: Rowman and Littlefield Publishers.

Jones, M. (2008). "Internal Control, Accountability and Corporate Governance: Medieval and Modern Britain Compared". *Accounting, Auditing & Accountability Journal* 21 (7): 1052–75.

Jones, T. (1991). "Ethical Decision Making by Individuals in Organizations: An Issue Contingent Model". *Academy of Management Review* 16 (2): 366–95.

Joseph, H. (1976). "The Unworkable Marriage". *ICAN* 8 (4): 5.

Jupe, R. (2000). "Self-Referential Lobbying of the Accounting Standards Board: The Case of Financial Reporting Standard No.1". *Critical Perspectives on Accounting* 11 (3): 337–59.

———. (2009). "New Labour, Network Rail and the Third Way". *Accounting, Auditing & Accountability Journal* 22 (5): 709–35.

Jupe, R., and G. Crompton. (2006). "'A Deficient Performance': The Regulation of the Train Operating Companies in Britain's Privatised Railway System". *Critical Perspectives on Accounting* 17 (8): 1035–65.

Kalpagam, U. (1999). "Temporalities, History and Routines of Rule in Colonial India". *Time and Society* 8 (1): 141–59.

———. (2000). "Colonial Governmentality and the 'Economy'". *Economy and Society* 29 (3): 418–38.

Kaplan, R., and D. Norton. (1996). *The Balanced Scorecard: Translating Strategy into Action.* Boston, MA: Harvard University Press.

Kaplan, S., and J. McEnroe. (1991). "Positive Theory, Rationality and Accounting Regulation". *Critical Perspectives on Accounting* 2 (4): 361–74.

Karch, C.A. (1985). "Class Formation and Class and Race-relations in the West Indies". In *Middle Classes in Dependent Countries*, edited by D.L. Johnson, 107–36. Beverly Hills, CA: Sage Publications.

Katz, F. (1989). "Implementation of the Holocaust: The Behavior of Nazi Officials". In *The Nazi Holocaust: Historical Articles on the Destruction of the European Jews*, edited by M. Marrus. Westport, CT: Meckler.

Kedslie, M. (1990a). *Firm Foundations: The Development of Professional Accounting in Scotland, 1850–1900.* Hull: Hull University Press.

———. (1990b). "Mutual Self Interest—A Unifying Force: The Dominance of Societal Closure over Social Background in the Early Professional Accounting Bodies". *Accounting Historians Journal* 17 (2): 1–19.

Keenan, M. (1998). "A Defence of 'Traditional' Accounting History Research Methodology". *Critical Perspectives on Accounting* 9 (6): 641–66.

Keynes, J.M. (1936). *The General Theory of Employment, Interest and Money.* London: Macmillan.

Khalifa, R., and L. Kirkham. (2009). "Gender". In *The Routledge Companion to Accounting History*, edited by J.R. Edwards and S.P. Walker, 433–50. London: Routledge.

Killian, S. (2010). "'No Accounting for These People,' Shell in Ireland and Accounting Language". *Critical Perspectives on Accounting* 21 (8): 711–23.

Kim, S. (2004a). "Imperialism without Empire: Silence in Contemporary Accounting Research on Race/Ethnicity". *Critical Perspectives on Accounting* 15 (1): 95–133.

———. (2004b). "Racialized Gendering of the Accountancy Profession: Toward an Understanding of Chinese Women's Experiences in Accountancy in New Zealand". *Critical Perspectives on Accounting* 15 (3): 400–37.

———. (2008). "Whose Voice Is It Any Way? Rethinking Oral History Methodology in Accounting Research on Race, Ethnicity and Gender". *Critical Perspectives on Accounting* 19 (8): 1346–69.

Kinealy, C. (1994). *This Great Calamity: The Irish Famine, 1845–1852.* Dublin: Gill and Macmillan.

King, M. (2003). *The Penguin History of New Zealand.* Auckland: Penguin.

Kipnis, K. (1981). "Engineers Who Kill: Professional Ethics and the Paramountcy of Public Safety". *Business & Professional Ethics Journal* 1 (1): 77–91.

Kirkham, L. (1992). "Integrating Herstory and History in Accountancy". *Accounting, Organizations and Society* 17 (3/4): 287–97.

———. (1997). "Through the Looking Glass: Viewing Sexual Harassment within the Accounting Profession". *Critical Perspectives on Accounting* 8 (3): 273–83.

Kirkham, L., and A. Loft. (1993a). "Accountancy and the Gendered Division of Labour: A Review Essay". *Accounting, Organizations and Society* 17 (3/4): 367–78.

———. (1993b). "Gender and the Construction of the Professional Accountant". *Accounting, Organizations and Society* 18 (6): 507–58.

———. (2001). "The Lady and the Accounts: Missing from Accounting History". *Accounting Historians Journal* 28 (1): 76–90.

———. (2004). "Who Is an Accountant? Accounting Occupations in the UK Census 1861–2001". Paper presented at the 27th Annual Congress of the European Accounting Association, Prague.

Kluger, B., and D. Shields. (1991). "Managerial Moral Hazard and Auditor Changes". *Critical Perspectives on Accounting* 2 (3): 255–72.

Knights, D., and D. Collinson. (1987). "Disciplining the Shopfloor: A Comparison of the Disciplinary Effects of Managerial Psychology and Financial Accounting". *Accounting, Organizations and Society* 12 (5): 457–77.

Knights, D., and H. Willmott. (1986). "Introduction". In *Labour Process Theory*, 1–45. London: Macmillan.

Knox, W. (1789). *Three Tracts Respecting the Conversion and Instruction of the Free Indians and Negroes Slaves in the Colonies.* London: J. Debrett.

———. (1790). *A Letter from W.K. Esq. to W. Wilberforce, Esq.* London: J. Debrett.

Koeppen, D. (1990). "Creating an Accounting Culture in the Classroom". *Accounting Historians Journal* 17 (1): 89–96.

Kogon, E. (1946). *Der SS-Staat, das System der deutschen Konzentrationslager.* Frankfurt am Main: Verlag Karl Alber.

———. (1950). *The Theory and Practice of Hell, The German Concentration Camps and the System behind Them.* New York: Farrar, Straus and Co.

Komori, N. (2007). "The 'Hidden' History of Accounting in Japan: A Historical Examination of the Relationship between Japanese Women and Accounting". *Accounting History* 12 (8): 329–58.

———. (2008). "Towards the Feminization of Accounting Practice: Lessons from the Experiences of Japanese Women in the Accounting Profession". *Accounting, Auditing & Accountability Journal* 21 (4): 507–38.

Kondo, D. (1990). *Crafting Selves: Power, Gender, and Discourses of Identity in a Japanese Workplace.* Chicago: University of Chicago Press.

Kornberger, M., C. Carter and A. Ross-Smith. (2010). "Changing Gender Domination in a Big Four Accounting Firm: Flexibility, Performance and Client Service Practice". *Accounting, Organizations and Society* 35 (8): 775–91.

Laine, M. (2009). "Ensuring Legitimacy through Rhetorical Changes?: A Longitudinal Interpretation of the Environmental Disclosures of a Leading Finish Chemical Company". *Accounting, Auditing & Accountability Journal* 22 (7): 1029–54.

Lambert, E., and S. Spooner. (2005). "Corporate Governance and Profit Manipulation: A Field Study". *Critical Perspectives on Accounting* 16 (6): 717–48.

Landau, N. (1988). "The Laws of Settlement and the Surveillance of Immigration in Eighteenth-Century Kent". *Continuity & Change* 3 (3): 391–420.

———. (1990). "The Regulation of Immigration, Economic Structures and Definitions of the Poor in 18th Century England". *Historical Journal* 33 (3): 541–72.

Lapsley, I. (1988). "Research in Public Sector Accounting: An Appraisal". *Accounting, Auditing & Accountability Journal* 1 (1): 21–33.

Larrinaga-Gonzales, C., and J. Bebbington. (2001). "Accounting Change or Institutional Appropriation?: A Case Study of the Implementation of Environmental Accounting". *Critical Perspectives on Accounting* 12 (3): 269–92.

Larson, M.S. (1977). *The Rise of Professionalism. A Sociological Analysis.* Berkeley: University of California Press.

Latour, B. (1987). *Science in Action: How to Follow Scientists and Engineers through Society.* Milton Keynes: Open University Press.

Laughlin, R. (1995). "Empirical Research in Accounting: Alternative Approaches and a Case for Middle-Range Thinking". *Accounting, Auditing & Accountability Journal* 8 (1): 63–87.

———. (1999). "Critical Accounting: Nature, Progress and Prognosis". *Accounting, Auditing & Accountability Journal* 12 (1): 73–78.

Lawrence-Lightfoot, S. (1988). *Balm in Gilead: Journey of a Healer.* New York: Addison-Wesley.

Lee, J. (1989). *Ireland 1912–1985: Politics and Society.* Cambridge: Cambridge University Press.

Lee, T. (1995a). "The Professionalization of Accountancy: A History of Protecting the Public Interest in a Self-Interested Way". *Accounting, Auditing & Accountability Journal* 8 (4): 48–69.

———. (1995b). "Shaping the U.S. Academic Accounting Research Profession: The American Accounting Association and the Social Construction of a Professional Elite". *Critical Perspectives on Accounting* 6 (3): 241–61.

———. (1997). "The Editorial Gatekeepers of the Accounting Academy". *Accounting, Auditing & Accountability Journal* 10 (1): 11–30.

———. (1999). "Anatomy of a Professional Elite: The Executive Committee of the American Accounting Association 1916–1996". *Critical Perspectives on Accounting* 10 (2): 247–64.

———. (2000). "A Social Network Analysis of the Founders of Institutionalized Public Accountancy". *Accounting Historians Journal* 27 (2): 1–48.

———. (2010). "Social Closure and the Incorporation of the Society of Accountants in Edinburgh in 1854". *Accounting, Business & Financial History* 20 (1): 1–22.

Lee, T., F. Clarke and G. Dean. (2008). "The Dominant Senior Manager and the Reasonably Careful, Skilful and Cautious Auditor". *Critical Perspectives on Accounting* 19 (5): 677–711.

Lee, T., and P. Williams. (1999). "Accounting from the Inside: Legitimizing the Accounting Academic Elite". *Critical Perspectives on Accounting* 10 (6): 867–95.

Lees, L.H. (1998). *The Solidarities of Strangers. The English Poor laws and the People, 1700–1948.* Cambridge: Cambridge University Press.

Lehman, C. (1992). "'Herstory' in Accounting: The First Eighty Years". *Accounting, Organizations and Society,* 17(3/4): 261–85.

———. (2006). "The Bottom Line". *Critical Perspectives on Accounting* 17(2/3): 305–22.

Lehman, C., and T. Tinker. (1987). "The 'Real' Cultural Significance of Accounts". *Accounting, Organizations and Society* 12 (5): 503–22.

Lehman, G. (1995). "A Legitimate Concern for Environmental Accounting". *Critical Perspectives on Accounting* 6 (5): 393–412.

———. (2006). "Perspectives on Language, Accountability and Critical Accounting: An Interpretative Perspective". *Critical Perspectives on Accounting* 17 (6): 755–79.

———. (2010). "Perspectives on Accounting, Commonalities & the Public Sphere". *Critical Perspectives on Accounting* 21 (8): 724–38.

Lengel, E. (2002). *The Irish through British Eyes: Perceptions of Ireland in the Famine Era.* Santa Barbara, CA: Greenwood.

Leonard, T. (1996). "American Progressives and the Rise of Expertocracy". Paper presented at Grinnell College for the History of Economics Society Meetings, Iowa, U.S.

———. 2006. American progressives and the rise of expertocracy. Paper presented at History of Economics Society Meetings. Available at: www.princeton.edu/~tleonard/papers/expertocracy.pdf

Levant, Y. and M. Nikitin. (2009). "Charles Eugene Bedaux (1886–1944): 'Cost Killer' or Utopian Socialist". *Accounting, Business and Financial History* 19 (2): 167–87.

Levy, C. (1971). "Obituary: John W. Cromwell Jr., Noted Dunbar Teacher". *Washington Post*, 22 December.

Lewis, L., and J. Unerman. (1999). "Ethical Relativism: A Reason for Differences in Corporate Social Reporting?" *Critical Perspectives on Accounting* 10 (4): 521–47.

Lightbody, M. (2009). "Turnover Decisions of Women Accountants: Using Personal Histories to Understand the Relative Influence of Domestic Obligation". *Accounting History* 14 (1/2): 55–78.

Linn, R. (1996). *Power, Progress & Profit. A History of the Australian Accounting Profession*. Blackwood: Historical Consultants.

Lippman, E. (2009). "Accountants' Responsibility for the Information They Report: An Historical Case Study of Financial Information". *Accounting Historians Journal* 36 (1): 61–79.

Lippman, E., and P. Wilson. (2007). "The Culpability of Accounting in Perpetuating the Holocaust". *Accounting History* 12 (3): 283–303.

Littler, C.R. (1982). *The Development of Labour Processes in Capitalist Societies: A Comparative Study of the Transformation of Work Organisation in Britain, Japan, and the USA*. London: Heinemann.

Llewellyn, S. (1996). "Theories for Theorists or Theories for Practice? Liberating Academic Accounting Research?". *Accounting, Auditing & Accountability Journal* 9 (4): 112–18.

Llewellyn, S., and S.P. Walker. (2000). "Household Accounting as an Interface Activity: The Home, the Economy and Gender". *Critical Perspectives on Accounting* 11 (4): 447–78.

Locke, J. (1764). *Two Treatises of Government*. London: H. Woodfall, I. Whiston.

Lodh, S., and M. Gaffikin. (1997). "Critical Studies in Accounting Research, Rationality, and Habermas: A Methodological Reflection". *Critical Perspectives on Accounting* 8 (5): 433–74.

Loft, A. (1986). "Towards a Critical Understanding of Accounting: The Case of Cost Accounting in the U.K., 1914–1925". *Accounting, Organizations and Society* 11 (2): 137–69.

———. (1990). *Coming into the Light: A Study of the Development of a Professional Association for Cost Accountants in Britain in the Wake of the First World War*. London: CIMA.

———. (1992). "Accountancy and the Gendered Division of Labour: A Review Essay". *Accounting, Organizations and Society* 17 (3/4): 367–78.

Lovell, A. (1995). "Moral Reasoning and Moral Atmosphere in the Domain of Accounting". *Accounting, Auditing & Accountability Journal* 8 (3): 60–80.

Low, M., H. Davey and K. Hooper. (2008). "Accounting Scandals, Ethical Dilemmas, and Educational Challenges". *Critical Perspectives on Accounting* 19 (2): 222–54.

Luft, J., and M. Shields. (2003). "Mapping Management Accounting: Graphics and Guidelines for Theory-Consistent Empirical Research". *Accounting, Organizations and Society* 28 (2/3): 169–249.

Lyons, F.S.L. (1973). *Ireland since the Famine*. Dublin: Fontana.

Macdonald, K.M. (1995). *The Sociology of the Professions*. London: Sage.

Macintosh, N. (1994). *Management Accounting and Control Systems*. Chichester: John Wiley & Sons.

———. (1995). "The Ethics of Profit Manipulation: A Dialectic of Control Analysis". *Critical Perspectives on Accounting* 6 (4): 289–315.

———. (2009). "'Effective' Genealogical History: Possibilities for Critical Accounting History Research". *Accounting Historians Journal* 36 (1): 1–27.

Macintosh, N., and R. Scapens. (1990). "Structuration Theory in Management Accounting". *Accounting, Organizations and Society* 15 (5): 455–77.

Macintosh, N., N. Sherer and A. Riccaboni. (2009). "A Levinasian Ethics Critique of the Role of Management and Control Systems by Large Global Corporations: The General Electric/Nuovo Pignone Example". *Critical Perspectives on Accounting* 20 (6): 751–61.

Macve, R. (1999). "Capital and Financial Accounting: A Commentary on Bryer's 'A Marxist Critique of the FASB's Conceptual Framework'". *Critical Perspectives on Accounting* 10 (5): 591–613.

Malsch, B., and Y. Gendron. (2009). "Mythical Representations of Trust in Auditors and the Preservation of the Social Order in the Financial Community". *Critical Perspectives on Accounting* 20 (6): 735–50.

Maltby, J. (2005). "Showing a Strong Front: Corporate Social Reporting and the Business Case in Britain 1914–1919". *Accounting Historians Journal* 32 (2): 145–71.

Maltby, J., and M. Tsamenyi. (2010). "Narrative Accounting Disclosure: Its Role in the Gold Mining Industry on the Gold Coast 1900–1949". *Critical Perspectives on Accounting* 21 (5): 390–401.

Margavio, G. (1993). "The Savings and Loan Debacle: The Culmination of Three Decades of Conflicting Regulation, Deregulation and Reregulation". *Accounting Historians Journal* 20 (1): 1–32.

Markus, H.B. (1997). *The History of the German Public Accounting Profession*. New York: Garland Publishing.

Marshall, J.D. (1985). *The Old Poor Law, 1795–1834*. Basingstoke: Macmillan.

Martens, S., and J. McEnroe. (1992). "Substance over Form in Auditing and the Auditor's Position of Public Trust". *Critical Perspectives on Accounting* 3 (4): 389–401.

Martin, I. (1933). "Accounting as a Field for Colored Men". *Journal of Accountancy* 112–16.

Martin, R. (1998). "Fragmentation and Fetishism: The Post Modern in Marx". *Critical Perspectives on Accounting* 9 (1): 77–93.

Marx, K. (1867). *Capital: A Critique of Political Economics*. Vol. 1. New York: Vintage Books.

Masocha, W., and P. Weetman. (2007). "Rhetoric in Standard Setting: The Case of the Going Concern Audit". *Accounting, Auditing & Accountability Journal* 20 (1): 74–100.

Mathews, M. (1995). "Social and Environmental Accounting: A Practical Demonstration of Ethical Concern". *Journal of Business Ethics* 14 (8): 663–71.

———. (1997). "Twenty-Five Years of Social and Environmental Research: Is There a Silver Jubilee to Celebrate?" *Accounting, Auditing & Accountability Journal* 10 (4): 481–531.

———. (2001). "Some Thoughts on Social, Economic and Environmental Accounting Education". *Accounting Education* 10 (4): 335–52.

Mattessich, R. (1995). "Conditional-Normative Accounting Methodology: Incorporating Value Judgments and Means-End Relations of an Applied Science". *Accounting, Organizations and Society* 20 (4): 259–84.

———. (2003). "Accounting Representation and the Onion Model of Reality: A Comparison with Baudrillard's Orders of Simulacra and his Hyperreality". *Accounting, Organizations and Society* 28 (5): 443–70.

———. (2008). *Two Hundred Years of Accounting Research*. New York: Routledge.

Matthews, D., M. Anderson and J.R. Edwards. (1998). *The Priesthood of Industry: The Rise of the Professional Accountant in British Management*. Oxford: Oxford University Press.

Matz, A. (1938). "The Position of the German Accountant". *Accounting Review* 13 (4): 392–95.

———. (1940). "Accounting as a Tool for Economy in German Business". *Accounting Review* 15 (2): 177–85.

Mayston, D. (1993). "Principals, Agents, and the Economics of Accountability in the New Public Sector". *Accounting, Auditing & Accountability Journal* 6 (3): 68–96.

———. (1999). "The Private Finance Initiative in the National Health Service: An Unhealthy Development in New Public Management?" *Financial Accountability and Management* 15 (3): 249–74.

McKeen, C.A., and A.J. Richardson. (1998). "Education, Employment and Certification: An Oral History of the Entry of Women into the Canadian Accounting Profession". *Business and Economic History* 27 (2): 500–21.

McKernan, J. (2007). "Objectivity in Accounting". *Accounting, Organizations and Society* 32 (1/2): 155–80.

McKinlay, A. (2006). "Managing Foucault: Genealogies of Management". *Management and Organizational History* 1 (1): 87–100.

McKinlay, A., and E, Pezet. (2010). "Accounting for Foucault". *Critical Perspectives on Accounting* 21 (4): 486–95.

McNicholas, P., M. Humphrey and S. Gallhofer. (2004). "Maintaining the Empire: Maori Women's Experiences in the Accountancy Profession". *Critical Perspectives on Accounting* 15 (1): 57–93.

McSweeney, B., and S. Duncan. (1998). "Structure or Agency? Discourse or Meta-Narrative? Explaining the Emergence of the Financial Management Initiative". *Accounting, Auditing & Accountability Journal* 11 (3): 332–61.

McWatters, C. (2008). "Investment Returns and *la Traite Négrière*: Evidence from Eighteenth Century France". *Accounting, Business & Financial History* 18 (2): 161–85.

McWatters, C., and Y. Lemarchand. (2009). "Accounting for Triangular Trade". *Accounting, Business & Financial History* 19 (2): 189–212.

Meisel, B. (1992). *Geschichte der deutschen Wirtschaftsprüfer: Entstehungs—und Entwicklungsgeschichte vor dem Hintergrund einzel—undgesamtwirtschaftlicher Krisen.* Cologne: Verlag Dr. Otto Schmidt.

Mercredi, O., and M.E. Turpel. (1993). *In the Rapids, Navigating the Future of First Nations.* Toronto: Viking.

Merino, B. (1998). "Critical Theory and Accounting History: Challenges and Opportunities". *Critical Perspectives on Accounting* 9 (6): 603–16.

Merino, B., and S. Kenny. (1994). "Auditor Liability and Culpability in the Savings and Loan Industry". *Critical Perspectives on Accounting* 5 (2): 179–93.

Merino, B., and A. Mayper. (1993). "Accounting History Empirical Research". *Accounting Historians Journal* 20 (2): 237–75.

———. (2001). "Securities Legislation and the Accounting Profession in the 1930s: The Rhetoric and Reality of the American Dream". *Critical Perspectives on Accounting* 12 (4): 301–26.

Messner, M. (2009). "The Limits of Accountability". *Accounting, Organizations and Society* 34 (8): 918–38.

Miles, R. (2000). "Apropos the Idea of 'Race'. . . Again". In *Theories of Race and Racism: A Reader*, edited by L. Back and J. Solomos, 125–43. London: Routledge.

Mill, J.S. (1859/1946). *On Liberty.* Oxford: Blackwell.

Miller, M. (1999). "Auditor Liability and the Development of a Strategic Evaluation of Going Concern". *Critical Perspectives on Accounting* 10(3): 355–75.

Miller, P. (1990). "On the Interrelations between Accounting and the State". *Accounting, Organizations and Society* 15 (4): 315–38.

———. (1998). "The Margins of Accounting". *European Accounting Review* 7 (4): 605–21.

———. (2001). "Governing by Numbers: Why Calculative Practices Matter". *Social Research* 68 (2): 379–96.

Miller, P., T. Hopper and R. Laughlin. (1991). "The New Accounting History: An Introduction". *Accounting, Organizations and Society* 16 (5/6): 395–403.

Miller, P., and C. Napier. (1993). "Genealogies of Calculation". *Accounting, Organizations and Society* 18 (7/8): 631–47.

Miller, P., and T. O'Leary. (1987). "Accounting and the Construction of the 'Governable Person,'" *Accounting, Organizations and Society* 12 (3): 235–65.

———. (1993). "Accounting Expertise and the Politics of the Product": Economic Citizenship and Modes of Corporate Governance". *Accounting, Organisations and Society*, 18 (2/3): 187–206.

———. (1994). "Accounting, 'Economic Citizenship', and the Spatial Reordering of Manufacture". *Accounting Organizations and Society* 19 (1): 15–43.

Miller, P., and N. Rose. (1990). "Governing Economic Life". *Economy and Society* 19 (1): 1–31.

Milloy, J. (1983). "The Early Indian Acts: Developmental Strategy and Constitutional Change". In *As Long as the Sun Shines and Water Flows: A Reader in Canadian Native Studies*, edited by I.A.L. Getty and A.S. Lussier, 56–63. Vancouver: University of British Columbia Press.

———. (1999). *A National Crime: The Canadian Government and the Residential School System, 1879 to 1986*. Winnipeg: University of Manitoba Press.

Mills, S., and M. Bettner. (1992). "Ritual and Conflict in the Audit Profession". *Critical Perspectives on Accounting* 3 (2): 185–200.

Milne, M. (1996). "On Sustainability: The Environment and Management Accounting". *Management Accounting Review* 7 (1): 135–61.

Milne, M., H. Tregidga and S. Walton. (2009). "Words Not Actions! The Ideological Role of Sustainable Development Reporting". *Accounting, Auditing & Accountability Journal* 22 (8): 1211–57.

Mitchell, A., and P. Sikka. (1993). "Accounting for Change: The Institutions of Accountancy". *Critical Perspectives on Accounting* 4 (1): 29–52.

Mitchell, A., P. Sikka and H. Willmott. (1998). "Sweeping It under the Carpet: The Role of Accountancy Firms in Money Laundering". *Accounting, Organizations and Society* 23 (5/6): 589–607.

Mitchell, B. (1969). "The Black Minority in the CPA Profession". *Journal of Accountancy* 128 (4): 41–48.

Mobus, J. (2005). "Mandatory Environmental Disclosure in a Legitimacy Theory Context". *Accounting, Auditing & Accountability Journal* 18 (4): 492–517.

Montano, D. (1978). "Accounting Education in Trinidad and Tobago". *ICAN* 4:31–34.

Montgomery, D. (1987). *The Fall of the House of Labor: The Workplace, the State, and American Labor Activism, 1865–1925*. New York: Cambridge University Press.

Moore, D. (1991). "Accounting on Trial: The Critical Legal Studies Movement and its Lessons for Radical Accounting". *Accounting, Organizations and Society* 16 (8): 763–91.

Morgan, G., and H. Willmott. (1993). "The 'New' Accounting Research: On Making Accounting More Visible". *Accounting, Auditing & Accountability Journal* 6 (4): 3–36.

Morris, A. (1991). *The Treaties of Canada with the Indians of Manitoba and the North-West Territories: Including the Negotiations on which They Were Based, and Other Information Relating Thereto*. Saskatoon: Fifth House.

Morrison, A. (1998). *Theories of Post-Coloniality: Edward W. Said and W.B. Yeats*. Belfast: School of English, Queens University Belfast. http://www.qub.ac.uk/en/imperial/ireland/saidyeat.htm.

Morrison, M. (2004). "Rush to Judgment: The Lynching of Arthur Andersen & Co.". *Critical Perspectives on Accounting* 15 (3): 335–75.

Mouck, T. (1989). "The Irony of 'the Golden Age' of Accounting Methodology". *Accounting Historians Journal* 16 (2): 85–106.

———. (1992). "The Rhetoric of Science and the Rhetoric of Revolt in the 'Story' of Positive Accounting Theory". *Accounting, Auditing & Accountability Journal* 5 (4): 35–56.

———. (1993). "The 'Revolution' in Financial Reporting Theory, a Khunian Interpretation". *Accounting Historians Journal* 20 (1): 33–57.

———. (1994). "Corporate Accountability and Rorty's Utopian Liberalism". *Accounting, Auditing & Accountability Journal* 7 (1): 6–30.

MSc Accounting Association. (1990). *The MSc Accounting Programme at the University of the West Indies in Perspective*. Unpublished paper.

Muhlen, N. (1959). *The Incredible Krupps: The Rise, Fall, and Comeback of Germany's Industrial Family*. New York: Holt.

Mukhopadhyay, A. (2002). "Child Labour: A Problem Structural to Economy". *Socialist Perspective* 30 (1–2): 1–6.

Muller-Hill, B. (1994). "The Final Solution and the Role of Experts". In *The Final Solution: Origins and Implementation*, edited by D. Cesarani. London: Routledge.

Munro, R. (1995). "Managing by Ambiguity: An Archaeology of the Social in the Absence of Management Accounting". *Critical Perspectives on Accounting* 6 (5): 433–82.

Murphy, R. (1988). *Social Closure: The Theory of Monopolisation and Closure*. Oxford: Clarendon Press.

Murray, F. (1913). "The Position of Women in Medicine and Surgery". *New Statesman: Supplement on the Awakening of Women* (November): xvi–xvii.

Naipaul, V.S. (1970) *A flag on the island*. London Andre Deutsch.

Nandam, R., and M. Alam. (2005). "Accounting and the Reproduction of Race Relations in Fiji: A Discourse on Race and Accounting in a Colonial Context". *Accounting, Business and Political Interest* 4 (1): 283–303.

Napier, C. (1989). "Research Directions in Accounting History". *British Accounting Review* 21(3): 237–54.

———. (1998). "Giving an Account of Accounting History: A Reply to Keenan". *Critical Perspectives on Accounting* 9 (6): 685–700.

———. (2006). "Accounts of Change: 30 Years of Historical Accounting Research". *Accounting, Organizations and Society* 31 (4/5): 445–507.

Neal, M., and J. Morgan. (2002). "The Professionalization of Everyone? A Comparative Study of the Development of the Professions in the United Kingdom and Germany". *European Sociological Review* 16 (1): 9–26.

Neimark, M. (1990). "The King is Dead: Long Live the King". *Critical Perspectives on Accounting* 1 (1): 103–14.

———. (1994). "Regicide Revisited: Marx, Foucault and Accounting". *Critical Perspectives on Accounting* 5 (1): 87–108.

Neimark, M., and T. Tinker. (1986). "The Social Construction of Management Control Systems". *Accounting, Organizations and Society* 11 (4/5): 369–95.

———. (1987). "Identity and Non-Identity Thinking: A Dialectical Critique of the Transaction Cost Theory of the Modern Corporation". *Journal of Management* 13 (4): 661–73.

Nelson, R.L. (1959). *Merger Movements in American Industry 1895–1956*. Princeton, NJ: Princeton University Press.

Neu, D. (1991). "Trust, Impression Management, and the Public Accounting Profession". *Critical Perspectives on Accounting* 2 (3): 295–313.

———. (1999). "Discovering Indigenous Peoples: Accounting and the Machinery of Empire". *Accounting Historians Journal* 26 (1): 53–82.

———. (2000a). "Accounting and Accountability Relations: Colonization, Genocide and Canada's First Nations". *Accounting, Auditing & Accountability Journal* 13 (3): 268–88.

———. (2000b). "'Presents for the Indians': Land, Colonialism and Accounting in Canada". *Accounting, Organizations and Society* 25 (2):163–84.

Neu, D., D. Cooper and J. Everett. (2001). "Critical Accounting Interventions". *Critical Perspectives on Accounting* 12 (6): 735–62.

Neu, D., and C. Graham. (2004). "Accounting and the Holocausts of Modernity". *Accounting, Auditing & Accountability Journal* 17 (4): 578–603.

———. (2006). "The Birth of a Nation: Accounting and Canada's First Nations 1860–1900". *Accounting, Organizations and Society* 31 (1): 47–76.

Neu, D., and M. Heincke. (2004). "The Subaltern Speaks: Financial Relations and the Limits of Governmentality". *Critical Perspectives on Accounting* 15 (1): 179–206.

Neu, D., and C. Simmons. (1996). "Reconsidering the 'Social' in Positive Accounting Theory: The Case of Site Restoration Costs". *Critical Perspectives on Accounting* 7 (4): 409–35.

Neu, D., and R. Therrien. (2003). *Accounting for Genocide: Canada's Brutal Assault on Aboriginal People*. Black Point, NS: Fernwood Publishing.

Neu, D., H. Warsame and K. Podwell. (1998). "Managing Public Impressions: Environmental Disclosures in Annual Reports". *Accounting, Organizations and Society* 23 (3): 265–82.

Neumann, R., and J. Guthrie. (2002). "The Corporatization of Research in Australian Higher Education". *Critical Perspectives on Accounting* 13 (5/6): 721–41.

Nichols, D., R. Robinson, B. Reithal and G. Franklin. (1997). "An Explanatory Study of Sexual Behavior in Accounting Firms: Do Male and Female Critical Perspectives on Accountings Interpret Sexual Harassment Differently?" *Critical Perspectives on Accounting* 8 (3): 249–64.

Niel, D. (1792). *The African Slave Trade: Or a Short View of the Evidence, Relative to that Subject, Produced before the House of Commons*. Edinburgh: Guthrie J.

Noguchi, M., and J.R. Edwards. (2008). "Professional Leadership and Oligarchy: The Case of the ICAEW". *Accounting Historians Journal* 35 (2): 1–42.

O'Dwyer, B., and M. Canning. (2008). "On Professional Accounting Body Complaints Procedures: Confronting Professional Authority and Professional Insulation within the Institute of Chartered Accountants in Ireland (ICAI)". *Accounting, Auditing & Accountability Journal* 21 (5): 645–70.

Ó Gráda, C. (1989). *The Great Irish Famine*. London: Macmillan.

———. (1994). *Ireland, A New Economic History, 1780–1939*. Oxford: Oxford University Press.

———. (1999). *Black '47 and Beyond: The Great Irish Famine in History, Economy and Memory*. Princeton, NJ: Princeton University Press.

O'Neill, T.P. (1956). "The Organisation and Administration of Relief, 1845–52". In *The Great Famine: Studies in Irish History, 1845–52*, edited by R.D. Edwards and T.D. Williams, 209–59. Dublin: Browne Nolan.

O'Regan, P. (2003). "Accountability and Financial Control as 'Patriotic' Strategies: Accomptants and the Public Accounts Committee in Late Seventeenth and Early Eighteenth-Century Ireland". *Accounting Historians Journal* 30 (2): 105–31.

———. (2008). "Elevating the Profession: The Institute of Chartered Accountants in Ireland and the Implementation of Social Closure Strategies 1888–1909". *Accounting, Business & Financial History* 18 (1): 35–59.

———. (2010). "A Dense Mass of Petty Accountability: Accounting in the Service of Cultural Imperialism during the Irish Famine 1846–1847". *Accounting, Organizations and Society* 35 (4): 416–30.

Oakes, L., M. Covaleski and M. Dirsmith. (1999). "Labor's Changing Responses to Management Rhetorics: A Study of Accounting-Based Incentive Plans during the First Half of the Twentieth Century". *Accounting Historians Journal* 26 (2): 133–62.

Oakes, L., and T. Hammond. (1995). "Biting the Epistemological Hand: Feminist Perspectives on Science and Their Implications for Accounting Research". *Critical Perspectives on Accounting* 6 (1): 49–75.

Oakes, L., B. Townley and D. Cooper. (1998). "Business Planning as Pedagogy: Language and Control in a Changing Institutional Field". *Administrative Science Quarterly* 43 (2): 257–292.

Oakes, L., and J. Young. (2008). "Accountability Re-Examined: Evidence from Hull House". *Accounting, Auditing & Accountability Journal* 21 (6): 765–90.

———. (2010). "Reconciling Conflict: The Role of Accounting in the American Indian Trust Fund Debacle". *Critical Perspectives on Accounting* 21 (1): 63–75.

Okike, E. (2004). "Management of Crisis: The Response of the Auditing Profession in Nigeria to the Challenge to Its Legitimacy". *Accounting, Auditing & Accountability Journal* 17 (5): 705–30.

Oldroyd, D. (1998). "John Johnson's Letters: The Accounting Role of Tudor Merchants' Correspondence". *Accounting Historians Journal* 25 (1): 52–72.

———. (1999). "Historiography, Causality, and Positioning: An Unsystematic View of Accounting History". *Accounting Historians Journal* 26 (1): 83–102.

Oldroyd, D., R. Fleischman and T. Tyson. (2008). "The Culpability of Accounting Practice in Promoting Slavery in the British Empire and Antebellum United States". *Critical Perspectives on Accounting* 19 (5): 764–84.

Olson, S., and C. Wootton. (1991). "Substance and Semantics in the Auditor's Standard Report". *Accounting Historians Journal* 18 (2): 85–111.

Omi, M., and H. Winant. (1994). *Racial Formation in the United States: From 1960s to the 1980s.* New York: Routledge.

Orange, C. (1987). *The Treaty of Waitangi.* Wellington: Allen and Unwin.

Orij, R. (2010). "Corporate Social Disclosure in the Context of National Cultures and Stakeholder Theory". *Accounting, Auditing & Accountability Journal* 23 (7): 868–89.

Owen, D. (2008). "Chronicles of Wasted Time?: A Personal Reflection on the Current State of, and Future Prospects for, Social and Environmental Accounting Research". *Accounting, Auditing & Accountability Journal* 21 (2): 240–67.

Owen, D., R. Gray and J. Bebbington. (1997). "Green Accounting: Cosmetic Irrelevance or Radical Agenda for Change?". *Asian Pacific Review of Accounting* 4 (2): 346–73.

Oxley, G.W. (1974). *Poor Relief in England and Wales 1601–1834.* Newton Abbot: David and Charles.

Paige, K.L. (1991). "Integration of Blacks in the Accounting Profession: A Framework for the '90s". *CPA Journal* (September): 14–26.

Paldiel, M. (1993). *The Path of the Righteous: Gentile Rescuers of Jews During the Holocaust.* Hoboken, New Jersey: Ktav.

Parker, L. (1997). "Informing Historical Research in Accounting and Management: Traditions, Philosophies, and Opportunities". *Accounting Historians Journal* 24 (2): 111–49.

———. (2008a). "Interpreting Interpretive Accounting Research". *Critical Perspectives on Accounting* 19 (6): 9–14.

———. (2008b). "Strategic Management and Accounting Processes: Acknowledging Gender". *Accounting, Auditing & Accountability Journal* 21 (4): 611–31.

Parker, L., J. Guthrie and R. Gray. (1998): "Accounting and Management Research: Passwords from the Gatekeepers". *Accounting, Auditing & Accountability Journal* 11 (4): 371–402.

Parker, R. (1988). "Select Bibliography of Works on the History of Accounting 1981–87". *Accounting Historians Journal* 15 (2): 1–81.

Pasewark, W., R. Shockley and J. Wilkerson. (1995). "Legitimacy Claims of the Auditing Profession vis-à-vis the Behaviour of Its Members: An Empirical Examination". *Critical Perspectives on Accounting* 6 (1): 77–94.

Patten, D. (2002). "The Relation between Environmental Performance and Environmental Disclosure: A Research Note". *Accounting, Organizations and Society* 27 (8): 763–73.

Perkin, H. (1969). *The Origins of Modern English Society 1780–1880*. London: Routledge and Kegan Paul.

Piore, M., and C. Sabel. (1984). *The Second Industrial Divide: Possibilities for Prosperity*. New York: Basic Books.

Planter. (1789). *West-India Trade and Islands. Commercial Reasons for the Non-Abolition of the Slave Trade in the West-India Islands*. London: W. Lane.

Pois, R. (1989). "The Holocaust and the Ethical Imperative of Historicism". In *The Nazi Holocaust: Historical Articles on the Destruction of the European Jews*, edited by M. Marrus. Westport, CT: Meckler.

Ponemon, L. (1990). "Ethical Judgments in Accounting: A Cognitive-Developmental Perspective". *Critical Perspectives on Accounting* 1 (2): 191–215.

Popay, J., S. Escorel and M. Hernandez. (2008). *Defining and Measuring Social Exclusion*. Final Report to the WHO Commission on Social Determinants of Health from the Social Exclusion Knowledge Network. www.who.int/social_determinants/knowledge_networks/final_reports/sekn_final%20report_042008.pdf (accessed 29 May 2011).

Potter, B. (1999). "The Power of Words: Explaining Recent Accounting Reforms in the Australian Public Sector". *Accounting History* 4 (2): 43–72.

Poullaos, C. (2009). "Profession, Race, and Empire: Keeping the Centre Pure, 1921–1927". *Accounting, Auditing & Accountability Journal* 22 (3): 429–68.

Power, M. (1991). "Auditing and Environmental Expertise: Between Protest and Professionalisation". *Accounting, Auditing & Accountability Journal* 4 (3): 30–42.

———. (1992). "After Calculation? Reflections on Critique of Economic Reason by Andre Gorz". *Accounting, Organizations and Society* 17 (5): 477–99.

———. (1996). "Making things Auditable". *Accounting, Organizations and Society* 21 (2/3): 289–315.

———. (1997a). *The Audit Society: Rituals of Verification*. Oxford: University of Oxford Press.

———. (1997b). "Expertise and the Construction of Relevance: Accountants and Environmental Auditing". *Accounting, Organizations and Society* 22 (2): 123–46.

———. (2003). "Auditing and the Production of Legitimacy". *Accounting, Organizations and Society* 28 (4): 379–94.

Power, M., and R. Laughlin. (1996). "Habermas, Law and Accounting". *Accounting, Organizations and Society* 21 (5): 441–65.

Poynter, J.R. (1969). *Society and Pauperism. English Ideas on Poor Relief, 1795–1834*. London: Routledge and Kegan Paul.

Preston, A. (1992). "The Birth of Clinical Accounting: A Study of the Emergence and Transformation of Discourses on Costs and Practices of Accounting in U.S. Hospitals". *Accounting, Organizations and Society* 17 (1): 63–100.

———. (2006). "Enabling, Enacting and Maintaining Action at a Distance: An Historical Case Study of the Role of Accounting in the Reduction of the Navajo Herds". *Accounting, Organizations and Society* 31 (6): 559–78.

Preston, A., W. Chua and D. Neu. (1997). "The Diagnosis-Related Group-Prospective System and the Problem of the Government of Rationing Health Care to the Elderly". *Accounting, Organizations and Society* 22 (2): 147–64.

Preston, A., D. Cooper and S. Combs. (1992). "Fabricating Budgets, a Study of the Introduction of Budgeting in the National Health Service". *Accounting, Organizations and Society* 17 (6): 561–93.

Preston, A., D. Cooper, D. Scarborough and R. Chilton. (1995). "Changes in the Code of Ethics of the U.S. Accounting Profession, 1917 and 1988: The Continual Quest for Legitimation". *Accounting, Organizations and Society* 20 (6): 507–46.

Preston, A., and L. Oakes. (2001). "The Navajo Documents: A Study of the Economic Representation and Construction of the Navajo". *Accounting, Organizations and Society* 26 (1): 39–71.

Previts, G., and B. Merino. (1979). *A History of Accounting in America: An Historical Interpretation of the Cultural Significance of Accounting*. New York: Wiley.

Previts, G., L. Parker and E. Coffman. (1990a). "Accounting History: Definition and Relevance". *Abacus* 26 (1): 1–16.

———. (1990b). "Accounting History: Subject Matter and Methodology". *Abacus* 26 (1): 136–58.

Price, R., Indian Association of Alberta, & Treaty & Aboriginal Rights Research Centre of Manitoba. (1975). *Spirit and Terms of Treaties 6, 7 & 8: Alberta Indian Perspectives*. Edmonton: Indian Association of Alberta.

Prince, M. (1831). *The History of Mary Prince, a West Indian Slave*. London: Westley and Daviseckley.

Puxty, T., and R. Laughlin. (1983). "A Rational Reconstruction of the Decision-Usefulness Criterion". *Journal of Business Finance and Accounting* 10 (4): 543–59.

Puxty, T., P. Sikka and H. Willmott. (1994). "Reforming the Circle: Education, Ethics and Accountancy". *Accounting Education* 3 (1): 77–92.

———. (2004). "Systems of Surveillance and the Silencing of UK Radical Accounting Labour". *British Accounting Review* 26 (2): 137–71.

Puxty, A., H. Willmott, D. Cooper and T. Lowe. (1987). "Modes of Regulation in Advanced Capitalism: Locating Accountancy in Four Countries". *Accounting, Organizations and Society* 12 (3): 273–91.

Quattrone, P. (2004). "Accounting for God: Accounting and Accountability Practices in the Society of Jesus (Italy, XVI–XVII Centuries)". *Accounting, Organizations and Society* 29 (7): 647–83.

Rabinow, P., and N. Rose, eds. (2003). *The Essential Foucault: Selections from the Essential Works of Foucault, 1954–1984*. New York: New Press.

Radcliffe, V. (2008). "Public Secrecy in Auditing: What Government Auditors Cannot Know". *Critical Perspectives on Accounting* 19 (1): 99–126.

Rahaman, A. (2010). "Critical Accounting Research in Africa: Whence and Whither". *Critical Perspectives on Accounting* 21 (5): 420–27.

Ramirez, C. (2001). "Understanding Social Closure in its Cultural Context: Accounting Practitioners in France (1920–1939)". *Accounting, Organizations and Society* 26 (4/5): 391–418.

Ramsay, J. (1789). *An Address to the Publick on the Proposed Bill for the Abolition of the Slave Trade*. London: J. Phillips.

Randolph, F. (1788). *A Letter to the Right Honourable William Pitt on the Proposed Abolition of the Slave Trade*. London: T. Cadell.

Rayburn, M., and G. Rayburn. (1991). "Contingency Theory and the Impact of New Accounting Technology in Uncertain Hospital Environments". *Accounting, Auditing & Accountability Journal* 4 (2): 55–75.

Razek, J. (1985). "Accounting on the Old Plantation". *Accounting Historians Journal* 10 (1): 19–36.

Reiter, S. (1996). "The Kohlberg-Gilligan Controversy: Lessons for Accounting Ethics Education". *Critical Perspectives on Accounting* 7(1/2): 33–54.

———. (1997). "The Ethics of Care and New Paradigms for Accounting Practice". *Accounting, Auditing & Accountability Journal* 10 (3): 299–324.

———. (1998). "Economic Imperialism and the Crisis in Financial Accounting Research". *Critical Perspectives on Accounting* 9 (2): 143–71.

Report from the Select Committee of the House of Lords on the Poor Laws. (1818). *British Parliamentary Papers*. Vol. 5.

———. (1831). *British Parliamentary Papers*. Vol. 8.

Report of the Royal Commission on Aboriginal Peoples. (1996). Ottawa: Canada Communications Group.

Reports of Assistant Commissioners, Report from His Majesty's Commissioners for Inquiry into the Administration and Practical Operation of the Poor Laws. (1834). *British Parliamentary Papers*. Vols. 28–29, Appendix A.

Rex, J. (1986). *Race and Ethnicity*. Milton Keynes: Open University Press.

Richardson, A. (1987a). "Accounting as a Legitimating Institution". *Accounting, Organizations and Society* 12 (4): 341–55.

———. (1987b). "Professionalization and Intraprofessional Competition in the Canadian Accounting Profession". *Work and Occupations* 14 (4): 591–615.

———. (1989). "Canada's Accounting Elite: 1880–1930". *Accounting Historians Journal* 16 (1): 1–20.

———. (2008). "Strategies in the Development of Accounting History as an Academic Discipline". *Accounting History* 13 (3): 247–80.

Roberts, J. (1991). "The Possibilities of Accountability". *Accounting, Organizations and Society* 16 (4): 355–68.

———. (2009). "No One is Perfect: The Limits of Transparency and an Ethic for 'Intelligent' Accountability". *Accounting, Organizations and Society* 34 (8): 957–70.

Roberts, J., and J.A. Coutts. (1992). "Feminization and Professionalization: A Review of an Emerging Literature on the Development of Accounting in the United Kingdom". *Accounting, Organizations and Society* 17 (3/4): 379–95.

Robson, K. (1992). "Accounting Numbers as 'Inscription': Action at a Distance and the Development of Accounting". *Accounting, Organizations and Society* 17 (7): 685–708.

Robson, N. (2007). "Adapting Not Adopting: 1958–74, Accounting and Managerial Reform in the Early NHS". *Accounting, Business & Financial History* 17 (3): 445–67.

Rodgers, J., and P. Williams. (1996). "Patterns of Research Productivity and Knowledge Creation at *The Accounting Review*: 1967–1993". *Accounting Historians Journal* 23 (1): 51–88.

Rodrigues, L. and Craig, R. (2007). "Assessing International Accounting Harmonization using Hegelian Dialectic, Isomorphism, and Foucault". *Critical Perspectives on Accounting* 18(6):739–757.

Roscoe, W. (1788). *A General View of the African Slave-Trade, Demonstrating its Injustice and Impolicy: With Hints towards a Bill for Its Abolition*. London: R. Faulder.

Rose, M. (1985). "Introduction: the Poor and the City, 1834–1914". In *The Poor and the City: The English Poor Law in its Urban Context, 1834–1914*, edited by M. Rose, 2–17. Leicester: Leicester University Press.

Rose, N. (1991). "Governing by Numbers: Figuring out Democracy". *Accounting, Organizations and Society* 16 (7): 673–92.

———. (1993). "Government, Authority and Expertise in Advanced Liberalism". *Economy and Society* 2 (3): 283–89.

Rosenberg, A. (1983). "The Philosophical Implications of the Holocaust". In *Perspectives on the Holocaust*, edited by R. Braham. Boston, MA: Kluwer-Nijhoff Publishing.

Rosenberg, A., and P. Marcus. (1988). "The Holocaust as a Test of Philosophy". In *Echoes from the Holocaust, Philosophical Reflections on a Dark Time*, edited by A. Rosenberg and P. Marcus, 201–22. Philadelphia, PA: Temple University Press.

Rosenblum, N. (1989). *Liberalism and the Moral Life*. Cambridge, MA: Harvard University Press.

Roslender, R., and J. Dillard. (2003). "Reflections on the Interdisciplinary Perspectives on Accounting Project". *Critical Perspectives on Accounting* 14 (3): 325–51.

Roslender, R., and J. Stevenson. (2009). "Accounting for People: A Real Step Forward or a Case of Wishing and Hoping". *Critical Perspectives on Accounting* 20 (7): 155–69.

Ross, A. (1967). "The Negro in the American Economy". In *Employment, Race, and Poverty*, edited by A. Ross and H. Hill, 3–48. New York: Harcourt Brace.

Rutterford, J., and J. Maltby. (2006). "Frank Must Marry for Money: Men, Women, and Property in Trollope's Novels". *Accounting Historians Journal* 33 (2): 169–99.

Ryan, S. (1972). *Race and Nationalism in Trinidad and Tobago*. Toronto: University of Toronto Press.

———. (1991a). "Race and Occupational Stratification in Trinidad and Tobago". In *Social & Occupational Stratification on Contemporary Trinidad and Tobago*, edited by S. Ryan, 166–90. St. Augustine: Institute of Social and Economic Research.

———. (1991b). "Social Stratification in Trinidad and Tobago: Lloyd Braithwaite Revisited". In *Social & Occupational Stratification on Contemporary Trinidad and Tobago*, edited by S. Ryan, 58–79. St. Augustine: Institute of Social and Economic Research.

Said, E. (1944). *Culture and Imperialism*. London: Fontana.

———. (1978). *Orientalism*. New York: Vintage Books.

———. (1979). *Orientalism*. New York: Vintage Books.

———. (1988). "Nationalism, Colonialism and Literature: Yeats and Decolonization". Field Day Pamphlets, Series, 5, *Nationalism, Colonialism and Literature*. Londonderry: Field Day.

———. (1993). *Culture and Imperialism*. New York: Vintage Books.

Sample, R.J. (2003). *Exploitation. What It Is and Why It's Wrong*. Oxford: Rowman and Littlefield Publishers.

Samuelson, R. (1999). "The Subjectivity of the FASB's Conceptual Framework: A Commentary on Bryer". *Critical Perspectives on Accounting* 10 (5): 631–41.

Saravanamuthu, K. (2004). "Gold-Collarism in the Academy: The Dilemma of Transforming Bean-Counters into Knowledge Consultants". *Critical Perspectives on Accounting* (15 (4/5): 587–607.

Sarcee Indian Agency Clerk. (1885). *Diary 1885*. Calgary: Glenbow Archives.

Sargiacomo, M. (2008). "Institutional Pressures and Isomorphic Change in a High- Fashion Company: The Case of Brioni Roman Style 1945–89". *Accounting, Business & Financial History* 18 (2): 215–41.

Scapens, R. (2008). "Seeking the Relevance of Interpretive Research: A Contribution to the Polyphonic Debate". *Critical Perspectives on Accounting* 19 (6): 15–19.

Scott, J.W. (1987). "Rewriting History". In *Behind the Lines: Gender and the Two World Wars*, edited by M.R. Higonnet, J. Jensen, S. Michel and M.C. Weitz, 19–30. Newhaven: Newhaven University Press.

———. (1988). *Gender and the Politics of History*. New York: Colombia University Press.

Select Committee. (1791). *An Abstract of the Evidence Delivered to the Select Committee of the House of Common, in the Years 1790 and 1791 on the Part of the Petitioners for the Abolition of the Slave Trade*. Edinburgh.

Sen, A. (1981). *Poverty and Famines: An Essay on Entitlement and Deprivation*. Oxford: Clarendon Press.

Shackleton, K. (1999). "Gendered Segregation in Scottish Chartered Accountancy: The Deployment of Male Concern about the Admission of Women, 1900–1925". *Accounting, Business & Financial History* 9 (1): 135–56.

Shapiro, B. (1998). "Toward a Normative Model of Rational Argumentation for Critical Accounting Discussions". *Accounting, Organizations and Society* 23 (7): 641–63.

———. (2002). "Rash Words, Insincere Assurances, Uncertain Promises: Verifying Employers' Intentions in Labor Contracts". *Critical Perspectives on Accounting* 13 (1): 63–88.

———. (2009). "A Comparative, Analysis of Theological and Critical Perspectives on Emancipatory Praxis through Accounting". *Critical Perspectives on Accounting* 20 (8): 944–55.

Shenkin, M., and A. Coulson. (2007). "Accountability through Activism: Learning from Bourdieu". *Accounting, Auditing & Accountability Journal* 20 (2): 297–317.

Shirer, W. (1960). *The Rise and Fall of the Third Reich*. New York: Simon and Schuster.

Sian, S. (2006a). "Inclusion, Exclusion, and Control: The Case of the Kenyan Accounting Professionalization Project". *Accounting, Organizations and Society* 31 (3): 295–322.

———. (2006b). "Reversing Exclusion: The Africanization of Accounting in Kenya 1963–70". *Critical Perspectives on Accounting* 18 (7): 831–72.

———. (2007). "Patterns of Prejudice: Social Exclusion and Racial Demarcation in Professional Accountancy in Kenya". *Accounting Historians Journal* 34 (2): 1–42.

Sikka, P. (2001). "Regulation of Accountancy and the Power of Capital: Some Observations". *Critical Perspectives on Accounting* 12 (2): 199–224.

———. (2008). "Corporate Governance: What about the Workers?" *Accounting, Auditing & Accountability Journal* 21 (7): 955–77.

Sikka, P., B. Wearing and A. Nayak. (1999). *No Accounting for Exploitation*. Basildon: Association for Accountancy and Business Affairs.

Sikka, P., and H. Willmott. (1995). "Illuminating the State–Profession Relationship: Accountants Acting as Department of Trade and Industry Investigators". *Critical Perspectives on Accounting* 6 (4): 341–69.

———. (1997). "Practising Critical Accounting". *Critical Perspectives on Accounting* 8 (1/2): 149–65.

———. (2005). "The Withering of Tolerance and Communication in Interdisciplinary Accounting Studies". *Accounting, Auditing & Accountability Journal* 18 (1): 136–46.

Sikka, P., H. Willmott and T. Lowe. (1989). "Guardians of Knowledge and Public Interest: Evidence and Issues of Accountability in the UK Accountancy Profession". *Accounting, Auditing & Accountability Journal* 2 (2): 47–71.

———. (1991). "Guardians of Knowledge and Public Interest: A Reply to Our Critics". *Accounting, Auditing & Accountability Journal* 4 (4): 14–22.

Sikka, P., H. Willmott and T. Puxty. (1995). "The Mountains are Still There: Accounting Academics and the Bearing of Intellectuals". *Accounting, Auditing & Accountability Journal* 8 (3): 113–40.

Silver, H. (1994). "Social Exclusion and Social Solidarity: Three Paradigms". *International Labour Review* 133 (5/6): 531–78.

Simmons, W. (1887). *Men of mark: eminent, progressive and rising.* New York: Geo. M. Rewell & Co. Reprinted by Arno Press, New York, 1968).

———. (1968). *Men of Mark: Eminent, Progressive and Rising.* New York: Arno Press.

Sinclair, K. (1991). *A History of New Zealand.* London: Allen Lane.

Singer, H. (1943). "Standardized Accountancy in Germany". In *National Institute of Economic and Social Research, Occasional Papers* V. London: Cambridge University Press.

Slocum, E., and R. Vangermeersch. (1996). "A Search for Lena E. Mendelsohn". *Accounting Historians Notebook* 19 (1): 10–11, 22–27.

Smith, A. (1776). *An Inquiry into the Nature and Causes of the Wealth of Nations.* New York: Modern Library.

Smith, L. (1950). *Trinidad Who What Why: Public Life, Business, People and Sport.* Port of Spain: L.S. Smith.

Solomons, D. (1991). "Accounting and Social Change: A Neutralist View". *Accounting, Organizations and Society* 16 (3): 287–95.

Spence, C. (2009). "Social Accounting's Emancipatory Potential: A Gramscian Critique". *Critical Perspectives on Accounting* 20 (6): 205–27.

Spence, C., J. Husillos and C. Correa-Ruiz. (2010). "Cargo Cult Science and the Death of Politics: A Critical Review of Social and Environmental Accounting Research". *Critical Perspectives on Accounting* 21 (1): 76–89.

Spencer, H. (1851). *Social Statics: or The Conditions Essential to Human Happiness Specified, and the First of Them Developed.* London: John Chapman.

Spraakman, G., and R. Davidson. (1998). "Transaction Cost Economics as a Predictor of Management Accounting Practices at the Hudson's Bay Company 1860 to 1914". *Accounting History* 3 (2): 69–101.

Spruill, W.G., and C.W. Wootton. (1995). "The Struggle of Women in Accounting: The Case of Jennie Palen, Pioneer, Accountant, Historian and Poet". *Critical Perspectives on Accounting* 6 (4): 371–89.

———. (1996). "Jennie M. Palen". *CPA Journal* 66 (6): 74–75.

Statutes of Canada. (1860). Ottawa: Government of Canada.

Stevenson, J. (1984). *British Society 1914–1945.* London: Allen Lane.

Stewart, L. (2010). "Contingency Theory Perspectives on Management Control System Design among U.S. Ante-Bellum Slave Plantations". *Accounting Historians Journal* 37 (1): 91–120.

Stewart, R. (1992). "Pluralizing Our Past: Foucault in Accounting History". *Accounting, Auditing & Accountability Journal* 5 (2): 57–73.

Streeter, D. (1990). *The History of Black Accountancy: The First 100 Black CPAs.* Washington, DC: National Association of Black Accountants.

Strom, S.H. (1992). *Beyond the Typewriter: Gender, Class and the Origins of Modern American Office Work 1900–1930.* Urbana: University of Illinois Press.

Swanson, T. (1972). *Touche Ross: A Biography.* New York: Touche Ross and Co.

Sy, A. and Tinker, T. (2005). "Archival Research and the Lost World of Accounting". *Accounting History* 10(1): 47–69.

Taket, A., B.R. Crisp, A. Nevill, G. Lamaro and S. Barter-Godfrey, eds. (2009). 'Introduction'. In *Theorising Social Exclusion*, edited by A. Taket, B.R. Crisp, A. Nevill, G. Lamaro and S. Barter-Godfrey, 3–11. London: Routledge.

Talmon, J.L. (1989). "European History- Seedbed of the Holocaust". In *The Nazi Holocaust: Historical Articles on the Destruction of the European Jews*, edited by M. Marrus. Westport, CT: Meckler.

Tate, W.E. (1969). *The Parish Chest. A Study of the Records of Parochial Administration in England.* Cambridge: Cambridge University Press.

Taylor, A.J.P. (1965). *English History 1914–1945*. Harmondsworth: Pelican.
———. (1970). *English History 1914–1945*. Harmondsworth: Pelican.
Taylor, F.W. (1903). *Shop Management*. New York: Harper and Row.
Te Ara. (1966a). *An Encyclopaedia of New Zealand*. Edited by A.H. McLintock, section on John Ballance. www.teara.govt.nz/1966/B/BallanceJohn/Balance John/en (accessed 4 January 2007).
———. (1966b). *An Encyclopaedia of New Zealand*. Edited by A.H. McLintock, section on land settlement. www.teara.govt.nz/1966/L/LandSettlement/Land-Settlement/en (accessed 21 September 2006).
———. (2006). *The Encyclopedia of New Zealand*. Section on New Zealand History in Brief. www.teara.govt.nz/NewZealandInBrief/History/5/en (accessed 20 September 2006).
Thane, P. (1992). "The History of the Gender Division of Labour in Britain: Reflections on 'Herstory' in Accounting: The First Eighty Years". *Accounting, Organizations and Society* 17 (3/4): 299–312.
Thompson, E.P. (1967). "Time, Work-Discipline and Industrial Capitalism". *Past and Present* 38 (1): 56–97.
———. (1993). *Customs in Common*. London: Penguin Books.
Thomson, I., and J. Bebbington. (2004). "It Doesn't Matter What You Teach?" *Critical Perspectives on Accounting* 15 (5): 609–28.
———. (2005). "Social and Environmental Reporting in the UK: A Pedagogic Evaluation". *Critical Perspectives on Accounting* 16 (5): 507–33.
Thornton, D. (1984). "A Look at Agency Theory for the Novice—Part 1". *CA Magazine*, November, 90–97.
Tilly, C. (1994). "The Time of States". *Social Research* 61 (2): 269–95.
Tinker, A.M. (1980). "Towards a Political Economy of Accounting: An Empirical Illustration of the Cambridge Controversies". *Accounting, Organisations and Society* 5 (1): 147–60.
Tinker, T. (1985). *Paper Prophets: A Social Critique of Accounting*. New York: Praeger.
———. (1988). "Panglossian Accounting Theories: The Science of Apologising in Style". *Accounting, Organizations and Society* 13 (2): 165–89.
———. (1991). "The Accountant as Partisan". *Accounting, Organizations and Society* 16 (3): 297–310.
———. (1999). "Mickey Marxism Rides Again". *Critical Perspectives on Accounting* 10 (5): 643–70.
———. (2001). "*Paper Prophets*: An Autocritique". *British Accounting Review* 33 (1): 77–90.
———. (2002). "Critical Research in the United States". *Critical Perspectives on Accounting* 13 (4): 517–26.
———. (2005). "The Withering of Criticism: A Review of the Critical Renewal of Professional, Foucauldian, Ethnographic, and Epistemic Studies in Accounting". *Accounting, Auditing & Accountability Journal* 18 (1): 100–35.
Tinker, T., and A. Koutsoumandi. (1997). "A Mind is a Wonderful Thing to Waste: 'Think Like a Commodity', Become a Critical Perspectives on Accounting". *Accounting, Auditing & Accountability Journal* 10 (3): 454–67.
Tinker, T., C. Lehman and M. Neimark. (1991). "Falling Down in the Hole in the Middle of the Road: Political Quietism in Corporate Social Reporting". *Accounting, Auditing & Accountability Journal* 4 (2): 28–54.
Tinker, T., M. Niemark and B. Merino. (1982). "The Normative Origins of Positive Theories: Ideology and Accounting Thought". *Accounting, Organizations and Society* 7 (2): 167–200.
Tinker, T., and M. Neimark. (1987). "The Role of Annual Reports in Gender and Class Contradictions at General Motors 1917–1976". *Accounting, Organizations and Society* 12 (1): 71–88.

———. (1988). "The Struggle over Meaning in Accounting and Corporate Research: A Comparative Evaluation of Conservative and Critical Historiography". *Accounting, Auditing & Accountability Journal* 1 (1): 55–74.

Tinsley, J. (1983). *Texas Society of Certified Public Accountants: A History, 1915–1981.* College Station: Texas A&M University Press.

Tobias, L. (1983). "Protection, Civilization, Assimilation". In *As Long as the Sun Shines and Water Flows: A Reader in Canadian Native Studies*, edited by I.A.L. Getty and A.S. Lussier, 39–55. Vancouver: University of British Columbia Press.

Toms, S. (2006). "Asset Policy Models, the Labour Theory of Value and Their Implications for Accounting". *Critical Perspectives on Accounting* 17 (7): 947–65.

———. (2010a). "Calculating Profit: A Historical Perspective on the Development of Capitalism". *Accounting, Organizations and Society* 35 (2): 205–21.

———. (2010b). "The Labour Theory of Value, Risk, and the Rate of Profit". *Critical Perspectives on Accounting* 21 (1): 96–103.

Trevelyan, C.E. (1848). *The Irish Crisis.* London: Macmillan.

Trevelyan, G.M. (1966). *Illustrated History of England.* London: Longman.

Trials of War Criminals Before the Nuremberg Military Tribunals under Control Council Law No.10, Nuremberg, 1946–1949 Vol. 5. (1950). Washington, DC: United States Government Printing Office.

Tucker, St. George. (1796). *A Dissertation on Slavery with a Proposal for the Gradual Abolition of it in the State of Virginia.* Philadelphia, PA: Mathew Carey.

Tyson, T. (1990). "Accounting for Labor in the Early 19th Century: The U.S. Arms Making Experience". *Accounting Historians Journal* 17(1): 47–59.

———. (1993). "Keeping the Record Straight: Foucauldian Revisionism and Nineteenth Century U.S. Cost Accounting History". *Accounting, Auditing & Accountability Journal* 6 (2): 4–16.

———. (1995). "An Archivist Responds to the New Accounting History: The Case of the US Men's Clothing Industry". *Accounting, Business & Financial History* 5 (1): 17–38.

———. (1998a). "Mercantilism, Management Accounting, or Managerialism? Cost Accounting in Early Nineteenth-Century US Textile Mills". *Accounting, Business & Financial History* 2:211–29.

———. (1998b). "The Nature and Environment of Cost Management among Early Nineteenth Century U.S. Textile Manufacturers". *Accounting Historians Journal* 19 (2): 1–24.

———. (2000). "Accounting History and the Emperor's New Clothes: A Response to Knowing More as Knowing Less?". *Accounting Historians Journal* 27 (1): 159–71.

Tyson, T. and Oldroyd, D. (2007). "Straw Men and Old Saws—An Evidence-Based response to Sy and Tinker's Critique of Accounting History". *Accounting Historians Journal* 34(1): 173–193

Tyson, T., R. Fleischman and D. Oldroyd. (2004). "Theoretical Perspectives on Accounting for Labor on Slave Plantations of the USA and the British West Indies". *Accounting, Auditing & Accountability Journal* 17 (5): 758–78.

Tyson, T., D. Oldroyd and R. Fleischman. (2005). "Accounting, Coercion, and Social Control during Apprenticeship: Converting Slave Workers to Wage Workers in the British West Indies, c.1834–1838". *Accounting Historians Journal* 32 (2): 201–31.

UN War Crimes Commission. (1948). "Noteworthy War Criminals. Second World War-Europe SS". In *History of the UN War Crimes Commission and the Development of the Laws of War.* London: HMSO. http://www.ess.uwe.ac.uk/WCC/warcrimindss.htm.

Unerman, J., and M. Bennett. (2004). "Increased Stakeholder Dialogue and the Internet: Towards Greater Corporate Accountability or Reinforcing Capitalist Hegemony". *Accounting, Organizations and Society* 29 (7): 685–707.

University of the West Indies. (1991). *The MSc Accounting Programme at the UWI, St. Augustine*. Unpublished paper.

Velayutham, S. (2003). "The Accounting Profession's Code of Ethics: Is it a Code of Ethics or a Code of Quality Assurance?" *Critical Perspectives on Accounting* 14 (4): 483–503.

Verma, S., and S. Gray. (2006). "The Creation of the Chartered Accountants of India: The First Steps in the Development of an Indigenous Accounting Profession Post- Independence". *Accounting Historians Journal* 33 (2): 131–56.

Viator, R. (2001). "An Examination of African-American Access to Public Accounting Mentors: Perceived Barriers and Intentions to Leave". *Accounting, Organizations and Society* 26 (6): 541–61.

Vollmers, G. (2003). "Industrial Slavery in the U.S.: The North Carolina Turpentine Industry, 1849–61". *Accounting, Business & Financial History* 13 (3): 369–92.

Von Lang, J. (1983). *Eichmann Interrogated*. London: Bodley Head.

Wacquant, L. (1997). "Towards an Analytic of Racial Domination". *Political Power and Social Theory* 11:221–34.

Walby, S. (1986). *Patriarchy at Work: Patriarchy and Capitalist Relations in Employment*. Cambridge: Polity Press.

Walker, S.P. (1988). *The Society of Accountants in Edinburgh, 1854–1914. A Study of Recruitment to a New Profession*. New York: Garland Publishing.

———. (1991). "The Defence of Professional Monopoly: Scottish Chartered Accountants and Satellites in the Accountancy Firmament, 1854–1914". *Accounting, Organizations and Society* 16 (3): 257–83.

———. (1995). "The Genesis of Professional Organization in Scotland: A Contextual Analysis". *Accounting, Organizations and Society* 20 (4): 285–310.

———. (1996). "The Criminal Upperworld and the Emergence of a Disciplinary Code in the Early Chartered Accountancy Profession". *Accounting History* 1 (2): 7–35.

———. (1998). "How to Secure your Husband's Esteem: Accounting and Private Patriarchy in the British Middle Class Household during the Nineteenth Century". *Accounting, Organizations and Society* 23 (5/6): 485–514.

———. (2000). "Encounters with Nazism: British Accountants and the Fifth International Congress on Accounting". *Critical Perspectives on Accounting* 11 (2): 215–45.

———. (2003a). "Agents of Dispossession and Acculturation. Edinburgh Accountants and the Highland Clearances". *Critical Perspectives on Accounting* 14 (8): 813–53.

———. (2003b). "Identifying the Woman behind the 'Railed-in Desk': The Proto-Feminisation of Bookkeeping in Britain". *Accounting, Auditing & Accountability Journal* 16 (4): 609–59.

———. (2003c). "Professionalisation or Incarceration? Household Engineering, Accounting and the Domestic Ideal". *Accounting, Organizations and Society* 28 (7/8): 743–72.

———. (2004a). "Expense, Social and Moral Control: Accounting and the Administration of the Old Poor Law in England and Wales". *Journal of Accounting and Public Policy* 23 (1): 85–127.

———. (2004b). "The Genesis of Professional Organisation in English Accountancy". *Accounting, Organizations and Society* 29 (2): 127–56.

———. (2005). "Accounting in History". *Accounting Historians Journal* 32 (2): 233–59.

————. (2006). "Philanthropic Women and Accounting: Octavia Hill and the Exercise of 'quiet power and sympathy'". *Accounting, Business & Financial History* 16 (2): 163–94.

————. (2008a). "Accounting Histories of Women: Beyond Recovery? *Accounting, Auditing & Accountability Journal* 21 (4): 680–710.

————. (2008b). "Accounting, Paper Shadows and the Stigmatized Poor". *Accounting, Organizations and Society* 33 (4/5): 453–87.

————. (2008c). "Innovation, Convergence and Argument without End in Accounting History". *Accounting, Auditing & Accountability Journal* 21 (2): 296–322.

————. (2011). Professions and Patriarchy Revisited. Accountancy in England and Wales, 1887–1914". *Accounting History Review* 21 (2): 185–225.

Walker, S.P., and G. Carnegie. (2007). "Budgetary Earmarking and the Control of the Extravagant Woman in Australia, 1850–1920". *Critical Perspectives on Accounting* 18 (2): 233–61.

Walker, S.P., and S. Llewellyn. (2000). "Accounting at Home: Some Interdisciplinary Perspectives". *Accounting, Auditing & Accountability Journal* 13 (4): 425–49.

Walker, S.P., and F. Mitchell. (1998). "Labor and Costing: The Employees' Dilemma". *Accounting Historians Journal* 25 (2): 35–62.

Walker, S.P., and K. Shackleton. (1998). "A Ring Fence for the Profession: Advancing the Closure of British Accountancy 1957–1970". *Accounting, Auditing & Accountability Journal* 11 (1): 34–71.

Wallage, P. (2000). "Assurance on Sustainability Reporting: An Auditor's View". *Auditing: A Journal of Practice and Theory* S53–S65.

Walsh, E., and R. Stewart. (1993). "Accounting and the Construction of Institutions: The Case of a Factory". *Accounting, Organizations and Society* 18 (7/8): 783–800.

Walters, M., and J. Young. (2008). "Metaphors and Accounting for Stock Options". *Critical Perspectives on Accounting* 19 (6): 805–33.

Ward, A. (1974). *A Show of Justice*. Auckland: Auckland University Press.

Ward, J. (1991). *British West Indian Slavery, 1750–1834: The Process of Amelioration*. Oxford: Clarendon Press.

Watts, R., and J. Zimmerman. (1978). "Toward a Positive Theory of the Determination of Accounting Standards". *Accounting Review* 53 (1): 112–34.

————. (1979). "The Demand for and Supply of Accounting Theories: The Market for Excuses". *Accounting Review* 54 (2): 273–305.

————. (1986). *Positive Accounting Theory*. Englewood-Cliffs. NJ: Prentice Hall.

Webb, S., and B. Webb. (1927). *English Local Government: English Poor Law History: Part I. The Old Poor Law*. London: Longman, Green and Co.

Wellers, G. (1978). "Reply to the Neo-Nazi Falsification of Historical Facts Concerning the Holocaust". In *The Holocaust and the Neo-Nazi Mythomania*, edited by S. Klarsfeld. New York: Beate Klarsfeld Foundation.

Wells, M.C. (1978). *Accounting for Common Costs*. Urbana, IL: Center for International Education and Research in Accounting.

Wertheimer, A. (1996). *Exploitation*. Princeton, NJ: Princeton University Press.

Whiteley, H. (1833). *Excessive Cruelty to Slaves. Three Months in Jamaica in 1832: Comprising a Residence of Seven Weeks on a Sugar Plantation*. Philadelphia, PA: publisher not known.

Whitley, R. (1988). "The Possibility and Utility of Positive Accounting Theory". *Accounting, Organizations and Society* 13 (6): 631–45.

Wiencek, H. (2003). *An Imperfect God: George Washington, His Slaves, and the Creation of America*. New York: Farrar, Straus and Giroux.

Wiesel, E. (1988). "Some Questions That Remain Open". In *Comprehending the Holocaust*, edited by A. Cohen, Y. Gelber and C. Wardi. Frankfurt am Main: Verlad Peter Lang.

Wilberforce, W. (1792). *Speech in the Debate on a Motion for the Abolition of the Slave Trade in the House of Commons on Monday and Tuesday April 18 and 19, 1791, Reported in Detail*. London: James Phillips.

Williams, E. (1969). *Inward Hunger: The Education of a Prime Minister*. London: Andre Deutsch.

Williams, P. (2004a). "Recovering Accounting as a Worthy Endeavor". *Critical Perspectives on Accounting* 15 (4/5): 113–17.

———. (2004b). "You Reap What You Sow: The Ethical Discourse of Professional Accounting". *Critical Perspectives on Accounting* 15 (6/7): 995–1001.

Williams, P., and J. Rodgers. (1995). "The *Accounting Review* and the Production of Accounting Knowledge". *Critical Perspectives on Accounting* 6 (3): 263–87.

Williams, P., G. Jenkins and L. Ingraham. (2006). "The Winnowing Away of Behavioral Accounting Research in the US: The Process for Anointing Academic Elites". *Accounting, Organizations and Society* 31 (8): 783–818.

Williams, S. (2003). "Assets in Accounting: Reality Lost". *Accounting Historians Journal* 30 (2): 133–74.

Williamson, O. (1985). *The Economic Institutions of Capitalism*. New York: Free Press.

Willmott, H., T. Puxty and D. Cooper. (1993). "Maintaining Self-Regulation: Making 'Interests' Coincide in Discourses on the Governance of the ICAEW". *Accounting, Auditing & Accountability Journal* 6 (4): 88–93.

Windsor, C., and S. Auyeung. (2006). "The Effect of Gender and Dependent Children on Professional Accountants' Career Progression". *Critical Perspectives on Accounting* 17 (6): 828–44.

Wood, P. (1985). "Finance and the Urban Poor Law: Sunderland Union, 1836–1914". In *The Poor and the City: The English Poor Law in its Urban Context, 1834–1914*, edited by M.E. Rose, 20–56. Leicester: Leicester University Press.

Wood, P. (1991). *Poverty and the Workhouse in Victorian Britain*. Stroud: Alan Sutton.

Wootton, C., and B. Kemmerer. (1996). "The Changing Genderization of Bookkeeping in the United States, 1870–1930". *Business History Review* 70 (4): 541–86.

———. (2000). "The Changing Genderization of the Accounting Workforce in the U.S., 1930–90". *Accounting, Business & Financial History* 10 (2): 169–90.

Wootton, C., and W. Spruill. (1994). "The Role of Women in Major Public Accounting Firms in the United States during World War II". *Business and Economic History* 23 (1): 241–52.

Young, J. (1997). "Defining Auditors' Responsibilities". *Accounting Historians Journal* 24 (2): 55–63.

Young, J., and M. Annisette. (2009). "Cultivating Imagination: Ethics, Education and Literature". *Critical Perspectives on Accounting* 20 (1): 93–109.

Young, J., and T. Mouck. (1996). "Objectivity and the Role of History in the Development and Review of Accounting Standards". *Accounting, Auditing & Accountability Journal* 9 (3): 127–47.

Young, J., and A. Preston. (1996). "Are Accounting Researchers under the Tyranny of Single Theory Perspectives?". *Accounting, Auditing & Accountability Journal* 9 (4): 107–11.

Young, J., and P. Williams. (2010). "Sorting and Comparing: Standard-Setting and 'Ethical' Categories". *Critical Perspectives on Accounting* 21 (6): 509–21.

Zan, L. (2004). "Writing Accounting and Management History: Insights from Unorthodox Music Historiography". *Accounting Historians Journal* 31 (2): 171–92.

Zeff, S. (1998). "Independence and Standard Setting". *Critical Perspectives on Accounting* 9 (5): 535–43.

———. (1999). "The Evolution of the Conceptual Framework for Business Enterprises in the United States". *Accounting Historians Journal* 26 (7): 89–131.

Zelinschi, D. (2009). "Legitimacy, Expertise and Closure in the Romanian Accountant's Professionalization Project 1900–1916". *Accounting History* 14 (4): 381–403.

Zimmeck, M. (1988a). "Get Out and Get Under": The Impact of Demobilisation on the Civil Service, 1919–32". In *The White Blouse Revolution: Female Office Workers since 1870*, edited by G. Anderson, 88–120. Manchester: Manchester: University Press.

Zimmeck, M. 1988b. The 'New Woman' in the machinery of government: a spanner in the works. In R. MacLeod (ed) *Government and Expertise: Specialists, Administrators and Professionals: 1860–1919*. pp. 185–202. Cambridge: Cambridge University Press.

Index

Note: Page numbers ending in "f" refer to figures. Page numbers ending in "t" refer to tables.

An environmentally friendly book printed and bound in England by www.printondemand-worldwide.com

This book is made entirely of sustainable materials; FSC paper for the cover and PEFC paper for the text pages.

#0028 - 090513 - C0 - 229/152/15 [17] - CB